RACISM, MODERNITY AND IDENTITY

ON THE WESTERN FRONT

For Zubeida, Aziz and Parin Rattansi

RACISM, MODERNITY AND IDENTITY

On the Western Front

Edited by

Ali Rattansi and Sallie Westwood

POLITY PRESS

First published in 1994 by Polity Press
in association with Blackwell Publishers.

Editorial office:
Polity Press
65 Bridge Street
Cambridge CB2 1UR, UK

Marketing and production:
Blackwell Publishers
108 Cowley Road
Oxford OX4 1JF, UK

238 Main Street
Cambridge, MA 02142, USA

ISBN 0 7456 0941 4
ISBN 0 7456 0942 2 (pbk)

A CIP catalogue record for this book is available from the British Library and
the Library of Congress

Phototypeset in 10½ on 12 pt Caslon
by Intype, London
Printed in Great Britain by T.J. Press, Padstow, Cornwall

This book is printed on acid-free paper.

CONTENTS

THE CONTRIBUTORS

Cathie Lloyd is a Research Fellow at the Centre for Research in Ethnic Relations at the University of Warwick. She is working on anti-racist movements and strategies in Europe, focusing on the history of anti-racist ideas in France. She has published widely on anti-racism in the context of the history of ideas and public order. Between 1988 and 1991 she worked as a senior researcher at the Commission for Racial Equality.

Robert Miles is Professor and Head of the Department of Sociology at the University of Glasgow, and Visiting Professor at Glasgow Caledonian University. He has published many articles and several books on racism and migration, including *Racism and Migrant Labour* (1982); *Capitalism and Unfree Labour: Anomaly or Necessity?* (1987); *Racism* (1989) and *Racism after 'Race Relations'* (1993). He also co-authored (with Annie Phizacklea) *Labour and Racism* (1980) and (with Diana Kay) *Refugees or Migrant Workers?* (1992)

Jan Nederveen Pieterse is author of *White on Black: Images of Africa and Blacks in Western Popular Culture* (1992) and *Empire and Emancipation* (1989), and editor of *Christianity and Hegemony* (1992), *Emancipations, Modern and Postmodern* (1992) and, with Bhikhu Parekh, *The Decolonization of Imagination* (forthcoming). In 1990 he received the JC Ruigrok Award of the Netherlands Society of Sciences for *Empire and Emancipation*. He is Senior Lecturer at the Institute of Social Studies in The Hague.

Ali Rattansi teaches Sociology at City University, London. He has written widely on social and cultural theory and on racism and ethnicity. His books include *Marx and the Division of Labour* (1982); *Ideology, Method and Marx* (1989); (with Roy Boyne) *Postmodernism and Society* (1990); (with James Donald) *'Race', Culture and Difference* (1992); (with Peter Braham and Richard Skellington) *Racism and Antiracism* (1992); and (with David Reeder) *Rethinking Radical Education* (1992).

David Slater is Professor of Social and Political Geography at Loughborough University of Technology, Leicestershire, author of *Territory and State Power in Latin America* (1989) and editor of *New Social Movements and the State in Latin America* (1985). Currently, he is preparing a manuscript on *Politics, Post-Modernity and the Periphery*.

Sallie Westwood teaches Sociology at the University of Leicester and has conducted research in Ghana, India and the UK in the field of ethnic and gender studies. She is currently working on racisms and nationalisms in Latin America. Her work has been published widely in book chapters and journals, and she is the author of *All Day, Every Day: Factory and Family in the Making of Women's Lives* (1984). She has also co-authored (with Parminder Bhachu), *Enterprising Women: Gender, Ethnicity and Economic Relations* (1988); (with E. J. Thomas) *Radical Agendas? The Politics of Adult Education* (1991); (with John McIlroy) *Border Country: Raymond Williams in Adult Education* (1993); and (with Sarah Radcliffe) *Viva: Women and Popular Protest in Latin America* (1993).

Michel Wieviorka is Professor at the Ecole des Hautes Etudes en Sciences Sociales and (with George Balandier) the Director of 'Les Cahiers Internationaux de Sociology'. He is the author of several books, including (with Alan Touraine and Francis Dubet) *The Working Class Movement* (1987); *Sociéties et Terrorisme* (forthcoming in translation); *L'Espace Du Racisme* (1991); and *La France Raciste* (1992). He is also editor of *Racisme et Modernité* (1993).

Howard Winant teaches sociology at Temple University. He is the author of *Racial Conditions: Politics, Theory, Comparisons* (1994) and *Stalemate: Political Economic Origins of Supply Side Policy* (1988). He is co-author (with Michael Omi) of *Racial Formation in the United States: From the 1960s to the 1990s* (1994).

Robert Young teaches English at Wadham College, Oxford. He is the author of *White Mythologies: Writing History and the West* (1990), and *Colonial Desire: Hybridity in Culture, Theory and Race* (1994).

ACKNOWLEDGEMENTS

This book would not have been possible without the patience and enthusiasm of our contributors and our editors at Polity Press. We owe special thanks to the authors in this volume and to David Held and Anthony Giddens for their warm support.

Ali Rattansi and Sallie Westwood

MODERN RACISMS, RACIALIZED IDENTITIES

Ali Rattansi and Sallie Westwood

The spectre that haunts the societies of 'the West' is no longer communism but, both within and outside their frontiers, a series of racisms and ethno-nationalisms. These are part of the fall-out from the crisis of the institutions and settlements which provided 'the West' with a period of unprecedented prosperity and global dominance in the second half of the twentieth century. Both the 'internal' and 'external' settlements have come under increasing pressure. Economic recessions, the aftermath of decolonization, new forms of globalization, the collapse of the former Soviet bloc, the failure of a new equitable or stable world order and the increasing heterogeneity of Euro-American societies have combined to undermine the certainties of material comfort, space and time, territory and history, which underpinned for white, especially male Westerners a sense of what must have appeared to be unshakeable security and superiority.

Much of this volume is concerned to explore a variety of aspects of the new racisms and nationalisms which have disfigured the contemporary period, as neofascist parties have gained electoral ground and as racialized violence has escalated to alarming proportions on the streets of cities and towns all over Europe (Cheles *et al.*, 1991; Ford, 1992). In the East End of London a candidate from the neofascist British National Party gained office in September 1993 in a local election, several black and Asian young men have been murdered in the capital by racist thugs, and anti-racist protestors have fought pitched battles with police and members of neofascist groups. In the USA, the continuing significance of the Ku-Klux-Klan, the support

for figures such as David Duke and, above all, the events in Los
Angeles following the Rodney King trial have once again highlighted
the fragile and changing forms of ethnic and racialized antagonism
which have been a constitutive feature of its history (Goodings-
Williams, 1993; Madhubuti, 1993). No doubt, to this catalogue of what
one might call *interethnicine* conflict must be added the horrific events
in the former Yugoslavia, especially as they appear to contradict a
view widely held that ethno-nationalist and racialized genocide was,
in Europe, an aberration which the defeat of Nazism had irrevocably
eradicated.

However, the presumption of commonality which enables the com-
pilation of a catalogue of events of this kind cannot be regarded as
unproblematic. That is, it can no longer be assumed that the conceptual vocabulary of 'racism' of 'ethnicity' or 'nationalism' can provide
the basis of a viable taxonomy of these events, or that any catalogue
based on such forms of classification will enable the creation of convincing, all-encompassing explanatory frameworks. Such scepticism is
itself intrinsically connected with a wider loss of confidence in the
West's metanarratives, which has often been taken to be the defining
feature of a new, 'postmodern' era.

'Modernity' and 'postmodernity' have in recent times become part
of the new intellectual terrain which has enabled a number of exceed-
ingly complex questions to be posed about the philosophical foundations, genealogy, transformation and prospects of 'the West' in a
novel period. They have also begun to transform the nature of discussions about racism, ethnicity and identity. There are several reasons
for the prominence of modernity and postmodernity as organizing
themes in contemporary debates, including the discussions to be
found in this collection.

In part, modernity and postmodernity have emerged as attempts to
replace political and social scientific metanarratives such as Marxism,
Weberianism, liberalism, social democracy and varieties of conserva-
tism which have come to be regarded as no longer adequate to the
explication and control of events in an era characterized by culturally
heterogeneous, rapidly changing social configurations, structured by
new forms of globalization and the all but complete collapse of communist blocs.[1] Moreover, there has been a sense that most older
metanarratives have given an emphasis to economic forces and antagonisms which can no longer be sustained in the face of an acknowledgement of the constitutive role of the discursive, as well as the
social explosions accompanying the emergence of new collective subjects only loosely connected with older class-based movements: chief

among the new collective subjects are women and ethnic and racialized minorities whose own movements are having a profound, destabilizing cultural impact on the societies of 'the West'.

These considerations are closely connected, indeed may be said to derive from and reinforce, a further, much wider sense of unease. That is, there is a growing, although uneven, sense that what is at stake as we enter a new phase in the history of the globe is not just this or that Western metanarrative, or just the role of a particular collective subject represented by labour movements, but the viability, the self-understanding and self-justification of a global project: 'Western modernity' (including socialism as a particular variant). This is conceptualized as a whole set of cultural, political and economic transformations symbolically set in motion by the European Enlightenment of the eighteenth century with its boundless confidence in the capacity of a stable individualized subject, 'Western Man', to conjoin Reason with Progress, harnessing the natural and social sciences as key transformative agencies. This is a confidence seriously disturbed by a growing suspicion that Western modernity, however impressive its achievements, not only is incapable of providing solutions to basic problems of war and violence, environmental damage, economic exploitation, bureaucratic mismanagement and corruption, and equitable material comfort and security at national and global levels, but also chronically generates them as an almost inseparable part of its mode of operation.[2]

Issues around racism are crucially implicated in the question mark over Western modernity, for another side of this modernity has been its close involvement with, indeed its legitimation of, Western genocide against aboriginal peoples, slavery, colonial domination and exploitation, and the Holocaust, in all of which Western doctrines of 'racial' and cultural superiority have played a constitutive role.

Nevertheless, it is just at this point that a range of nagging questions reappear. What sense does it make to run all these forms of domination, exploitation, inferiorization and genocide together? If older, often class- and economically-based metanarratives are inadequate to the understanding of these phenomena, can frameworks which take modernity or alleged new phases, such as 'post-industrialism' or 'postmodernity', as their starting points lead to any greater illumination? If modernity is characterized by rapid change and new types of globalization, what new forms does racism take, and again can they be understood within the parameters of a singular theorization? And if Enlightenment-derived values such as forms of humanist universalism can be questioned because they installed Western Man as the norm and measure of humankind, and if Western liberalism and individualism were complicit with racialized domination, what does this imply for attempts to mobilize values of human rights, as derived from the Enlightenment, against racialized discriminations, inequalities and violence? Moreover, how should the 'social', and individual and collective identities now be theorized when the previously privileged role of class-based identities can no longer be taken as axiomatic? In an age of multiple and shifting subjectivities and identifications, and new interconnections between the 'local' and the 'global', what meaning can be given to 'identity' at all?

These are among the questions which the contributors to this volume have addressed. Not surprisingly, their approaches to these complex issues differ. But as we shall see, the gulf between them is not as unbridgeable as might at first be apparent.

Ali Rattansi's essay explores the implications of recent debates around modernity and postmodernity for a new understanding of racism, ethnicity and identity in 'Western' social formations. This is achieved through the construction of what he calls a 'postmodern' frame, which is then deployed in an analysis of very broad scope. The 'postmodern' frame as theorized in the essay draws upon a wide range of authors. Bauman, Giddens, Foucault, Derrida and Laclau and Mouffe all figure in a framework which emphasizes the significance of a set of key themes: the 'postmodern' condition as a reflection on the nature and limits of Western modernity; an analysis of modernity which focuses on its typical dualities, for example the chronic disembedding and reinvention of traditions and collective identities; the marginalization of Western modernity's Others in the construction of Western identities; the impact of new forms of globalization; the decentring and de-essentialization of both subjects and the 'social'; an appreciation of temporality and spatiality as constitutive of identities and the 'social'; a consideration of the relation between the 'psychic' and the 'social'; and an engagement with questions of sexuality and sexual difference.

Each of these elements is shown to have a significant bearing for rethinking questions of racism, ethnicity and identity. Some examples will suffice in giving an indication of the form of analysis that emerges from this exercise. A consideration of sexuality and sexual difference yields a critique of colonial discourse analysis and Bauman's justly celebrated discussion of the Holocaust, as well as a novel focus on the sexualization of contemporary racial and ethnic discourses. A de-essentialization of the 'social' provides a theoretical infrastructure which enables a break with reproductive models of racism as well as providing a framework which, by emphasizing the lack of political belongingness of racializing and ethnic discourses, makes otherwise incongruous alliances between racist and racialized groups intelligible. Forms of discrimination engaged in by public agencies are reconceptualized as part of the operation of modern social formations as disciplinary networks of biopolitics and power-knowledge. Temporality and spatiality are shown to be crucial for understanding the ways in which sexuality, 'otherness' and conceptions of 'modernity' can combine to create ambivalences in the representation of diasporic minorities such as British South Asians. And the need for understanding the profound interconnections between time and space, narrative and place, and their dislocations in an era of new global configurations, is emphasized in a commentary on the new racisms which also highlights the articulations between racism and masculinity.

David Slater's chapter elaborates upon a theme which is signalled in Rattansi's essay as crucial to any project which attempts to appropriate the 'postmodern' for analyses of the contemporary period: a displacement of the ethnocentrism, or what Slater calls the Euro-Americanism, of so much 'postmodern' discourse. Slater's critical reading of some key 'postmodernist' figures – Rorty, Vattimo, Baudrillard – exposes the extent to which their work, references to the significance of the 'Other' not withstanding, remains imprisoned within assumptions which treat 'the West' as a self-contained entity, an 'enclosure sufficient to itself'. These intellectuals fail to 'anthropologize' 'the West'. They display an ignorance of the extent to which 'the West' or 'the North' – these geographical slippages being indicative of the imaginary unity of these intellectual and political configurations – have actually been formed by 'the South'. At the same time they exhibit a profound arrogance, for in their work 'the South' only ever functions as an *object* of knowledge. Especially, there never seems to be any acknowledgement that 'the West's' Others might actually be a source of theory. Slater calls for Euro-American intellectuals to engage in a project that genuinely treats 'the West' as Other, a theme that is implicit in the idea of the 'postmodern'. Slater contributes to this anthropologizing project by exploring the writings of a number of figures from that other America, Latin America, habitually erased by the 'postmodernists' who treat the USA as synonymous with America. Among other things, Slater demonstrates the extent to which Latin American debates have prefigured and developed those taking place in 'the North', and the degree to which Latin American social and cultural formations have long exhibited features of hybridity and heterogeneity which in their ethnocentrism many 'postmodernists' have seen as unique to the contemporary 'North'.

To anthropologize 'the West' is, in part, to deconstruct its pretensions to unity, uniqueness and wholeness. It is this form of undoing 'the West's' front, its façade, that is pursued in the two contributions to the second part of the book. Jan Nederveen Pieterse in the first of these points out that 'to deconstruct Europe is to deconstruct modernity, its leading self-definition'. The strategy of Pieterse's unpacking of 'the West', as he calls it, is to expose the very profound degree to which the West has actually borrowed and been formed by the cultures of 'the South'. Often, these borrowings took the form of 'fashions' – turquerie, 'Ethiopianism', chinoiserie – which influenced art, music, architecture and aesthetics. Equally significant have been the scientific and technological influences without which the achievements of 'the West' would have been impossible. As Pieterse puts it, the 'Occident' was historically 'multicultural' long before it was demographically diverse in the more contemporary sense of the term. Ironically, unpacking 'the West' reveals the extent of modernity's formation by cultures which it reviled as archaic and 'premodern'.

One form of disavowal by 'the West' of its indebtedness to the Rest has been the writing out of these other contributions in many of its most influential historical narratives, which have tended to privilege Greece as the main point of origin of the genius of 'Western Man'. An unravelling of this invention of 'the West' has recently been undertaken by Martin Bernal in *Black Athena*, which, as the sub-title to the work highlights, aims to expose the Afro-Asiatic roots of European classical civilization. Bernal's project has become embroiled in a set of controversies which have demonstrated the intertwining of scholarship and politics which Edward Said and other proponents of colonial discourse analysis have long been concerned to expose.

But Robert Young argues that colonial discourse analysis appears to have reached an impasse, for it seems to homogenize a complex set of colonial formations and tends to ignore altogether the Latin American and especially the African experiences. Moreover, it remains evasive on questions of truth and representation. As Young points out, Bernal's *Black Athena* appears to be a project that could help us to move beyond the impasse. In showing how the classical scholars of the nineteenth century attempted to write out of the historical record the indebtedness of Greece to African, particularly Egyptian culture, Bernal unravels the racism that reinvented 'the West' in the nineteenth century and affirms the possibility that the Other can be a source of knowledge – something that, as Slater argues, even the 'postmoderns' have failed to appreciate properly. Bernal's entire argument is premised on the assumption that in some form or other it is possible to know the truth about other cultures, in this case Ancient Greece. However, Young argues that Bernal is unable to escape many of the dilemmas that have confronted colonial discourse analysis. Especially, Bernal, although critical of the underlying racialized politics that influenced the nineteenth-century classicists, is curiously oblivious of the political context of his own work. He remains evasive on the question of what the term 'Black' signifies in his own work, and therefore is unable to clarify the implications of his historical investigations for contemporary debates about the role of 'black' cultures in the formation of 'the West'. Young takes the argument further by insisting that what is required is a much more thorough going discussion of the racial categories that permeated nineteenth-century academic disciplines and general Victorian assumptions about culture. He makes a valuable contribution to this project by exposing the development of racial theory in nineteenth-century American archaeology and anthropology, which attempted to provide a scholarly justification for slavery. One strategy pursued by these racial theorists was to deny the 'blackness' of Egypt. Thus Young is able to argue that the 'whitening' of Egypt that Bernal investigates in *Black Athena* emerged not only from European academic racism, but also from efforts to create an academically respectable rationale for American slavery. At the same time Young shows the degree to which fears of miscegenation, in particular, condensed the anxieties but also provided metaphors for the forms of cultural exchange, economic exploitation and physical domination that colonialism and slavery involved. Young concludes his essay by drawing out important implications from his own historical research for the project of colonial discourse analysis.

There has been much debate in recent years concerning the degree to which the discrediting of nineteenth-century doctrines of 'scientific racism' has given rise to racializing discourses that now rely on notions of cultural difference. These are the 'new racisms' that have been espoused by a variety of new right and neofascist organizations that have gained an increasing purchase on the national politics of almost all European states. The three chapters that form the section on 'Racism and Modernity in Contemporary Europe' explore a range of questions that have arisen as a result of reflection and research on the resurgence of racism in Europe and on the debates that have emerged as anti-racist movements have sought to mobilize against the influence

of the new racist organizations and the collusion of national governments and European Community organizations.

Michel Wieviorka suggests that any analysis of contemporary racism
in Europe has to recognize the connections between modernity and
racism. It is not merely that scientific racism was obviously a post-
Enlightenment phenomenon, but, according to Wievieorka, that the
logics of present-day racism operate in a 'space' in which social groups
are differentially positioned in relation to the modern European
nation-state.

Wievieorka distinguishes four forms of racism as they articulate
with modern social and political conditions: a universalist one, which
inferiorizes others as non- or pre-modern; another, which he calls
the 'poor white' response, which derives from anxieties about being
excluded from the material benefits of modern industrial society; a
third, which has anti-modernist inflexions, appeals to traditions of
community, religion and nation, and demonizes those thought to be
excessively 'modern'; and finally intergroup hostilities that have complex, cross-cutting relations with the conditions of modernity. These
broad types of racism have now taken particular forms. The present
European context is defined by what Wievieorka calls *le grande
mutation*, manifested in crises and the 'destructuration' of industrial-
ism, national identity and the welfare state, which have allowed each
type of racism to flourish as the 'space' of racism has itself expanded
in these conditions. As he puts it, 'Reason, progress, development
become divorced from nation, identity, subjectivity, and in this split,
racism may easily develop.'

For Wieviorka contemporary European racism fuses with a variety
of elements – nationalism, regionalism, populism – and is forced to
present a front of respectability. These factors have prevented racism
from posing the kind of threat that Europe experienced during the
interwar period, but Wieviorka is far from complacent. Moreover, he
is well aware of the complexities created by national specificities,
although he contends that these do not fundamentally challenge his
overall framework.

Robert Miles, just as much as Wieviorka, is concerned to find a
general theorization that might enable an understanding of current
European racism without erasing the historical peculiarities which
each national discourse and polity exhibits. Miles is critical both of
what he calls the 'colonial paradigm' and Wieviorka's post-industrialist
framework. The former is said, among other things, to externalize the
problem of racism through the imperial connection, one consequence
being its inability to explain anti-Semitism; to the latter, Miles pro-

poses an alternative theorization which posits a 'disorganization of capitalism' rather than the transition to a new era of post-industrialism.

Miles's own model regards racism as integral to the development of capitalist social formations, for racisms mediate a series of contradictions that are said to arise chronically out of the commodifying logic of capitalism. The universalization of the commodity form creates ideologies of formal equality which are contradicted by the endemic inequalities of capitalism; racism enables a justification of inequalities by naturalizing them through conceptions of fixed attributes. Moreover, resistance to commodification and capitalist transformation allows recalcitrant populations to be racialized as primitive, thus underwriting the forcible expropriation of their labour, or even the genocide of the stigmatized populations. And the contradiction between the universalizing thrust of capitalist relations and the formation of nation-states creates populations that are constantly being collectivized through identifications that posit national and 'racial' essences.

Miles's thesis as far as contemporary European racisms is concerned is that what we are witnessing is not so much an increase in racism as an intensification of nationalist, cultural racisms that have arisen out of the crisis of the nation-state in a new period of globalization. The state plays a crucial role in the generation of these new racisms as it attempts to contain the contradictions, which have now moved beyond the power of the nation-state, by appeals to fictitious conceptions of sovereignty and unity. For Miles this is a 'classic inversion in which the imagination denies the real conditions of existence'.

For all their differences, there are some notable similarities between the arguments of Miles and Wieviorka. A major theoretical difference is that what the latter regards as attributes of modernity and post-industrialism are seen by Miles to be specific to capitalism: but in many instances the mechanisms which drive the racialization process are identical – crises of the nation-state, the racialization of populations resisting capitalist modernization, and divisions and restructuring within national working classes.

One of Miles's arguments is that the 'spaces' for anti-racism in Europe are created from the same contradictions between the forces and ideologies of capitalist universalism and its chronic inequalities that also constantly generate the conditions for racism. Or, to put it in other terms, anti-racism has involved in part a struggle over how the universalist humanism of the Enlightenment and the liberalisms of its aftermath can be turned to anti-racist advantage. These struggles are the central focus of Cathie Lloyd's chapter on anti-racist movements in France and Britain. As becomes clear from her account of many of the debates, Enlightenment-derived universalism, as a basis for anti-racism, encounters a number of difficulties. It is in tension with the multiculturalist valorization of cultural difference. And the new racisms have turned both universalist and differentialist arguments to their own advantage by making claims for a universal human nature which supposedly dictates that populations 'naturally' prefer to interact with their own (national-cultural) kith and kin. Superimposed upon these difficulties have been problems of possible neutralization by incorporation by the state, fragmentations within racialized communities, and divisions over strategy and leadership. Cathie Lloyd disentangles these various threads in an analysis of the commonalities and differences between the French and British anti-racist movements, and demonstrates how the legacy of the Enlightenment is at much at stake in this context as in the debates about modernity and postmodernity. We need to confront the possibility, she argues, that a new European anti-racist politics of citizenship cannot be created without a transformation and reconstruction of the ideas of 'liberty, equality and fraternity' inherited from the Enlightenment.

The final part of the book brings us back to many of the themes broached in the first section, but with a particular emphasis on the interconnections between the local and the global. Sallie Westwood's chapter returns to issues of decentred subjects and identities central to Rattansi's concerns, but in a specific context: that of a racialized psychiatric complex, experienced as a set of powerful and painfully exclusionary discourses and practices in the lives of people of African-Caribbean and South Asian descent in Britain. The debate about the overrepresentation of, especially, British African-Caribbean groups in the category 'schizophrenic' is recontextualized by Sallie Westwood within the dilemmas and oppressions of belonging and unbelonging, the pain and humiliation of racist and psychiatric objectifications. The local and the global intersect here. These are migrants or descendants of migrants from Britain's former colonies, propelled thousands of miles by the search for work or ties of kinship, only to encounter the racialized exclusions of nation, city, locale and psychiatric institutions. But these are not merely narratives of victimage. Resistance emerges constantly as a source of strength in otherwise oppressive encounters, a strategy for living in the complexities of ethnicity, gender, class and racialization which define the lives of the narrators around whose accounts the paper is structured.

Howard Winant's chapter connects up the multiplicity and fragility of identities, at both local and global levels, with the processes of racial formation. To accomplish this, he borrows, like Rattansi earlier, from the poststructuralists, and he also deploys what he refers to as a decentred concept of hegemony, which does not privilege class or any other subject. The formation of subjects is seen as a complex, multidimensional process which requires an understanding of racial time as an articulation between genealogical time and contingent time. Winant is concerned to elucidate the formation of both 'white' and 'non-white' identities. With regard to the former, Winant discusses the crisis of 'whiteness' in the USA, and specifies some of the reasons for the re-emergence of fascism in an analysis which bears some striking similarities to that of Wieviorka: *inter alia*, Winant argues that race becomes more significant as class recedes as an organizing force in politics, and he emphasizes that the collapse of corporatist settlements and downward mobility are also important destabilizing forces, although Winant is more concerned to highlight the undermining of middle- rather than working-class material prospects in a new period of recession and restructuring. Winant includes a 'local' case study of changing identities in the USA in the post-civil rights era. He focuses on the contradictory pulls of 'panethnicity' and ethnic alliances on the one hand, and the growing class divisions within the black communities on the other, and raises some profoundly important queries about the potentialities of new forms of radical democratic politics for containing the tensions growing out of the crisis of white ethnicity and the white backlash, as well as the inequalities and discriminations faced by racialized minorities. A new radical democracy will require, as he emphasizes, a vision 'in which greater equality permits more flexibility and uncertainty about individual, and collective, racial identity and meaning'; above all, it is going to need a destabilization of any sense that one could be 'comfortable' with one's racial identity, a 'common sense' that needs to be exposed as a key component of local hegemonic orders.

Modern racisms and racialized identities thus form the fulcrum for this collection, but, to change metaphors, in a new vein. These questions are discussed in a form that puts at centre stage the interconnections between all three terms that appear in our title: racism, modernity and identity. In doing this, we hope that the book exhibits the relevance of a new terrain of debate for understanding racisms in a period of crisis in 'Western' social formations.

Notes

We are indebted to Anthony Giddens for valuable comments on an earlier version of the Introduction.

1 It is implicit in our remarks that 'modernity' and 'postmodernity' are indeed metanarratives. Whatever else the present period is characterized by, it is certainly not the death of metanarratives, although we would agree with Lyotard (1984) if his argument were construed to mean that there is a new scepticism towards the claims of metanarratives. Some of the difficulties of Lyotard's careless use of relevant concepts are discussed in Kellner (1988).
2 The literature on the debates over Western modernity is now vast, and it is impractical here to provide an adequate bibliography. For useful overviews, see Ross (1988); Boyne and Rattansi (1990); Nicholson (1990); Best and Kellner (1991); Smart (1992); Lash and Friedman (1992).

References

Best, S., and Kellner, D. (1991) *Postmodern Theory: Critical Interrogations*, London: Macmillan.
Boyne, R., and Rattansi, A. (eds) (1990) *Postmodernism and Society*, London: Macmillan.
Cheles, L., Ferguson, R., and Vaughan, M. (1991) *Neo-Fascism in Europe*, London: Longman.
Ford, G. (1992) *Fascist Europe: The Rise of Racism and Xenophobia*, London: Pluto Press.
Gooding-Williams, R. (ed.) (1993) *Reading Rodney King, Reading Urban Uprising*, London: Routledge.
Kellner, D. (1988) 'Postmodernism and social theory: some challenges and problems', *Theory, Culture and Society*, vol. 5, nos 2–3.
Lash, S., and Friedman, J. (eds) (1992) *Modernity and Identity*, Oxford: Basil Blackwell.
Lyotard, J.-F. (1984) *The Postmodern Condition: A Report on Knowledge*, Manchester: Manchester University Press.
Madhubuti, H. (ed.) (1993) *Why LA Happened*, Chicago: Third World Press.
Nicholson, L. (ed.) (1990) *Feminism/Postmodernism*, London: Routledge.
Ross, A. (ed.) (1988) *Universal Abandon? The Politics of Postmodernism*, Edinburgh: Edinburgh University Press.
Smart, B. (1992) *Modern Conditions, Postmodern Controversies*, London: Routledge.

Part I

RACISM AND 'POSTMODERNITY'

1

'WESTERN' RACISMS, ETHNICITIES AND IDENTITIES IN A 'POSTMODERN' FRAME

Ali Rattansi

Introduction

The debates around postmodernism and postmodernity, given great impetus by Lyotard's *The Postmodern Condition* (1984), continue apace, although with little apparent agreement about the terms of reference. This paper explores some aspects of their relevance for issues around racism and ethnicity. In particular, it asks whether, despite important caveats, a 'postmodern' frame can be constructed as a convenient device to bring a number of important recent developments in social and cultural theory into focus, and to enable a productive discussion of their relevance for questions of racism, ethnicity and identity.

My project, as begun in this contribution, is born of the conviction that there is much bold, innovative theorizing being undertaken in sociology, the relevance of which for understanding racialization and ethnic and national mobilization is becoming apparent and is clearly in need of greater exploration and development. At the same time, greater interdisciplinarity in the social sciences and humanities, which might perhaps be taken to indicate a 'postmodern' turn in these forms of inquiry, is also creating opportunities which allow old questions to be considered in new ways and points up the manner in which racialization and ethnic identifications may be taking new forms.

While much valuable research on these issues has been conducted under the rubric of, especially, Marxist and Weberian paradigms of various kinds, I share the growing sense of many that they exhibit an exhaustion that requires quite fundamental reconceptualization. This need not involve an erasure of what is valuable in these types of analysis, or result in a modish endorsement of all that is new. What is required is a rigorous engagement with new forms of theorization to assess their fruitfulness in illuminating questions of racism, ethnicity and identity. This paper begins to chart a way of engaging in this all too necessary project.

What I propose to do in this paper, then, is to provide both a particular take on the 'postmodern' turn, by constructing what I call a 'postmodern' frame, and a particular optic on issues around racism and ethnicity by deploying this 'postmodern' frame. By placing the term 'postmodern' consistently in quotes, I am registering reservations about its distinctiveness and indicating a provisionality about its use which are discussed more fully in what follows.

I make no apology for the relatively detailed discussion of the 'postmodern' frame provided here, for the purpose of this essay is twofold: the construction of a selective 'postmodern' frame, and an indication of its value in exploring questions of racism and ethnicity.

The 'Postmodern' Frame

My construction of the 'postmodern' frame as an analytical device highlights the following features:

1   The 'postmodern condition' as a reflection on the nature and limits of Western modernity.
2   'Modernity' as an analytical category: the form of conceptualization adopted here analyses especially the constitutive dualities of Western modernity.
3   The role of Western modernity's Others, both internal and external, real and imagined, in the formation and continuous reconstruction of Western identities, in particular by processes of marginalization of Others as binary opposites.
4   An exploration of the profound impact of new phases and conceptualizations of globalization.
5   The project of decentring and de-essentializing both 'subjects' and the 'social'.
6   Analyses of temporality and spatiality as constitutive features of the social, of subjectivity and of processes of identification.

7 A reconsideration of the relation between the 'psychic' and the 'social'.
8 An engagement with questions of sexuality and sexual difference.

Most of these elements are obviously intertwined. Thus my outline of the 'postmodern' frame as interpreted here is brought together under three broad rubrics. The bearing of each on questions of racism, ethnicity and identity is discussed after these fundamental elements of a 'postmodern' framing have been put in place.

The 'postmodern' frame I: the condition of 'postmodernity'

Lyotard's *The Postmodern Condition*, the founding text for most contemporary debates on postmodernism, has often found itself an easy target for a key 'performative contradiction', to borrow Habermas's (1987) telling phrase: that is, for reinstating a grand narrative-type distinction between modernity and postmodernity as epochal transformations of the contemporary age, while at the same time positing an 'incredulity towards metanarratives' as a key defining element of the postmodern condition. But Lyotard's position has always been more evasive on this question. In the appendix to the English translation of *The Postmodern Condition*, Lyotard asserts that the 'postmodern' is 'undoubtedly part of the modern', referring to it as modernism in 'the nascent state' (1984, p. 79). Elsewhere, he defines 'the post of postmodernity' as a process of 'ana-lysing, ana-mnesing, of reflecting' (1986, p. 6).

It is this sense of the 'postmodern' condition as a critical reflection on the character, foundations and limits of modernity that provides one of the basic underpinnings of the 'postmodern' frame deployed in my discussion of racism, ethnicity and related issues.

There is inevitably some disagreement about both the naming and character of this reflexivity towards modernity. Giddens (1990a) refers to the heightened reflexivity of contemporary intellectual life, in the West in particular, as a phase in the 'radicalization' of modernity, ushering in a period in which there is a recognition of, and anxiety surrounding, a collapse of Enlightenment confidence in the capacities of Reason and the certitude of Progress. The super-reflexivity of the current phase of modernity is seen by Giddens to have intrinsic connections with the social sciences, in so far as they are crucial to a process involving 'the chronic revision of social practices', in the light of those practices, which is part of 'the very tissue of modern institutions' (p. 40). But the anxieties surrounding the collapse of faith in Enlightenment certitudes is seen as a current having its fundamental roots in the Enlightenment feature of treating all beliefs and knowledges as provisional and revisable in the light of further theoretical and empirical advances, especially in the natural and social sciences. In this sense the anti-foundationalism often regarded as symptomatic of a transition to 'postmodernity' is seen by Giddens as a trend emerging in the heart of the modern project, and particularly evident in the work of Nietzsche in the mid-nineteenth and Heidegger in the early twentieth century. 'Postmodern' scepticism is only the 'self-clarification of modern thought', a radicalization of the Enlightenment trust in Reason.

While Giddens denies credibility to the term 'postmodernity', the notion that modernity has now entered a phase of chronic crisis appears intrinsic to his discussion. It is this crisis of confidence in the Enlightenment ideals of Reason, Progress and the possibilities for penetrating the secrets of nature, including 'human nature', and of remoulding the social order on the basis of the truths revealed by the natural and social sciences, that Bauman labels 'postmodernity'. Thus, for both Giddens and Bauman the present period is characterized not so much by radically new institutional configurations – although these are significant – as by a new intellectual sensibility. Bauman, however, appears to be more sceptical about the transformative possibilities underwritten by Giddens in 'Modernity and Utopia' (1990). The similarities and differences between Giddens and Bauman are strikingly exhibited in the latter's *Modernity and Ambivalence*:

> Postmodernity is modernity coming of age: modernity looking at itself at a distance rather than from inside, making a full inventory of its gains and losses, psychoanalysing itself, discovering the intentions it never before spelled out, finding them mutually cancelling and incongruous. Postmodernity is modernity coming to terms with its own *impossibility*: a self-monitoring modernity, one that consciously discards what it was once unconsciously doing. (1991, p. 272, emphasis added).

The difference between Giddens and Bauman may be characterized by referring to Habermas' famous early intervention: while Giddens appears to hold out some hope for modernity completing its project, Bauman baldly asserts its impossibility.

For the purposes of this essay it is not necessary to adjudicate between Giddens and Bauman, although I cannot resist the temptation to point out that in any case there is no vantage point from which it might be confidently concluded that 'modernity' can or cannot complete its project(s). Bauman appears here to be caught in a performative contradiction not untypical of postmodernists who seem to have boundless confidence in their generalizations while proclaiming the impossibility of prediction.

The point I wish to emphasize is that my construction of the 'postmodern' frame draws out that which is common to Bauman and Giddens. Thus the first theme of the 'postmodern' frame as deployed here is that it interrogates the nature, the foundations and the limits of (Western) modernity. Giddens, Bauman and others tend to conflate modernity with *Western* modernity *tout court*, a point to which I return, and which is also discussed by Slater in chapter 2.

One of the consequences of my mode of framing the 'postmodern' is that both Foucault and Derrida can be constructed as 'postmoderns', and indeed throughout this essay 'poststructuralism' will be regarded as a key element of the 'postmodern' frame.

Another is that there is an intrinsic connection between modernity and the 'postmodern' frame: the latter is a mode of being both inside and outside modernity, of stepping back, or out, and looking in, while still having one foot and eye, so to speak, inside modernity. This is a point that may be expressed by deploying a variety of representations. For instance, the 'postmodern' frame may be said to be one of the many proliferating language games of modernity, or a 'frame within a frame', and modernity might be regarded as becoming both object and subject within this frame.

However, to leave matters there would be to neglect some important considerations. Once the issue of modernity's complicity with, and constitution by, imperialist and colonialist projects is fully acknowledged, the form of distantiation and reflexivity that must be achieved cannot be captured by metaphors which merely refer to the 'postmodern' as a frame inside a frame. This would leave untransformed the many ways in which the 'postmodern' frame as derived from Bauman, Giddens, Foucault, Derrida and others is deeply ethnocentric, particularly in its failure to grasp the profound significance of imperialism, colonialism and their associated racisms as constitutive of modernity. A 'postmodern' frame which reflexively distances itself from modernity *and* from ethnocentric 'postmodern' frames thus has to engage in a more complex set of moves, and to set up locations which open up other 'spaces' from which to interrogate both modernity and its own reflexivities. In some sense this is a 'frame inside a frame inside another frame'. There is here the construction of a particular form of hybridity for which a new term could be invented. However, to avoid the proliferation of inelegant neologisms, I will continue to use the term 'postmodern frame', but with the understanding that it is always in an actual or potential state of internal displacement, that there is always a kind of counter-discourse operating as a sub-text within it, which can be mobilized to 'interrupt' the forms of reflexivity and interrogation of modernity found in the major sources I have drawn upon.

The spatial metaphors of displacement, other spaces and new locations, with which I have attempted to capture the complexity of the manoeuvres required by a 'postmodern' frame that is appropriate to analyses of modernity and its racisms, although suggestive of the forms of internal distantiation required, do not actually provide a proper specification of the epistemological questions that arise. That is, I am aware that a number of issues are left unresolved as to the nature of these sites of enunciation and the knowledges they supposedly produce. To take just one instance, it is arguable that the kind of frame that is being proposed here positions itself in the 'margins' of not only 'modernity', but 'postmodern' reflexivities as well. But what, epistemologically speaking, is 'marginality', and how does it manage to avoid various traps, for example an empiricism which epistemologically privileges marginalized groups and their subjectivities, or a kind of foundationalism which locates the margin in the subjectivity of diasporic intellectuals, as seems sometimes to be implied in the writings of figures such as Said, Bhabha and others discussed later in this essay?

I do not have the space here to tackle these complex issues beyond registering my awareness of them and stating my dissatisfaction with the lack of elaboration they have so far received.

This issue is itself embedded in three wider epistemological and theoretical questions concerning the construction of a 'postmodern' frame. First, is there a contradiction involved in interrogating the nature, foundations and limits of Western modernity while still using some of its own logics and devices? Second, to what extent does the questioning of modernity and its characteristic rationalities and epistemological foundations – that is, the 'anti-foundationalism' – of many of the 'postmoderns' as defined here collapse into a self-defeating relativism, an 'anything goes' nihilism and 'irrationalism'? Third, and related, how strongly can the 'postmodern' frame be specified as a form of theorization separate from other modes of analysis current in the social sciences and humanities? All three questions arise much more dramatically for the poststructuralist elements of the 'postmodern' frame as proposed here, and my – inevitably brief – comments on these issues focus on the work of Foucault and Derrida.

On the first issue, Derrida has clarified his position in a number of texts, most especially in the essay 'The principle of reason: the university in the eyes of its pupils' (1983), where he displays his commitment to the project of reasoned critique, which, as Norris has pointed out, is 'strictly inconceivable outside the tradition of enlightened rational critique whose classic formulations are still to be found in Kant' (1987, p. 162). Foucault, having resolutely set himself against the Enlightenment in many of his earlier works, came partially to revalorize the Enlightenment project, especially what he referred to as the Enlightenment 'attitude' and 'philosophical ethos' of 'permanent critique of our historical era' (1984, p. 42), admitting also that any modern project of critique had to accept its partial determination by the Enlightenment (p. 43). Thus although both Derrida and Foucault have consistently attempted to probe the limits of modern forms of 'rationality', they have not, in the final instance, placed themselves entirely outside many of their protocols.

With regard to questions of truth and accusations of adopting an 'anything goes' philosophical discourse, again Derrida has unequivocally distanced himself from appropriations of his work which saddle him with an irresponsible relativism and a licensing of unconstrained 'free play' in matters of interpretation and the hooking up of language to the external world – a key text here being 'Afterword: toward an ethic of discussion' in *Limited Inc* (1988). Foucault, on the other hand, remained ambiguous and elusive on questions of epistemology, but as Barrett (1991, p. 145) among others has emphasized, he was far from being a relativist, and it is worth pointing out that his own 'genealogical' and 'archaeological' investigations, while aware of their own historicity, partiality and provisionality, are inconceivable without an implicit grounding in truth-claims of some sort.

In other words, the 'postmodern' frame as constructed here should not be construed as relativist or 'irrationalist', although given the scope of this essay I am unable to offer any elaborate epistemological discussion and justification of it. The issue has necessarily to be 'bracketed'.

However, some remarks on the theoretical specificity of this framework are called for. It is intrinsic to the forms of poststructuralism that have influenced the construction of my 'postmodern' frame that 'strong' boundaries cannot be drawn around it. Inherent to the deconstructive 'attitude' which informs this frame is the project of exposing the relative arbitrariness of boundary formation in social and intellec-

tual configurations, and an interrogation of the policing of these borders by disciplinary apparatuses of power/knowledge. Thus, although
the theoretical framing adopted here obviously privileges particular
conceptions of the subject, the social and so forth, many of the
arguments advanced, inferences made and conclusions drawn about
racism, ethnicity and identity have resonances with claims made in
other theoretical frameworks. Moreover, there is no suggestion here
that specific historical, sociological and other forms of field-work
research are so determined by their theoretical frameworks that they
cannot be 'read' and deployed as part of an argument that purports
to come from what I shall construe as a 'postmodern' frame, despite
differences of theorization between the latter and the conceptual
architecture of the field research. In other words, the 'postmodern'
frame adopted here is against theoretical reductionism. By the same
token, the arguments emerging from my own analyses may be appropriated as part of discussions drawing upon other theorizations.

Thus, the classification involved in delineating the 'postmodern'
frame may be regarded as 'weak' rather than 'strong', positing
inherently permeable boundaries and areas of overlap with other
forms of conceptualization, and liable to internal inconsistencies and
incoherences of various kinds. As we shall see, the 'postmodern' frame
proposed here – to change metaphors – is composed of loosely knit
strands and no doubt always vulnerable to being unravelled.

The 'postmodern' frame II: modernity – and its Others

There appear to be just as many contestations over defining and
periodizing the 'modern' as there are uncertainties surrounding the
nature and timing of the 'postmodern', with some even tracing
the beginning of the 'modern' era to Augustine in the fourth century
(Smart, 1992, p. 8). On the other hand, given the significance of
the legacy of the European Enlightenment to debates between the
moderns and postmoderns, it is not surprising that most participants,
while mindful of pre-Enlightenment antecedents, tend to privilege a
conception of modernity as an era characterized by the fateful conjoining of an Enlightenment faith in the capacity of Reason and science
to penetrate the essential character of nature and humanity, with the
development of industrial society.

It is inappropriate here to rehearse controversies over the meaning
of 'modernity' as they have developed in recent years. Rather, it is
my purpose to indicate the distinctiveness of my 'postmodern' take on

modernity – although always with the caveat that this is an inevitably selective exercise open to debate and modification.

The 'modern' condition

The interpretation of 'modernity' in my version of the postmodern frame draws in part on Bauman's conception, but also highlights Foucauldian and Derridean themes which tend to get somewhat muted in Bauman's more Weberian inflections, and makes reference to some of Giddens's recent commentaries on the nature of what he variously terms 'late' or 'high' or 'radicalized' modernity. To begin with, it is worth pointing out that I concur with authors like Bauman and Giddens that industrialization, urbanization, commodification and constant and increasingly rapid social change are constitutive of Western modernity, and that modernity is in diverse ways a global phenomenon, the significance of which is commented upon in greater detail later.

However, it is immediately necessary to enter at least two important caveats. First, there has been a pronounced tendency in the work of Bauman in particular to neglect issues that derive from the specific pressures of capitalist social relations. As we shall see, this becomes evident in Bauman's interpretation of the Holocaust. I certainly do not wish to reduce modernity to capitalism, or to resurrect earlier notions of 'capitalist society' which gave an overriding significance to a particular organization of production relations in defining the character and trajectory of national polities. Rather, I wish to register that the stick does indeed seem to have been bent too far the other way.

My second reservation relates in part to a point made earlier about the ethnocentrism of so many 'postmodern' analyses: their astonishing silence on the migrations to the societies of advanced modernity from impoverished parts of the globe, especially the ex-colonies of these very polities. The effect is an equally damaging neglect of questions of racism and the new politics of cultural difference that are endemic features of western European societies, and which are also transforming the political contours of the United States, Canada and Australia.

With these caveats in mind, I want to turn to other aspects of 'postmodern' analyses which open up fruitful avenues for theorization and substantive investigation.

Modernity, ambivalence and Otherness

I want to begin with Bauman's suggestion that modernity is in part driven by a powerful striving for classificatory and social order, hence an uneasiness with ambiguities and ambivalences which disturb and destabilize neat boundaries and borders. There is, underlying this, according to Bauman, a fear of chaos, generated paradoxically by an awareness of diversity and the possibility of transformation.

Bauman's point needs to be supplemented by the more general observation that modernity is characterized by a duality in which rapid and incessant change, and the fragmentation that ensues from the power of market forces, are also accompanied by constant projects which attempt the conservation and indeed invention of traditions (Lash and Urry, 1987, p. 86, and 1994, pp. 246–8; Giddens, 1994). It is valuable to connect up this duality with Bauman's emphasis on modernity's striving for classificatory order and the ambivalence it generates, for it yields important insights, as we shall later see, in understanding processes by which particular segments of a population – for instance, diasporic communities – fall foul of one side of the duality of modernity: its drive for cultural assimilation.

Bauman refers to 'ambivalence' as a 'disorder of language' stemming from the inherent problem of imposing classificatory order on an inherently reclassifiable world (1991, p. 1). I would argue in Derridean terms that ambivalence is also inherent in *différance*, the ever-present possibility of re-inscribing and stretching and re-interpreting meaning in different contexts (as well as in the workings of the psychic economy, of which more later). The potential chaos of the infinitely mobile signifier constantly lurks in the interstices of language.

Among other things, this argument establishes the significance of the discursive, and the power of culture and its codes in constituting and ordering the experience of modernity – an emphasis on 'culture' and its codes which is a distinctive feature of the 'postmodern' frame.

However, Bauman exaggerates the 'acute discomfort' of ambivalence. My argument, instead, is that modernity's subjects are able to occupy different discursive positions, to switch codes and registers, and to negotiate between cultural modalities with far greater facility and reflective skill than is allowed for in Bauman's scheme. Thus, modernity's ambivalence is generated not by occupying only the first term of the binary between 'order' and 'chaos', *but by inhabiting both terms simultaneously* – there is a striving for order while at the same time there is an excitement, exhilaration and anxiety produced by rapid change and the proliferation of choices inherent in modernity's discursive and institutional configurations.

Moreover, drawing upon Bauman and Foucault, it can be seen that modernity's striving for social and intellectual order, beginning as it did in the seventeenth and eighteenth centuries, has become thoroughly intertwined with three distinctly modern projects: the *nation-state*, the *'gardening' state* and the *disciplinary society*. *Nation-states* have been driven by cultural assimilationism, and thus a form of strong cultural ordering, a point that hardly needs labouring, although it has a profound significance for understanding the formation of Western racism. In referring to the *gardening* metaphor for one of the key sets of projects of the modern European state, Bauman not only highlights the will to find technical, managerial solutions to all problems, but draws attention to what Foucault calls biopolitics and the 'management of populations': in this particular instance, a form of management that uses the metaphors of plants and breeding to embark on a project of 'weeding out' and 'decontamination'. The conception of the *disciplinary* society as I use it here draws heavily, of course, on Foucault's analysis of the modern social as a network of power/knowledge configurations that both produce and regulate a modern form of individuation, one which installs social scientific technologies of government to produce a new form of power, disciplinary bio-power, which regulates the social not so much by centralized coercion as by the institutional production and surveillance of individuals and their bodies in the fields of education, the economy, medicine, mental health, criminal justice, welfare and so forth.

These features of the modern are crucial to an understanding of a set of processes that are of key significance in my 'postmodern' framing. That is, the striving for stable classificatory systems, articulated with the modern projects of constructing disciplined, managed, healthy nations has consistently involved the weeding out of contaminating 'Others' who appear to disturb the social order, who fall foul either of cultural/ethnic boundaries or seem to transgress conceptions of the 'normal' as defined by discourses such as biology, medicine, psychology and psychiatry, sociology, criminology, pedagogy and economics, and their associated disciplinary and regulatory institutions such as hospitals, prisons, schools and factories. Remember in this context that in the nineteenth century phrenology was an important discipline, while in the early twentieth century eugenics played a significant part in processes of normalization and the management of populations. Both have had important effects on processes of racialization.

To pursue the point further, the identities of Western modernity must be seen as constructed through processes of 'normalization', to borrow Foucault's term, but which have the effect of marginalizing those Other populations – among a diverse group, the insane, the sick, the criminalized, the educational failures or the 'ineducables', and those workers labelled incompetent or disabled. This allows consideration of a crucial element of the 'postmodern' frame applicable not only to modernity but to the social in general; identities, individual and collective, are here conceptualized (in Derridean mode) as tending to be constructed in processes involving comparison, alterity, marginalization and opposition to other identities, a point elaborated upon in the next section and whose ramifications are explored at many other points.

Now it is notorious that, in writing the genealogies of normalizing technologies and the processes of the marginalization of Others, Foucault was conspicuously silent about Europe's *other* Others, the 'native' populations subjected to the brutal forces of slavery, colonial domination and racism.[1] However, as we shall see, this should not be regarded as a necessary bar to an extension of his work in exploring questions of racism and the effects of Europe's imperial expansion on both the West and 'the Rest'.[2] A similar argument applies, of course, to the work of Bauman and others, although as I discussed at some length earlier, this does mean that these 'postmodern' analyses need always to be approached with a certain vigilance and in a potentially 'interruptive' mode.

There are two other constitutive features of modernity that I wish to set out as visualized in a postmodern frame. The first, in contrast to the Foucauldian theme of surveillance and disciplinary power, and the constitutive role of imperialism and colonialism, acknowledges that *the period of modernity is also the period of democratic transformations*, in which forms of politics have become institutionalized, more strongly in some societies than othes, and usually allied with liberalism or social democracy, that undermine the certainty of describing that society from a singular viewpoint, thus allowing a multiplicity of political institutions and subject positions (Mouffe, 1989). Of course, in the case of polities with colonial possessions this was always a case of democratic projects at home – achieved after protracted struggles by disenfranchised groups – rather than in the imperial possessions, which were usually regarded, even by liberals such as Mill, as incapable of democratic self-government (Parekh, 1993).

Modernity and globalization

The second is globalization, already prefigured in the suggestion that imperialism and colonialism have been constitutive of modernity. While it is easy to dismiss as 'global babble' some of the banalities about growing interdependence on a world scale, it is clear that serious new issues are at stake. Of course, discussions of globalization have inevitably found themselves swamped in profound disagreements around periodization (when did it start, are we experiencing a significantly new phase?), generative forces, and mechanisms and logics of development (see McGrew, 1992 for a useful review). For the purpose of framing globalization within the 'postmodern' turn as conceived of here, I wish to emphasize only the following key themes, which will be interwoven at appropriate points in the discussion of racism, ethnicity and related concerns in subsequent sections.

The first is a refusal to reduce globalization to a singular or primary determinant, whether this is posited as the capitalist world economy, as in Wallerstein's analysis (e.g. Wallerstein, 1984), or technology, in the form of information technology and the means of travel, such as jet-powered airliners, as in other accounts (McGrew, 1992). That is, multidimensional analyses of the sort suggested by Appadurai (1990) are intrinsic to a 'postmodern' frame, with no necessary connections assumed to exist between the forces involved, or any necessary logic of development presumed to inhere in any particular driving force, whether this is said to be the economic, the political, the cultural or the geopolitical.

Moreover, globalization is framed here as sets of uneven, contradictory, confused and uncertain processes which in their complexity and heterogenity can make a mockery of the usual analytical binaries, such as universalization/particularization, homogenization/differentiation, centralization/decentralization, and stability/instability, which are deployed in discussions of most global transformations.

In addition, the postmodern frame acknowledges the full significance of cultural processes in the formations of globalization not merely in the new forms of the circulation of knowledges and images, but in the complex interrelation of these to the formation and reformation of collective identities, whether based on ethnicity, nationalism or other forms of identification. This emphasis is congruent with the general point made earlier about the importance ascribed to 'cultural' transformations in the 'postmodern' frame.[3]

Globalization means, among other things, that the cultural boundaries of nation-states are breached in myriad ways, creating opportunities for cultural cosmopolitanisms of various kinds, but also generating anxieties which are experienced in different ways by locales and their populations, and managed and mobilized through a range of strategies by local and national state agencies, political parties, including especially racist ones, 'new' social movements such as the Greens, and commercial enterprises.

Within these dynamics of global cultural formation and the transformation of national cultures, the 'postmodern' frame is particularly sensitive to *new* forms of hybridization, syncretism, fusion, difference and incommensurability, as cultural collectivities, imaginations, fantasies and agencies are driven to rub up against each other, leading to fracturing and recomposition, a redrawing of boundaries, and the creation and re-creation of new forms and antagonisms. These processes are not only cultural, but *political* in the broadest sense, being constitutive of a variety of practices: defensive, affirmatory or transformative, whether in the arts (including music, as we shall see) or involved more explicitly in the conventional systems of political representation, in the form of movements which mobilize collectivities in civil society, the public sphere, and across the artificialities of the public-private divide.

Postmodernist aesthetics are crucial here. They simultaneously enable and are in part constituted by these new cultural formations, involving as they do irreverent deconstructions, fusions and recompositions, producing new cultural forms which take popular culture seriously and debunk the absolutist claims of high culture. (For a justification of the use of 'postmodernism' to characterize particular contemporary cultural and aesthetic currents, see Boyne and Rattansi, 1990b.)

The processes and effects of globalization cannot be fully understood without grasping the profound significance of the temporal and spatial transformations that are involved. These are discussed later as part of the general conceptualization of time/space as a defining element of the 'postmodern' frame.

The 'postmodern' frame III: decentring, de-essentialization, sexuality and identities

I have argued earlier that a 'postmodern' framing regards the production and representation of particular identities as relational: that is, as constructed through alterity, comparison, opposition and possible marginalization of other identities. To put it in different terms, this creation takes the form of representations which construct a kind of mirroring, in which collective and individual identities are formed as much by 'reflections' of, and on, what the perceiving subject is not, as by what it is, as 'seen' in the mirror of self-regarding and other-regarding texts and practices.

Decentring and de-essentializing the subject and the social

In a 'postmodern' framing, this mode of analysing identities is intrinsically connected to a decentring and de-essentializing of the subject and the social. *Decentring* refers here in the first instance to the deflation of a rationalist/Cartesian pretension to unproblematic self-knowledge. It also involves a critique of the conception of a linear connection of subjects to the external world, in which reality is made transparent from a uniquely privileged vantage point through the application of rationality and empirical disciplines. *De-essentialization* is an intimately related manoeuvre, cutting the ground away from conceptions of subjects and social forms as reducible to a timeless, unchanging, defining and determining element or ensemble of elements – 'human nature', for example, or in the case of the social, the logic of the market or mode of production. Alterity is important here because subjects and the social, and thus both individual and collective identities, are seen not as essentially given, but as constantly under construction and transformation, a process in which differentiation from Others is a powerful constitutive force.

In Foucauldian terms, the decentering and de-essentialization of the *subject* is undertaken on the one hand by exposing the many 'sites' – understood to include discourses and practices – of enunciation and positioning which fragment the subject and challenge the possibility of a singular, non-contradictory identity, and on the other by constructing genealogies of subject-formation. These de-essentialize by exposing how different have been the conceptions of 'human nature' – with regard to mental and physical characteristics and capacities, sexualities and so forth – installed in different historical periods by discursive regimes and their associated institutions of power and knowledge (e.g. Foucault, 1977, 1979, 1980a). The *social* in Foucault is decentred and de-essentialized by a series of moves, partly via the methodology of 'genealogy' and the denial of the possibility of reducing the social to any one causal principle of operation and determination; also by emphasizing the heterogeneity of sources of power and the operation of power as a form of microphysics always subject to a diversity of strategies and resistance; and by an emphasis upon the social as a product of practices of regulation, resistances and representation rather than a pre-given structure which reproduces itself through agencies of socialization, as conceptualized in conventional sociology and most versions of Marxism (Foucault, 1977, 1980b).

Decentring and de-essentialization, as undertaken through Derridean deconstruction, are also central features of the 'postmodern' frame as conceived in this essay.[4] Derrida also famously de-essentializes and decentres identities by a range of theoretical manoeuvres: by his critique of logocentrism and phallocentrism; by invoking *différance* as intrinsic to the operation of language and meaning; and by exposing and undoing, or *deconstructing*, the binarities by which attempts are constantly made to hold identities in place. Derrida's critique of logocentrism undermines the consistent Western metaphysical attempt to find a pure origin. For Derrida there can be no pure origin: any identity to *be* at all must presuppose difference from something else. Moreover, instead of a stable polarity between identity and difference, Derrida coins the term *différance*, which combines the sense of 'to differ' with that of 'to defer', thus introducing an element of temporality, and highlighting the mobility of language, meaning and identity. The concept of *différance* draws attention to various features: the ever-present potential of a play of signification by reference to other related concepts; reinscription in a different context; and thus, a stretching of meaning, and forms of transformation of identity. In a Derridean conceptualization, all determinate identities always involve *provisional* closure; thus they are always open to reinterpretation and transformation.

And to return briefly to the question of binarity, Derrida's argument is that the construction of identities in Western culture is thoroughly permeated by the erection of binary oppositions such as nature/culture, rational/irrational, man/woman, good/evil, etc., in which the first term is regarded as superior, and the second usually involves features that pose a threat to the first. Derridean *deconstruction* of binary oppositions involves various moves: an exhibition of 'marginal' cases which are undecidable with reference to the binary as posited; a demonstration of the difficulties of defining the first term without including elements of the other; and, rather then a reversal of the binary, a strategy that attempts to question fundamentally the very grounds on which the binary is erected (e.g. Derrida 1977, 1978, 1981; Gasché, 1986; Norris, 1987; Ryan, 1982).

While Derrida gestures towards a connection between Western 'logocentrism' and 'ethnocentrism' (1981, pp. 24–5), and has explicitly

written about racism and apartheid (1985), it has been left to others
to draw out the relevance of deconstruction for understanding questions of racism, ethnicity, Western colonial domination and so on –
work which is discussed separately in this essay.

The decentring and de-essentialization of the subject and the social,
and the related critiques of the search for universal guarantees and
foundations of knowledge, lead on to a critique, as Laclau and Mouffe
(1985) have highlighted, of epistemologically privileged subject positions, and politically privileged collective subjects – classes, nations,
'races' – charged with a unique role in political opposition and transformation.

Laclau and Mouffe's work represents an important advance in the
construction of a decentred, de-essentialized conception of the social,
extending in particular the work of Derrida, and it undoubtedly has
relevance for issues of racism, ethnicity and forms of anti-racist politics. In the present context it is possible to provide only the briefest
reference to their important project; a more elaborate consideration
will appear in another publication (Rattansi, forthcoming). Most
immediately, then, I wish to endorse an undoing of the 'social' which
posits 'not an interaction or determination between fully constituted
areas of the social, but a field of relational semi-identities in which
"political", "economic" and "ideological" elements all enter into
unstable relations of imbrication without ever managing to constitute
themselves as separate objects' (Laclau, 1990, p. 24). There is a play
between necessity and contingency such that 'the boundaries between
the contingent and the necessary are constantly displaced' (p. 27),
and the field of the social is a sort of 'trench war' in which 'different
political projects strive to articulate a greater number of social signifiers around themselves' to 'fix meanings around a nodal point' (p. 28).
The social is never simply repetitive and reproductive, but always
subject to subversion. Identities, relationally and contingently formed,
are constituted by power relations, and are always open to 'dislocation'
and threatened by the 'outside' or 'other' which in part defines the
positive elements. In effect, the social is a 'decentred structure' composed of practices of centring, the construction of power centres
around nodal points of articulation (pp. 30–1, 39–40). (For another
project of 'undoing the social', see Game, 1991.)

Identities and time/space

The Derridean concept of *différance*, as I have remarked above, and Laclau's notion of dislocation crucially introduce the significance of temporality in the constitution and possible transformation of identities. Of course, these emphases are not unique to Derrida and Laclau, although both provide original – and related – theoretical infrastructures to establish the point.

In a variety of contemporary social theorizations the role of spatiality is also being acknowledged, and I would argue that the complex intertwining of time and space in constituting the 'social' and modes of individuation, taken together with the social constructions of temporality and spatial organization, have to be given due emphasis in a 'postmodern' frame. However, it is simply not possible to engage here with what is now a voluminous literature on these issues, beyond making some general points.

'Time' and 'space' have to be regarded as equally important. The implausible privileging of one or the other, implicit or otherwise – for example, temporality in the work of Laclau (rightly taken to task by Massey, 1993) and Giddens (see Soja, 1989, and Urry, 1991, for critiques), or spatiality in the 'postmodernism' of Jameson and others (Jameson, 1984, 1991) – has to be avoided. Relatedly, time cannot be *opposed* to space, with the former connoting movement and the latter being seen as static; if space is seen as socially constituted, then it has to be conceptualized as intrinsically dynamic and in a continuous process of transformation. These deconstructions of the time/space binary also enable an undoing of the moves by which the supposed dynamism of Time has been connotatively linked to History, Progress, Reason and the Male in Western culture, and whereby Space has been either seen simply as not-Time – that is, as lack – or filled out with categories like stasis, nostalgia, emotion and the body, which also allows them to be construed as Female (Massey, 1993, pp. 148–50). Moreover, as Foucault (1980b, 1986) and others have emphasized, considerations of spatiality cannot be neglected in analyses of power.

Additionally, and crucially, there are strong emotional investments in 'spaces', and thus in particular national and local landscapes, architecture, forms of spatial organization and so forth, around which identities are constructed and valorized by temporal and spatial narratives and representations. The places, and the individual and collective identities involved in these narratives, representations and processes, are in crucial senses 'imaginary' in form. They are sites of fantasy, pleasure, ambivalence, anxiety and paranoia. In conditions of contemporary, advanced Western modernity, there is a constant if uneven restructuring of the 'local' and the 'global' that leads to a constant reconfiguration of time/space relations, which may heighten anxieties while opening up tempting and exciting possibilities.

This last point is a formulation in spatial and temporal terms of more general points about modernity, and its relation to globalization, that I have endorsed earlier. Among other things, we have here the phenomenon of what Harvey (1989) has called 'time-space compression', in which the extraordinary speeding up produced by contemporary technologies of transportation, communication and information transfer has the effect of shrinking global spatiality. The almost instantaneous, often 'live' transmission of images of momentous events around the globe by the mass media now have the effect, in my view, of heightening anxieties by representing a world of almost terrifying contingency and danger, thus producing even greater incoherences in the public narratives and images of time and space through which individuals and 'local' communities can create secure identities. The loss of 'anchorage' involved here may be amplified by often devastating transformations in locales produced by the internationalization of production and the globalization of capital flows. Juxtaposed with the settlement of migrant populations, also part of the spatial reconfigurations produced by global flows of populations, the results can be explosive in relation to the racialization of such locales. One important element, also discussed later, is the way the global reach of mass communication technologies creates a desire for self-insertion in the images and spectacles being transmitted, leading to a 'staging' of events by 'locals' to gain international and national recognition, again with consequences for racialized conflict and violence. The fragmenting effects of mass communicated narratives of global contingency, danger and risk are exacerbated by the intrinsic element of chaos in the spatial, which is the result of unintended consequences and the juxtaposition of sites structured by divergent contingencies and causalities (Massey, 1993, pp. 156–7).

Psychoanalysis and identity

Any 'postmodern' decentring of the subject has to engage with psychoanalytic contributions to the understanding of the formation of identities and processes of identification, especially in the forms they have been analysed in poststructuralism and poststructuralist feminism. But thereby a 'postmodern frame' not only must include a consideration of the relation between the psychic and the social, but also has to regard questions of sexuality and sexual difference as of vital importance. The effects of these questions on the understanding of racism and ethnicity are explored in the second half of this essay.

The 'postmodern' significance of psychoanalysis lies in displacing the centred, rational subject with a subject whose unconscious desires, including sexual desire, constantly disrupt the conscious logic of intention and rationality. Second, and this is particularly true of the Lacanian version, the emphasis on unconscious desires and processes of imaginary constructions of coherence allows considerable play for fantasy in the formation of identities and the operation of subjectivities (for a discussion of the concept of fantasy in psychoanalytic terms, see Laplanche and Pontalis, 1986). Coherence is constantly attempted through *narratives* of the self and identities: that is, by way of *representations*. Third, the fantasy of coherence fails to neutralize the effects of the myriad forms of splitting – especially between the masculine and the feminine, and 'good' and 'bad' parts of the self – which remain with the subject and find expression in complex ways in processes of identification, ambivalence and disavowal (Lacan, 1977; Laplanche and Pontalis, 1973, pp. 205–8, 427–9, 1986; Hall, 1992b): in other words, in shifts and splits in identity.

'Postmodern' feminism

Versions of especially Lacanian psychoanalysis have had a profound influence on feminist analyses of sexuality and sexual difference, although not without controversy (Rose, 1986; Grosz, 1990; Butler, 1990). My purpose here is not to comment on these debates, but to outline the general impact of poststructuralism on feminist theory and thereby to indicate how aspects of the analysis of sexual difference are constitutive of the 'postmodern' frame.

Poststructuralist feminism's de-essentializing, and decentring and thus anti-foundationalist moves have, in the first place, had the effect of putting a question mark over the founding subject of earlier feminism: woman (Riley, 1988). Any possible consensus on the category of woman has been challenged by the general poststructuralist premise that all subjects are *produced* by relations of power and knowledge, *including feminism* as a discursive formation. But second, even the plural 'women' cannot survive as a stable signifier, because gender is not constructed in a consistent form in varying historical contexts. Moreover, it is criss-crossed by ethnic, class and national and other divisions, thus rendering 'gender' problematic as a separable dimension of social relations. Third, the notion of patriarchy as a singular form of trans-historical and cross-cultural male domination has also been challenged for its totalizing and ethnocentric essentialism (Butler, 1990, p. 3). This deflation of the explanatory claims of 'patriarchy' has been accompanied, in postmodern feminisms, by a displacement of the search for the ultimate, definite origins of male domination by a more historically and culturally nuanced analysis of particular forms and contexts of domination, subordination and resistance (Fraser and Nicholson, 1988). And finally, the poststructuralist emphasis on the cultural production of bodily characteristics and capacities has undermined the biological basis of the sex/gender distinction ubiquitous in early feminist theory (Butler, 1990, pp. 6–7).

It will become apparent in what follows that many of these anti-foundationalist, de-essentializing and decentring moves have considerable relevance for, and resonance in, contemporary analysis of racism and ethnicity. None more so, in fact, than a further element of the feminist project (and this is not necessarily confined to versions of poststructuralist or postmodern feminism): the fundamental and perhaps fatal undermining of the Enlightenment equation between masculinity and rationality, the construction of Woman as the Other of Reason.

The 'postmodern' project invites a deconstruction of precisely these sorts of *superimposition* of binaries upon one another – reason/irrationality, rational/emotional, culture/nature, masculine/feminine and others – which have not merely underwritten the Western placing of women in subordination (see, for example, the discussion by Hekman, 1990), but have also marked out an inferiorizing and marginalizing location for the subjects of the West's imperial and colonial domination of large parts of the globe.

Having constructed a 'postmodern' frame, it is now possible to explore the distinctiveness of some of what it reveals about questions of racism, ethnicity and identity.

Imperial and colonial alterities: formations of 'the West' – and its 'Others'

The 'discourses' of the West

Just as feminists, partly under the influence of poststructuralism, have exposed the masculinism of the binarities which enthroned the European male at the centre of rationality, so too, especially in the wake of the struggles for decolonization throughout the twentieth century, has it become increasingly clear how the formation of 'Western' identities has been a process profoundly shaped by European encounters with those other 'Others', met, pillaged and subjugated during voyages of 'discovery'. The 'discoveries' the West made were as much discoveries, and productions, of *itself* as of the peoples and lands encountered.

Arguably, what defines the inauguration of Western modernity is the emergence of rationalism, symbolized by the Cartesian ego. But this is also the period of imperial expansion, in which European encounters with these 'Others' determines in part the *meaning* of rationality, thus giving these initial encounters as much claim to heralding the beginning of modernity as any other set of events (Todorov, 1984, p. 5).

To put it differently, most forms of Western racism are inconceivable and incomprehensible without an understanding of how 'Western' identities – and those of its Others – have continually been formed and created by actual and imagined encounters with the non-Western Others of modernity. Identities such as 'the West' and 'European', even 'white', their conflation with conceptions of rationality, 'civilization' and Christianity, and the superimposition upon these of images of paganism and savagery as constituted by binaries such as naked/clothed, oral/literate, technologically backward/advanced, were not already 'in place' – they came into being in processes of imperial exploitation and colonial domination.

Moreover, temporality and spatiality have been crucially imbricated in these processes. Spatially, these 'other spaces' of Western modernity became *extensions* as well as the *outside* of Western identities, and as we shall see, they had profound effects on identities inside the geographical boundaries of the West. In temporal terms, the non-Western Other could be denied *coevalness*, as Fabian (1983) has put it in his critique of Western anthropology, by being treated as a 'primitive': child-like both in the sense of being at a stage of development that 'the West' had already passed through and as indicative of a state requiring tutelage and governance. Note too, that the early encounters between 'the West' and 'Others' occurred at a time when the 'civilizing' process as described by Elias (1978) – particular forms of bodily technique, hygiene, clothing, physical organization of domestic and public spaces, modes of consuming food with implements, etc. – were themselves in a process of formation, allowing a projection of anxieties about these social codes on to populations with quite different conceptions of relations with nature and of social intercourse.

'Postmodern' frame work has been a crucial element in more recent analyses of the set of processes by which 'the West' has continually 'discovered' and formed itself, while at the same time violating and irrevocably transforming 'the Rest'. A range of poststructuralist intellectual resources have been brought to bear on this question, supplemented by forms of feminism, psychoanalysis and Marxism.

Some of this work, especially that of Edward Said, Homi Bhabha and Gayatri Chakravorty Spivak, is by now well known and will be very briefly discussed here. But my purpose is also to highlight elements which are either ignored or seriously underplayed in these better-known analyses.

Several fundamental premises are shared by poststructuralist/'postmodern' analyses of Western imperialism and colonial adventures: that these have been as much subject-constituting projects as those of territorial expansion and economic exploitation; that questions of identity-formation have thus been of critical importance in shaping, legitimating and also destabilizing the whole enterprise; that the encounters between 'the West' and 'the rest' have been mutually constitutive – the cultures of both have been profoundly shaped by colonialism and imperialism; that the 'Western' identities so formed have been framed relationally, in difference (and *différance*) – that is, by conceptions of what 'the West' is not like, by way of constructions of the supposed attributes of the subjugated or colonized Other; that an analysis of imperial and colonial discourses is therefore indispensable, for subjects are constituted in and through discourses, which provide 'speaking' positions, subject-positions, identities and identifications; and that, while discourses clearly have institutional locations, the Marxist base-superstructure schema has limited scope within analyses which conceive of discourses (in poststructuralist as well as other terms) as object-constituting, thus breaking the cultural/material or words/things binaries (Barrett, 1992).

While much of the work discussed in this section refers to earlier historical periods, the significance of its fundamental premises for

understanding contemporary forms of ethnicity and racism will
become apparent in subsequent sections. However, it must be pointed
out that any project of deconstructing and destabilizing Western cultural hegemonies has in any case to engage with their *formations* and
continuing effectivities – such analyses cannot be dismissed as 'merely
historical'. Rather, they should be understood also as investigations
of processes by which identities and cultural locations have come to
be relatively 'fixed', and as continuing to provide cultural resources
and discursive repertoires in the formation of contemporary ethnicities and racisms. An important illustration of this point is provided by
the manner in which AIDS came to be seen as an 'African' disease,
a form of representation that drew upon a range of colonial discourses
regarding African 'primitiveness' and supposedly associated sexualities, linked in a chain of connotations with more recent anxieties
around homosexuality (Watney, 1990).

'Colonial discourse analysis': Said, Bhabha and Spivak

Edward Said's *Orientalism* (1978), despite the reservations expressed
by its critics (Clifford, 1988; Mani and Frankenberg, 1985; Young,
1990 and in this volume; Ahmad, 1992) and the self-criticism of its
author (1985) remains a key source of inspiration for what has come
to be called 'colonial discourse analysis'. For Said, 'Orientalism' is a
vast assemblage of cultural and institutional networks, comprised of
historical, philosophical, linguistic, anthropological and other forms
of scholarship, supplemented by other narratives such as travellers'
accounts and fiction, which created 'the Orient' as an object of both
study and government. Orientalists and their knowledges were, and
to some degree continue to be, deeply implicated in the way the
West administered and exploited 'Oriental territories' – Said's own
work refers primarily to the 'Arab' Orient – and appropriated their
cultures. Among other resources, Said uses Foucault's concept of
discourse to analyse a creation at once intellectual and politico-administrative, a form of power/knowledge which underwrote Western domination by producing the Orient as always inferior, according to Said,
whether in religious belief, intellectual capacity or political talent, and
thus as requiring and benefiting from Western domination. In the
nineteenth century, biological theories fused with other discourses to
racialize the discourses and practices of Orientalism, thus reinforcing
its capacity to create an epistemological and ontological binary
between Occident and Orient, on to which were heaped a series of

antinomies, some of them deriving from European fears of the internal 'Others' so well analysed by Foucault (Said, 1978). The Orient has thus been one of the poles of difference that has given Europe and 'the West' fundamental elements of its identity, and especially its continuing sense of superiority over 'the Rest'.

Said's work has by now inspired a vast body of what one might broadly call deconstructive scholarship, which has engaged in intellectually 'undoing the West' – exposing its dependence on external and internal Others for a positive identity as well as exploring the role of particular politico-administrative discourses in establishing its hegemony. A brilliant instance and development is Gauri Viswanathan's genealogy of the creation of English literary studies for the Indian middle classes as a strategy for stabilizing British rule through a process of co-optation and mediated rule by acculturation (1987). The strategy both drew upon and furthered the establishment of literary studies in British education, and was represented as the dissemination of a literary knowledge that was in the interests of 'humanity' and was 'objective, universal and rational' (Viswanathan, 1987, pp. 18, 20–1). Here we see English literary studies as simultaneously a humanist, Enlightenment (and 'enlightenment') and political project, conjoining the 'interests' of Reason, Humanity, Government and Imperialism, and forming both British cultural institutions and one of their most significant Others.

In this form of the West's undoing, serious epistemological and ontological questions immediately surface. To reiterate a point made earlier, what sort of epistemological stance allows an appropriation of 'Western' frames of analysis such as poststructuralism, and their transformation and deployment in deconstructing Western knowledges and their disciplinary foundations from the point of view of the West's Others? And ontologically, what is now the status of entities such as the 'Orient' or 'Occident', 'East' and 'West'?

It is arguable that Said's attempts to work through these epistemological and ontological considerations have been less than convincing (Young 1990; Clifford, 1988). If other poststructuralist inspired 'colonial discourse' analysts have also been evasive in the face of these seemingly intractable issues, they have nevertheless managed to rework Said's powerful but flawed theses in genuinely original and productive ways.

Bhabha, drawing ingeniously and variously upon Derrida, Fanon, Foucault, Freud and Lacan, has focused on the chronic instability of the binaries constructed in colonial discourses. What emerges from his readings of various episodes in the colonial project is not so much the operation of relatively fixed divisions and inversions into Orient, not-Orient or Occident, of powerless/powerful, as implied by Said, but the movements of *différance*, ambivalence, disavowal and resistance which insert themselves at the very point that colonial authority bears down on and interacts with native cultural practices. The destabilization of colonial authority, created by the production of questioning, 'hybrid' versions of colonial impositions such as Christianity (Bhabha, 1984), operates alongside the complexities of anxiety and ambivalence. These are generated partly by the creation of 'colonial subjects' – especially by practices of acculturation of the type discussed by Viswanathan – who 'mimic' the colonizers, thus upsetting a simple grid of inferiority and superiority, for 'mimicry' is at once resemblance and menace (Bhabha, 1986); and partly through the workings of a psychic economy which produces the colonized Other as both familiar and strange, as knowable and inscrutable, as contemptible and desirable, the object of both paranoia and fantasy, and thus of fear and pleasure (Bhabha, 1983; see also Nandy, 1983, p. 72).

In Bhabha's work are found dimensions of the workings of power which take the analysis decisively beyond not only Said, but Foucault and Derrida as well, while retaining their fundamental interest in interrogating processes of enunciation and address, and the associated multiple subject-positions and formations of contradictory subjects and identities.

These are motifs that Bhabha has now developed in relation to a more explicit concern with temporality and modernity as they connect with the ambivalences of the 'nation' as a cultural and political form (1990a, 1990b). The nation appears in Bhabha's account as chronically riven with ambivalences as it attempts to contain the fissures that animate its very being. To paraphrase his argument in terms of the framing adopted in my essay, the nation is a decentred *cultural* artefact that constantly endeavours to *naturalize* its artifice by rhetorical and administrative strategies. Mythological origins, supposedly 'lost in the mists of time', are constantly constructed in narratives, literary and historical, or enacted in exercises of power over populations. Forms of address are produced which attempt to construct a national unity out of a diversity of 'peoples'. But the culturally bounded and politically policed space and time of the nation are constantly breached. The artifice can be exposed in deconstructive readings of significant texts, which is precisely the purpose of Bhabha's collection, *Nation and Narration* (1990a), and is challenged in counter-narratives of subordinated and 'hybrid' populations. The 'people' thus must be thought of as existing in 'double-time', for the project of producing the nation as a community involves a tension between a 'pedagogic' authority of continuity and a 'performative' strategy (1990b, p. 297) in which the ragged, potentially transgressive cultures of everyday life are constantly brought under the sway of a narrative of what one might call a national 'comm*unity*'.

What Bhabha refers to as his 'growing, if unfamiliar, sense of the nation as one of the major structures of ideological ambivalence within the cultural representations of modernity' (1990c, p. 4) is by no means unconnected with his interest in colonialism. A special place is occupied by 'minority discourse' in Bhabha's account of those liminal regions of the national culture from which the pedagogy of the nation is contested (1990b, pp. 306–8). Minority discourse appears to be the product of minorities displaced to the metropolitan culture from the former colonies. While Bhabha acknowledges that minority cultures might generate 'a history of the people' and become 'the gathering points of political solidarity', 'minority discourse' is *defined* by Bhabha as incapable of engaging in a homogenizing of cultural experience (1990b, p. 308).

This is a convenient, if perplexing move, for no serious theorization is offered of the relation between minority cultures and minority discourse. Moreover, the later is always referred to in the singular. At this point the reader has a growing, familiar sense of the epistemological problems elided in much colonial discourse analysis and other writings claiming a certain authority and authenticity for their origins in relations of marginality – a difficulty I have referred to earlier in this essay. It is now appropriate to turn to the work of another, equally influential figure in colonial discourse analysis.

In exposing the 'violent episteme' of an imperialism that produced 'the colonial subject as history's nearly selved other', Gayatri Chakravorty Spivak also engages in a deconstruction which attempts to displace rather than merely reverse the opposition colonizer/colonized (1985, pp. 134, 147). 'Who is the native?' she asks (1985, p. 134) and explores possible answers in a series of interviews and essays on colonial discourse which exhibit the variety of representations and fabrications by which colonial systems of authoritative, discursive practices constructed natives as the 'subjects' of imperial rule (1987, 1990). With an even more self-conscious eclecticism than that of Bhabha, Spivak refers to herself as a *bricoleur*, with deconstruction, Foucauldian archaeology and genealogy, Marxism, psychoanalysis and feminist frames 'interrupting' each other in her explorations. These breach disciplinary boundaries between literary analysis, historical research, political economy and philosophy to produce a range of interventions

that quite deliberately defy easy summary, assimilation and critical
interrogation. Issues of class, 'race', gender (1900, 1987, p. 81) and the
politics of the contemporary Western academy figure more prominently than in Bhabha's work in interventions which constantly
attempt to unsettle and disrupt the reader – and listener, many of her
essays being originally presented as lectures – with shifts of theory
and register and in objects and modes of analysis. Her work ranges
from engagements with French feminisms to translations of Derrida,
from deconstructivist readings of canonical English literary texts to
historical retrievals of 'subaltern' women in colonial India, and readings of contemporary Bengali women writers.

Spivak's most recent work has become famous for a question related
to that of 'who is the native?': 'Can the subaltern speak?' (1988). This
thematizes a series of concerns about the forms in which 'native'
resistances to the networks of imperial and indigenous class and
patriarchal power can be read and written about, 'retrieved' that is,
without collapsing the narratives into humanist discourses of supposedly authentic consciousness, or myths of pure nativist cultures of
origin which might form the basis of overly essentialized oppositional
politics, possibly reworked within nationalist or fundamentalist discursive structures.

For detailed overviews and assessments of Spivak's work, the reader
should turn elsewhere (Parry, 1987; Young, 1990). Here, for the time
being, I only wish to make the point that, as with Said and Bhabha,
questions of 'race' and sexuality are rarely confronted directly, either
remaining as taken-for-granted elements of the colonial project or
emerging in tantalizing gestures. In Spivak's work 'race', though often
invoked, appears only briefly in connection with the British project
of representing a race-differentiated India which would cement a
collusive relationship with the dominant Aryans against exploitable
aboriginals (1984, pp. 141–2); in a short commentary on a colonial
document which attempted to create a chromatic taxonomy to determine eligibility for employment in the East India Company (1986,
pp. 236–8); and in some incidental remarks on anti-racism (1990,
pp. 125–9).

Equally surprisingly, while there are critiques of French feminisms
as well as references to masculinist and patriarchal ideologies, both
imperial and 'native', and an intriguing set of reflections on the silenc-
ing of the subaltern women thus subordinated, Spivak, like Bhabha
– and Said only less so – offers relatively little on what one might call
the 'sexualization' of colonial discourse or the sexual dynamics of
various elements of imperial and colonial projects.

The sexualization and gendering of colonial discourse

This relative neglect of the sexualization of colonial discourses is in part related to the absence of an understanding of the power of premodern European fantasies and anxieties about mythic figures such as 'monstrous races' and Wild Men and Wild Women, almost demonic, imagined internal 'Others', always invested with lascivious sexuality and extraordinary sexual powers, which formed European preconceptions about non-European peoples (Mason, 1990; Cohen, 1988). These fantasies became intertwined with imagined encounters with, and imagined accounts of, 'the East' or Africans, and exerted a powerful formative influence on figures such as Columbus. This has led to recent suggestions that a great part of the 'observations' of Columbus and his contemporary imperial adventurers simply 'confirmed' the fantasized representations of extraordinary, monstrous, sub-human creatures imagined in published tracts consulted by Columbus and his contemporaries, which created grids through which they were then found and 'seen'.[5] Peter Mason's poststructuralist analysis in *Deconstructing America* (1990) is particularly acute in its account of these representations, and in its emphasis on the articulations between images of Wildness, Monstrosity and the fears generated by other internal demons, especially witches and the insane (pp. 41ff).

Mason's account reveals, too, the ambivalence lurking in many of these conceptions, especially of the Wild Man, whose supposed savagery was thought to be combined with a potential for civilization, a mastery over beasts, a certain folk wisdom and an enviable freedom from the constraints of conventional civilization (pp. 46–7). In other words, what we see here is a foreshadowing of the ambiguity of Western conceptions of the 'noble savage', soon to be discovered and represented in other continents.

The bestial, threatening but fascinating sexuality of Wild Men and Women in the European imagination had a powerful influence on conceptions of the 'natives' of Other lands encountered by Europeans. Accounts abound of the supposed sexual appetites and powers of Africans and North American 'Indians'. These were very often given visual force in the illustrations which were included in the texts of the explorers. To take just one instance, a woodcut in the 1509 edition of Amerigo Vespucci's account shows a 'young member of the crew who is solicited by a group of native women while another woman stands behind him with a club ready to fell him ... The text of Vespucci also relates the use of venomous insects and spices by Indian women to enlarge the penises of their mates, . . . once again a sign of the sexual lasciviousness assigned to the European Wild Woman, as well as referring to the power of European witches to cause impotence in males' (Mason, 1990, pp. 48–9; see also Carr, 1985, p. 52). As with the fears and fascination engendered by representations of African sexuality (Jordan, 1974), what can be read here perhaps more specifically is the anxiety of the *white European male*; but also his attraction to modes of sexuality supposedly untrammelled by the restraints of 'civilization'. The pulling apart of the 'European' psyche around the axis of desire and repulsion when confronted by the Other is a recurrent theme in Western culture: some of its contemporary forms feature in my later discussion of racism and ethnicity.

Several other elements of the gendering and sexualization of the colonial project deserve more elaborate treatment than can be provided here, but reference to them serves to highlight the lacunae in some of the best-known examples of colonial discourse analysis.

First, the selective *effeminization* of the non-European Others, and their spaces, legitimating their penetration, appropriation and subjugation (a discourse which often overlapped with their infantilization – a point I have already referred to when discussing the denial of coevalness to non-Western Others – thus rendering them further incapable of self-government). This effeminization, the production of the Other as metaphorically and metonymically female, is evident in the gender of territory names – America (which is Amerigo's name feminized), Virginia, Florida, Guiana, to take a few instances – constructing the territories as objects available to the appropriating thrust of European masculinity. This is a form of imagery articulating with woodcuts and paintings, in which the territories are often represented as eroticized females, and in voyeuristic texts that are a kind of respectable and 'authenticated' form of pornography (Hulme, 1985; Carr, 1985).

A contrasting form of feminization constructed the Other male as lacking appropriate masculinity, as evidenced by lack of bodily hair, in the case of North American 'Indians', contrasted with their supposedly cannibalistic women (Mason, 1990, p. 173; Carr, 1985, p. 47); or as displaying a passive or contemplative rather than militaristic culture, a tactic that was used to construct, divide and govern the ethnic geography of India. In India, in this process, some of those designated as masculine and martial were co-opted, while others fought out their resistance to colonialism within the same reconstruction of a powerful Indian masculine tradition (Nandy, 1983, pp. 7–8, 18–27).

These constructions and representations of masculinity and femininity were part of a process of cultural and political reconstruction of sexual difference both at 'home' and in the colonies, displaying the very complex interplay between the formations of 'the West' and 'the Rest'. The selective effeminization of *natives*, for instance, articulated with a class-divided reconstruction of *British* masculinities in which hegemonic conceptions of upper-class males, especially those charged with running the Empire, emphasized sexual self-restraint and lack of emotional display, while the lower-class male was constructed as prone to sexual excess and indeed was expected to affirm his masculinity in demonstrations of sexual prowess (Ballhatchett, 1980). At the same time, the masculinism of the imperial project enabled a reinforcement of the construction of middle-class English women as chaste, frail and in need of protection, a representation which in the colonies and at home could be played off both against the sexually predatory native and the sexually available 'native' woman – those fantasies of Oriental and other eroticism acted out by colonial administrators and travellers, gaining wide circulation at home through lurid accounts (think of Flaubert's *Voyage en Orient*) (Terdiman, 1985; Kabbani, 1986; Mills, 1991). Moreover, the supposed threat to the white woman in the colonies enabled a legitimation of some of the most repressive measures against 'natives', usually at moments when colonial authority seemed particularly vulnerable, moments especially exemplified in the Indian mutiny of 1857 and the Morant Bay rebellion in Jamaica in 1865 (Ware, 1992, pp. 38–42; Hall, 1992).

It is possible to see in much of this the significance of the 'postmodern' framing of identities as formed in relations of alterity with Other subjects regarded as marginal and secondary. The historical researches drawn upon here show how those Others, deemed to be outside the time of Western modernity and ruthlessly governed and exploited in other spaces, came in fact to be formative influences on the imperial culture as a whole: *in other words, how the 'premodern' 'Rest', whatever the attempts to inferiorize, exclude and expel it, came to inhabit 'the West'*.

The forms of governmental discourse and construction of genders involved here need to be seen in their articulation with a wider *sexualization* of the discourses of 'race' and the *racialization* of the discourses around sexual differentiation that occurred especially in the nineteenth century, with continuing reverberations. Stepan's researches (1990), for instance, have demonstrated the analogic reasoning in nineteenth-century sciences which presented the 'lower races' as similar to the female of the human species – in facial structure, in having a 'narrow, childlike and delicate skull, so different from the robust and rounded heads characteristic of males of superior races', and in being innately 'impulsive, emotional, imitative rather than original, and incapable of the abstract reasoning found in white men' (Stepan, 1990, pp. 40–1).

Gilman (1992) has similarly explored the forms in which medical and psychological discourses and artistic representations created an imagery in which female sexuality, blackness and prostitution came together to create a powerful connotative chain between blackness and the sexualized female in imperial cultures of the nineteenth century:

> The 'white man's burden' thus becomes his sexuality and its control, and it is this which is transferred into the need to control the sexuality of the Other, the Other as sexualised female. The colonial mentality which sees 'natives' as needing control is easily transferred to 'woman' . . . when Freud, in his *Essay on Lay Analysis* (1926), discusses the ignorance of contemporary psychology concerning adult female sexuality, he refers to this lack of knowledge as the 'dark continent' of psychology . . . In using this phrase in English, Freud ties the image of female sexuality to the colonial black and to the perceived relationship between the female's ascribed sexuality and the Other's exoticism and pathology. (pp. 194–5)

To this one could add fears of 'miscegenation', especially as expressed by upper-class males, both disgusted and fascinated by working-class women and their black partners in England (Rattansi, 1992b, p. 53), and which also fed into anxieties about racial degeneration and underpinned by the discourses of eugenics and more generally by class discourses about codes of breeding (Cohen, 1988, pp. 63–78). Among other things, this enabled attempts to construct white women as reproducers of the 'race', as mothers whose proper place was in the domestic sphere (Davin, 1989).

Travellers' tales: femininity and the interruption of colonial discourse

But the attempt to fulfil the white man's burden, to return to Gilman's point, was continually disrupted, not least by some of the white women who, in part defiance of hegemonic cultural constructions of white middle-class womanhood, travelled and worked in the colonies, and whose accounts and activities, operating in the play and clash of the discourses of imperialism and femininity, managed to breach the masculinist governmentalism of the Empire (Mills, 1991; see also Ware, 1992). Mills's fascinating archaeology of women travel writers of the nineteenth century demonstrates that many of these women, while colluding with imperial discourses in important ways, nevertheless introduced elements of contradiction and ambivalence by deploying the conventions of contemporary discourses of femininity. They initiated personal relationships in an attempt to explore the individuality of the 'natives', and tried to write with some semblance of empathy.

Women writers, moreover, according to Mills (1991, p. 98), 'because of their socialisation as sexualised objects of a male gaze', tended to be more aware of the way they might have appeared to the natives – a taking of the place of the Other which was another disrupting force, an ambivalence perhaps matched only by those other marginals of dominant Victorian and Edwardian culture, homosexuals such as E. M. Forster, and others, like Orwell, ambiguous about their commitment to the 'hyper-masculinity' of imperial Britain (Nandy, 1983, pp. 35–44). Even Kipling can be seen as a far more complex figure than a straightforward ideologue of the colonial project (Nandy, 1983, pp. 35–44, 64–71; Said 1993). The ambivalence produced by the undercurrent of homo-eroticism in the relation of male colonizers to the 'natives' has received some attention (Nandy, 1989; Hyam, 1990) and is clearly an axis of cultural dislocation which deserves far greater exploration.

Not all the studies I have drawn upon in discussing the sexualization of colonial discourse can be theoretically assimilated to poststructuralism of the kind evident, say, in the writings of Bhabha, although many, like Sarah Mills's important work (1991), draw explicitly upon poststructuralist resources. The point, however, is that they can all be read and re-read as constitutive of a 'postmodern' frame which attempts to highlight and destabilize the overlapping and cross-cutting binaries which were put into place in Western culture, and which defined its identities during its formative encounters with non-Western Others. The binaries have been of various kinds – white/black, civilized/savage, rational/irrational, adult/child, for example – but always potentially unstable and held in place by networks of power and knowledge, discursive structures and strategies that feminists have consistently exposed and deconstructed in their attempts to challenge the forms of male domination in Western cultures (see, for instance, Hekman, 1990). What I have done in my own account is to bring into particular focus the significance of the male/female and masculine/feminine binaries, and the sexualization of the discourses and strategies which were imbricated both in the government of the colonized and in the formation of Western cultures at 'home'.

at this point an obvious shortcoming of the analysis pur-
section cannot pass without comment: the 'culturalism'
investigation for which identity and subject-formation
little or no reference to a massive body of earlier and
esearch on the political economy of the processes involved
s domination of the Rest. It is my view that this is neither
a necessary nor an irreparable omission. Nevertheless, the terms in
which an adequate articulation with the concerns of political economy
can be accomplished remain to be worked out.

Racism and modernity: the Holocaust

Once viewed through a 'postmodern frame', the formation of modernity becomes inconceivable without a deep sense of the constitutive
role of 'internal' and 'external' Others. To give a different emphasis,
modernity cannot be understood without grasping racism as its other,
'darker' side.

But this begs a nagging question about the significance of anti-
Semitism in Western culture. The European persecution of Jewish
communities clearly predates the advent of modernity as understood
here. How, then, can a 'postmodern' frame help in understanding this
phenomenon? One response is to see the figure of the Jew as one of
those 'internal' Others whose representation and treatment in European culture fed into the growth of modern racism. While no doubt
plausible, this only serves to raise further questions: how can this
seemingly perennial Otherness be understood, and is there a specificity to modern 'Western' anti-Semitism? Should the Holocaust be
seen as an 'aberrant', even premodern irrational eruption in modernity's otherwise relatively smooth narrative of rationality, progress
and civilization? Perhaps most crucially, given the purpose of this
essay, what can the category of 'modernity' yield in an analysis of
anti-Semitism and especially the Holocaust?

The Holocaust is sometimes taken to be symbolic in some sense
of the 'end' of the modern project, by its horrific demonstration of
the grotesque truth behind modernity's progressive mask. It is one
of the signal achievements of Bauman's recent (1989) work to interpret
the Holocaust in a manner that allows an appreciation of the specificity
of the Holocaust's *modernity*, and in doing so to give a strong sense of
the productiveness of a 'postmodern' frame. This is not to argue that
he furnishes answers to all the questions posed earlier, but to suggest
that henceforth it becomes impossible to talk about the Holocaust

without acknowledging modernity's inextricable complicity in its perpetration.

Any 'postmodern' framing has to accept Bauman's judgement that the Holocaust was not a *failure*, but a *product* of modernity (1989, p. 5), or at least that it was not *simply a failure* but *also a product of modernity*. Modernity may not have been its sufficient condition, but it was undoubtedly a necessary condition (p. 13). While Western modernity represents itself as civilized, and therefore as a project of 'humanity against barbarism, reason against ignorance, objectivity against prejudice, progress against degeneration, truth against superstition, science against magic, rationality against passion' (p. 96), and more especially projects a mythology of itself as a tamer of cruelty and violence, this is only by restructuring the forms and access to the means of violence, now vested in a centralized state and redistributed to containable and, as far as possible, 'invisible' spaces.

Elimination of Jews was a Nazi goal legitimized by typically 'modern' projects – scientific racism and centralized social engineering – and given rhetorical power by a metaphor of the 'gardening state' which underwrote the 'weeding out' of alien breeds which upset the 'spiritual and moral equilibrium' of the national culture (Bauman, 1991, p. 27). Once this 'rational' and 'scientific' plan of the destruction and elimination of the Jew from the body politic was in place, some of modernity's other central features were routinely involved in its implementation. Among these, most crucially, was instrumental reason, in the form of the 'rationality' of bureaucratic procedure, which detached itself from the obscenity of the ultimate goals and focused on the best means with which to make Germany *judenrein* – 'clean of Jews'. Distanciation from the moral issues involved in this project of racial 'cleansing' was bureaucratically achieved in two ways. The minute functional division of labour involved in modern organization meant that most contributors to the genocide worked with little or no personal experience, or sometimes even knowledge, of the final goal of the collective activity (Bauman, 1989, p. 98). Second, there was a substitution of technical for moral responsibility, again typical of modern bureaucracies, so that acts were judged on grounds of rationality, in the name of technical efficiency, rather than ethics (pp. 180–1).

Moreover, 'Science', when put to the test as a safeguard of civilization, failed dismally, and again in ways inherent in modernity, with its emphasis on the separation of 'reason' from 'emotions' and morality. Doctrines of the value-neutrality of science made it 'morally blind and speechless', while the institutional imperatives and personal temptations of well-funded and officially sanctioned research proved

potent forces in eliciting the collaboration of scientists in the range
of research spawned by the project of racial cleansing (pp. 108–9).

For Bauman, the Holocaust was a paradigm of modern, bureaucratic
rationality and scientific reason, a narrative that 'could be made into
a textbook of scientific management', and had the Nazis won, he
avers, 'There would be no shortage of distinguished scholars vying to
research and generalise its experience for the benefits of an advanced
organisation of human affairs.' They would, indeed, have made it into
a textbook (p. 150).

Bauman draws much of his theorization of modernity and bureauc-
racy from the work of Weber. Surprisingly, despite some of the similarities between Weber's and Foucault's analysis of modernity
(Dreyfus and Rabinow, 1982, pp. 165–6; Smart, 1983, pp. 123–32;
Gordon, 1987), Bauman makes little use of Foucault's conception of
the disciplinary society, networks of power/knowledge, the operations
of power on bodies and so on, to augment his discussion of the Nazi
project, although Foucault's neglect of Nazism and the Holocaust is
equally astonishing.

Bauman's discussion of the inextricable links between modernity
and the Holocaust is not confined to a demonstration of the constitutive role of bureaucratic rationality and its practices in genocide. He
points also to the forms in which modern Jewry as a diaspora fell
foul of the assimilationist thrust of the nation-state and constantly
destabilized the boundary-fixing obsession and the anxiety and ambivalence intrinsic to modernity, which articulated with the growth of
nationalism and the nation-state. The advent of modernity unleashed
a highly dislocating set of processes: the Jew as eternal 'stranger' came
to symbolize in various and often contradictory ways the tensions,
antagonisms and insecurities thus generated. The Jew came to
embody the contradictions, but only because of his (sic) 'multi-dimen-
sional unclarity' (Bauman, 1989, pp. 40–1). No wonder that the Jew
' "could be represented as everything to be resented, feared or
despised. He was a carrier of bolshevism, but curiously enough, he
simultaneously stood for the liberal spirit of rotten Western bureauc-
racy. Economically, he was both capitalist and socialist. He was blamed
as the indolent pacifist but, by a strange coincidence, he was also the
eternal instigator of wars" '(p. 41).

Bauman's analyses are rich not only in their acute perception of the
many-sidedness of the connections between modernity, anti-Semitism
and the Holocaust, but as I shall show later, in their suggestiveness
for understanding the racialization of other, especially South Asian
diasporic minorities in Europe.

However, Bauman's emphasis on the uniqueness of the Jewish diasporic condition and its relation to European modernity and racism, and thus his lack of attention – in both *Modernity and the Holocaust* and his other commentaries on modernity – to the constitutive influence of slavery (see Gilroy, 1993a) and colonial racisms on Western modernity and the formation of other diasporas, is indicative of an ethnocentrism not only in his own work, but in that of many of those who fall within my framing of the 'postmodern'. I have discussed this issue earlier and, as I pointed out, it requires that any attempt at a 'postmodern' account of racism engage in a constant vigilance and be ever ready to 'interrupt' the flow of 'postmodern' analyses like Bauman's with an interrogation and a counter-discourse which displaces such elements of ethnocentrism.

I cannot engage in a lengthy critical commentary on Bauman's seminal work here, except to enter three further reservations. In his discussions of the destabilizing effects of diasporic Jewry on modernity's intolerance of ambivalence, Bauman fails to grasp the other sides of ambivalence as explored in discussions of colonial discourses – that is, ambivalence as constituted also by fascination and desire – to put it briefly, a lacuna deriving in part from Bauman's complete neglect of contemporary psychoanalytic frameworks. Bauman conceptualizes what he calls the 'scandal of ambivalence' as a 'language specific disorder', the excess of things over words making for a world intractable to definite classification, an inherently uncomfortable condition further destabilized by the ambiguity of diasporic Jewry. While this echoes poststructuralism, Derrida in particular, it is innocent of psychoanalytic possibilities.

A second difficulty in Bauman's analysis is that the dynamics of sexuality and sexual difference are totally absent: Bauman's 'Jew' is a taken-for-granted male whose forms of persecution and response are limited by being discussed in 'gender-blind' terms. Thus is missed the significance of Jewish male sexuality as symbolizing pollution and disease – Jews were popularly associated with the spread of syphilis in nineteenth-century Europe – and the chain of connotations of commerce, outsiderness, danger and deviant sexuality which linked the male Jew to the female prostitute, a form of symbolization condensed, for example, in popular and official images of Jack the Ripper as an East European Jew (Gilman, 1991, pp. 104–27). neglected too is the masculinism of fascist ideologies, and of Nazism in particular, and the forms of masculine desire, anxiety and dread and fear of women which animated at least some of the anti-Semitic, anti-communist and anti-working class violence of the 'foot-soldiers' of Nazism (see

Theweleit's interpretation (1987) of the fantasies of Freikorps officers, and Carter and Turner's important critical commentary on this study (1986)).

One of the many merits of Theweleit's analysis is its attempt to situate the production of male desire in the historical context of Germany after the First World War, with its unique capitalist and patriarchal formations. This throws into relief a further weakness in Bauman's analysis, one which is again evident in *Holocaust* as well as in the other writings. That is, there is a tendency in his analyses for 'modernity' to function as a rather abstract category – in particular, one which eschews analyses of historically specific capitalisms and class formations. In part, this may be a case of 'bending the stick too far' in reaction against earlier modes of class reductionist accounts which, for example, overprivileged the significance of 'monopoly capitalism' and the supposed role of particular class 'fractions' in Hitler's rise to power. But any analysis of Nazism, or modernity in general, which neglects the articulations between capitalist relations, class formations, 'modern' bureaucratic forms of organization and processes of racialization has to be deemed singularly flawed.

Hence my insistence at the beginning of this essay on the need to supplement the category of 'modernity' with specifications such as capitalist relations (and sexual difference), without which the category is left to carry an analytical burden it cannot bear.

Nevertheless, the value of 'modernity' as albeit a selective optic with which to understand key aspects of one of the most horrific forms of recent racism can now hardly be doubted. By the same token, a 'postmodern' analytical frame, for which 'modernity' is a central feature, is valorized.

Of ethnicities and racisms

A 'postmodern' frame's intrinsic suspicion of doctrines of 'pure' origins makes it inherently corrosive of discourses that invoke notions of historically formed cultural essences. Its de-essentializing and decentring tendencies inevitably provoke conflict with political projects which rely on strong classificatory systems, whether based on conceptions of 'ethnicity', 'nation' or 'race'. Moreover, conventional ideas of ethnicity and racism as elaborated in the truth-regimes of the human sciences find themselves equally vulnerable to the deconstructive power of 'postmodern' analysis.

The social sciences have had predictably little success in furnishing uncontentious definitions of ethnicity and racism. There is little agreement except around the points that the term 'ethnicity' derives from the Greek *ethnos*, meaning a *people*, a collectivity sharing certain common attributes, and that ethnicity ought essentially to be regarded as a cultural marker or, indeed, container in which some conception of shared origin and characteristics is crucial (Rex, 1986, pp. 26–9, 79–98). But what precisely is meant here by 'culture'? Is any particular shared 'cultural' attribute more important than any other – for instance, language, territoriality or religion? Do not notions of 'shared origin' smuggle in ideas of shared *biology* (Nash, 1989, p. 5)? How is 'ethnicity' to be consistently and usefully distinguished from 'race', and 'ethnocentrism' from 'racism', and both of these from 'xeno-phobia' and 'nationalism'? How distinctive is the current notion and practice of 'ethnic cleansing' from the Nazi project of 'racial cleansing'?

The inherent conceptual difficulties of strong classificatory pro-grammes in the human sciences have, around these questions, been hopelessly exacerbated by becoming intertwined and having to come to terms with the astonishingly complex manner in which populations appear to draw and redraw, maintain and breach, narrow and widen the boundaries around themselves and others.

Decentring and de-essentializing ethnicity, 'race' and racism

In this context the first 'postmodern' move must be to decentre and de-essentialize, by postulating what is often glimpsed but rarely acknowledged and accepted with any degree of comfort: that there are no unambiguous, water-tight definitions to be had of ethnicity, racism and the myriad terms in-between (cf. Omi and Winant, 1986, pp. 68–9). Indeed, all these terms are permanently 'in-between', caught in the impossibility of fixity and essentialization. There is a 'family resemblance' between them, a merging and overlapping of one form of boundary formation with another, coupled with strong contextual determination. One programmatic conclusion would be for 'postmodern' frame analyses to eschew tight definitions, and instead to engage in Foucauldian genealogical and archaeological projects, exploring the accretion of meanings, political affiliations, subject posi-tions, forms of address, regimes of truth and disciplinary practices involved in the construction of particular myths of origin, narratives of evolution and forms of boundary-marking and policing engaged in by different 'communities' in particular historical contexts. 'Ethnicity', 'race', 'the nation', and so on, carry infinitely rich connotations and continue to be harnessed to a wide variety of political and cultural projects, and such genealogies and achaeologies can and have explored the continuities and discontinuities in the discursive practices involved.

The debate about whether there is now a 'new racism' provides an illustration of the necessity for decentring and de-essentalizing concepts of 'race', 'ethnicity' and 'nation'.

Racisms 'old' and 'new': undoing a binary opposition

The political projects and the disciplinary matrices involved in the formation of 'race' as a marker in Western modernity have, of course, been extensively studied, and particular reference has already been made to the forms of 'scientific racism' of the nineteenth and early twentieth centuries, which were intertwined with conceptions of non-European Others, sexual difference, anti-Semitism and the culturally assimilationary thrust of the nation-state. 'Scientific racisms' have had two enduring characteristics: first, a biological definition of 'race', therefore 'racializing' the body and conceiving of a population as having a commonality of 'stock' and phenotypical features, such as coloration, hair type, shape of nose and skull, and even type of foot in the case of representations of Jewishness, as Gilman (1991, pp. 38–59) has pointed out; and second, attempts to create a *hierarchy* of races which, despite representing some 'white' races as racially inferior to others, have consistently consigned 'non-white' populations to the lowest rungs of the racial ladder (Banton and Harwood, 1975).

But the difficulty of extrapolating from 'scientific racism' to contemporary forms of inferiorization, discrimination and exclusion in order to define racism is evident in the controversy over the 'new racism' as well as in attempts to provide legislative and judicial protection to populations subjected to discriminatory practices. The term 'new racism' is already burdened by having two different referents. Martin Barker (1981), who appears to have first used the label, mainly targeted the recent appropriation of the doctrines of sociobiology by the British New Right, who have deployed sociobiological conceptions in postulating a supposedly 'natural' equivalence between cultural, especially *national* difference, and cultural and political antagonisms against those deemed to be 'obviously different': that is, foreign and alien. They have attempted thereby to legitimize policies for the repatriation of British Asian and British African-Caribbean populations, and to underwrite *de facto* segregation in schooling, especially in areas with a large concentration of British Asian, particularly Muslim populations. Balibar (1991), also keen to highlight the relatively novel phenomenon in which overt doctrines of biological inferiority have been abandoned in Europe, but where legitimation for domination, discrimination, repatriation and forms of segregation or separation continue to be found, speaks of the new racism as primarily a form of 'cultural racism'; a 'differentialist racism', in which cultural difference replaces the earlier and now scientifically discredited biological theorizations. Support for culturalist interpretations of new forms of racism has come from a number of other influential commentators (e.g. Gilroy, 1987, pp. 43–51).

But how 'new' is the 'new racism'? Its credentials for novelty have been questioned by Miles (1987), whose argument challenges the claims of Barker, Balibar and the rest. Miles maintains that the 'scientific racism' of the nineteenth and twentieth centuries, although rooted in biological features, always revolved around a conception of cultural/national character and uniqueness, and that there has always been a powerful connection between racist and nationalist discourses.

My purpose in referring to this discussion is not to adjudicate between these particular disputants – I return to some of these questions later, as part of a wider commentary on forms of racism in conditions of a possible 'crisis' of modernity – but to suggest that inside a 'postmodern' frame it seems clear, on the one hand, that without a very detailed archaeological and genealogical exercise it would be impossible to grasp the continuities and discontinuities between the two, but also that a simple old/new binary homogenizes each discourse and delimits its field of application, effectiveness and articulation in a singularly unhelpful manner. Both 'scientific racism' and 'differentialist racism' are complex enough formations to merit being referred to in the plural, and any effective comparative exercise requires an understanding of their articulation with discourses and disciplinary practices not merely around the 'nation', as has hitherto been the case, *but also around sexual difference, and the cultural codes of social class difference.*

My argument acquires particular relevance at a period in European history that has seen the resurgence of racisms which combine older fascist, anti-Semitic ideologies with a differentialist rhetoric mobilized against migrant communities with 'Third World' origins. Some of these movements are not afraid to speak openly of a commitment to racism, while still maintaining a rhetoric of differentialism. Thus Derek Beackon, elected as councillor for the British National Party

in the Millwall ward in London's East End in September 1993, is
reported to have said, 'I am happy to describe myself as a racist. I
just want to live amongst my own people' (*The Sun*, 18 September
1993, p. 7). Elsewhere his rhetoric appeals to a nationalism of Britishness and a territorialization which invites racist mobilization to return
Britain to the British and cleanse the streets of 'rubbish' – that is, the
Asian communities (see the report in the *Daily Mirror*, 18 September
1993, p. 2).

The discourses of 'race', nation and ethnicity: no necessary political belonging

Note, too, the ways in which racializing, exclusionary discourses can
take anti-racist campaigning principles based on multiculturalism and
equal respect for all cultures, and egalitarian appeals based on rights
of citizenship, and turn them around so that multiculturalism becomes
transmuted into a defence of the rights of white cultures to retain
their 'purity', and the rhetoric of citizenship is mobilized to underwrite
demands for forms of segregation in schooling and housing. This can
then be conjoined with claims that the real problem is that whites
have become 'second-class citizens' in their own countries. These
ploys are evident in the discourse of the Ku-Klux-Klan and in the
appeals of the British extreme right, as well as in British popular
culture (on the latter, see Cohen (1993) and British National Party
statements, such as in the wake of their victory in the Millwall council
election (*Daily Mirror*, 18 September 1992)).

Moreover, while the British extreme right has generally espoused
a traditional stance on the role of women and 'family values', there
has in fact been an internal struggle over attempts by some members
to articulate their racism with feminism, and attract more women
members, by arguing for more egalitarian approaches (Durham, 1991,
p. 274).

The only way to make sense of these complex and ever-changing
reconfigurations of what one might call colour, culture and political
discourse is to decentre and de-essentialize concepts of 'race', ethnicity and nation as recommended here. Although it is arguable that,
historically, concepts of 'race' have contained a strong biological
element, the degree of centrality accorded to biology is obviously
subject to enormous variation, as is its articulation with conceptions
of nationality, sexual difference, class and democratic rights. There
are, moreover, shifts of discourse and policy depending upon targeted

populations – 'Black', 'Asian', 'Oriental', 'Celtic' and so on. In other words, there are racisms, not a singular racism.

Nor can it be assumed that the concept of 'race' and nation will function only in a manner that underwrites projects of domination and inferiorization. Their capacity for mobilization as resources for resistance is evident in conceptions of Afrocentrism and in other projects which rely on a notion of an African 'race' and nation, particularly in the populations of the African diaspora in the United States and Britain. And it certainly cannot be ruled out that some of the discourses and practices of those committed to doctrines of racial and cultural purity among the ethnic minorities might be regarded in some respects and contexts as 'racist'. Hence, in part, the futility of merely proclaiming the scientific falsity of the concept of 'race'. From 'postmodern' perspectives, as from others, such attributions of fixed origin appear reprehensible in their attempts at closure around mythic collectivities, but there is no denying their potential for cultural and political mobilization.

Thus, as with 'race', the various elements that go to make up the notion of ethnicity – language, religion, notions of common origin, codes of kinship, marriage and dress, forms of cuisine and so forth – *have no necessary political belonging* (see Laclau, 1977, pp. 160–72, and 1990, pp. 28–9, for a discussion of the relative mobility of various discursive figures in the 'trench war' of political struggles), and can be mobilized for apparently incongruous alliances. Examples are the alliances between the 'cultural racists' of the British New Right and British Muslim communities demanding the right to separate schooling; between the black nationalism of the African-American Louis Farrakhan and elements of the white American extreme right, anti-Semitism being one of the uniting political strands; and in South Africa, at the time of writing, between sections of the Zulu population and white right-wing groups, each demanding separate 'homelands'. This demonstrates the complex articulations that become possible around projects of nationalism, racism and ethnicity, white and black. The language of cultural difference, as part of ethnicity, 'race' and nation, has no necessary political belonging.

Ethnicity, representation and racialization

A 'postmodern' framing conceptualizes *ethnicity* as part of a *cultural politics of representation*, involving processes of 'self-identification' as well as formation by disciplinary agencies such as the state, and

including the involvement of the social sciences, given their incorporation in the categorization and redistributive activities of the state
and campaigning organizations.

'Representation' in this conceptualization is being used in a double
sense. On the one hand, it refers to issues of authority and account-
ability in the articulation of communal views and 'interests'. It poses
questions about who is authorized to speak for whom, and immediately opens up the issue of conflicts within designated ethnic communities. It also encourages analyses of projects of hegemony within
and between ethnic communities (Cohen, 1988, pp. 26–7). Moreover,
by foregrounding institutional politics, it reveals what is so often at
stake in the conflicts within and between collectivities: a voice in the
allocation and redistribution of resources, often from local and national
state agencies.

But the emphasis on 'representation' is also important because it
focuses attention on the significance of the construction and constant
re-creation of ethnic identities through the production of images and
narratives in visual and written texts of 'popular' and 'high' culture:
newspapers, novels, television documentaries and drama, cinema, the
theatre, music, painting and photography. Ethnic identity is a 'social
imaginary', to adapt a term from Castoriadis (1987), or to borrow
Anderson's (1983), an 'imagined community': that is, among other
things, a collectivity bonded together by forms of literary and visual
narration which locate in time and space, in history, memory and
territory.

The formation of ethnic identities may be regarded as part of a
process of *racialization* when categories of 'race' are explicitly invoked,
or when popular or specialized biological and quasi-biological discourses are drawn upon to legitimate projects of subject-formation,
inclusion and exclusion, discrimination, inferiorization, exploitation,
verbal abuse, and physical harassment and violence. However, individual acts and collective projects of boundary-formation, discrimination, exploitation and violence may or may not involve explicit
inferiorization, and may or may not contain references to biological
notions of 'stock', 'blood', genetic differences and bodily attributes
such as colour, and capacities such as 'intelligence'. Note, too, that
appeals to ethnicity and cultural difference, by invoking ideas of
shared origin, 'kith and kin' and 'nation', may in fact smuggle in
quasi-biological conceptions. Moreover, as Cohen (1988) in particular
has emphasized, rhetorics of social class have often contained appeals
to biology, enshrined in ideas of 'codes of breeding'.

The decentring and de-essentialization of 'race' and 'ethnicity' that is being recommended here makes for a much more fruitful analytical engagement with these processes of flux, contextual transformation and dislocation, and the complex overlapping and cross-cutting of boundaries that characterizes the formation of ethnic and racialized identities. This is not to argue that definitions of racism are not necessary, both for purposes of legal protection and redress, and for the specification of objects of social, political and economic analysis, but to recognize that strict definitions are always liable to find themselves confounded by the complex intertwining of the very wide range of cultural repertoires being drawn upon by individuals and collectivities.

The difficulties of drawing neat boundaries around concepts such as ethnicity, ethnocentrism, race, racism, etc. are now becoming more widely acknowledged, as are the difficulties of finding unambiguous and acceptable ethnic labels in practices of regulation and policy, such as in census questions. Some have even doubted the value of the notion of ethnicity (e.g. Omi and Winant, 1986). Others (Anthias, 1992) appear to regard ethnicity as the primary concept, with 'race' as a sub-set, although this then leads to another set of classificatory conundrums around definitions of racism (see Mason's (1992) critique of Anthias).

The significance of a 'postmodern' framing of these difficulties lies in elaborating a framework that makes these problems intelligible in a specific manner, and in proposing avenues for research. The 'postmodern' point is not merely one of highlighting a perennial excess of 'things' over 'words' – that is, that definitions and analyses are always partial – but one of exhibiting particular forms of interpenetration between 'words' and 'things', in which discourses of 'race' and ethnicity are *productive* of objects of analysis in forms that prevent simple 'empirical' adjudication between competing discourses. This involves an undermining of the cultural-material distinction, and is overlain by the potential destabilizing effects of *différance* as a property of language and discourse, both in everyday life and in specialized disciplines, and deconstruction as an analytical strategy that allows the unravelling and displacement of binaries such as that of 'old/new' racism.

These general aspects of a 'postmodern' framing raise a number of questions and open up several avenues for elaboration. Given the constraints of space, four issues only are now briefly highlighted to exhibit further the particular emphases of 'postmodern' framing. The discussion that follows will thus be confined to the following:

1 The effects of a 'postmodern' decentring, de-essentialization and 'detotalization' or 'undoing' of the social.
2 A decentring of the racist subject.
3 Issues of sexual difference, ambivalence and pleasure in racializing processes, in the context of time/space relations and new forms of global/local configuration.
4 The phenomenon of the so-called 'new ethnicities'.

Racism and the decentring of the social

Decentring and detotalizing the social, as remarked upon earlier in this chapter, has the consequence of treating the 'social' within a 'postmodern' frame as always relatively open, in the process of becoming 'closed', but always subject to the play of contingency, dislocation, opposition and disintegration, which prevents closure around discursive practices within and between contextual, institutional sites. Framed in this mode, the variety and contradictions of ethnic and racialized discourses, as constitutive of the social, are particularly highlighted, pointing up the complexity and relative contingency and openness of the processes by which identities are constructed in 'routine' everyday practices, as well as in more explicit political projects of ethnic and racialized hegemony.

Take the case of 'stereotypes' of British Asians and British African-Caribbeans, as part of the cultural repertoire of inferiorization, exclusion, abuse and discrimination in contemporary Britain. A 'postmodern' framing is alert to significant *dislocations* in a process often portrayed as all-encompassing and monolithic, smoothly reproducing racialized stereotypes and practices of discrimination in institutional sites, such as schools. To put it differently, a 'postmodern' framing requires that we break with 'reproductive' models in which, say, the academic performance, suspension rates, etc. of British Asian and British African-Caribbean pupils are portrayed as an outcome of 'stereotypes' of these pupils held by teachers which lead to acts of discrimination against them: for example, placing them in less academic streams and sets. This picture oversimplifies (Rattansi, 1992a). Racialization processes in schools are coming to be seen as uneven and contradictory in their operation. Not all teachers hold stereotypes; the stereotypes are often contradictory in their attributions of characteristics such as 'lazy', 'unacademic', 'stupid' and 'bright', as between different British Asian and British African-Caribbean pupils; other forms of discrimination may or may not follow from the expression of stereotyping abuse in the classroom; and the 'reproduction' of racialized stereotypes and discourses more generally is negotiated and resisted by pupils through a varied repertoire of strategies. Some of these appear to be gendered, with some British African-Caribbean female pupils 'settling' for a truce in which resistance to racialized and gendered schooling practices is strategically controlled to prevent an open confrontation which could lead to serious disciplinary measures. Codes of black masculinity drawn upon in disciplinary contexts *may* prevent some black male pupils adopting the relatively conciliatory pose of young black females (see Rattansi, 1992a, for a more detailed discussion of relevant research).

While research monographs in the social sciences (Jenkins, 1986, 1992; Genders and Player, 1989) have noticed the occurrence of contradictory stereotypes, neither their general significance nor the import of their gendered mode has been sufficiently noticed; nor, as we shall see, have the role of 'modernity' as a constitutive category and the significance of time and space in the operation of these dislocations and contradictions.

In understanding these problems, a shift from a conventional social science vocabulary to a more poststructuralist one is useful. One translation to make here is Foucauldian: studies of the recruitment of ethnic minorities to employment (e.g. Jenkins, 1986, 1992), of discriminatory treatment in schools (Rattansi, 1992a) and of allocation procedures for public housing (Henderson and Karn, 1984, 1987), for example, may be said to point up the extent to which stereotyping discourses, working as legitimation for exclusion from jobs, higher streams and sets in schools, and better council housing, are based on *normalizing, disciplinary* judgements. They are part of what Foucault has called 'bio-politics', enshrined in managerial and allocatory practices which regard good time-keeping, lack of 'trouble-making' and possible attributes of cleanliness, hygiene, bodily deportment and technique as the relevant criteria which determine access to and allocation of resources. These considerations override conceptions of skill, academic ability and need, and neglect the possibility of greater acceptance of cultural relativism in matters of 'taste' and life-style. Moreover, these judgements are gendered and class specific as well as racialized: to elaborate upon just one of the instances mentioned above, it is clear that judgements which have worked against certain families being allocated public housing on the basis of size of family, type of 'taste' in decoration, lifestyle, etc. are the product of a form of 'middle-class' disciplinary, biopolitical gaze and practice, routinized

in the procedures of modern public bureaucracies, which have disadvantaged both ethnic minorities *and* particular sections of the white
working class. This is how Henderson and Karn's research (1984,
1987) may be read within a 'postmodern' frame.

Institutional racism

The concept of 'institutionalized racism', of course, has been deployed
to point up processes of this kind, but a 'postmodern' frame sees
this not as a smooth, reproductive machine, but as an internally
contradictory set of processes. These are bound up with the specificity
of *modern* disciplinary institutions, which among other things embody
particular 'standards' of deportment and hygiene, involving not merely
racialized, but gendered and class-specific discursive practices of
judgement and discrimination, including bodily attributes, everyday
aesthetics, capacities for self-control (drinking, time-keeping, lack of
disruptive behaviour) and ordering of the immediate environment
(tidiness, cleanliness, etc.). Moreover, the assumption of 'uniform'
judgements, consistently 'applied', cannot necessarily be made,
although the consistently discriminatory outcomes of allocatory processes may provide particular clues to the forms of 'normalizing'
discrimination involved.

Undoing the social in this manner has, of course, general implications for the way in which the operation of racialized power relations
is theorized. That is, it cannot be conceptualized as working and
reproducing through a small number of tightly knit sites, such as
those of state and capital, aided and abetted by a capitalist media
supposedly interested only in dividing black and white workers, as
set out in some influential Marxist works (for cruder versions of this
thesis, see Sivanandan, 1974; for a more sophisticated but nevertheless
class-reductionist rendering of this type of argument, see Sarup, 1986,
pp. 40, 95–8). Instead, racialized power relations may be seen more
usefully in neo-Foucauldian terms which do not deny the importance
of the state and capital, but see these as far more fragmented and
internally divided, together with a multiplication of sites for the operation of racisms – playgrounds, streets, classrooms, doctor's surgeries,
mental hospitals, offices, etc. An important constitutive role is assigned
to specialized configurations of power/knowledge such as psychiatry
or educational psychology, and professional ideologies. For example,
among teachers there is the popular liberal notion of treating individual students in supposedly 'colour-blind' terms, which has the

effect of ignoring the effects of racism and racialized economic disadvantage on students (a form of 'professionalism' criticized in the Rampton Report (DES, 1981).

Moreover, attempts to understand struggles to improve the treatment of ethnic minorities – for instance, in the workplace – have to give much greater importance to the question of discursive contestations. Jewson and Mason's (1992) analysis of the rhetorical ploys and counter-moves in struggles over the meaning of 'equal opportunities' in particular workplaces furnishes an especially well-researched illustration of a widespread strategy of resistance by those opposed to such policies.

Sexuality, time/space, the body, pleasure, ambivalence and the spectacular in racialization

The question of the gendering of racialized discursive practices has already featured in the above discussion. Several other dimensions can be highlighted: for instance, the ways in which the black and Asian presence in British inner cities – in other words, 'the inner city' as a *racialized* 'place' – is also *sexualized* by reference to the 'threat' posed to white women by black men in a variety of discourses, including those of the popular press, politicians and the police (Ware, 1992). The British extreme right has certainly been adept at exploiting this particular form of appeal to its male and female members, in texts likely to generate fear among women and masculine protectiveness among men. Thus, the National Front youth paper *Bulldog* covered its front page with a story headlined 'Black pimps force White girls into prostitution', while *National Front News* consistently carries reports of alleged sexual offences perpetrated by black men against white women. The front page was used to caption a photograph of a white family with the appeal: 'White man! You have a Duty to Protect Your Race, Homeland and Family!' *Bulldog* advised its readers to 'think of the safety of your White womenfolk . . . think of your mother, your sister, your girlfriend' (Durham, 1991, p. 272). Among other things, these examples convey the significance of the articulations between 'family' and 'home' as symbols of race and space (Cohen, 1993). They also repeat, at a temporal and spatial distance, the colonial discourse whereby the idea of the Empire as a dangerous place where women needed protection and were to stay at 'home' allowed the construction of aggressive and protective masculinities, with a privileged placing in the 'public' arena, confining women to the 'domestic' sphere.

Of course, the racializing of space, especially in the city, takes a variety of forms, from the relative segregation of communities by housing policies and the phenomenon of 'white flight' (Cohen, 1993), as well as black expulsion – ethnic minority families forced out by vicious harassment – to the connotative 'fixing' of drug and crime issues to the black presence. And the sexualization of the inner city also has an autonomous logic involving prostitution, the activities of pornographers, and 'panics' around the gay and lesbian presence, although here again the racialization and the sexualization can be articulated to each other via the supposed power of black pimps. This representation is circulated by various forms of media including film – take the case of the highly popular *Mona Lisa*, whose racializing and sexual dynamics, involving a world of black pimps and black and white prostitutes, are acutely explored by Pajaczkowska and Young (1992). It also appears in panics about black homophobia (Burston, 1993).

The gendering and sexualization of the nation is another important element in the dynamics of the sexualization of 'race'. Women, as Yuval-Davis and Anthias (1989, pp. 8–10) have pointed out, and as is evident from the discussion of the discourse of the extreme right above, play a pivotal role in the construction of ethnicity and nationality: as biological reproducers; as boundary markers – hence the attempts to police their sexual relations with 'others'; as transmitters of the culture; as crucial symbols, for example in notions of the motherland; and, of course, as actual participants in national struggles.

Hence, surely, the significance of the metaphor of 'rape' in discussions of the impact of immigration on British culture (see, for example, the speech by John Stokes, MP, reproduced, although not with this point in mind, by Barker, 1981, p. 18), and the actuality of rape in so many projects of what have come now to be called 'ethnic cleansing'. If 'woman' is a key signifier of both culture and territory, then the sexual violation of her body is an assertion of masculinist ethnicity, or nationality, or 'race', which emasculates the other (although thereby enmeshing the rapist in the contradictions of defilement by such biological intercourse and the probable birth of a 'miscegenated' population). But masculinization may function in an oppositional mode – for example, in struggles for nationhood – while simultaneously being part of the discursive practices which subordinate women in that community. An instance may be found in Yuval-Davis and Anthias's recounting of a popular, presumably male, Palestinian saying of the 1980s which referred to the higher birth rates among the Palestinian population: 'The Israelis beat us at the borders but we beat them in the bedrooms' (1989, p. 8).

Space, then, is not only feminized but masculinized. This too feeds into the racialization of locales. In British cities this often happens through the staking out of territorial claims, and their continued policing by young working-class males to keep an area 'clean' of 'wogs', 'Pakis' and 'niggers'. Among other things, the discursive practices involved attempt to humiliate these Others by physical assaults and verbal abuse, which 'prove' the masculinity of the attackers and 'reduce' the victims to 'cissies': a form of emasculation and effeminization (Willis, 1978). And the significance of masculinist cultures was emphasized by the Macdonald Inquiry into the murder of an Asian pupil at Burnage High School in Manchester, England, by a white school-mate: a strong masculinist culture of violence in the all-boys school was, the report argued, an important constitutive feature of the racism in the school (Macdonald *et al.*, 1989).

But it is important to remember that there may be complex variations in the racializing dynamics involved, with alliances between white and African-Carribean males against Asians or, as in some areas, the skirmishes being confined to whites and Asians, co-existing with the presence of African-Carribeans in local colleges of further and higher education (Cohen, 1993). And as we shall see in the next section, the Macdonald Inquiry also had some interesting remarks on the complexity of racialized networks of alliance and co-operation.

There is precious little research on the connections between classed masculinities, the territorialization of social relations and racism (Cohen's work being a notable exception). I would suggest that among the elements that such research would need to consider are the *pleasures* of male bonding and violence in various urban contexts, where there is a perennial search for excitement thwarted by a chronic lack of material and cultural resources and opportunities. The possibilities for gaining fame and notoriety through media coverage gives added pleasure and affirmation, and provides motivation for a continuation of the violence, despite the threat and actuality of prison and other sanctions. (What applies to racist activities can surely also be true of the pleasures of anti-racist involvements. For discussions of 'pleasure' in cultural politics, see the pioneering attempt in Bennett *et al.*, 1983.)

Some of this becomes evident in recent accounts of those involved in soccer violence and in the activities of Britain's far right organizations. Here, for example, are extracts from an interview with a soccer 'hooligan':

He talks of his days with the Subway Army (so named because of the way they ambushed opposition fans in Wolverhampton's subway network) . . . with an unmistakable air of nostalgia. They were heady days of male bonding. You looked after your mates, and they looked after you . . . The fighting would go on for as long as the police would let it. Tony freely admits he wasn't much interested in the football. What attracted him was the thrill of the violence. 'It's just a buzz. A feeling of power. Knowing you are with a bunch of geezers who can do another firm.' (Weale, 1993; see also Williams *et al.*, 1987)

The same report explores the attractions of participating in violence abroad, and the pleasures of national and international notoriety in a world of international media coverage:

The up-and-coming soccer yobs (sic) have . . . been looking abroad for action, where they can be sure of a bigger stage which will attract widespread media attention and where they can make their names. Some, like Paul Scarrot from Nottingham, who earned the title of super-yob after being expelled from the 1990 World Cup in Italy, go on to achieve international notoriety.

And a contemporaneous account of a neo-Nazi group not only recounted the pleasures of violence and listening to racist rock bands, but contained the following remarks on the significance to the group of media coverage:

This is a fan club whose cult is itself and its own doings. No group was ever more besotted by its reflection in the media, whether it is in its own *Blood and Honour* fanzine or in the furiously hostile publicity granted to the skinhead racist scene by the mainstream press and television. When they are in jail, which is fairly frequently, members devour the anti-racist magazine *Searchlight*, which is devoted to exposing the neo-Fascist right. They find their own names and doings and are happy. (Ascherson, 1993)

A globalized, media-saturated world is in some senses constitutive of this group: its name, Blood and Honour, is in fact borrowed from the South African neo-Nazi party, the AWB, while some of the pleasures of media coverage are bound up with a sense of connection with an international network of neofascist organizations, but are also perhaps a compensation for the drab anonymity of an ordinary existence in a soulless new English town, Milton Keynes.

The body and its insertion into an economy of the cultural politics of pleasure and spectacle thus emerges as an important site for exploration that future research into racializing processes must address. Think, for example, of the ways in which so many younger members of the extreme right fashion distinctive bodily adornments from tattoos to skinhead and 'mohican' haircuts, 'badges' of membership, identification and affirmation directly imprinted on the body, but allied to particular conceptions of bodily hygiene and a lifestyle which allows them to construct their identities in often imaginary differentiation from blacks, 'Pakis' and groups like 'new age travellers' (see again Ascherson, 1993, on the Blood and Honour Group). Musical preferences for raucous rock and modes of dance – often accompanied by violence – set their bodies in motion, to borrow a phrase from Mort (1983).

These accounts give added weight to Silverman's recent suggestion that an understanding of contemporary forms of racism, and racist violence in particular, requires an acknowledgement of Bauman's emphasis on the symbolic nature of the 'struggle for survival' today and its desire to imprint itself on 'the public imagination' (Silverman, 1993). A shift to a relatively novel racism in which the symbolic has a more privileged role, whether in the form of the desecration of Jewish graves or attacks on Muslim and other places of worship, takes place as part of a change of emphasis in racialized discourses to the language of 'difference', which I have discussed earlier.

Silverman usefully yokes his argument to recent discussions of economic and political transformations in western Europe, whether theorized in terms of 'postmodernization', or, as Wieviorka has done in this volume and in his *L'Espace du Racisme* (1991), under the rubric of 'post-industrialism', an analysis which points to the marginalization of older labour movements and the numerical decline and fragmentation of the communities built around the male manual working class, due to a fundamental restructuring of the industrial and urban infrastructure, combined with crises of national identity and state institutions. This is the 'space' in which there is a relatively new politics of cultural difference organized around 'new' social movements, including racist and anti-racist movements well aware of symbolic gestures and the staging of events, operating in a political environment in which governments, too, are enmeshed in a strategy of the symbolic management of racialized discrimination and conflict.

One consequence of the new industrial, urban and cultural transformations is a disembedding of traditions and a collapse of employment and other infrastructures, and feelings of rootlessness, generating anxieties which become exploited and mobilized around endless searches for 'roots' and projects of racialized nationalisms. There is a sense in which this gives rise to particular racisms that are novel, and which enable the thesis of a 'new racism' to be reformulated in a more convincing fashion.

But as I have argued above, such analyses will have to accomplish far more than document some of these processes of 'postmodernization' or the crisis of 'modernity'. We need to theorize them rigorously by a more direct rethinking of the formation of identities, subjectivities and the social, in which issues of sexuality, pleasure, temporality and spatiality have a role entirely neglected in the work not only of Wieviorka but also of Silverman. It is important to note, too, that the form of analysis I am recommending is different in quite fundamental ways from discussions of urban racism based either on albeit sophisticated versions of the 'false consciousness' thesis as posited by Phizacklea and Miles (1980; for an appreciative but critical discussion, see Rattansi 1992a, pp. 31–3) or on a resource-conflict model of the type proposed by Wellman (1977), in which white racism is seen primarily as a legitimating ideology for white privilege.

This is even more so once the question of *ambivalence* and its great significance is appreciated. Racialized discourses, and those involving degrees of sexualization in particular, are not merely differentiating, inferiorizing and legitimating, but involve forms of ambivalence which interrupt their subordinating charge, a point emphasized earlier with regard to the general 'postmodern' conception of self-Other relations, and colonial discursive practices.

I have remarked elsewhere on the ambivalence around the figure of the British Asian woman, at once the guardian and pillar of the 'tightly knit' Asian family – much admired, especially by the right, for its 'family values' and discipline – but also a symbol of Asian 'backwardness'. She is seen as subject to extraordinary subordination and, by her adherence to Asian conventions, is regarded as an obstacle to the assimilation of Asians into British culture or 'the English way of life'; she is also considered sexually alluring, the dusky heiress to the Kama Sutra and the Oriental harem (Rattansi, 1992a).

The ambivalence surrounding the British Asian family, especially on the right, is nicely captured by a recent headline in the conservative *Daily Mail*: 'Britain's traditional family is now Asian' (29 January 1993). The accompanying text, drawing upon *Social Trends 1992* continues: 'Asians have taken over from whites as the traditional British family, a new report reveals. Seventy per cent of Pakistani and Bangladeshi households here consist of husband, wife and children – the accepted norm for generations – compared with only 25 per cent of whites.' The discourse combines a nostalgia for a golden age, and an implicit admiration for the 'family values' of Asians, with the anxiety of being 'taken over' as well as overtaken by a population not granted the status of really belonging – they are still described as Pakistani and Bangladeshi households who happen to be 'here'.

But in this instance and others around the discussion of 'the Asian woman', we can also see how the category of 'modernity', conceptions of time and space, and the sexualization of discourses around cultural 'Others' can combine in distinctive ways. That is, discourses around British Asians, their families, 'their women', their supposed business success and so forth can be understood by analogy with Bauman's analysis of the Jew as eternal 'stranger', falling foul of modernity's drive for classificatory order and its abhorrence of the disruptive, unassimilable figure. It is arguable, that is, that British Asians generate a series of contradictory responses in discourses in modern British culture, partly because of their transgression of a series of culturally produced boundaries which attempt to hold British modernity in place: *British Asians are, in effect, too pre-modern, too modern and too postmodern.* The 'premodernity', *the lack of coevalness in time*, of British Asians is symbolized by the supposedly all-effective subjugation of 'their women', as well as by patterns of dress, religious 'fundamentalism', 'uncivilized' and 'backward' practices of ritualized animal slaughter and so forth. Their *modernity-in-excess* is symbolized, as with the Jews, by their supposedly disproportionate involvement in commerce, by their eagerness to accumulate, and by their shops replacing the 'traditional' English cornership, symbol of the cosy British working-class community/neighbourhood – the kith and kin element is important here. But they are also too 'postmodern', too mobile, a diasporic, 'deterritorialized' community with links in India, Pakistan, Canada, the USA, Singapore, Hong Kong and elsewhere, disturbing the settledness of Britain's 'island race' culture, bringing in brides and husbands from India, while setting up transnational businesses and refusing to support the British cricket team in its (currently disastrous) encounters with India, Pakistan and the West Indies. And yet, this is a form of cultural disruption always overlain with the ambivalence of unconscious desire and the more explicit pulls of admiration and envy.

So there is not just the often-noted *double-bind* of racist discourses which traps the racialized subject into inferiorization and transgression – as Fanon put it, 'When people like me, they tell me it is in spite of my colour. When they dislike me, they point out it is not because of my colour. Either way, I am locked into the infernal circle' (1986, p. 116). But there is also a *triple-bind* which is revealed when temporality and spatiality are more explicitly built into the analysis of racializing processes.[6]

Decentring the racist subject

If the proliferation of contradictory and ambivalent discourses is
indicative of disclocations internal to and constitutive of the social
and its relative openness, it is also to be seen as part of the structuration which makes available a series of different 'subject positions'.
In effect, it is part of the process by which, in this instance, racist
identities are decentred by being invited to occupy a variety of enunci-
ative modes and to engage in a range of practices. A 'postmodern'
frame posits racist identities, like other identities, including that of
the 'anti-racist', as decentred, fragmented by contradictory discourses
and by the pull of other identities. It sees them, therefore, as not
necessarily consistent in their operation across different contexts and
sites, and not available in the form of transparent self-knowledge to
the subjects.

Researchers like Billig (1978, 1984), more aware of the complexities
of racialized identity formation, have furnished a range of examples of
relevant subjects and contexts: for instance, the trade union official,
a member of the explicitly racist National Front, who appeared to
have been elected to his union position by both blacks and whites
because of his record of fighting equally for both sets of members,
and his personal relations of friendliness to black colleagues; and the
white girl interviewed at school, who expressed strong racist views,
but was then seen leaving school arm in arm with an Asian girl (see
also Jones, 1988, pp. 177–227). Even the Macdonald Inquiry into
the murder of a British Pakistani pupil at Burnage High School in
Manchester was forced to conclude that the racism of his killer, a
white fellow pupil, was not of a 'simple' kind: he had earlier established alliances and friendships with other black and Asian pupils (see
Rattansi, 1992a, for a more detailed discussion). Moreover, as I pointed
out earlier, the inquiry also in effect argued that what has to be
understood is not only the complexity of his racism, but the effect of
his masculinity as embedded in the aggressive and violent culture
of his all-boys school.

The form of decentredness of racist and racializing subjectivities
and identities cannot, however, be understood simply in Foucauldian
terms as the structured effects of different discourses and the subject
positions thus made available, for example, around both 'race' and
masculinity. Disavowal statements of the kind, 'I'm not a racist,
but . . . (there are too many of them)' or 'Some of my best friends are
black, but . . . (it's the rest)', etc., need to be seen as part of complex
rhetorical strategies by subjects as reflexive *agents*, attempting to

articulate different subject positions within a framework of perceived interests, and drawing upon a variety of what Weatherall and Potter (1993) have called interpretive repertoires. Discourses of liberalism and even egalitarianism may be rhetorically mobilized not merely against racialized forms of discrimination and exclusion, but to legitimate them.[7]

Weatherall and Potter's discourse analysis frame for the exploration of the highly complex rhetoric involved in the 'working out' of white New Zealanders' construction of Maoris as racial problems, and their legitimation of exclusionary and exploitative practices against Maoris, may be regarded as a particularly fruitful illustration of a type of 'postmodern' analysis of racism. Eschewing reductive accounts of racism as simply 'false consciousness', and the 'racist' as a unified subject, they explore how social categories and arguments are deployed by white New Zealanders around specific instances and fields such as education, crime and land claims, but for Weatherall and Potter always with a view to understanding these rhetorical moves in a historical context of relations of power, domination and advantage, while drawing out the tension of contradictory pulls of 'racist' and 'anti-racist' positions.

Among other things, Weatherall and Potter's *Mapping the Language of Racism* accomplishes a critique of the common conception of racism as 'prejudice', with its psychologically reductive, individualistic and pathologizing tendency. It reveals, at the same time, the Enlightenment residue of the 'rational/prejudiced' binary which underlies much of this type of analysis (see also Rattansi, 1992a, for a critique of 'prejudice' as used in the discourse of 'multicultural education'). And it establishes the productiveness of the strategy recommended in this essay, of avoiding supposedly water-tight definitions of racism in favour of actually examining how racial logics and categories work in relation to specific events and social fields.

However, among a number of my reservations with regard to their project, three interrelated ones are particularly relevant here. First, while justifiably sceptical of attempts within social psychology to construct typologies of subjects along a spectrum of adherence to racist views (1993, p. 194), Weatherall and Potter by default end up not merely decentring but almost completely denuding subjects of identities altogether: 'Conflict, ambivalence, inconsistency and contradiction seem to be endemic. They do not, that is, seem to be associated with just one group of individuals or one type of person. Everybody is a dilemmatician – anti-racist to the same extent as racist' (1993, p. 198). But this evades the issue of the different 'investments' that indi-

viduals may have in particular identities and identifications in a wide
range of contexts. To take rather extreme cases to illustrate the point,
while both the long-standing National Front activist and the 'liberal'
or other kind of anti-racist activist may both draw on conflicting logics
and face discursive dilemmas in justifying their (subject) positions, to
homogenize them as 'dilemmaticians' – Weatherall and Potter's term
– is to ignore vital differences in how each may engage in social
practices towards racialized groups at work and in other fields, and
the degree to which each is likely to initiate and respond to various
projects of racialized or racializing mobilizations. Unwittingly no
doubt, Weatherall and Potter appear to be aligned to the crasser
postmodernist conceptions of 'multiple identities', mainly as a consequence of wanting to avoid equally problematic theorizations of
'identity' in social psychology (pp. 43–9).

At this point a second difficulty becomes apparent: the neglect of
psychoanalytic accounts. Weatherall and Potter distance themselves,
not without good reason, from the 'authoritarian personality' studies
(pp. 49–57), but apart from a passing nod of approval to the possibilities of mobilizing Horney's 'neo-Freudian' work for reading racist
discourse (p. 54), they fail to engage with the psychoanalytic possibilities that might prove fruitful. Not surprisingly, while borrowing from
aspects of Bhabha's work (pp. 142–3), his use of psychoanalytic theory
and the related emphasis on 'ambivalence' go unnoticed, and it is
tempting to attribute Weatherall and Potter's complete neglect of the
gendering and sexualization of racial discourse – and this is my third
reservation – in part to the absence of psychoanalytic theory in their
construction of discourse analysis.

Psychoanalysis and the decentred racist subject

Psychoanalytic theorizations, as an earlier part of this essay has suggested, must be regarded as important to a 'postmodern' decentring
of the subject and in principle could yield interesting accounts of
decentred, 'racialized' subjects – here to include those with investments in racist *and* anti-racist positions, and also those who are the
objects of racism. Franz Fanon's *Black Skin, White Masks* is a key
reference point for understanding some of the psychic costs of racism
to its victims – I use the latter term without imputing passivity to
them. However, it is not at all clear that, to date, the psychoanalytic
literature has produced work of serious power and scope in understanding the psychic economy of racism, although Fanon himself

offers some interesting observations, and the work of Kovel (1988), Rustin (1991, pp. 57–84), Kristeva (1991) and others (see Gordon, 1992, and Young, 1993, for brief surveys) may be regarded as having made a start. Among those I have already discussed, Bhabha, Gilman and Cohen, from different theoretical stances, have deployed psychoanalytic concepts productively.

The *ambivalence* of racism, although deriving from a variety of sources that I have remarked upon, is particularly open to psychoanalytic interpretation, for it is in psychoanalysis that the notion has its strongest roots. Curiously, the Klein-influenced commentators, Gordon, Young and Rustin, appear not to grasp its significance; indeed, they neglect it altogether, one consequence being their noticeable pessimism (this being slightly less true of Rustin), the effect of reducing racism to an uncontradictory pathology.

'Postmodern' framing obviously requires a form of psychoanalytic theorization which, in addition to being aware of the racist involvements of psychoanalytic theory and politics, does not merely reduce all racisms to supposedly eternal and universal psychic mechanisms, but also reflects on the specificity of modernity and its constitutive role in the formation of racism. Psychoanalytic attempts to grapple with colonialism and the Holocaust have been forced to confront racism in a more historically specific register, with the Frankfurt School's 'Authoritarian Personality' studies perhaps being the most explicit in their efforts to delineate some of the interconnections between modernity and racism.

One of the more interesting recent attempts is that by Stephen Frosh (1989, and also 1987 and 1991), who sketches out the links between racism and modernity, sexuality and masculinity, while mindful of the significance of ambivalence, although his account is written with little engagement with 'colonial discourse analysis'. Frosh analyses racism as one response of the threatened ego, an ego that is generically fragile, split and fragmented in both Kleinian and Lacanian senses, but under further pressure from the multiplicitous, disintegrating, constantly changing, fast-moving forces of social life under conditions of modernity. Sexuality is crucially important in his account: in the Fanonian sense, with the white man seeing the black man as biological Other – a vehicle for the projection of unwanted feelings about the body – as well as a sexual threat (Fanon, 1986, pp. 163–78). Repressed homosexual desire creates an ambivalence that connects up with other forms of ambivalence that permeate feeling towards others, whether Jews, black people or Asians. Modernity is one of the other sources of ambivalence. It is experienced as threatening, but in

part exciting. Other forms of ambivalence see the hated objects as
not only disgusting and hateful, but powerful, fascinating, erotic and
possessors of qualities admired by racist subjects. Hence the plausi-
bility of conspiracy theories in which the enemy is seen as having
conquered what terrifies the racist – chaos, change, disorder, fragmentation, disintegration.

This is not an appropriate place to enter into a lengthy consideration
of the merits of psychoanalytic approaches to issues of racism. Here
I only wish to register the general point that in my view neither the
general decentredness of the (racist) subject nor the sexualization and
ambivalences of racism can be fully grasped without some hypothesiz-
ation of the self as constitutively divided between the conscious and
the unconscious, without understanding the centrality of sexuality,
and without some consideration of splitting, fantasy, pleasure, introjec-
tion, projection and so on, as possible mechanisms by which identifications and subjectivities operate and change. Clearly, complex issues
arise for practices of anti-racism, too, if psychoanalytic insights are
granted credibility.

Ethnicities, 'new' and 'old'

The 'decentring' and 'de-essentializing' moves of the 'postmodern'
frame have played a key role in this essay: in mobilizing a general
conception of identities; in exploring its effects on the dissolution of
'woman' as a figure in feminism; in suggesting its possible ramifications for understanding the nature of 'race', the formation of racist
identities, subjectivities and discourses; and in emphasizing that ethnicities, nationalisms and other forms of collective identity are products of a process to be conceptualized as a cultural politics of
representation, one in which narratives, images, musical forms and
popular culture more generally have a significant role.

Contemporary forms of globalization, the formation of diasporas
and diasporic identities, and the creation of new hybrid and synthetic
cultural forms, I have earlier argued, are also of key interest within a
'postmodern' frame, as is Hall's conception of the 'new ethnicities'
(1992c) for similar reasons, in what he now refers to as a 'notorious'
piece (1992d).

Written in the context of a debate on the place of 'Black film'
in British cinema, Hall's 'New ethnicities' (1992c) reflects on the
particularities of an apparently curious conjunction between poststructuralism, a series of iconoclastic 'Black' cinematic projects – Hanif

Kureishi's *My Beautiful Launderette* and Sankofa's *Passion of Remembrance* being two outstanding examples – and the formation of a new configuration in ethnic minority politics in Britain, where the saliency of 'Black' as a unifying signifier has been gradually losing its potency. This is in effect a double interwoven transition. There is a shift, first, from an earlier period characterized by *a struggle over relations of representation* – taking the form of demands for access to the apparatuses and technologies of representation, and the contestation of gross stereotypes and their replacement with 'positive' images – to *a politics of representation* where the demands of the 'positive' image are now regarded as suffocating the possibilities for exploring the huge variety of ethnic, sub-cultural and sexual identities pulsating in the minority communities. Moreover, there is an experimentation with modernist and postmodernist forms which break from an equally stifling aesthetic of 'realism' imposed by the demands of the 'positive image' (usually privileging middle-class heterosexuality). And relatedly, we see the beginnings of a new phase which Hall describes as the demise of 'the essential black subject', in which the oppositional political unity forged by ethnic minorities of African-Caribbean and South Asian descent under the sign of blackness – influenced by the Black Power movement in the USA – is giving way to new types of political 'subject' involving new forms of identity-formation and a new phase in the politics of cultural difference.

Poststructuralism doubles here as both a *form of analysis*, which reads this as a de-essentializing moment, and a *constitutive element* in the formation of the new ethnicities in so far as some of the cultural workers and activists involved have themselves been influenced by poststructuralist currents (not least by the writings of Hall himself). By the same token, the 'postmodern' frame as defined here is also doubly valorized (although I hasten to add that the essential black subject is being undermined by rather more than the adoption of versions of poststructuralism by artists and film-makers).

Questions of sexuality have been crucial to the projects comprising the new ethnicities, for many of the de-essentializing cultural and political projects have been produced by black feminists and gay and lesbian activists intent upon challenging the codes of black masculinity that had hitherto marginalized other sexual identities in the minority communities.

Issues of globalization and diaspora are also central, given the impetus provided by decolonization processes in general, the influence of 'Third World' cinema, and the creation of new 'hybrid' cultural

forms by borrowing from Western, Asian, African, African-American
and other cultural practices.

Commenting on these new cultural politics, and indeed deploying
the term 'new ethnicities', is for Hall also a way of rescuing the
concept of ethnicity from its connotative links with nation and 'race'.
Here we encounter another doubling, for at the same time that Hall
himself contributes to a de-essentialization of the black subject by
pointing to the cultural and political possibilities opened up by the
new cultural politics, he also wants to emphasize that there can be no
form of representation, no sort of political enunciation, no kind of
positioning, which does not have to operate with historically given
languages and cultural codes: in other words, with ethnicities.

The 'new ethnicities', then, is Hall's way of conceptually inserting
the minority communities into the more generally commented upon
politics of cultural difference of late modernity or 'postmodernity',
a politics that has also seen the demise and fracturing of other
previously essentialized subjects: social classes and women.

The precise meaning of 'ethnicity' still remains elusive, but in my
view Hall's general project is nevertheless indispensable, for it
attempts to chart and indeed to recommend new, more open, non-
absolutist forms of cultural politics within and between the minority
communities and their articulation with the politics of the 'centre'.
This is a project to which Paul Gilroy has also made powerful contributions (see Gilroy, 1992 and 1993b), while not falling into the trap
of assuming a utopian emancipation from all forms of cultural essentialization, an escape from the positionings of time and space, narrative, memory and territorialization which make cultural production
and politics possible. It is here that the 'strategic essentialism' recommended by Spivak and others finds its place in an oppositional politics
of coalition and co-operation rather than an endless multiplication of
identities and fragments incapable of effective collective mobilization.
In all these senses, Hall's account of the 'new ethnicities' can be
mined for its suggestiveness for what in very general terms may
be regarded as the political implications of the 'postmodern' frame,
especially as they relate to questions of 'race' and ethnicity.

But this is a politics that has to contend with a variety of different
political projects of cultural difference in the minority diasporic communities of Britain and the USA, and the 'backlash' they have had to
endure. For one thing, versions of the 'old' ethnicities are very much
alive, a point hardly to be laboured in the wake of the Rushdie affair,
in which revamped Islamic 'fundamentalisms' were met in turn with
a retreat into virulent assimilationism by some white liberals. Fay

Weldon's *Sacred Cows* (1989) provides an instructive illustration of the arguments of Mendus (1989) and Parekh (1993) about the strong limits to 'liberal' toleration. At the same time, many new black cultural forms and projects, from rap to the films of Spike Lee have attempted to reconstruct traditional masculinities: they have colluded with or actively promoted mysogynistic and homophobic currents and have supported black nationalisms which run quite counter to the optimistic openness tracked in Hall's 'new ethnicities' (on Spike Lee, see for instance the critiques by Michelle Wallace, 1992, and Paul Gilroy, 1993c).

Rap is clearly a contradictory cultural form. There is on the one hand the misogyny of Ice-T and others, with some black cultural critics making a particularly strong stand against 2-Live Crew (Baker, 1992, 1993). Stephens (1991), on the other hand, regards rap as a 'clearly postmodern artform', characterized by 'indeterminacy, decanonisation, hybridisation, performance and participation, and immanence', although his oxymoronic construction of rap as a form of Afrocentric postmodernism fails to convince. A more likely candidate for the label 'postmodernist' rap in the sense used in this essay is the music and performance of the British South Asian rapper Apache Indian who not only mocks the misnaming of native Americans – although this may be an unwitting consequence of borrowing the name from an Indo-Caribbean musical hero (see Back, 1993a) – and borrows a musical form produced by members of the African diaspora, but in songs like 'Arranged marriage', 'Sharabi' (alcoholic) and 'Caste system' challenges cultural practices among the British South Asian communities which subordinate women, valorize hard-drinking and displays of masculinity, and reinforce boundaries of caste, class and ethnicity (Back, 1993a, 1993b). More recently, he has become involved in the anti-racist campaigns provoked by the victory of the British National Party and the serious escalation in racist violence in London's East End, and has released a single, 'Moving on', with part of the proceeds going to a variety of grass-roots East End Bengali campaigning organizations (Back, 1993a).

This is not to argue that only 'progressive' forms of rap can qualify as 'postmodernist', but that the essentialism of a strongly committed form of Afrocentrism surely disqualifies. Stephens (1992), however, does usefully place rap as a 'postmodern' musical form and reflects on the mixed audiences for it, and now the 'interracial' performers of the music.

Not yet concluded

This essay, though lengthy, can be regarded only as a beginning. It has merely sketched out the manner in which sets of emergent theorizations and substantive investigations enable new, productive directions to be taken in the analysis of Western racisms, ethnicities and identities. I have loosely codified these novel theoretical moves and explorations in what I term a 'postmodern' frame, and have set out some of the ways in which forms of racialization and ethnic and national mobilization may be made more intelligible in terms of this type of framing.

I have not suggested that this framing is entirely unproblematic, or that it represents something completely novel, or that work done under the rubric of other types of theorization should somehow be regarded as redundant. Such presumptuousness is entirely inimical to the pluralist, detotalizing and deconstructive spirit of any stance that claims a connection or affiliation with the 'postmodern', even one that dilutes what often passes for postmodernism as much as I have done.

I am also aware that a large number of issues remain to be discussed, especially around the problems of effective anti-racism in the West and their relation to other types of struggle, and how these might be reconsidered by way of a 'postmodern' framing. Elsewhere I have explored some of the ways in which new forms of theorization can enable a rethinking of conventional debates and divisions: for example, those between 'multiculturalists' and 'anti-racists' in education (Rattansi, 1992a). More generally, difficult questions remain about 'new social movements' and 'identity' politics (see Westwood, and Winant in this volume). There is justified questioning, for example, about the real difference to racist discrimination and injustice that a 'postmodern' politics of cultural difference can make. And there are nagging 'postmodern' scepticisms about the degree to which 'social engineering' and social reforms, especially those confined within national boundaries, can hope to succeed. These issues are broached in a publication of rather different scope (Rattansi, forthcoming).

Nevertheless, I hope to have given a strong indication of why attempts to confront questions of racialization, ethnicity and identity in the contemporary West need to give serious consideration to the type of framing proposed here.

Notes

Versions of this chapter have been presented on a number of occasions: as a paper at the Theory, Culture and Society 10th Anniversary Conference at Seven Springs, Pennsylvania; as lectures at the Institute of Social Studies at the Hague and the University of Lancaster; and as Keynote Addresses at the Annual Conference of the Canadian Anthropological Society, York University, Toronto, and the ' "Others" in Discourse' conference at the University of Toronto. I am grateful to the participants at all these events for helpful discussions. I owe special thanks to Anthony Giddens and Sallie Westwood for their detailed comments on an earlier version of the chapter.

1 It is worth remembering, though, that Foucault was active in a number of anti-racist campaigns in Paris in the 1970s and 1980s (Eribon, 1991).
2 The formulation 'The West and the Rest' is borrowed from the title of Hall's essay (1992a).
3 For a debate on the significance of 'culture' in processes of globalization, see Boyne (1990) and Wallerstein (1990).
4 There are, of course, some important differences between Foucault and Derrida. However, for present purposes these can be set aside.
5 Columbus brought back parrots from the Caribbean, and these were taken as 'proof' that he had reached 'the East' (Mason, 1990, p. 23).
6 For an interesting attempt to understand racialization in Britain in spatial and temporal terms, see Hesse (1993).
7 For general discussions of the connections between liberalism and racism, see Goldberg (1993, pp. 4–8, 213–37) and Parekh (1993).

References

Ahmad, A. (1992) 'Orientalism and after', in Ahmad, A., *In Theory: Classes, Nations and Literatures*, London: Verso.

Anderson, B. (1983) *Imagined Communities: Reflections on the Origins and Spread of Nationalism*, London: Verso.

Anthias, F. (1992) 'Connecting "race" and ethnic phenomena', *Sociology*, vol. 26, no. 3.

Anthias, F. and Yuval-Davis, N. (1992) *Racialised Boundaries*, London: Routledge.

Appadurai, A. (1990) 'Disjuncture and difference in the global cultural economy', in Featherstone, M. (ed.), *Global Culture*, London: Sage.

Ascherson, N. (1993) 'Scenes from Domestic life', *Independent on Sunday*, 17 October.

Back, L. (1993a) 'X amount of Sat Siri Akal!: Apache Indian, reggae music and intermezzo culture', mimeo.

Back. L. (1993b) 'The unity beat', *Guardian*, 13 October.

Baker, H. Jr., (1992) ' "You caint' trus' it": experts witnessing the case of rap', in Wallace, M., and Dent, G. (eds), *Black Popular Culture*, Seattle: Bay Press.

Baker, H., Jr. (1993) *Black Studies, Rap and the Academy*, Chicago: University of Chicago Press.

Balibar, E. (1991) 'Is there a neo-racism?' in Balibar, E., and Wallerstein, I., *Race, Nation and Class*, London: Verso.

Ballhatchett, K. (1980) *Race, Sex and Class Under the Raj: Imperial Attitudes and Policies and their Critics: 1793–1905*, London: Weidenfeld & Nicolson.

Banton, M., and Harwood, J. (1975) *The Race Concept*, Newton Abbot: David and Charles.

Barker, M. (1981) *The New Racism*, London: Junction Books.

Barrett, M. (1991) *The Politics of Truth: From Marx to Foucault*, Cambridge: Polity Press.

Barrett, M. (1992) 'Words and things: materialism and method in contemporary feminist analysis', in Barrett, M., and Phillips, A. (eds) *Destabilising Theory*, Cambridge: Polity Press.

Bauman, Z. (1989) *Modernity and the Holocaust*, Cambridge: Polity Press.

Bauman, Z. (1991) *Modernity and Ambivalence*, Cambridge: Polity Press.

Bennett, T., Burgin, V., and Donald, J. (eds) (1983) *Formations of Pleasure*, London: Routledge.

Bhabha, H. (1983) 'The other question', *Screen*, vol. 24, no. 6.

Bhabha, H. (1985) 'Signs taken for wonders: questions of ambivalence and authority under a tree outside Delhi', in Barker, F., Hulme, P., Iversen, M., and Loxley, D. (eds), *Europe and Its Others*, Vol. 1, Colchester: University of Essex.

Bhabha, H. (1986) 'Of mimicry and man: the ambivalence of colonial discourse', in Donald, J., and Hall, S. (eds) *Politics and Ideology*, Milton Keynes: Open University Press.

Bhabha, H. (ed.) (1990a) *Nation and Narration*, London: Routledge.

Bhabha, H. (1990b) 'DissemiNation: time, narrative and the margins of the modern nation', in Bhabha, H. (ed.), *Nation and Narration*, London: Routledge.

Bhabha, H. (1990c) 'Introduction: narrating the nation', in Bhabha, H. (ed.) *Nation and Narration*, London: Routledge.

Billig, M. (1978) *Fascists: A Social Psychological View of the National Front*, London: Harcourt, Brace, Jovanovich.

Billig, M. (1984) 'I'm not National Front, but . . .', *New Society*, no. 68.

Boyne, R. (1990) 'Culture and the world system', in Featherstone, M. (ed.) *Global Culture*, London: Sage.

Boyne, R., and Rattansi, A. (eds) (1990a) *Postmodernism and Society*, London: Macmillan.

Boyne, R. and Rattansi, A. (1990b) 'The theory and politics of postmodernism', in Boyne, R. and Rattansi, A. (eds), *Postmodernism and Society*, London: Macmillan.

Burston, P. (1993) 'Batties bite back: gays, homophobia and racism', *Guardian Weekend*, 20 November.

Butler, J. (1990) *Gender Trouble: Feminism and the Subversion of Identity*, London: Routledge.

Carr, H. (1985) 'Woman/Indian: "The American" and his Others', in Barker, F.,

Hulme, P., Iversen, M., and Loxley, D. (eds), *Europe and Its Others*, Vol. 2. Colchester: University of Essex.

Carter, E., and Turner, C. (1986) 'Political semantics: notes on Klaus Theweleit's *Male Fantasies*', in Burgin, V., Donald, J., and Kaplan, C. (eds) *Formations of Fantasy*, London: Routledge.

Castoriadis, C. (1987) 'The imaginary', in Appignanesi, L. (ed.), *The Real Me: Postmodernism and the Question of Identity*, London: Institute of Contemporary Arts.

Clifford, J. (1988) 'On Orientalism', in Clifford, J., *The Predicament of Culture*, Cambridge, Mass.: Harvard University Press.

Cohen, P. (1988) 'The perversions of inheritance: studies in the making of multi-racist Britain', in Cohen, P., and Bains, H. (eds), *Multi-Racist Britain*, London: Macmillan.

Cohen, P. (1993) *Home Rules: Some Reflections on Racism and Nationalism in Everyday Life*, London: The New Ethnicities Unit, University of East London.

Davin, A. (1989) 'Imperialism and motherhood', in Samuel, R. (ed.), *Patriotism: The Making and Unmaking of British National Identity*, Vol. 1, London: Routledge.

Derrida, J. (1977) *Of Grammatology*, Baltimore: Johns Hopkins Press.

Derrida, J. (1978) *Writing and Difference*, London: Routledge.

Derrida, J. (1981) *Positions*, Chicago: University of Chicago Press.

Derrida, J. (1983) 'The principle of reason: the university in the eyes of its pupils', *Diacritics*, vol. 13, no. 3.

Derrida, J. (1985) 'Racism's last word', *Critical Inquiry*, no. 12.

Derrida, J. (1988) 'Afterword: toward an ethic of discussion', in Derrida, J., *Limited Inc*, Evanston: Northwestern University Press.

DES (1981) *West Indian Children in Our Schols* (The Rampton Report), London: Department of Education and Science.

Dreyfuss, H. L., and Rabinow, P. (1982) *Michel Foucault: Beyond Structuralism and Hermeneutics*, Brighton: Harvester Press.

Durham, M. (1991) 'Women and the National Front', in Cheles, L., Ferguson, R., and Vaughan, M. (eds) *Neo-Fascism in Europe*, London: Longman.

Elias, N. (1982) *The History of Manners: The Civilizing Process*, New York: Pantheon.

Eribon, D. (1991) *Michel Foucault*, London: Faber.

Fabian, J. (1983) *Time and the Other: How Anthropology Makes Its Object*, New York: Columbia University Press.

Fanon, F. (1986) *Black Skin, White Masks*, London: Pluto Press.

Foucault, M. (1977) *Discipline and Punish*, London: Allen Lane.

Foucault, M. (1979) *The History of Sexuality*, Vol. 1, London: Allen Lane.

Foucault, M. (1980a) *Power/Knowledge: Selected Interviews 1972–77* (ed. Gordon, C.), Brighton: Harvester Press.

Foucault, M. (1980b) 'Questions on geography' in Foucault, M. *Power/Knowledge* (ed. Gordon, C.), Brighton: Harvester Press.

Foucault, M. (1984) 'What is Enlightenment?' in Rabinow, P. (ed.), *The Foucault Reader*, Harmondsworth: Penguin.

Foucault, M. (1986) 'Of other spaces', *Diacritics*, vol. 16.

Fraser, N. and Nicholson, L. (1988) 'Social criticism without philosophy: an encounter between feminism and postmodernism', *Theory, Culture and Society*, vol. 5, nos 2–3.

Frosh, S. (1987) *The Politics of Psychoanalysis*, London: Macmillan.

Frosh, S. (1989) 'Psychoanalysis and racism', in Richards, B. (ed.) *Crises of the Self*, London: Free Association Books.

Frosh, P. (1991) *Identity Crisis: Modernity, Psychoanalysis and the Self*, London: Macmillan.

Game, A. (1991) *Undoing the Social: Towards a Deconstructive Sociology*, Milton Keynes: Open University Press.

Gasché, R. (1986) *The Tain of the Mirror: Derrida and the Philosophy of Reflection*, Cambridge, Mass.: Harvard University Press.

Genders, E., and Player, E. (1989) *Race Relations in Prisons*, Oxford: Clarendon Press.

Giddens, A. (1990a) *The Consequences of Modernity*, Cambridge: Polity Press.

Giddens, A. (1990b) 'Modernity and utopia', *New Statesman and Society*, 2 November.

Giddens, A. (1994) 'Living in a post-traditional society', in Beck, U., Giddens, A., and Lash, S., *Reflexivity and Its Doubles: Structures, Aesthetics and Community*, Cambridge: Polity Press.

Gilman, S. (1991) *The Jew's Body*, London: Routledge.

Gilman, S. (1992) 'Black bodies: white bodies: towards an iconography of female sexuality in late nineteenth century art, medicine and literature', in Donald, J., and Rattansi, A. (eds), *'Race', Culture and Difference*, London: Sage.

Gilroy, P. (1987) *There Ain't No Black in the Union Jack*, London: Hutchinson.

Gilroy, P. (1992) 'Cultural studies and ethnic absolutism', in Grosserg, L., Nelson, C., and Treicher, P. (eds) *Cultural Studies*, London: Routledge.

Gilroy, P. (1993a) *The Black Atlantic: Modernity and Double Consciousness*, London: Verso.

Gilroy, P. (1993b) *Small Acts: Thoughts on the Politics of Black Cultures*, London: Serpent's Tail.

Gilroy, P. (1993c) 'Spiking the arguments: Spike Lee and the limits of racial community', in Gilroy, P., *Small Acts: Thoughts on the Politics of Black Cultures*, London: Serpent's Tail.

Goldberg, D. (1993) *Racist Culture*, Oxford: Blackwell.

Gordon, C. (1987) 'The soul of the citizen: Max Weber and Michel Foucault on rationality and government', in Whimster, S., and Lash, S. (eds) *Max Weber, Rationality and Modernity*, London: Allen and Unwin.

Gordon, P. (1992) 'Souls in armour: towards a psychoanalytic understanding of racism', mimeo.

Grosz, E. (1990) *Jacques Lacan: A Feminist Introduction*, London: Routledge.

Habermas, J. (1987) *The Philosophical Discourse of Modernity*, Cambridge: Polity Press.

Hall, C. (1992) *White, Middle Class and Male: Explorations in Feminism and History*, Cambridge: Polity Press.

Hall, S. (1992a) 'The West and the Rest: discourse and power', in Hall, S., and Gieben, B. (eds) *Formations of Modernity*, Cambridge: Polity Press.

Hall, S. (1992b) 'The question of cultural identity', in Hall, S., Held, D., and McGrew, A. (eds), *Modernity and Its Futures*, Cambridge: Polity Press.

Hall, S. (1992c) 'The new ethnicities', in Donald, J., and Rattansi, A. (eds), *'Race', Culture and Difference*, London: Sage.

Hall, S. (1992d) 'What is this "Black" in Black popular culture?', in Wallace, M., and Dent, G. (eds), *Black Popular Culture*, Seattle: Bay Press.

Harvey, D. (1989) *The Condition of Postmodernity*, Oxford: Blackwell.

Hekman, S. (1990) *Gender and Knowledge: Elements of a Postmodern Feminism*, Cambridge: Polity Press.

Henderson, J., and Karn, V. (1984) 'Race, class and the allocation of public housing in Britain', *Urban Studies*, vol. 21.

Henderson, J., and Karn, V. (1987) *Race, Class and State Housing*, Aldershot: Gower.

Hesse, B. (1993) 'Black to front and black again: racialization through contested times and spaces', in Keith, M., and Pile, S. (eds), *Place and the Politics of Identity*, London: Routledge.

Hulme, P. (1985) 'Polytropic man: tropes of sexuality and mobility in early colonial discourse', in Barker, F., Hulme, P., Iversen, M., and Loxley, D. (eds), *Europe and Its Others*, Vol. 2, Colchester: University of Essex.

Hyam, R. (1990) *Empire and Sexuality: The British Experience*, Manchester: Manchester University Press.

Jameson, F. (1984) 'Postmodernism, or the cultural logic of late capitalism', *New Left Review*, no. 146.

Jameson, F. (1991) *Postmodernism or The Cultural Logic of Late Capitalism*, London: Verso.

Jenkins, R. (1986) *Racism and Recruitment*, Cambridge: Cambridge University Press.

Jenkins, R. (1992) 'Black workers in the labour market: the price of recession', in Braham, P., Rattansi, A., and Skellington, R. (eds), *Racism and Antiracism: Inequalities, Opportunities and Policies*, London: Sage.

Jewson, N., and Mason, D. (1992) 'The theory and practice of equal opportunities policies: liberal and radical approaches', in Braham, P., Rattansi, A., and Skellington, R. (eds), *Racism and Antiracism: Inequalities, Opportunities and Policies*, London: Sage.

Jones, S. (1988) *Black Culture, White Youth*, London: Macmillan.

Jordan, W. (1974) *The White Man's Burden*, Oxford: Oxford University Press.

Kabbani, R. (1986) *Europe's Myths of Orient*, London: Macmillan.

Kovel, J. (1988) *White Racism: A Psychohistory*, London: Free Association Books.

Kristeva, J. (1991) *Strangers to Ourselves*, New York: Columbia University Press.

Lacan, J. (1977) *Ecrits*, London: Tavistock.

Laclau, E. (1990) *New Reflections on the Revolution of Our Time*, London: Verso.

Laclau, E. and Mouffe, C. (1985) *Hegemony and Socialist Strategy*, London: Verso.

Laplanche, J., and Pontalis, J.-B. (1973) *The Language of Psychoanalysis*, London: The Hogarth Press.

Laplanche, J. and Pontalis, J.-B. (1986) 'Fantasy and the origins of sexuality', in Burgin, V., Donald, J., and Kaplan, C. (eds) *Formations of Fantasy*, London: Routledge.

Lash, S. and Urry, J. (1987) *The End of Organized Capitalism*, Cambridge: Polity Press.

Lash, S., and Urry, J. (1994) *Economies of Sign and Space*, London: Sage.

Lyotard, J.-F. (1984) *The Postmodern condition: A Report of Knowledge*, Manchester: Manchester University Press.

Lyotard, J.-F. (1986) 'Defining the postmodern', in Appignanesi, L. (ed.), *Postmodernism*, London: ICA.

Macdonald, I., Bhavnani, R., Khan, L., and John, G. (1989) *Murder in the Playground*, London: Longsight Press.

Mani, L. and Frankenberg, R. (1985) 'The challenge of Orientalism', *Economy and Society*, vol. 14, no. 2.

Mason, D. (1992) *Some Problems With the Concept of Racism*, Leicester University Discussion Papers in Sociology.

Mason, P. (1990) *Deconstructing America: Representations of the Other*, London: Routledge.

Massey, D. (1993) 'Politics and space/time', in Keith, M. and Pile, S. (eds), *Place and the Politics of Identity*, London: Routledge.

McGrew, A. (1992) 'A global society?', in Hall, S., Held, D., and McGrew, A. (eds), *Modernity and Its Futures*, Cambridge: Polity Press.

Mendus, S. (1989) *Liberalism and the Limits of Tolerance*, Cambridge: Cambridge University Press.

Miles, R. (1987) 'Recent Marxist theories of nationalism and racism', *British Journal of Sociology*, vol. 38, no. 1.

Mills, S. (1991) *Discourses of Difference: An Analysis of Women's Travel Writing and Colonialism*, London: Routledge.

Mort, F. (1983) 'Sex, signification and pleasure', in Bennett, T., *et al.* (eds), *Formations of Pleasure*, London: Routledge.

Mouffe, C. (1989) 'Radical democracy: modern or postmodern?', in Ross, A. (ed.), *Universal Abandon? The Politics of Postmodernism*, Edinburgh: Edinburgh University Press.

Nandy, A. (1983) *The Intimate Enemy: Loss and Recovery of Self Under Colonialism*, Delhi: Oxford University Press.

Nandy, A. (1989) *The Tao of Cricket: On Games of Destiny and the Destiny of Games*, New York: Viking.

Nash, M. (1989) *The Cauldron of Ethnicity in the Modern World*, Chicago: University of Chicago Press.

Norris, C. (1987) *Derrida*, London: Fontana.

Omi, M., and Winant, H. (1986) *Racial Formation in the United States: From the 1960s to the 1980s*, New York: Routledge.

Pajaczkowska, C., and Young, L. (1992) 'Racism, representation and psychoanalysis', in Donald, J., and Rattansi, A. (eds), *'Race', Culture and Difference*, London: Sage.

Parekh, B. (1993) 'Decolonising liberalism', in Pieterse, J. N., and Parekh, B. (eds) *Decolonising the Imagination*, Zed Press.

Parry, B. (1987) 'Problems in current theories of colonial discourse', *Oxford Literary Review*, vol. 9, nos 1–2.

Phizacklea, A., and Miles, R. (1980) *Labour and Racism*, London: Routledge and Kegan Paul.

Rattansi, A. (1992a) 'Changing the subject? Racism, culture and education', in Donald, J., and Rattansi, A. (eds), *'Race', Culture and Difference*, London: Sage.

Rattansi, A. (with Donald, J.) (1992b) *The Question of Racism*, Milton Keynes: Open University Press.

Rattansi, A. (forthcoming) *The Other Sides of Modernity*, Cambridge: Polity Press.

Rex, J. (1986) *Race and Ethnicity*, Milton Keynes: Open University Press.

Riley, D. (1988) *'Am I That Name?' Feminism and the Category of 'Women' in History*, London: Macmillan.

Rose, J. (1986) *Sexuality in the Field of Vision*, London: Verso.

Rustin, M. (1991) *The Good Society and the Inner World*, London: Verso.

Ryan, M. (1982) *Marxism and Deconstruction*, Baltimore: Johns Hopkins University Press.

Said, E. (1978) *Orientalism*, London: Routledge.

Said, E. (1985) 'Orientalism reconsidered', in Barker, F., Hulme, P., Iversen, M., and Loxley, D. (eds), *Europe and Its Others*, Vol. 1, Colchester: University of Essex.

Said, E. (1993) *Culture and Imperialism*, London: Chatto and Windus.

Sarup, M. (1986) *The Politics of Multiracial Education*, London: Routledge.

Silverman, M. (1993) 'Symbolic violence and the new communities', paper presented to workshop on 'Antiracist Strategies and Movements in Europe', University of Greenwich, September.

Sivanandan, A. (1974) *Race, Class and the State*, London: Institute of Race Relations.

Smart, B. (1983) *Foucault, Marxism and Critique*, London: Routledge.

Smart, B. (1992) *Modern Conditions: Postmodern Controversies*, London: Routledge.

Soja, E. (1989) 'Spatializations: a critique of the Giddensian version', in Soja, E., *Postmodern Geographies*, London: Verso.

Spivak, G. (1985) 'The Rani of Sirmur', in Barker, F., Hulme, P., Iversen, M., and Loxley, D. (eds), *Europe and Its Others*, Vol. 1, Colchester: University of Essex.

Spivak, G. (1986) 'Imperialism and sexual difference', *Oxford Literary Review*, vol. 8, nos. 1–2.

Spivak, G. (1987) *In Other Worlds: Essays in Cultural Politics*, London: Methuen.

Spivak, G. (1988) 'Can the subaltern speak?' in Nelson, C., and Grossberg, L. (eds) *Marxism and the Interpretation of Culture* London: Macmillan.

Spivak, G. (1990) *The Post-Colonial Critic: Interviews, Strategies, Dialogues*, London: Routledge.

Stepan, N. L. (1990) 'Race and gender: the role of analogy in science', in Goldberg, D. (ed.), *Anatomy of Racism*, Minneapolis: University of Minnesota.

Stephens, G. (1991) 'Rap music's double-voiced discourse: a crossroads for interracial communication', *Journal of Communication Inquiry*, vol. 15, no. 2.

Stephens, G. (1992) 'Interracial dialogue in rap music', *New Formations*, no. 16.

Terdiman, R. (1985) 'Ideological voyages: concerning a Flaubertian dis-orientation', in Barker, F., Hulme, P., Iversen, M., and Loxley, D. (eds) *Europe and Its Others*, Vol. 1, Colchester: University of Essex.

Theweleit, K. (1987) *Male Fantasies*, Cambridge: Polity Press.

Todorov, T. (1984) *The Conquest of America: The Question of the Other*, New York: HarperCollins.

Urry, J. (1991) 'Time and space in Giddens' social theory', in Bryant, C. and Jary, D. (eds), *Giddens' Theory of Structuration*, London: Routledge.

Viswanathan, G. (1987) 'The beginnings of English literary study in British India',

Oxford Literary Review, vol. 9, nos. 1–2; also in Donald, J., and Rattansi, A. (eds) (1992) *'Race', Culture and Difference*, London: Sage.

Wallace, M. (1992) 'Boyz n the hood' and 'Jungle fever', in Wallace, M., and Dent, G. (eds), *Black Popular Culture*, Seattle: Bay Press.

Wallerstein, I. (1984) *The Politics of the World Economy*, Cambridge: Cambridge University Press.

Wallerstein, I. (1990) 'Culture in the world-system: a reply to Boyne', in Featherstone, M. (ed.), *Global Culture*, London: Sage.

Ware, V. (1992) *Beyond the Pale: White Women, Racism and History*, London: Verso.

Watney, S. (1990) 'Missionary positions: AIDS, Africa and race', in Ferguson, R., Gever. M., Minh-ha, T. T., and West, C. (eds), *Out There: Marginalisation and Contemporary Cultures*, New York and Cambridge, Mass.: New Museum of Contemporary Art and MIT Press.

Weale, S. (1993) 'Foreign fields of violent dreams', *Guardian*, 16 October.

Weatherall, M., and Potter, J. (1993) *Mapping the Language of Racism*, Hemel Hempstead: Harvester Wheatsheaf.

Weldon, F. (1989) *Sacred Cows: A Portrait of Britain, Post-Rushdie, Pre-Utopia*, London: Chatto and Windus.

Wellman, D. (1977) *Portraits of White Racism*, Cambridge: Cambridge University Press.

Wieviorka, M. (1991) *L'Espace du Racisme*, Paris: Seuil.

Williams, J., Dunning, E., and Murphy, P. (1987) *Hooligans Abroad*, London: Routledge.

Willis, P. (1978) *Learning to Labour*, Farnborough: Saxon House.

Young, R. (1990) *White Mythologies: Writing History and the West*, London: Routledge.

Young, R. M. (1993) 'Psychoanalysis and racism: a loud silence', mimeo.

Yuval-Davis, N. and Anthias, F. (eds) (1989) *Woman-Nation-State*, London: Macmillan.

2

EXPLORING OTHER ZONES OF THE POSTMODERN: PROBLEMS OF ETHNOCENTRISM AND DIFFERENCE ACROSS THE NORTH-SOUTH DIVIDE

David Slater

Introduction

It is clear that discussions of the postmodern have expanded out from the domains of art, architecture and literature to cover a very broad social and political terrain; indeed it has been suggested that the postmodern has become equivalent to a 'general sign of radical critique concerning styles of discourse and research in all the disciplines of the humanities and social sciences' (Marcus, 1991 p. 1). At the same time, it is equally clear that the term 'postmodern', as a 'state of mind' (Bauman, 1992, p. vii), inscribes an elusive, ambiguous, elastic, equivocal, enigmatic sense of presence that defies any consensual definition. It is itself a *site* of continuing controversy and reflection. Nor can we assume that it is only the recent contributions to such a debate that are necessarily the most germane. Take the following passage, for example:

> This grave dissociation of past and present is the generic fact of our time and the cause of the suspicion, more or less vague, which gives rise to the confusion characteristic of our present-day existence. We feel that we actual men have suddenly been left alone on the earth; that the dead did not die in appearance only but effectively; that they can no longer help us. Any

remains of the traditional spirit have evaporated. Models, norms, standards
are no use to us. We have to solve our problems without any active collaboration of the past, in full actuality... The European stands alone, without
any living ghosts by his side.

In the above passage, written just over 60 years ago, and elsewhere
in his diagnosis of the 'rebellion of the masses', Ortega y Gasset (1957,
p. 36) captured a sense of indeterminancy, of a continuing present, an
evaporation of fixed markers, and a feeling of intense discontinuity,
within which we can discern a postmodern spirit. But how might we
interpret, in today's world, Ortega y Gasset's notion of the European
standing alone?

Surely, one of the symptomatic features of today's postmodern is the
collapse of the Eurocentric imperative. For instance, one observer notes
that postmodernism is like the 'Toyota of thought: produced and as-
sembled in several different places and then sold everywhere' and again
that 'Postmodernism is a sign of the loss of the colonial model of a
universal culture spread out to educate the world at large.'[1] In a
similar vein, Young (1990, p. 19), in his text on 'white mythologies',
argues that 'Postmodernism can best be defined as European culture's
awareness that it is no longer the unquestioned and dominant centre
of the world.' Equally, Murphy (1991, p. 124), in his examination of
postmodern perspectives on justice, writes that 'Postmodernism is,
in some fundamental sense, postcolonial in its mentality.'

My first question here is: to what extent can we accept the idea
that postmodernity constitutes or is expressive of the end of Western
ethnocentrism? With the advent of the postmodern ethos, is Eurocentrism, that peculiarly self-centred form of knowledge that is directed
outwards to colonize and assimilate the non-West 'other', in eclipse?
My purpose in exploring what I shall refer to as some other zones of
the postmodern is twofold.

First, I want to examine the question of ethnocentrism in the
context of the interpretative work of one or two of the more prominent
exponents of the postmodern turn; my position in this respect will be
that Western ethnocentrism does not terminate with the modern,
and that its presence in the postmodern genre requires far more
critical analysis. Second, moving to one part of the South, namely
Latin America, I shall consider some of the debates that have evolved
in this part of the periphery in order to ascertain to what extent there
are parallel concerns, together with thematic specificities and, more
important, emerging positions which can help us to develop a greater
degree of understanding of the postmodern across the North-South

divide.[2] For example, how can we learn from the discussions in Latin America so that we might be in a better position to pursue a genuine global expansion of meaning? It must be emphasized that to assume that, in the postmodern debate, reflexivity and analytical innovation originate only within the heartlands of the capitalist West not only is representative of an ethnocentric mode of thought, but by the same token, vitiates the broader development of global knowledge and understanding which is so needed in today's world.

The purpose of this kind of enquiry is not, within the process of critical analysis, or what Said (1992, p. 19) has termed the 'deconsecrating' of Eurocentrism, to replace one modality of centrism by another. Nor is it a case of substituting one kind of essentialism for another – for example, a notion of an essential 'white, bad First World social subject' by the idea of an essential 'black, good Third World social subject'. Rather, the broader objective is to subvert the continuation of the varying forms of Occidental enclosure, and to strive toward the stimulation of genuine dialogue, which unavoidably entails a restless decolonization of the imagination. Through the bringing to life of some of the rich potential of North-South encounters, the framework of interpretative meaning, in which the First World's postmodern debate unfolds, can be fissured and remapped.

Tracing Euro-Americanism on a postmodern terrain

Although it is more customary to employ the term 'Eurocentrism' when referring to that particular form of universalist thought which is rooted in Europe, in this case I prefer to use the term 'Euro-Americanism' as a way of encompassing a broader tendency of First World or Northern reflection. I shall organize the argument into two interrelated components: initially, I shall trace the lines of exclusion behind which the West is represented as a world unto itself, as a self-contained entity of universalist theorization; and second, in a much shorter section, the related mode of inclusion of the non-West will be interpreted in the context of containment through assimilation. The argument will be illustrated via a reading of relevant positions taken by a number of authors whose work can be seen as emblematic, in not entirely dissimilar ways, of the postmodern mode of thought- primarily, for this particular analysis, Rorty, Baudrillard and Vattimo. I shall concentrate on certain specific texts of these writers, since they amply provide a number of key examples of the web of problems that emerge from connecting the postmodern with Euro-Americanist discourses.[3]

Contours of exclusion

One of the themes that permeates any consideration of the West/non-West historical dynamic concerns the ways in which the West has been and continues to be interpreted as a self-contained entity, as an enclosure sufficient unto itself, and as a transcendental meeting point of all particular histories.[4] In reflecting on one aspect of this theme, and in direct relation to a discussion of Foucault, Spivak (1988, p. 291) suggests that 'to buy a self-contained version of the West is to ignore its production by the imperialist project'. In a similar vein, although in the context of an examination of universalist elements within Western feminism, Mohanty (1992, p. 80) writes that 'universal sisterhood seems predicated on the erasure of the history and effects of contemporary imperialism'. In both cases, 'imperialism' is used as a signifier of absence, and of exclusion; in fact, Spivak (1988, p. 291) stresses the continual need to confront the 'sanctioned ignorance' of the imperialist project.

If we turn to Rorty's explicit thoughts on ethnocentrism and his exchange with Geertz, as well as to other related interventions, it is possible to substantiate and further develop the above-mentioned criticism.

Rorty (1991a, p. 13) argues that one consequence of his anti-representationalism is the 'recognition that no description of how things are from a God's eye point of view, no skyhook provided by some contemporary or yet-to-be-developed science, is going to free us from the contingency of having been acculturated as we were'. Rorty believes that it is only possible to go beyond our acculturation if our culture contains splits which can be due to 'disruptions from outside' or 'internal revolt' (p. 13). For Rorty, if no such splits emerge, if there are no tensions which make people listen to unfamiliar ideas in the hope of finding the means to overcome these same tensions, then we shall not be able to go beyond our acculturation. He goes on to state that 'our best chance for transcending our acculturation is to be brought up in a culture which prides itself on *not* being monolithic – on its tolerance for a plurality of subcultures and its willingness to listen to neighbouring cultures' (p. 14). Or, as he expresses it in an essay on solidarity, we can try to 'extend our sense of "we" to people whom we have previously thought of as "they" ' (Rorty, 1989, p. 192).

It is in this context that the reader is invited to contemplate the idea of two types of ethnocentrism: first, as an inescapable condition – basically equal to 'human finitude'; and second, as a reference to the *ethnos* of the West, which is conceived as being universally superior. Rorty distances himself from the latter variant and places himself very much within the realm of the first form of ethnocentrism. It is contended that to be ethnocentric is to split the human race into the people to whom one must legitimate one's beliefs and the others. The first group – one's *ethnos* – consists of those people who share enough of one's beliefs to allow 'fruitful conversation' to be possible (Rorty, 1991a, p. 30). Elaborating on this position, Rorty argues that it is not feasible to justify our beliefs to everybody, but only to 'those whose beliefs overlap ours to some appropriate extent' – to those linked together by 'previously-shared premises' (p. 31, footnote 13). It is appropriate at this point to ask: how do these shared premises evolve and become sedimented in a given society? And also, to what extent, within Rorty's chosen frame of Western liberal democracy, or more specifically the idea that 'American democracy is the embodiment of all the best features of the West' (p. 211), has another kind of essentialism been established? From studying his debate on ethnocentrism with Geertz, his comments on Lyotard and a short chapter on what he refers to as 'postmodern bourgeois liberalism', we may be in a better position to answer these and related questions.

Rorty, in his exchange with Geertz, asserts that 'our bourgeois liberal culture' takes a pride in 'constantly enlarging its sympathies', and its estimation of its own moral value is rooted in its posited 'tolerance of diversity' (Rorty, 1991a, p. 204). Furthermore, the reader is informed that the majority of the globe's inhabitants simply do not believe in human equality: 'such a belief is a Western eccentricity' (p. 207). In a subsequent chapter on Lyotard, and the theme of cosmopolitanism without emancipation, Rorty includes an important reference to force, noting that 'we Western liberals have had the Gatling gun, and the native has not'; hence, 'we *have* used force rather than persuasion to convince natives of our own goodness' (p. 219). But, Rorty goes on, 'it is also the case that we Western liberals have raised up generations of historians of colonialism, anthropologists, sociologists, specialists in economic development... who have explained to us in detail just how violent and hypocritical we have been' (p. 219). This latter position conflicts somewhat with an earlier commentary on Chomsky and the Vietnam War, wherein Rorty asserts that Chomsky's position contributed to a marginalization of intellectuals from the 'moral consensus of the nation'; to refer to such a war as immoral was to indulge in pointless 'self-castigation' (p. 201).[5] There are four issues I want to raise in the context of Rorty's above-summarized position.

1   As regards the portrayal of Western liberal democracy, and the United States in particular, its content and contextualization are constructed within a frame that is cut off from the constitutive history of its relations with the non-West Other. For example, from the Monroe Doctrine of 1823 onward, with the deployment of ideas of the 'manifest destiny' of the United States in the Western hemisphere, to the recent invasion of Panama and the destabilization of Nicaragua, the reality of US external relations disrupts the series of settled meanings and images that Rorty attaches to his treatment of American liberal democracy. Moreover, the violent internal history of the sociopolitical constitution of the United States would also tend to subvert the major emphasis of Rorty's representation. Symptomatically, in his essay on solidarity, Rorty observes that solidarity is thought of as the 'ability to see more and more traditional differences (of tribe, religion, race, customs, and the like) as unimportant when compared with similarities with respect to pain and humiliation' (Rorty, 1989, p. 192). But surely it can be argued that very often it is the deployment of, for example, a racist discourse which causes the 'pain and humiliation' that Rorty sees as a potential bond of solidarity. In this sense, then, solidarity needs to be seen as including a continuing struggle against those discourses based on race or religion which carry within them the seeds of the subordination or in extreme cases outright rejection of the rights of the ethnic or religious Other (Castoriadis, 1992).

2   Using Rorty's own term of the 'outsider', or referring to other non-West communities, the resistance and struggle against Western force has been precisely a crucial part, a global part of the struggle for 'human equality', which Rorty characterizes as being somehow only a 'Western eccentricity'. Non-Western struggles for human equality and dignity could be taken, in Rorty's own terminology, as one possible 'split' or 'disruption from outside' which could aid us in the transcending of our own acculturation, giving, as Rorty might put it, 'toeholds for new initiatives' (Rorty, 1991a, p. 13). However, Rorty, not unlike other metropolitan theorists, as Said (1993, p. 368) has recently reminded us, remains silent on the history of other non-Western struggles for human equality and political recognition. The posited equivalence of the West with the belief in human equality, abstracted from the historical record of the Western dissemination of structures of *in*equality, and the rich historical tradition of non-West resistance to such structures, reflects a widely held presupposition that, on the terrain of the social, the West has nothing to learn from the non-West.[6]

3   Characteristically, within the analytical confines of Occidental enclosure, critical examination and understanding of the West's colon-

izing force is safely relocated inside the West itself. Whatever pain and humiliation the West may have caused through its colonial encounters with the non-West, at least it has also produced and trained the intellectuals who are able and morally propelled to reflect on such encounters, thus developing a resource of critical knowledge that can be shared with the world as a whole. What is excluded from such an interpretation is the presence of other agents of knowledge and reflection, located in the periphery, who have also developed a wide range of critiques of the West/non-West encounter. Further, since these critiques have come from outside the Western liberal community, they have often been able to disrupt the inner images and representations of that community; and, as a consequence of such a disruption, we are placed in a better position to rethink and recontextualize, as Rorty himself might put it, in often quite fundamental ways, the constitution of the West's imaginary. Thus, for example, Rorty's earlier conviction that the philosophers' moral concern should be with continuing the 'conversation of the West' (Rorty, 1980, p. 394) could be interrupted by a potentially enabling West/non-West dialogue. I shall return to this theme below.

4   Finally, there is in Rorty's work an apparent foreclosing of narratives of emancipation and a prioritization of the narratives of increasing cosmopolitanism. One key effect of such a position, situated as it is within a decidedly positive view of Western liberal democracy, is to help legitimate the contemporary discourse of neoliberalism, even though tolerance and solidarity with sufferers and outsiders may still be advocated. In an era marked by the passion to acquire and to consume, or what Connolly (1991, p. 172) refers to as the 'universalization of the drive to affluence', it would seem important to distinguish individualism from individuality. The possessive individualism that accompanies the sanctity of property, the sovereignty of the market, and the drive to affluence, an individualism that Macpherson (1988, p. 3) defined in terms of a conception of the individual as basically the proprietor of his (sic) own person or capacities, owing nothing to society for them, needs to be kept separate from the concept of individuality. Individuality can be seen in terms of the existence of a space of being, within which resistance and opposition to the encroachments of state and corporate institutions can develop. Individuality, partially expressed through, for example, the emergence of the critical citizen, opposed to the tendencies of neoliberal normalization, can then be associated with the discussion of the intervening social agent, whose horizon has not been blocked by an individualism that ignores or degrades the politics of identity and difference.

Rorty argues that a commitment to Rawlsian procedural justice, including the development of the principle of religious toleration and the institutions of large market economies, is not only an attractive feature of Western culture, but also the best we can aim for (Rorty, 1991a, pp. 209–10). When Rorty presses for increasing cosmopolitanism and tolerant reciprocity, he contends that there has been nothing to emancipate: 'there is no human nature which was once, or still is, in chains' (p. 213). Rather, our species, according to Rorty, has lately been making up a particularly good nature for itself: 'that produced by the institutions of the liberal West' (p. 213). As one of the tasks for Rorty's 'postmodern bourgeois liberals', loyalty to Western liberal society is seen as quite sufficient for morality; indeed, our society ought to be convinced that it 'need be responsible only to its own traditions' (p. 199). It is in this kind of interpretative context that Rorty goes on to suggest that the 'ultimate political synthesis of love and justice may . . . turn out to be an intricately-textured collage of private narcissism and public pragmatism' (p.210).

One of the major difficulties with the above argument is that, if we prioritize loyalty to Western liberalism and responsibility to our own traditions, the process of recontextualization will tend to be much more severely curtailed. By an unwarranted emphasis on loyalty, the potentially enabling splits and disruptions from outside will tend to be much more easily foreclosed. Moreover, in such a setting the potential for a radical interrogation of Western liberalism, or what Derrida (1992, p. 107) might refer to as an illumination of the 'nocturnal face' of Western democracies, will hardly be enlarged.

A sense of private, perhaps cynical, narcissism, and an ethnocentric underwriting of the West as universal project, are clearly found in the more recent texts of Baudrillard. It is important to signal that his earlier writing expressed a much more critical attitude towards Western ethnocentrism. Discussing Western culture in general, Baudrillard noted that other cultures were entered into its museum 'as vestiges of its own images . . . it reinterpreted them on its own model, and thus precluded the radical interrogation these "different" cultures implied for it'; further 'its reflection on itself leads only to the universalization of its own principles' (Baudrillard, 1975, pp. 88–9).

It is somewhat ironic that, while these remarks could be most appropriately employed against Rorty's thesis, as well as against the work of a wide range of modern and postmodern theorists, in his later interpretations Baudrillard has in an important sense re-entered the Occidental enclosure of privileged reflection. Hence, in his book *America*, we read that 'the countries of the Third World will never internalize the values of democracy and technological progress' (Baudrillard, 1989,p. 78), but in any case this would not seem to be particularly important since the Third World has been decolonized, and 'human rights have been won everywhere'; 'the world is almost entirely liberated; there is nothing left to fight for' (p. 112).

In a companion volume, entitled *Cool Memories*, where it is suggested that, while Nietzsche grappled with the death of God, all we have to deal with is 'the *disappearance* of politics and history' (Baudrillard, 1990, p. 186), the expression of ethnocentric sentiment becomes ever more virulent.

On Africa, the reader is informed that 'the West will be hard-pressed to rid itself of this generation of simiesque and prosaic despots born of the monstrous crossing of the jungle with the shining values of ideology', that 'there is no hope for this continent', and that 'politicians – power itself – are abject because they merely embody the profound contempt people have for their own lives' (p. 15).

On Recife and Brazil, we read of a 'cannibalistic, amorous, seductive culture', learn that 'there is nothing more beautiful than a blonde half-caste with blue eyes: the surprise of an illogical conjunction and a purer model', and are informed that a 'cannibalistic society has no unconscious' (pp. 61–2). Moving to another part of the South, Baudrillard writes, 'Asia so degraded, so corrupted by the colonial era and by its own crowdedness that it can only choose between depravity and the puritan orgy of communism' (p. 168); or on the predicament of Thai men, when the women of that country are so beautiful, 'what is left for these men but to assist in the universal promotion of their women for high-class prostitution' (p. 168).

Finally, along these lines, Baudrillard allows himself a further generalization, noting that there is an unequal scale of passions between North and South. For the author of *Cool Memories*, the weak are imbued with 'contempt for themselves by a sort of capillary action from the superior race' (p. 71). In addition, 'in the order of passions (which is the true order of power), the same countries and peoples are eternally doomed to resentment, to the hysteria of impotence in the face of the arrogant efficiency of the Whites' strategies' (p. 71). And in sum, 'it is this inequality in passions, in virtue, in courage (all they have left is their deaths) which means that the oppressed peoples will never actually measure up to their own power' (p. 71).

Elsewhere in this particular text, Baudrillard remarks that the United States has a 'fantastic capacity for absorbing violence', and he goes on to suggest that the truth of 'our societies is that they can no longer cut away evil: they have to absorb it' (p. 176). By the same

token, Baudrillard has absorbed and projected not only a confining
ethnocentrism, but also, it has to be said, a racist inscription. Defining
postmodernity as 'renovation within ruination' (p. 171), but in a context where politics and history are supposed to have disappeared, and
where apparently human rights have been won everywhere, we are
left with what Baudrillard calls the 'hysterical obsession with events'
(p. 37), and renewal is little more than ever more sophisticated forms
of cynical manipulation.

It is exactly these kinds of glaciating, cynical interventions in which
the social and the political have been effectively closed down, that
provide a background for writers like Stuart Hall to reject this form of
ideological postmodernism; 'it is what happens to ex-Marxist French
intellectuals when they head for the desert' (Hall, 1991, p. 33). But it
must not be assumed that Baudrillard, as terminator of the social and
political, necessarily epitomizes the postmodern spirit. Certainly on
the question of market ideology Jameson, for example, is very clear,
writing that the surrender to the various forms of this ideology has
been 'imperceptible but alarmingly universal'; the proposition that
'the market is in human nature', cannot, for Jameson, be allowed to
stand unchallenged: 'it is the most crucial terrain of ideological
struggle in our time' (Jameson, 1991, pp. 263–4).

Finally, in this first part of my discussion of some postmodern lines
of exclusion, I want to consider the relevance of two recent texts by
the Italian philosopher Vattimo, whose work has been closely associated with new theorizations of postmodernity.

In his book *The End of Modernity*, Vattimo (1991) argues that, while
Nietzsche and Heidegger found themselves obliged to adopt a critical
distance from Western thought in so far as it was foundational, at the
same time they found themselves unable to criticize Western thought
in the name of another and truer foundation. It is in this sense that
Vattimo considers Nietzsche and Heidegger to be the early philosophers of postmodernity. He develops his position by suggesting that
the notions of progress and its overcoming both belong to modernity,
and therefore that the spirit of the postmodern is more effectively
captured by seeing it in terms of the 'dissolution of the category of
the new' (p. 4). For Vattimo the idea of history as a unitary process
is rapidly dissolving, and we are moving into an era of 'post-historicity'
(p. 4). Since it is posited that there is no longer any unitary or
privileged history, (echoing Lyotard's (1986) notion of the death of
metanarratives), but only different histories, it can also be proposed
that we are now living the 'dissolution of history'. In other words, the
end of *universal* history is equated with the dissolution of history as

such. As an illustration of this idea, Vattimo refers to the fact that the world of the mass media, which extends across the face of the earth, is also the world 'in which the "centres" of history have multiplied'. These 'centres' are defined as the 'powers capable of collecting and transmitting information on the basis of a unitary vision which is always the result of specific political choices' (Vattimo, 1991, p. 10). What this means, accordingly, is that the 'very conditions necessary for a universal history as a unitary process of events ... have ceased to exist' (p. 10). But what relation to the past does Vattimo posit for postmodern thought?

The twin concepts of *Andenken* and *Verwindung*, emanating from Heidegger, provide a central nucleus for Vattimo's approach to modernity, postmodernity and time. With the use of the concept of *Verwindung*, Vattimo attempts to underline the idea that, in the context of modernity and postmodernity, the philosophy of the latter is at one and the same moment reconciled to not being able to make a radical break with the philosophy of modernity, while at the same moment it deconstructs or destructures the categories belonging to that philosophy. Thus while postmodernity inevitably has to resign itself to the categories of modernity – to progress, overcoming and the new – it also tries to twist them in another direction and to turn them against themselves; in this way postmodernity is viewed as a 'field of possibility' (Vattimo, 1991, p. 12). *Andenken*, or recollection, is intimately connected to *Verwindung*, in that being is an experience of recollecting, receiving and distorting meanings from the past, responding to those signals that come flickering across the ruins of time.

It is symptomatic that, although Vattimo emphasizes the significance of distortion, of twisting past meanings in another direction, just as, in a related manner, Rorty stressed the importance of disruptions and splits, *Verwindung* is not deployed to deconstruct the supremacy of Western thought. However, Vattimo is certainly more critical of Westernization than Rorty.

For Vattimo (1991, p. 153), Westernization is seen in one key sense as a 'deplorable event triggered by the triumph of imperialistic capitalism in alliance with science and technology'. It occurs first through the expansion of political domination, and in particular in relation to the diffusion of cultural models. However, the political and cultural aspect is accompanied by another more scientific and methodological one, namely the fact that 'so-called primitive societies are regarded as the objects of a kind of knowledge that is completely dominated by "Western categories' (p. 152). I shall return to this last point in a moment.

In his more recent book entitled *The Transparent Society*, Vattimo (1992) re-emphasizes some aspects of the above-summarized approach, noting that the idea of universal history is no longer tenable, and including a series of critical remarks on colonialism and imperialism. But here we find ambivalence. In one passage we are informed that colonialism and imperialism have ended (p. 4), while subsequently they are seen as in crisis, and finally it is suggested that European imperialism has indeed ended, or at least has been radically transformed (p. 6). Vattimo writes of this transformation that 'the West is living through an explosive situation, not only with regard to other cultural universes (such as the"third world") but internally as well, as an apparently irreversible pluralization renders any unilinear view of the world and history impossible' (p. 6).

A related ambivalence can be located in Vattimo's attitude towards Western thought. On the one hand, he writes critically that more or less all Enlightenment thinkers, Hegel, Marx, positivists, historians of every type, judged the meaning of history 'to be the realization of civilization, that is, of the form of Western European man' (Vattimo, 1992, p. 3). Similarly, as regards modernity, the criterion has always been that of modern European man, 'as if to say: we Europeans are the best form of humanity and the entire course of history is directed towards the more or less complete realization of this ideal' (p. 4). But since the so-called primitive peoples have rebelled against European tutelage, 'the European ideal of humanity has been revealed as one ideal amongst others, not necessarily worse, but unable, without violence, to obtain as the true essence of man, of all men' (p. 4).

This critical stance on Westernization is a recurrent theme of Vattimo's reflections, especially, for example, in relation to notions of 'progress' and the diffusion of 'rationalization'. In a short discussion of myths, he notes that the idea that the history of Western reason is the history of an exodus from myth is a myth as well, and in this sense demythologization has itself been shown to be a myth (Vattimo, 1992, p. 39).[7] On technical advance and progress, it is argued that the rationalization of the world turns against reason and emancipation, 'precisely to the extent that it is more and more perfectly accomplished' (p. 78). At the same time, in a world of disenchantment and dissolution, where there are no longer any foundations, where the relation between theory and practice is oblique, and where there are many different cultural horizons, there is more hope for the possibilities of reciprocity and equality (a democratic 'heterotopia'). Vattimo explores this vision by giving importance to being, seen in terms of consensus, dialogue and interpretation rather than stability, fixity and permanence. The experience of oscillation in the postmodern world gives us the opportunity to find a new way of 'being (finally, perhaps) human' (p. 11).

On the other hand, the conventional association of the Third World with so-called primitive peoples, (even including the ironic insinuation), or the rather conformist representation of underdeveloped countries in terms of a lack,[8] display little evidence of the spirit of twisting or disrupting the normal meanings attached to the West/non-West split. This aspect of Vattimo's postmodern perspective is much more clearly revealed in his 1991 text on modernity.

Taking a brief text on 'primitive' societies written by the anthropologist Guidieri, Vattimo quotes a section in which it is argued that Westernization does not simply entail the disappearance of cultures that are other. Other cultures are interpreted as having found ways – 'paradoxical, irrational and caricatural', but 'authentic' – of entering our Western universe; and in this context, 'the non-Western contemporary world is an immense construction site of traces and residues, in conditions which have still to be analyzed' (Vattimo, 1991, p. 158). For Vattimo, we live in a world where the 'immense construction site of traces and residues' interacts with the unequal distribution of power and resources at the global level, so that the result is the 'growth of marginal situations that are the truth of the *primitive* in our world' (p. 159 emphasis added). The disappearance of alterity occurs as a condition of widespread contamination, so that what Vattimo sees as the increased homologation or sameness of the world takes on a weakened and contaminated form; 'it possesses neither the iron-clad unity of the total organization of the metaphysical and technological world, nor some sort of "authentic" unity which could be diametrically opposed to the former' (p. 159). Furthermore, in the process of homologation and contamination, the texts that belong to our Western tradition 'progressively lose their cogency as models and become part of this vast construction site of traces and residues, just as the condition of radical alterity of cultures that are other is exposed as an ideal which has perhaps never been realized, and is certainly unrealizable for us' (p. 161).

Even though the above passage points to the idea of change through increased cultural intersections, there is no notion that within non-Western traditions there may be models of thought and analytical reflection which can provide a critical and disrupting understanding of such interrelations.[9] At the same time, little if any distinction is made between so-called primitive societies and the Third World, and marginality and the condition of being primitive are made concomitant. Apart from a palpable lack of curiosity in non-Western thought,[10] no attempt is made to puncture the Western pretension to be the world's centre of reflection and philosophical development. There is no attempt, as Rabinow (1986, p. 241) has expressed it, 'to anthropologize the West', and show how 'exotic its constitution of reality has been'. As is known, such a position is not new. From the Hegelian notion of the 'principle of the North' – 'thought and the universal' – through Husserl's (1965, p. 178) conviction that 'philosophy has constantly to exercise through European man its role of leadership for the whole of mankind', to Habermas' erudite indifference to non-Western thought, there is a clearly visible connecting thread.

It is in this particular context that an associated contour of exclusion can be located. The problem I am referring to here concerns the question of knowledge – its source, production, relevance and recognition. Societies of the South are rarely seen as a source of scientific knowledge and analytical reflection. In postmodern times, it might well be expected that such an introverted and limiting predilection would be on the wane. With a plurality of voices, a vigorous eclecticism and the desire to juxtapose a variety of texts, might we not assume that there would be a genuine worldliness, a refreshing heterogeneity of origins and approaches? Along the various routes of feminist theory, it is not infrequently argued, and with good reason, that discussion of postmodern subjectivities, of decentred positionalities, of the plurality of resistance, tends to bypass the varied contributions of feminist theory – it is more a case of white males debating the postmodern deconstruction of the ungendered subject.[11]

With reference, then, to the place of the South, and in the specific context of the role of Third World intellectuals, how do we situate the postmodern and its politics? We have seen, in relation to our discussion of Rorty, Baudrillard and Vattimo, that the South is not constituted as a space of knowledge, let alone theoretical knowledge. Here too there is a parallel with the critique of the traditional canon in literature and philosophy in the United States.

Examining the latter domain, the Afro-American philosopher West (1992, p. 704) has recently commented that 'the idea of taking black people seriously in the life of the mind is a very new notion for white people, so they have to get used to it'. In her critical scrutiny of the literature of the United States, and the place of race therein, Toni Morrison (1992, p. 33) stresses the point that black or Africanist people have been predominantly represented as 'dead, impotent, or under complete control'. When recognition does take place, it is frequently a recognition of the capacity to resist, since, as Franco

(1988, p. 503) put it, in her insightful analysis of ethnocentrism, it would seem that 'the Third World is not much of a place for theory'. I shall take one short but revealing example to illustrate my argument at this point.

In one section of his conversations with the Italian journalist Trombadori, during the late 1970s, Foucault says that his experience in Tunisia where he lived for two and a half years was a 'decisive one' (Foucault, 1991, p. 132). The experience he relates concerns the political upsurge of Marxist students in the late 1960s in Tunisia; students who were deeply committed to political mobilization and to the objective of struggling against varying forms of social oppression. In Tunisia in the early part of 1968, Foucault recognized what became for him the central significance of a certain political perspective, which embodied the desire and the will to take radical action. He contrasts this sense of purpose and resolve with the 'hyper-marxism' and 'indomitable discursivity' of the Parisian situation (p. 139). On the basis of his Tunisian experience he decided to become actively involved politically in France; 'it wasn't May of '68 in France that changed me; it was March of '68 in a third world country' (p. 136).

Curiously, although the impact of political practice in a Third World country is underscored in these passages, and also a connection is made in a sense between peripherality and one kind of learning, the Third World in the example of Tunisia still remains a blank space as far as the agents of critical knowledge are concerned. Equally, there would appear to have been little impact in terms of a possible redirection or reorientation towards the effects of the non-West, the influence of the postcolonial on the study of Occidental discourses. The postcolonial Maghreb did not lend itself to the disruption, or interruption, of the Occidental definition of modernity.[12]

Containment through assimilation

As can be appreciated from my consideration of some aspects of the tendency to create a self-contained vision of the formation of the West, the lines of exclusion never function as impermeable boundaries. Interwoven into the constructions that exclude, we can find subordinating forms of incorporation of the non-West Other. In the context of literary theory, Franco (1988, p. 504) has suggested that metropolitan discourses on the Third World have generally been characterized by one of three devices: (a) exclusion – for example, the Third World is irrelevant to theory; (b) discrimination – the Third World is irrational

and therefore its knowledge must be subordinate to the rational
knowledge produced by the West; and (c) recognition – the Third
World is seen only as the place of the instinctual. From our previous
commentary on Rorty, Vattimo and Baudrillard it can be seen that, in
these postmodern interpretations, exclusion and discrimination are
intimately connected, and that the 'recognition' in Baudrillard can be
taken to conform to Franco's characterization.[13] I would argue then
that, in these representations of the postmodern, there is a dialectic
of exclusion and assimilation which is rooted in a particular discursive
construction of 'Northern' and 'Southern' or Occidental and non-
Occidental worlds.

The Occidental prerogative of inclusion is marked by the persistent
inclination to constitute the non-West Other as the Occidental self's
shadow. In commenting on the work of Foucault and Deleuze, Spivak
(1988, p. 292) draws our attention to the ways in which both these
authors write in a way which reflects the 'unacknowledged subject of
the West'. In other words, it is argued that when the thinking
(Western) subject is rendered transparent or invisible, the 'relentless
recognition of the Other by assimilation' is concealed (p. 294). What
is missing in these Occidental interpretations is the recognition of the
impossibility of any Oneness of thought. To admit to the notion of
an inevitable split in the thinking of the Occidental subject would
also be tantamount to positing a notion of lack. This recognition could
then provide a basis from which to dehegemonize Western positions.
Instead of difference and heterogeneity in thought and reflection
being erased or occluded, the ground could be opened up for sym-
biotic exchanges across a much broader interpretative world. This
entails, as Bhabha (1991, p. 217) might express it, the need to transform 'our sense of what it means to live, to be, in other times and
different spaces, both human and historical'. Equally, it is also important to stress that, in displacing and subverting hegemonic discourses,
Western critics need to 'learn how to occupy the subject position of
the other rather than simply say, "OK, sorry, we are just very good
white people, therefore we do not speak for blacks" '.[14] And, as McGee
(1992, p. 171) usefully adds, 'without this kind of radical self-critique,
teaching third-world texts becomes only another mode of assimilating
the Other'.

Within various expressions of the postmodern ethos, one may
encounter a notable celebration of difference, or the privileging of
plurality. But if that celebration carries with it the insistence that
synchronicity is the key site of historical evaluation, if the symbols,
products, and meanings of other cultures are decontextualized and

then juxtaposed or combined with similarly extracted elements, the historical and political vitality of the distinct and of the distinguishable will be erased. Moreover, under a new Occidental panoply of decontextualized and re-amalgamated meanings, there is the possibility that the potentially fissuring impact of the non-West on the hegemonic discourses of the West will be better resisted and contained.

Containment of difference through an ethnocentric mode of representation can be exemplified by referring to an apparently neutral statement in Lyotard's (1986) text, *The Postmodern Condition*. In explaining that the object of his study is the condition of knowledge in the 'most highly developed societies', Lyotard then conflates North America with the 'American continent' as a whole (p. xxiii). In this way, a crucial historical and political difference is dissolved, and that other – Latin – America becomes the not-one, the unnamed part of the American continent. When Heller and Fehér (1988, p. 6) write that a key factor furthering the 'relative universalism of the postmodern condition is the fact that there is no longer *terra incognita* in our political geography', they are adopting an overly sanguine perspective.[15] In fact, one such *terra incognita* in the domain of Euro-American reflections on the postmodern is formed by the debates on modernity and postmodernity in that part of the periphery which Lyotard unconsciously subsumes under the signifier of 'America'.

Inside the South: the politics of difference

In the field of literature studies, the work of a series of well-known Latin American writers has not infrequently been associated with a postmodern genre. The language of García Márquez, especially, for example, in *One Hundred Years of Solitude*, does not attempt to reveal or replace reality, but rather to indicate how it can both represent and disrupt a variegated *range* of realities. Similarly, and coming well before Jameson, Borges questioned the modernist notion of art as a totalizing entity, replacing it with the notion of the work of art as a deferred entity. Furthermore, the annotatory approach developed by Borges not only dissolved all codes, but actually dispensed with the very notion of coding itself (Ortega, 1988, p. 196). A parallel argument is developed by Zavala (1988) in her consideration of Hispanic modernism, in which, *inter alia*, she shows how much of the contemporary discussion of the modern/postmodern nexus in the Hispanic world as a whole has its precursors at the turn of the last century.[16]

Thus, in the context of literature at least, it can be shown that Latin America has been postmodern *avant la lettre* and also in a *sui generis* sense. However, in other fields of knowledge the situation would appear to be somewhat more ambiguous and ambivalent.

As a way of retaining a necessary connection with the first part of the analysis, and of carrying forward the previous thread of the argument, I shall concentrate my attention on the sociocultural and political/philosophical discussions of the modern and postmodern. At the same time, of course, it has to be remembered that in Latin America the dividing lines between domains of knowledge are, and have always tended to be, far more porous than in the West.

In her attempts to diagnose salient facets of the debate around the modern and the postmodern, Richard, in a related series of articles, captures the sense of ambivalence and perhaps critical perplexity that often seems to undercut current debates on the relevance of the postmodern to political thinking in Latin America. In an earlier article, it is argued that, although the postmodern critique of the universalizing project of capitalist modernity has been politically enabling in one sense, on the other hand, there has also been a tendency to dissolve centre-periphery distinctions, whereby the realities of imperialist domination have tended to be re-absorbed and anaesthetized within an apparently equivalent set of Other images and meanings. For Richard, there has been a tendency in the West for postmodernism to defend itself against the potentially disrupting influence of the Other by inserting it back into a framework which domesticates difference and contradiction (Richard, 1987/88).

At the same time, Richard (1991, p. 15) posits that the postmodern assumes a number of forms: suspicion in philosophy, parody and simulacrum in aesthetics, deconstruction in critical theory, scepticism in politics, relativism in ethics and syncretism in culture. She further argues that, for Latin America, these forms are concomitant with a matrix of interconnected crises; of totality and the pluralization of fragments; of unicity and the multiplication of differences; and of centrality and the proliferating overflow of margins (p. 15).[17] Insisting on the continuing necessity for critique, and for independence from official institutions and the market, Richard (1992) re-emphasizes the subversive role of the intellectual not only as interpreter, but as transgressor of the ordered deployment of normalizing knowledge. In societies such as Chile, which are characterized by various 'vectors of conflict', the intellectual must be able to open up 'points of flight' from the official projects of ordering knowledge.[18] In this context, Richard reads the postmodern as potentially enabling and progressive

for the way in which a uniform and subordinating 'story' of development and modernization can be destabilized and displaced. One of
the points that is being emphasized here is the significance of the
resisting and reflexive actor. In a related article on the 'crisis of
the original and the revenge of the copy', Richard has stressed how a
symptomatic problem of the centre's postmodern discourse is the
inclination to include the periphery under the tolerant slogan of
the Other, thus taking away the possibility that Latin Americans can
be actors in 'our own reformulation of discourses' (Richard, 1989,
p. 49).

The idea that the postmodern turn, as an imported mode of reflection, can be detrimental to the independent analysis of the specificities
of Latin America's own political scene finds expression in Reigadas'
(1988) contribution to an Argentinian text on postmodernity. In this
intervention, two incursory waves of Western penetration are identified: first, the neoliberal doctrine of modernization and development,
and second, the current adaptation of the postmodernity debate to
Latin American conditions. Reigadas shares with Richard a sharp
opposition to the precepts of neo-liberalism and Western individualism, but is more unequivocally negative towards the postmodern. She
asks the question:

> why should we uncritically assume the end of history, . . . entertain the crisis
> of the idea of the nation, proclaim the perversion of the State, renounce
> collective projects, celebrate the end of ideologies and utopias, declare that
> liberation and the Third World are old myths, hasten to interpret our cultural
> problems in terms of a very post-modern heterogeneity, declare ourselves
> the partisans of fragmentation, pastiche and syncretism, and passively
> enjoy the kingdom of uncertainty? (Reigadas, 1988, p. 142)

Taking the argument further, she asks: why should it be assumed that
nations are obsolete anachronisms when Latin America was always
prevented from constructing its own versions, and why should the
historical ideals of solidarity and justice be renounced in exchange for
a postmodern individualistic culture in which anything goes? For
Reigadas (p. 144) the 'iconoclastic irrationality' of the postmodern is
reflected in its totalitarian negation of totality. In Reigadas' vision, the
postmodern is linked to neoliberalism and the renewed Western project of dominating the periphery; seemingly, this double Occidental
move signifies a growing 'cultural colonization'.

Hence, while both Richard and Reigadas concur on the need to
interrogate neoliberalism and Western-led projects of modernization,

Richard adopts a more nuanced view of the postmodern, refusing simply to condemn it as another modality of cultural and political manipulation.

The same thematic surfaces in Hopenhayn's (1988) critical observations on culture and development. How, he asks, can we incorporate the postmodern debate in order to reactivate the cultural basis of development, without it leading us into a postmodernism that is functional to neoliberalism's project of political and cultural hegemony?[19] Or, how might it be possible to reinterpret the challenges of planning, state policy and the programmes of modernization in the light of the eventual cultural earthquake announced by the protagonists of postmodernity? Equally, how can a critique of ethnocentrism (including the critique of imitative patterns of development) be integrated into the analysis without culminating in regionalisms, particularisms and some form of 'wishful thinking' (Hopenhayn, 1988, p. 68).

Hopenhayn anticipates the embryonic elements of possible answers to these kinds of questions through drawing up the following register of connected themes: the revalorization of democracy; a reorientation of planning to accord with the new realities of social complexity; a change in the perception and attitude of social scientists faced by a multiple array of social actors; and a revalorization of social movements over political parties, and especially the so-called new social movements and base organizations. Through all these interconnected themes, Hopenhayn posits the importance of a cultural dimension.

The emphasis given to new social movements goes together with the need to accept the search for new forms of doing politics, whereby the constitution of collective identities and the recognition of cultural diversity figure prominently. The revalorization of democracy and pluralism point to the consolidation of a democratic culture, and not only a government elected by majorities. The reorientation of planning presupposes a change in the structure of perception, with a move away from the older mechanistic paradigms towards a more fluid approach that seeks a co-ordination rather than homogenization of diverse social energies. The rethinking of the social sciences also implies a move towards a more reflexive perspective on what is an increasingly complex, disarticulated and polymorphous social fabric. In all these examples, Hopenhayn expresses the belief that it is through insights from the postmodern debate that the cultural base on which modernization in Latin America has been constructed may be better understood. More concretely, he argues that through a postmodern problematization of the 'cultural cement of modernization' it may be easier to break through the neoliberal frame on development thinking (Hopenhayn, 1988, p. 68).[20]

Hopenhayn's approach is both interesting and somewhat unusual, in that it includes an attempt to connect discussions of culture with those of planning and economic development.[21] In this sense the potential relevance of the postmodern inflection is employed in the pursuit of a broader recontextualization of domains which are quite customarily kept apart.

In a not unrelated exploration of many of the most interesting but also problematic questions of thinking the modern and the postmodern for Latin America, Piscitelli (1988) has extended the debate somewhat further. He begins his discussion by arguing against closed schemas, and favouring a hybridization of knowledge and action. Such an orientation is placed in a setting where the modern is seen to be on the wane. The fading of the transforming value of the aesthetic, the increase in the distance that separates utopias and the vain promises of the vanguards from material misery, a growing dehumanization provoked by the non-correspondence between technological and social development and the satisfaction of immaterial needs, and the explosive return of irrational sentiments and beliefs that were assumed to be effectively overcome are, for Piscitelli (1988, p. 70), just some of the expressions that lend credence to the notion of the exhaustion of modernity. They are also some of the issues that any future social theory must tackle.

Thinking of the posited exhaustion of modernity, Piscitelli wonders to what extent this exhaustion was revealed in the original failure of modernity to recognize the multiple alterities that have resisted its disfiguring and destructive hegemony. It was so normal to think that the non-Occidental was also pre-rational that it became feasible to deny the idea that modern culture was always a culture of external and internal imperialism, which, perhaps, embodied totalitarianism in its purest form. Moreover, as Piscitelli (1988, p. 82) reminds the reader, the developed 'democracies' have always had their 'other scene' – the Cosa Nostra, the P2 and, we might add, the clandestine 'Gladio network' and the Oliver Norths – which, as I argued earlier, seldom appear on the agendas of Western theoretical debate.

Broadening the terrain of his anti-ethnocentric position, Piscitelli suggests that it may be considered time to invert our interpretative codes and change the terms of comparison. Hence, instead of seeing the 'imperfection' of our political forms in the limited and insufficient gaze of the North, let us make our comparative analyses the anticipation of what will be seen in the North in a few more years. In this

way, the South or, in this particular case, Latin America may be seen
as ahead of the North, as a world which offers to its supposedly more
advanced Northern Other a picture of what it, i.e. the North, may
become. Notions of the so-called Third Worldization of the First
World, the growth of 'informal sectors', and the increasing prominence
of cultural heterogeneity and hybridization or *mestizaje* point in the
direction of this kind of analysis, with all its destabilizing and innovative potential.

Intimately interwoven into Piscitelli's challenging of the negative
effects of Occidental ethnocentrism, it is possible to discern a recurrent concern with problems of political identity and social struggle. It
is suggested that a new conscience is required, different from that
kind of modernist intellectual approach which always expressed the
presumptuous confidence of being located on the cutting edge of
time. This 'new conscience' would be linked to the development of a
radical democratic politics, that might be both post-Marxist and postmodern. For Piscitelli (1988, p. 80) the novelty of postmodernity is
given by the end of monolithic projects, and the proliferation of
movements which express an intrinsic reappropriation of society itself.
However, at the same time, the postmodern is viewed with political
ambivalence, since, as with Hopenhayn, there is a realization that the
postmodern is itself open and polysemic; Piscitelli (p. 73) asks, for
example, 'how can we Latin Americans rescue post-modernism from
its re-appropriation by neo-conservatism'? A further dilemma takes
shape in the need, expressed by Piscitelli, to reconstruct a collective
imaginary, capable of orientating political action and social struggle,
in an epoch marked by the resulting confusion of the postmodern
critique of modernity. Moreover, Piscitelli (p. 72) goes on, from where,
and in the name of which principles, values and mandates, is it
possible to define the notions of reality, truth and legitimacy, and how
is a political project to be constructed in a way that will be appropriate
for solving the 'crisis and stagnation from which we are now suffering'?

In a time of mediocrity, opportunism and the absence of heroism,
Piscitelli (1988, p. 82) also locates interstices, antagonistic values and
the small flashes of happiness and audacity that 'invite the continuation of the dialogue humanity has with itself'. Together with this
pervasive sense of ambivalence and duality, there is also the paradox,
expressed by other writers too, of living in a time of increasing fluidity,
plurality, multiplicity, openness and perplexity, which seems to ground
the need for new bases, and the construction of new, freer horizons.
As Achugar (1991, p. 122), García (1991, p. 214) and Gómez (1988,
p. 93) all stress, these new horizons ought to include the continual

search for the specificities of the Latin American situation, with an adherence to the principle of 'liberation from the canons of metropolitan imposition' (Gómez, 1988, p. 93).[22]

Along with Piscitelli, Aricó (1992), Lechner (1988, 1991) and Portantiero (1992) underline the need to rethink the political within a difficult societal context of complex, fluid and unstable identities.[23] Lechner (1988, pp. 115–16), for example, suggests that postmodern culture expresses a crisis of identity. This is interpreted in the context of a growing disarticulation and fragmentation of society, and the increasingly enigmatic and multiple nature of the domain or space of the political. For Lechner (1991, p. 68), we are living a continuing present, a time characterized by a sequence of events and conjunctures, and devoid of a future horizon. It is posited that postmodern culture, with its critique of the notion of the subject, has tended to undermine the bases for a rethinking of the political. Influenced by the notion of the end of metanarratives and the crumbling of foundations, the construction of new political identities and horizons has been made much more problematic.

Aricó (1992) also expresses a sense of difficult times, believing that there is no longer a centre, a rear guard or an apparent way of 'integrating dispersed struggles' (p. 21). For Aricó, the left has to transform political culture, and if this proves to be impossible, the prospect is one of simply helping to administer an order it cannot change. Aricó (p. 23) points to what is for him the fundamental arena of struggle: 'the arena of culture, of values, and the legitimacy of a political and social order'.

Similarly, Portantiero (1992) emphasizes the question of values and ethics in any construction of a new politics. Today's crisis, he writes, which is at root a crisis of values, challenges us to 'invent a new political culture with new forms of collective action, which in turn could lead us to new modes of understanding' (p. 17). In his short but incisive intervention, Portantiero touches on a number of key issues, including the need to focus on the public sphere, as distinct from the binary split between the private and state spheres. It is within this public sphere that ideas for the autonomous organization of a self-managed society can emerge. The struggle to relocate discussions of the community and the citizen and to situate the policies of structural adjustment in a wider context of political ethics form two other connected themes on Portantiero's agenda.

Running through these various analytical reflections, there is a constant sense of involvement with all the problems of constructing a new politics that is independent and critical of the dominance of

possessive individualism. At the same time, there is a clear distancing
from those earlier socialist discourses that always presupposed an
unquestioned foundation, or ultimate ground, from which all political
meaning acquired its historical significance. The fact that Aricó
entitled his paper 'Rethink everything' gives expression to a pervasive
current of critical thought. In the search for new political identities
that can be constitutive of an emancipatory ethos, old allegiances are
radically questioned and remapped. For example, the meaning of
the Cuban revolution for Latin America can be seen as a point of
condensation for many interwoven debates on democracy and socialism, imperialism and national self-determination, and essentialism
versus difference. In the charting of new political identities for Latin
America, the remaining contours of an older mode of centralizing
truth – that which Lyotard (1988, p. 50) likened to a machine for
'producing universality out of particularity' – are being gradually
redrawn and resituated in a different problematic.[24]

So far, in my presentation of important elements of the debates
unfolding in Latin America, I have given some priority to the critique
of Western ethnocentrism, and to issues surrounding problems of
identity, difference and the rethinking of the political. These two
thematics have been quite strongly evident in the literature evolving
inside the Southern Cone countries, particularly in Argentina and
Chile, from where many of the texts originate. All that is possible
within the limited scope of this part of my exploration is to *introduce*
some facets of a rich and heterogeneous body of literature. I have
tried to summarize a number of arguments, incorporating a range of
cited passages as a way of conveying the actuality of this interpretative
world. My formulations could not possibly begin to cover the full
extent of the Latin American discussions of modernity and postmodernity, but hopefully they will at least provide me with a comparative
basis from which we can return to the earlier evaluation of certain
Occidental readings of the postmodern. Before making such a recon-
nection, however, there is one further thematic that requires some
consideration, if only in the briefest possible manner.

Moving north from the countries of the Southern Cone, it is noticeable that in Peru and Bolivia, and most strikingly perhaps in Mexico,
the issue of cultural hybridization and *mestizaje* figures much more
prominently in the relevant debates.[25] In societies suffused with the
shades of multiple social and cultural forms, concepts of national,
regional or religious identity cannot be realistically separated from a
mosaic of meaning and practice.

In the case of the Andean countries, Calderón (1987) and Quijano

(1988), sociologists from Bolivia and Peru respectively, emphasize the complex interweaving of the premodern and the (post)modern in the cultural configuration of these societies. For Calderón, social and cultural identities increasingly assume a kaleidoscopic form, rendering their recognition and comprehension ever more problematic.[26] But, at the same time, there is in the work of Quijano, for example, an attempt to rescue notions of reciprocity and collective solidarity, embedded in the cultural history of the Andes. For Quijano, these indigenous practices can be seen as forming the basis for a more enabling modernity *sui generis*, in which notions of the nation and of community can be rethought in the face of the challenge from neoliberalism.[27]

For García Canclini (1991, p. 24), writing of the Mexican experience, as far as both hegemonic and popular cultures are *hybrid cultures*, it is undeniable that in this sense Latin America is living in a postmodern epoch, in a 'time of *bricolage* where diverse epochs and previously separated cultures intersect with each other'; 'we Latin Americans . . . are also a combination of truncated memories and heterogeneous innovations'.

Interestingly, the Mexican writer and artist Gómez-Peña (1992) advances a related argument, noting that in Mexico we are immersed in syncretism, so that 'this multiple otherness within constitutes the very spinal cord of our personal and collective biography' (p. 70). Unlike García Canclini, however, he contrasts this vision of multiple Otherness, of the Other that exists within us, to the situation in Anglo-America. Here, postmodernism has to be learnt as theory, since the cultural experience of Anglo-Americans is not marked by a growing within and across multiple cultural strata. 'Today in 1992', he writes, 'the US still does not have a critical discourse to understand and explain its own *mestizaje*' (p. 70).

Also from a Mexican context, Bartra (1991), in his original, postmodern diagnosis of national identity and modernity – Mexico's 'cage of melancholy' – illuminates the imbrication of borders. Bartra asks the question: 'do we recreate national culture in accordance with "true" popular culture, or do we accept the transnational invasion of the new mass culture?' (p. 11). The answer he gives is that these are two false alternatives, for contemporary national culture is an amalgam of both these options. The *fotonovelas*, private television, comic books, commercial music, pornographic and romantic novels and so on, exert an enormous influence, but for Bartra, no matter how much they are stigmatized as 'foreign' manifestations, they are also an 'equally integral part of Mexican political culture' (p. 12). At the same time, the

'Mexican soul' – melancholy, negligence, fatalism, inferiority, violence, sentimentalism, resentment and evasiveness – has survived the avalanche of foreign influences to retain a stable place in the nation's political culture.

Moreover, with the crucial existence of a border territory between two cultures, one has the imbrication of 'Mexicanization' with 'Americanization', on the connected but other sides of that border. It is possible, Bartra argues, to be Mexican without subjecting oneself to a state or territory; 'this deterritorialization and denationalization of the intellectuals is beginning to define the profile of the postmodern experience' (p. 15). If, as Bartra suggests, modernization is the real state of capitalist development, and modernity is an 'imaginary country whose legitimating network traps civil society' (p. 15), perhaps the postmodern sensibility can function as an alternative imaginary which destabilizes the points and lines of such a network.

There is in both Bartra and Gómez-Peña a sense that the postmodern imagination can be enabling, that the emerging 'borderization' of the world can provide points for a more effective contestation of oppressive practices and official meanings. They are critical, but not cynical. As with other authors discussed above, there is a continual and propelling desire to engage with the present, and the past, as a way of thinking a future, no matter how problematic. Further, there is in so much of the Latin American discussion both an inside and an outside. On the one side, there is both a continuing analytical engagement with Western theory *and* an interrogation of the effects of Occidental penetration on the actual political and sociocultural structures of Latin American societies. On the other, there is a persistent examination of the internal specificities of these peripheral societies, so that the 'inside' and the 'outside', the 'included' and the 'excluded' tend to intertwine, separate and recombine. The West or North is not an unnamed Other; its presence is unavoidably interwoven into the South's own constitutive inside, but this intermingling incorporates a critical spirit of challenging the nature of the Occidental presence. Latin America is not contextualized as a self-contained entity, writing out its truths and agendas for the rest of the world.

It is at this juncture that we can return to our initial consideration of the West's treatment of the postmodern, and see to what extent a recontextualization, to employ Rorty's concept, can be imagined.

Arenas of knowledge and the North-South divide

Some readers of my mode of inclusion of Latin American interpretations of the modernity/postmodernity nexus might be seen to register a sardonic smile: 'well, perhaps there still is some hope down there.' In a somewhat unexpected turn in his argument, Rorty (1991b, p. 181), in his brief but revealing commentary on the Brazilian theorist Unger, is encouraged to entertain the Brazilian's intimation that, if there is hope, it lies in the Third World. Continuing this thought, Rorty (p. 187) muses that, while perhaps Orwell's 'democratic vistas' have ended in barbed wire, 'maybe the Brazilians (or the Tanzanians, or *somebody*) will be able to dodge around that barbed wire'. Concluding this particular chapter on Unger, Castoriadis and the romance of national futures, Rorty writes as follows:

> To say . . . that if there is hope it lies in the imagination of the Third World, is to say that the best any of us here in Alexandria can hope for is that somebody out there will do something to tear up the present system of imaginary significations within which politics in (and between) the First and Second Worlds is conducted. (p. 192)

And for such a possible outcome, 'only some actual event, the actual success of some political move made in some actual country, is likely to help' (p. 192).

In the light of our earlier appraisal of Rorty's work, this later publication might seem to herald a different vista, associating, as it seems to do, the 'exemplary instability of the Third World' with a horizon called 'hope'. However, earlier on in his discussion of Brazil and Unger, Rorty suggests that Brazil is a country that '*cannot hope* to achieve what the North Atlantic has achieved in the way of equality and decency by the same means: reliance on a free market in capital and on compromises between pressure groups' (Rorty, 1991b, p. 180, emphasis added). This view corresponds to the thoughts advanced in an earlier chapter on Heidegger, Kundera and Dickens, where Rorty reaffirms the 'West as a continuing adventure' (p. 67). It is argued here that we should not follow Heidegger's view of the exhaustion of the West, but rather stress the genre in which the West has excelled, as found in the novels of Dickens, where moral protest stands out.

In these passages, Rorty argues strongly against what he refers to as the negative essentialization of the West, which, he adds, is frequently placed in contradistinction to the idea of a redemptive non-West or

East. But in the same few pages, Rorty does not hesitate to essential-
ize the East, noting, for example, that Heideggerian themes such as
the need 'to escape from busyness' and 'to become receptive to the
splendor of the simple, are easy to find in the East' (Rorty, 1991b,
p. 71). This chapter, which was written a little later than the commentary on Unger, where we read of the Third World as a possible place
of hope, reasserts Rorty's earlier views on the West, which I discussed
in some detail in the opening section of my analysis.

Linking the arguments found in these two different chapters, it is
instructive to note that, whereas it is hoped that under the rubric of
'the romance of a national future' somebody out there in the Third
World might tear up the present system of imaginary significations
and create something new – 'the actual success of some political move
made in some actual country' – the *actual history* of such attempts in
a wide variety of Third World countries, against which the 'North
Atlantic' has consistently intervened, is excluded from the record.
Knowledge of such interventions, which are somewhat removed from
the notion of 'compromises between pressure groups', is available,
but its recognition is persistently absent. Recognition of the detrimental effects of Western interventions, military, economic, political and
cultural, especially in contexts where movements or governments in
the South have been making Rorty's 'actual political moves', can
help us destabilize that standardizing vision of a benevolent West,
dispensing justice, equality, decency and tolerance to a hopeful non-
West.

Along a connected route, there is another way of thinking about
hope. Across the expanding arenas of knowledge, the debate on multi-
culturalism and what Charles Taylor (1992) has aptly called the 'politics of recognition', can help us reassert the need to go beyond Euro-
Americanism.[28] Both in the evaluation of Rorty, Baudrillard and Vattimo, and in my shorter review of the Latin American literature, I have
been motivated by the desire to break down unhelpful separations
and to call into question that Occidental tendency towards 'self-
immurement within ethnocentric standards' (Taylor, 1992, p. 72). In
the emerging debate on postmodernity, it seems to me quite crucial
to focus more of the analysis on ethnocentrism and the politics of
recognition, and in the case of this discussion, on intellectual recognition. The agents of knowledge must not always be assumed to be
of an Occidental pedigree.[29] Further, as Lauer (1991, p. 3) puts it,
'who decides today what are the global themes?'; or, as Barbara Christian (1989, pp. 227–8) observes, in a different context, there has long
been a Western 'binary' frame 'which sees the rest of the world as

minor, and tries to convince the rest of the world that it *is* major, usually through force and then through language, even as it claims many of the ideas that we, its "historical" other, have known and spoken about for so long'.

In the Latin American literature, the critique of Western moderniz-ation and modernity is one such example of Christian's argument. If the Western-based authors of the postmodern interruption had stretched out and referred to this other, apparently invisible, critical tradition, they could have seen how many of their ideas had already been placed on the agenda. But that stretching outside our ourselves, with the capacity for self-reflection and self-distance, is not always present. It requires, among other things, the commitment to challenge and transform the perspectives from which we have previously viewed the world. In the Western debate on modernity and postmodernity, the Heideggerian concepts of *Andenken* and *Verwindung*, adapted by Vattimo, could also be deployed to help in the process of stretching out of the Occidental enclosure. Similarly, Rorty's notion of recontex-tualization is pregnant with potential for the opening up of enclosure and the fissuring of deeply sedimented meanings. The North-South divide may seem, for now, an obdurate geopolitical reality, but the enframing of the 'global themes' of today does not have to imitate the hierarchy on which that original divide has been forged.

The processes of reflexivity, of self-distancing, of stretching out towards new themes of dialogue, learning and recontextualization, could well be developed as a hopeful, emancipatory current of the postmodern ethos. In the North, the need to 'reinvent ourselves as Other', can be set in the context of taking historic responsibility for 'the social locations from which our speech and actions issue'; 'this', for Sandra Harding (1992, p. 189), 'is a scientific and epistemological issue as well as a moral and political one'. Exactly.

In the North, that process of reinventing ourselves as other requires the will and the desire to learn from the South, not uncritically or romantically, fuelled by some unconscious sense of culpability, but as a way of better understanding the North itself, and with it the South, *and* vice versa. This complex imbrication also intersects with the politics of intellectual recognition. Not that the themes, the theoretical issues, the conceptual frameworks in the South are fundamentally different. There are key interfaces – for example, in the attention given to the politics of identity and subjectivity in Latin America as elsewhere – but the social and historical locations from which theoreti-cal analysis has emerged in Latin America have tended to generate a critical specificity that can illuminate what is often occluded in the North.

That the non-West Other has contributed, is contributing and will in the future contribute to the global growth of analytical knowledge and reflection is an idea that often seems beyond the Occidental imagination.[30] The life of the mind does not begin and end inside the Occident; there can be no Western checkpoint to keep out non-Western thought. And in exploring some of those other zones of the postmodern in one world of the South, I hope I have been able to show not only that the 'Euro-American' does not stand alone, but that the reflexive spirit of the postmodern might help us to go beyond ethnocentrism and move towards a more genuinely global expansion of knowledge and understanding. For such an expansion to take place, self-reflexivity, dialogue, intellectual reciprocity and the willingness to respect and learn from thinkers who are located in different regions are all key prerequisites.

In the context of the international division of intellectual labour, the power of interpretation over other peoples, as Lazreg (1988) has suggested, reflects an Occidental privilege that is deeply rooted and continually pervasive. The lines of thought and terrains of enquiry that connect the modern with the postmodern continue to exhibit the traces of such privilege and philosophical solipsism. So far, the Occidental explorations of the postmodern have not disrupted and destabilized the will to ethnocentrism, and yet, as I have argued, within the postmodern sensibility one can locate lines of interruption, and potential sites of displacement. The critique, for example, of metanarratives and universalist projects, as has been argued in Latin America, gives the potential for a more enabling and liberating perspective on sociopolitical change.

From the Latin American discussions of modernity and postmodernity, there are a number of themes which have a wider relevance to our need to develop and nourish a global expansion of knowledge and understanding for postmodern times.

In the first place, the sociopolitical investigation of the modern/postmodern nexus reveals the continuing vitality of an articulation between an inside and an outside. While one can find an analytical engagement with changes in Western-based theory, a persistent interest in the trends and issues of metropolitan discourses, and in their potential relevance for other regions, at the same time Latin American intellectuals continue to produce analysis of the specificities of their societies, and of the complex texture of exogenous and endogenous patterns. Looking to the outside is not motivated by the desire to acquire other forms of empirical information to be incorporated into already constituted theoretical frames; nor is it fuelled by the search for an exotic Other. Rather, knowledge from outside is examined in terms of its analytical value and potential relevance in the construction of knowledge for the sociopolitical inside.

Second, as discussed previously, critical interrogation of the Western ethnocentrism present in many of the texts on postmodernity provides a series of pointers for wider discussions of the politics of knowledge. Equally, from the earlier dependency perspectives of the late 1960s (Cardoso and Faletto, 1969; Kay, 1989), through to the contemporary debates on identity and political subjectivity, Latin America has been home to some of the most crucial challenges to what García Canclini (1993, p. 9) refers to as 'imperial ethnocentrism'. The critical examination not only of Western development theory, but also of the everyday effects of imperialist penetrations of the Latin American continent provide a vital counter-analysis of West/non-West relations.

Third, with reference to the growing global interest in questions of hybridization, Latin American societies and the knowledges produced within them reflect and give substance to many of today's wider debates on cultural relations and the politics of difference. The mosaic of different ethnic, communal and religious identities within specific societies of the Andean region or Mexico has created highly complex and fluid social processes that find expression in the production of heterogeneous knowledges and subjectivities. There is here a sense of 'multiple Otherness', of the Other that exists within, and the theorization of *mestizaje* and hybridization that is being developed in Latin America is highly relevant for any reinvention of ourselves as Other.

Finally, with respect to the configuration and deployment of knowledge, especially in the social and political domains, there is a double point. In the same spirit of hybridization, the organization of knowledge within the fields of social and political enquiry has been less subject to the disciplinary power of division and compartmentalization. The intermingling and intersections of spheres of investigation, the development of problematics rather than the rise and fall of paradigms, and the porosity of the border lines between different terrains of knowledge all reflect a greater sense of openness and reciprocity. At the same time, there has also been and there continues to be a vital connection between political practice and analytical reflection. The politically engaged intellectual, the social scientist who focuses on issues of societal conflict, of oppression and subordination, and who is also a participant in social and political change, retains a significant place in the territory of knowledge. These are not, of course, exclusive trends; there are tendencies towards a growing specialization and compartmentalization of knowledge, and with foreign funding, in some cases, a trend towards a Westernization of research frameworks.

These four elements, taken together, and flowing out of my consideration of the politics of difference in Latin America, help to provide an answer to the question I posed at the outset of the analysis: namely, how can we learn from the Latin American discussions of modernity and postmodernity within the overall frame of social and political theory? Through examining certain features of the debates in Latin America, it has been possible to recontextualize analysis of the postmodern as conducted in the Euro-American centres of knowledge. My perspective leaves many openings for further enquiry, challenge and argument; hopefully, if may contribute to the much needed destabilization of one form of Euro-Americanist truth.

Notes

Earlier versions of this paper were read in the Centre for Theoretical Studies in the Humanities and the Social Sciences, University of Essex, and during a colloquium sponsored by the Sociology Board, Latin American Studies and the Center for Cultural Studies at the University of California, Santa Cruz. I wish to thank the participants in both seminars for providing such stimulating encounters.

1   The quotation comes from a paper by Rajchman, which is referred to in Marcus (1991, p. 10).
2   For a recent consideration of the interconnections between postmodernism and Islam, see Ahmed's (1992) important contribution which critically dissects aspects of the 'Occident-Orient' divide.
3   In a related analysis (Slater, 1992), I have examined some of the works of Lyotard and Jameson in the context of the periphery and the postmodern.
4   For example, writing towards the end of the eighteenth century, Kant, in the ninth proposition of his Idea for a Universal History, posited a line of continuity from the Greeks through the Romans, and including episodically the political history of other peoples, in so far as knowledge of them had come down through the enlightened nations, so that 'we shall discover a regular process of improvement in the political constitutions of our continent (*which will probably legislate eventually for all other continents*)' (my emphasis). See Kant, (1991, p. 52). Related notions were to reoccur in the development of Western thought.
5   At the same time, Rorty criticizes Chomsky and other North American

intellectuals for attempting to rehabilitate Kantian notions of morality in the field of war and the external relations of states. Specifically, Rorty is referring to Kant's seventh proposition in his Idea for a Universal History, where, for example, it is written that 'as long as states apply all their resources to their vain and violent schemes of expansion, thus incessantly obstructing the slow and laborious efforts of their citizens to cultivate their minds . . . no progress in . . . the direction of . . . becoming morally mature can be expected' (Kant, 1991, p. 49). One would have thought that such a position was not entirely irrelevant in the United States of the Vietnam War period.

6   Of course, I am not implying here that the non-West has nothing to learn from the West, but rather that in the social field it is necessary to destabilize the ethnocentric implication that the learning process can only be one-way, with the non-West looking up to the West.

7   In fact, following ideas from Nietzsche and Heidegger, Vattimo goes on to state that the demythologization of demythologization, 'may be taken as the true moment of transition from the modern to the postmodern' (Vattimo, 1992, p. 42).

8   For instance, underdeveloped countries are interpreted in terms of their lack of information technology, or means of communication, or capacity for knowledge production, thus tending to reinforce the conventional response of seeking then to 'fill' these gaps or lacks through new waves of Westernization.

9   In a consideration of the power of myth, it is suggested that, while it is politically dangerous and unacceptable to try to restore the 'traditional' culture, it is nevertheless the case that 'mythical knowledge, uncompromised by the rationalism of the capitalist West, remains a benchmark for the rejection of modernity and its errors' (Vattimo, 1992, p. 34). The fact that outside the West there may be agents of knowledge who have already developed critiques of Occidental modernity is not seen as a possibility. The life of the mind remains a feature of the 'conversation of the West'.

10 In an article on postmodernity in Latin America, Reigadas (1988, p. 139) notes, *en passant*, that in a conversation with Vattimo in 1987 in Argentina, the Italian philosopher maintained, according to Reigadas, that the South belonged to the Western metaphysical tradition. When Reigadas put it to him that his attitude seemed to be that the periphery was residual to Occidental history, and that those in the South are always seen as savage, exotic and non-conceptualizable within any reasonable theoretical scheme, Vattimo accepted the observation, but confessed a lack of knowledge of Latin American reality. But equally, for Reigadas, there was no hint of a change of position on Vattimo's part.

11 For instance, in the field of anthropology, Mascia-Lees *et al.* (1989) trace out some aspects of the problem of an androcentric postmodernism, and, in a somewhat more targeted language, bell hooks (1991, p. 23) writes that 'postmodernist discourses are often exclusionary even as they call attention to, appropriate even, the experience of "difference" and "otherness" to provide oppositional political meaning, legitimacy and immediacy when they are accused of lacking concrete relevance'.

12 It is possible to make an associated argument in relation to Lyotard's experience in Algeria. Here also the significance of political practice is stressed,

but the relevance of the postcolonial for the life of the mind remains an
empty space (see, for example, Lyotard, 1988).

13   A somewhat similar form of discrimination surfaces at the end of one of
Deleuze and Guattari's recent articles: they write, for example, that points
of 'nonculture or underdevelopment' are 'linguistic Third World zones by
which a language can escape'. The association that is made between notions
of nonculture and the Third World is not original to Deleuze and Guattari,
but it is worthwhile noting here that, in the work of even the most subversive
of Western philosophers, older narratives of Occidental supremacy remain
dormant (see Deleuze and Guattari, 1990, p. 68).

14   The quotation is from Spivak, and cited in McGee (1992, p. 171).

15   They go on to suggest that the 'collapse of the colonial system', as well as
the ' "museification" of Europe' have closed the 'long period of unashamed
cultural supremacy on a note of "the quest for the primitive" ', borrowing,
they suggest, a phrase from anthropology. They add that the 'third world'
has been sharply engraved, in both positive and negative senses, on the
'membrane of the consciousness of 'the first world' (Heller and Fehér, (1988,
p. 6). In this short passage, neocolonialism and imperialism, or more contemporary forms of Western domination, constitute a present absence, and again
the Third World is linked to the primitive, being placed in another previous
time.

16   Arguing strongly against Eurocentric universalization, characteristic of many
Western analyses of cultural politics and postmodernism, Zavala provides the
reader with a series of themes that had already emerged in *fin de siglo* writing
in both Spain and parts of Latin America. She refers to 'carnivalization,
dissolution of legitimized narratives, displacement, critique of reason, hetero-
doxy (theological and political), eclecticism, "open" works, performance,
reader's participation, pluralism, collage, pastiche . . . and the dissolution of
boundaries' (see Zavala, 1988, p. 95).

17   An earlier echo of Richard's invocation of the multiplicity of crisis can be
found in Joaquín Brunner's (1987) diagnosis of modernity, where he writes
that in Latin America there is a sensation of a permanent and total crisis –
of the economy, of institutions, of political regimes, of the universities, of
art, of the public services, of private enterprise and of the armed forces.
Latin America is a project of echoes and fragments, utopias and pasts, 'whose
present we can only perceive as already being in continual crisis' (p. 39).

18   Richard, it ought to be noted, is taking her immediate context from the
current nature of state-society relations in Chile. Here, for Richard (1992,
p. 7), many producers of knowledge with a market value (sociologists and
economists) have been incorporated into the state, which 'legalizes them as
experts'.

19   In the context of feminist theory, Soper (1991, pp. 99–101) raises a related
series of questions and dilemmas. She writes that one of the key problems for
the 'postmodernists' is that of internal coherence; 'how can a postmodernist
perspective consistently present itself as "liberating" while conducting such
an unyielding critique of the metaphysics which have grounded all talk of
liberation?' (p. 100). If the postmodernists are not advocates of any political

change or programme, they must indirectly support the continuance of the status quo, and thus implicitly underwrite a specific position.

20 In the original, Hopenhayn uses the phrase *'cerco neoliberal'*, which I have rather blandly translated as 'frame'. In fact the Spanish expression is richer, implying the idea of 'siege' or 'fence'.

21 In a similar fashion, the Chilean writer Subercaseaux (1991) stresses the primary significance of the cultural – 'the umbilical cord that sustains language, customs, values, historical memory and creativity' (p. 140) – for analyses of modernization and politics. For a more recent development of his argument on planning, social change and culture, see Hopenhayn (1992).

22 At the same time, we should not assume that such a view is held by all contributors to the Latin American debate on modernity and postmodernity. As one case in point, Brunner *et al.* (1989, p. 216) argue that in the Chilean case the cultural incorporation of modernity operates as a process of internationalization, which implies for the periphery the need to 'receive' and 'incorporate' rather than to 'reject' or 'prevent'.

23 Piscitelli (1988, p. 82), for instance, writes that the most precarious aspect of living in Latin American societies is not the danger of unexpected assault, or the sudden and unexpected collapse of fragile social threads, but the fact that one is never assured of one's own identity, either individually or societally.

24 However, as Aricó (1992, p. 23) reminds us, it has often been the case that independent discussion of Cuba has been hindered by the fear of giving succour to aggressively reactionary positions. Also, perhaps, the more authoritarian currents of radical political thought have themselves found sustenance in an experiment that has continually represented the possibility of a viable monocentrism in politics.

25 In the case of Brazil, Limonad (1991, p. 101), in her article on the city and technology in postmodernism, writes that one of today's paradoxes is that Brazilians live in a postmodern society that has not fully achieved modernity; in the past, one had the idea of the coexistence of archaic and modern forms in the context of combined and unequal development, whereas now 'we experience an almost organic articulation of such forms'.

26 For example, referring to a song of Rubén Blades, Calderón (p. 9) emphasizes how it may no longer be possible to find 'America'; or if it is found, it may no longer be recognized. Previous modes of thinking and framing are no longer sufficient to interpret the changing map of social and cultural relations.

27 For some further and more recent discussion of these and related issues, in the context of contemporary Peru, see, for example, Urbano (1991) and Franco (1991).

28 Perhaps a more accurate term would be 'Euro-North Americanism', as, in fact, used by Quijano (1988), and in accordance with the need to undermine the definition of 'America' as North America. I have used the shorter term, since in English at least it is less cumbersome, and hopefully, from the tenor of the text, it will be clear what I mean.

29 Felski (1992, p. 134), in her timely reflections on feminism and postmodernism, writes that 'there is an obvious ethnocentrism underpinning assumptions that Western notions of the postmodern exemplify the most advanced state

of contemporary knowledge against which the worldviews of other cultures can be measured and found wanting'.

30　For example, in her discussion of Gramsci, Marxism and postmodernism, Holub (1992, p. 182) sets up a dichotomy between Western intellectuals on the one hand and non-Western developing cultures on the other. She goes on to argue that the critical intellectuals of the West, the 'arbiters of hope', need to receive the messages that reach us from the developing worlds, and 'translate them, by way of our theoretical tools, for ours' (p. 190).

References

Achugar, H. (1991) 'La política de lo estético', *Nueva Sociedad*, no. 116, pp. 122–9.

Ahmed, A. S. (1992) *Postmodernism and Islam*, Routledge: London.

Aricó, J. (1992) 'Rethink everything' (Maybe it's always been this way), *NACLA Report on the Americas*, vol. 25, no. 5, pp. 21–3.

Bartra, R. (1991) 'Mexican oficio: the miseries and splendors of culture', *Third Text*, no. 14, Spring, pp. 7–15.

Baudrillard, J. (1975) *The Mirror of Production*, St Louis: Telos Press.

Baudrillard, J. (1989) *America*, London: Verso.

Baudrillard, J. (1990) *Cool Memories*, London: Verso.

Bauman, Z. (1992) *Intimations of Postmodernity*, London: Routledge.

Bhabha, H. K. (1991) ' "Race", time and the revision of modernity', *Oxford Literary Review*, vol. 13, nos. 1–2, pp. 193–219.

Brunner, J. J. (1987) 'Notas sobre la modernidad y lo postmoderno en la cultura latinoamericana', *David y Goliath – Revista del Consejo Latinoamericano de Ciencias Sociales*, no. 52, Sept., pp. 30–9.

Brunner, J. J., Barrios, A., and Catalan, C. (1989) *Chile: Transformaciones Culturales y Modernidad*, Santiago de Chile: FLACSO.

Calderón, F. (1987) 'América Latina: identidad y tiempos mixtos o cómo tratar de pensar la modernidad sin dejar de ser indios', *David y Goliath – Revista del Consejo Latinoamericano de Ciencias Sociales*, no. 52, September, pp. 4–9.

Cardoso, F. H., and Faletto, E. (1969) *Dependencia y Desarrollo en América Latina*, Siglo XXI, Mexico City.

Castoriadis, C. (1992) 'Reflections on racism', *Thesis Eleven*, no. 32, pp. 1–12.

Christian, Barbara (1989) 'The race for theory', in Kauffman, L. (ed.). *Gender and Theory: Dialogues on Feminist Criticism*, Oxford: Blackwell.

Connolly, W. E. (1991) *Identity/Difference: Democratic Negotiations of Political Paradox*, Ithaca: Cornell University Press.

Deleuze, G., and Guattari, F. (1990) 'What is a minor literatuare', in Ferguson, R., Gever, M., Minh-ha, T. T., and West, C. (eds), *Out There: Marginalization and Contemporary Cultures*, Cambridge, Mass.: MIT Press.

Derrida, J. (1992) *The Other Heading: Reflections on Today's Europe*, Bloomington and Indianapolis: Indiana University Press.

Felski, R. (1992) 'Whose postmodernism?' *Thesis Eleven*, no. 32, pp. 129–40.

Foucault, M. (1991) *Remarks on Marx: Conversations with Duccio Trombadori*, New York: Semiotext(e).

Franco, C. (1991) 'Exploraciones en "Otra Modernidad": de la migración a la plebe urbana', in Urbano, H. (ed.), *Modernidad en los Andes*, Cusco: Centro de Estudios Regionales Andinos 'Bartolomé de las Casas'.

Franco, J. (1989) 'Beyond ethnocentrism: gender, power and the Third World intelligentsia', in Nelson, C., and Grossberg, L. (eds), *Marxism and the Interpretation of Culture*, Urbana: University of Illinois Press.

García, L. B. (1991) *El Imperio Contracultural: Del Rock a la Postmodernidad*, Editorial Nueva Sociedad, Caracas.

García Canclini, N. (1991), 'Los estudios culturales de los 80 a los 90: perspectivas antropológicas y sociológicas en América Latina', *Iztapalapa – Revista de Ciencias Sociales y Humanidades*, vol. 11, no. 24, pp. 9–26.

García Canclini, N. (1993) *Transforming Modernity: Popular Culture in Mexico*, Austin: University of Texas Press.

Gómez, L. (1988) 'Deconstrucción o nueva síntesis: aproximación crítica a la noción de postmodernidad', in Calderón, F. (ed.) *Imagenes Desconocidas: La Modernidad en la Encrucijada Postmoderna*, Buenos Aires: CLACSO, pp. 85–93.

Gómez-Peña, G. (1992) 'A binational performance pilgrimage', *Third Text*, no. 19, Summer, pp. 64–78.

Hall, S. (1991) 'The local and the global: globalization and ethnicity', in King, A. D. (ed.), *Culture, Globalization and the World-System*, London: Macmillan.

Harding, Sandra (1992) 'Subjectivity, experience and knowledge: an epistemology from/for rainbow coalition politics', in Nederveen Pieterse, J. (ed.). *Emancipations, Modern and Postmodern*, London: Sage.

Heller, A., and Fehér, F. (1988) *The Postmodern Political Condition*, Cambridge: Polity Press.

Holub, R. (1992) *Antonio Gramsci: Beyond Marxism and Postmodernism*, London and New York: Routledge.

hooks, bell (1991) *Yearning: Race, Gender and Cultural Politics*, London: Turnaround.

Hopenhayn, M. (1988) 'El debate post-moderno y la dimensión cultural del desarrollo' in Calderón, F. (ed.), *Imagenes Desconocidas: La Modernidad en la Encrucijada Postmoderna*, Buenos Aires: CLACSO.

Hopenhayn, M. (1992) 'Pensar lo Social sin Planificación ni Revolución?', *Revista de la CEPAL*, no. 48, December, pp. 137–48.

Husserl, E. (1965) *Phenomenology and the Crisis of Philosophy*, New York: Harper and Row.

Jameson, F. (1991) *Postmodernism or The Cultural Logic of Capitalism*, London: Verso.

Kant, I. (1991) *Political Writings*, Cambridge Texts in the History of Political Thought, edited by Hans Reiss, first published in 1970, Cambridge: Cambridge University Press.

Kay, C. (1989) *Latin American Theories of Development and Underdevelopment*, London and New York: Routledge.

Lauer, M. (1991) 'La modernidad, un fin incómodo', in Urbano, H. (ed.). *Modernidad en los Andes*, Cusco: Centro de Estudios Regionales Andinos 'Bartolomé de las Casas'.

Lazreg, M. (1988) 'Feminism and difference: the perils of writing as a woman on women in Algeria', *Feminist Studies*, vol. 14, no. 1, pp. 81–107.

Lechner, N. (1988) *Los Patios Interiores de la Democracia: Subjectividad y Política*, Santiago de Chile: FLACSO.

Lechner, N. (1991) 'La democratización en el contexto de la cultura posmoderna', *Revista Foro*, no. 14, April, pp. 63–70.

Limonad, E. (1991) 'Asi camina lo urbano: el derrotero – ciudad y tecnología en el postmodernismo', *Revista Interamericana de Planificación*, vol. 24, no. 95, pp. 96–115.

Lyotard, J.-F. (1986) *The Postmodern Condition: A Report on Knowledge*, Manchester: Manchester University Press.

Lyotard, J.-F. (1988) *Peregrinations: Law, Form, Event*, New York: Columbia University Press.

Macpherson, C. B. (1988) *The Political Theory of Possessive Individualism: Hobbes to Locke*, Oxford: Oxford University Press.

Marcus, G. E. (1991) 'Notes on ideologies of reflexivity in contemporary efforts to remake the human sciences', workshop on 'Postmodern Anthropology', University of Utrecht, 18–20 December.

Mascia-Lees, F. E., Sharpe, P., and Cohen, C. B. (1989) 'The postmodernist turn in anthropology: cautions from a feminist perspective', *Signs*, vol. 15, no. 1, pp. 7–33.

McGee, P. (1992) *Telling the Other: The Question of Value in Modern and Postcolonial Writing*, Ithaca: Cornell University Press.

Mohanty, C.T. (1992), 'Feminist Encounters: Locating the Politics of Experience', in Barrett, M., and Phillips, A. (eds), *Destabilizing Theory-contemporary feminist debates*, Cambridge: Polity.

Morrison, Toni (1992) *Playing in the Dark: Whiteness and the Literary Imagination*, Cambridge, Mass.: and London: Harvard University Press.

Murphy, P. (1991) 'Postmodern perspectives and justice', *Thesis Eleven*, no. 30, pp.117–32.

Ortega, J. (1988) 'Postmodernism in Latin America', in D'Haen, T., and Bertens, H. (eds), *Postmodern Fiction in Europe and the Americas*, Amsterdam: Editions Rodopi.

Ortega y Gasset, J. (1957) *The Revolt of the Masses*, New York: W. W. Norton (originally published in Spanish in 1930).

Piscitelli, A. (1988) 'Sur, post-modernidad, y después', in Calderón, F. (ed.), *Imagenes Desconocidas: La Modernidad en la Encrucijada Postmoderna*, Buenos Aires: CLACSO.

Portantiero, J. (1992) 'Foundations of a new politics', *NACLA Report on the Americas*, vol. 25, no. 5, pp. 17–20.

Quijano, A. (1988) 'Modernidad, identidad y utopía en América Latina', in Calderón, F. (ed.), *Imagenes Desconocidas: La Modernidad en la Encrucijada Postmoderna*, Buenos Aires: CLACSO.

Rabinow, P. (1986) 'Representations are social facts: modernity and post-modernity in anthropology', in Clifford J., and Marcus, G. E. (eds), *Writing Culture: The Poetics and Politics of Ethnography*, Berkeley and London: University of California Press.

Reigadas, M. C. (1988) 'Neomodernidad y posmodernidad: preguntado desde América Latina', in Mari, E. (ed.), *¿Postmodernidad?*, Buenos Aires: Editorial Biblos., pp. 113–45.

Richard, N. (1987/88) 'Postmodernism and periphery', *Third Text*, no. 2, Winter, pp. 5–12.

Richard, N. (1989) *La Estratificación de los Margenes*, Santiago de Chile: Francisco Zegers Editor.

Richard, N. (1991) 'Latinoamérica y la postmodernidad', *Revista de Crítica Cultural*, no. 3, April, pp. 15–19.

Richard, N. (1992) 'Cultura, política y democracia', *Revista de Crítica Cultural*, no. 5, July, pp. 5–7.

Rorty, R. (1980) *Philosophy and the Mirror of Nature*, Oxford: Blackwell.

Rorty, R. (1989) *Contingency, Irony and Solidarity*, Cambridge: Cambridge University Press.

Rorty, R. (1991a) *Objectivity, Relativism and Truth*, Philosophical Papers, vol. 1, Cambridge: Cambridge University Press.

Rorty, R. (1991b) *Essays on Heidegger and Others*, Philosophical Papers, vol. 2, Cambridge: Cambridge University Press.

Said, E. (1992) 'Culture and the vultures', *Times Higher Education Supplement*, no. 1003, 24 January, pp. 15 and 19.

Said, E. (1993) *Culture and Imperialism*, London: Chatto and Windus.

Slater, David (1992) 'Theories of development and politics of the post-modern: exploring a border zone', *Development and Change*, vol. 23, no. 3, pp. 283–319.

Soper, K. (1991) 'Postmodernism and its discontents', *Feminist Review*, no. 39, pp. 97–108.

Spivak, G. (1988) 'Can the subaltern speak?' in Nelson, C., and Grossberg, L. (eds), *Marxism and the Interpretation of Culture*, Urbana-Champaign: University of Illinois Press.

Subercaseaux, B. (1991) 'Política y cultura: descencuentros y aproximaciones', *Nueva Sociedad*, no. 116, November-December, pp. 138–45.

Taylor, C. (1992) 'The politics of recognition', in Taylor, C., and Gutman, A., (eds), *Multiculturalism and 'The Politics of Recognition'*, Princeton: Princeton University Press.

Urbano, H. (1991) 'Modernidad en los Andes: un tema y un debate', in Urbano, H. (ed.), *Modernidad en los Andes*, Cusco: Centro de Estudios Regionales Andinos 'Bartolomé de las Casas'.

Vattimo, G. (1991) *The End of Modernity: Nihilism and Hermeneutics in Post-Modern Culture*, Cambridge: Polity Press.

Vattimo, G. (1992) *The Transparent Society*, Cambridge: Polity Press.

West, C. (1992) 'The postmodern crisis of the black intellectuals', in Grossberg, L., Nelson, C., and Treichler, P. (eds), *Cultural Studies*, New York and London: Routledge.

Young, R. (1990) *White Mythologies: Writing History and the West*, London: and New York: Routledge.

Zavala, I. M. (1988) 'On the (mis-)uses of the post-modern: Hispanic modernism revisited', in D'Haen, T., and Bertens, H. (eds), *Postmodern Fiction in Europe and the Americas*, Amsterdam: Editions Rodopi.

Part II

THE WESTERN FRONT

3

UNPACKING THE WEST: HOW EUROPEAN IS EUROPE?

Jan Nederveen Pieterse

> The future is perfectly certain, what is unpredictable is the past.
>
> Evita Bezuidenhout

The division between the West and the non-West, or between North and South, ranks as the greatest divide in contemporary history, the main boundary marking the difference between inside and outside, a global boundary which is reproduced in countless local frontiers of cultural pluralism. That the North is in the South is a common perception; here I propose to focus on the South in the North. The critique of Eurocentrism, Orientalism and Western views of the 'other' are well-established themes. Here I want to develop a different kind of argument and problematize Europe itself. That contemporary Europe is multicultural in composition because of immigration is obvious, but this also takes Europe at face value. Instead let us consider the extent to which European culture itself is multicultural in a historical sense.

If this is a controversial argument, so are other claims made about Europe. When Jean-Marie le Pen says that the majority of Europeans are white and he is proud to be white, it is old-fashioned racism. When the chairman of the Flemish Block says that this is our country and therefore immigrants must go, it is an argument cast in terms of national identity. When he adds that this is 'our continent', we come to the view: Europe for the Europeans. This kind of claim is often made as a cultural claim, in one breath with 'European civilization'. In this light, it is appropriate to ask: what is Europe and how European is it?

The faces of Eurocentrism and Western triumphalism are many, as in the imagery of North-South relations and the familiar stereotypes of the miserable Third World of depraved and impoverished lands from where barbarian warmongers, fundamentalist fanatics, drug-traffickers and migrant hordes are threatening 'us'. The 1992 commemorations of Columbus' journeys focused on 'the West', extending from Vladivostok to Los Angeles. The Columbus celebrations focused attention on five hundred years of European expansion, or outward movement. Now we turn our attention to the reverse, to Europe's imports, its intake – which have not just been raw materials. This query is part of a larger project, the deconstruction of the West. Elsewhere I have discussed this in terms of critique of Western theories of progress, modernization and development (Nederveen Pieterse, 1991); here the question is taken up in a historical context.

'Our' perspective on history is strongly shaped by nineteenth-century views. This was the formative period of disciplines such as archaeology, art history, philology, sociology and anthropology, as well as the gestation period of European narcissism and imperialism. Because of the shadow cast by the nineteenth-century regime of truth, we forget, we structurally overlook the ways in which Europe in its development has been standing on the shoulders of other cultures. Nineteenth-century historiography is a historiography drunk with the superiority of 'European civilization'. Its regime of truth only acknowledged the usual stations of Europe – Greece, Rome, Christianity, Renaissance, Enlightenment. It emphasized the classical lineages of 'European civilization'. The prestige of the classical tradition came to dominate in the course of the seventeenth and eighteenth centuries. The classics served as the basis of a cultural compromise between the nobilities and bourgeoisie, at the expense of the Church. Hence the prominence of classical education in the nineteenth-century curricula for European élites. Hence the cliché of Greece as the 'cradle of European civilization'. If non-European contributions were acknowledged, it was in relation to European themes, as in 'Judeao-Christian civilization', or circumscribed and white-washed, as in the 'Aryan model' of history, in which everything paled into insignificance next to the creativity and drive of the 'Nordic races'.

Thus, when Egypt's contributions to civilization were acknowledged, at the same time Egypt was white-washed and cut off from Africa. The same holds for Crete, Phoenicia and Carthage – all moments of a mixed world of antiquity which knew no racial boundaries or colour prejudice. And it holds for Greece, whose indebtedness to Asia and Africa, in particular to Egypt, is suppressed in the 'cradle of civilization' view. Of course, Greek civilization did not arise ready-made like Aphrodite from the foam of the waves; Greek and Hellenic civilization were synthetic civilizations.

In recent years, Eurocentric historiography has come under review on several points. The Aryan model has been cast overboard; the contributions of the Arabic world are also increasingly being acknowledged in mainstream scholarship. Significant studies have appeared presenting a radical critique of Eurocentric historiography, such as Martin Bernal's *Black Athena* (discussed by Robert Young in this volume). African scholars and Africanists have contributed to revisions of Africa's contributions to world history (e.g. Diop, 1991; Sertima, 1989; Mokhtar, 1990). It all adds up to a decolonization of history which is still under way. Earlier, anthropologists had drawn up lengthy lists of items in Western culture that derive from non-Western sources – from food items and language to customs (e.g. Linton, 1936). The current revisions of Eurocentric history go further and show that to a considerable extent European knowledge, philosophy, physics, chemistry, technology, medicine, metallurgy, etc. are derived from non-European sources. The alphabet, the numerical system, algebra, mathematics (Ghevergese Joseph, 1987, 1991; Bishop, 1990), astronomy, architectural styles – the list is long. How could it be otherwise if we realize that until the fourteenth century Europe was invariably the *recipient* of knowledge and technology? The first item of technology exported *from* Europe to the Orient was a clock in 1338 (Cipolla, 1980, p. 222); meanwhile in China mechanical clocks had been in use since at least the eleventh century (Needham, 1987).

The real frontiers between Europe and non-European worlds have been much more blurred and porous than the rhetoric and imagery of 'European civilization' suggest. European culture developed in the context of several forms of osmosis. If we review the Afro-Asiatic roots of European civilization and look at Europe as part of Eurasia, European culture itself becomes more transparant. After all, like Arabia, India and Indo-China, Europe is only a peninsula of the great landmass of Eurasia. The notion of a singular and unique Europe is a blockage to understanding not just world history, but European history as well.

A query such as this could well take the form of a voluminous study. This essay is no more than an exploratory sketch of non-European influences in European culture. Several of these are on record as so many 'fashions' in European culture, such as turquerie, Ethiopianism, chinoiserie, Egyptianism, Orientalism, japonisme, *l'art nègre* and primitivism. This essay is confined to reviewing these fashions, at the same time reinterpreting 'fashions' as indicators of

:ebergs extending deep below the surface. While the emphasis here
s on the extent of influence of 'the South' in 'the North', this cannot
be separated from the changing perceptions of non-European cultures
in the West – a subject on which there is an extensive literature. The
emphasis on culture in this discussion does not mean that other
spheres are excluded from this dynamic. That much of the material
in this treatment concerns arts and crafts reflects the unevenness in
the Western reception of non-Western cultural influences. 'In the field
of art, especially the visual arts, western avant-gardes treated non-
western cultures entirely as equals.' Referring to the late nineteenth
century, Hobsbawm (1987, p. 181) adds, 'They were indeed largely
inspired by them in this period.' Consequently in art history, at least
in many of the better sources, there has been little inhibition in
crediting non-European inspirations and much work has been done
to uncover such connections. In general history this is much rarer,
with the exception, to a degree, of historians such as Toynbee (1972,
cf. Barraclough, 1979). The history of culture and civilization is deeply
preoccupied with 'the West' (e.g. Clark, 1969). In political economy
acknowledgement of non-Western influences is virtually absent
(economic histories routinely start with 1500 as the starting point of
'the rise of the West').[1] Likewise in histories of science and technology, the work of figures such as Joseph Needham is exceptional.
Military histories, on the other hand, often do acknowledge non-
European sources of invention (e.g. McNeill, 1982). Otherwise it is
mainly in anthropology that this nexus is thematized.

Afro-Asiatic lineages of Europe

Islam and turquerie

The world of Islam was both a successor to Hellenism and the recipient of cultural emanations from Asia and Africa, which it forged
into a formidable synthesis, witness the cultural achievements of
the emirate of Baghdad and Moorish Spain. European architecture
imitating Moorish and Arabic styles – mosques in European palatial
gardens, the fascination of the Alhambra (Koppelkamm, 1987) – is
part of a wider European fascination with the Arab world. In popular
entertainment culture, European theatres and cinemas with names
such as Alhambra and Roxy are reminders of this: windows of illumination, windows with a view on Europe's dreamland. Byzantium,

likewise on a crossroads of civilizations, also represents such a synthesis.

The relationship between Christendom and Islam is too often viewed in the light of the Crusades. The Crusades themselves denote a complex set of relations in which borrowing from the world of Islam played a considerable part. The relationship between Christendom and Islam was one not of animosity but rather of osmosis. The twelfth-century Renaissance and later Renaissance periods in Europe emerged out of a lengthy interpenetration with the worlds of Islam and Byzantium. The areas which pioneered these developments were those which stood in direct contact with these much more highly developed worlds – the trading cities of Italy, Portugal, northern Spain and the Provence. Thus, the caravels with which Prince Henry the Navigator undertook the pioneering explorations of the African coasts were designed on the model of Arab dhows with their lateen sails (*caravos* in Arabic, hence caravels) and also incorporated features of the Chinese junk, passed on by the Arabs (the stern-post rudder, watertight bulkheads and the compass for navigation) (Merson, 1989, pp. 72, 74). He took a notion of the contours of Africa as a continent from Arab sailors in Ceuta.

From the fall of Constantinople in 1453 into the nineteenth century, Turkey held an enduring fascination for Europeans, first as threat, later as gateway to the Orient. Countless objects and styles refer to this legacy, such as Turkish coffee, tobacco, honey, headwear, paper, decorative arabesks, ceramics and plants (above all, the tulip). Turkish artefacts were imported and later imitated in Europe, such as Candiana ware manufactured in Padua in the sixteenth century, imitating Iznik ceramics. In the 1500s arabesque engravings were published in Paris and England; 'Turkey carpets figured in the inventories and on portraits of dignitaries. Not only did they figure in the paintings, as in the still-lives and portraits of the Dutch masters of the seventeenth century (Theunissen, 1989), but they also seem to us a natural part of them:

> The Turkey carpets which became an almost essential feature of late Elizabethan or Jacobean portraits do not stand out as exotic objects but fit naturally into pictures in which the creation of a glowing mosaic of different patterns seems at least as important as the portrayal of an individual ... Certainly, many Elizabethan patterns could have come straight off a Persian or Turkish plate or tile. (Girouard, 1988)

In the 1500s the Levant trade became increasingly important to

northern Europe. Venice no longer dominated the trade because
Lisbon and Antwerp now also played a part in it. The English Levant
Company was founded in 1581. This was a time when the nexus
between the Protestant powers north of the Alps and the Ottoman
Turks was significant politically and militarily: they united forces
against the Catholic dominion of the Spanish Habsburg empire and
the Pope. The Dutch saying 'Better Turkish than Popish' dates from
this period. The Ottomans supported the Dutch revolution against
the Spanish Habsburg empire, and Sephardic Jews from the Porte
and Istanbul helped to finance the Dutch anti-imperialist war. Indeed,
Christendom at the time was no longer united and 'Europe' did not
yet exist.

In north European iconography, subtle but remarkable changes in
style and fashion occur over this period. Fashions changed to the
point that faces changed: beards became thinner (Reynolds, 1949).
Sixteenth-century paintings in the Low Countries show peasant types
with round faces and boorish costumes, whereas many figures in
seventeenth-century portraits are depicted with long narrow faces,
often with thin beards – in fact resembling Sephardic Jewish or Arab
styles and physiognomies. The Sephardim who were expelled from
Spain and Portugal trekked north to Antwerp, until the reach of the
Spanish army drove them further, to Amsterdam, Bologna and Istanbul. With them they brought their extensive transnational trade connections (in Lisbon they controlled the spice trade of the East Indies)
and the culture which had developed through the centuries of Moorish
culture in Andalusia (Raphael, 1985; Tanja, 1987). In other words,
Andalusia came north, and this is a neglected part of the story of the
rise of northern Europe: the politics, economics and culture of
the Ottoman connection, of the Sephardim and *al Andalus* also put
their stamp on the rise of modern capitalism.

The Ottoman Turks stood before the gates of Vienna until they
were defeated in 1683. Occidental hegemony is recent, much more
recent than we care to remember. More precisely, the Occident did
not yet exist: it is only a nineteenth-century fabrication. Thus, while
the Ottomans threatened the axis of Catholic powers from Spain
to Vienna, they entertained diplomatic and political relations and
sometimes alliances with the Protestant powers in France, England,
the Low Countries and the Rhineland. By the eighteenth century,
turquerie had become so much a part of European fashion that Augu-
ste Boppe noted: 'La Turquie est devenue un instant/une des prov-
inces du rococo.' European élites turned Ottoman culture into an
accessory of their repertoire. Turcomania involved dressing up in

Turkish costumes for parties and portraits, drinking Turkish coffee, and attending operas and plays with a Turkish motif – witness Mozart, Voltaire and Goethe (Kopplin, 1987; Schöning-Kalender 1987; Schiffer, 1982).

Ethiopianism

The thirteenth to fifteenth centuries were a period of pronounced Ethiopianism, in the sense of 'enthusiasm or preference for things Ethiopian'. Unlike the Ethiopianism of antiquity – for instance, among the Greeks of Homer's time – this was a Christian Ethiopianism. Hence the legend of Prester John, the popularity of the King of the Moors, the Queen of Sheba becoming a black figure in contemporary paintings, and the emergence of numerous black saints such as Saint Maurice (Nederveen Pieterse, 1992, ch. 1; Devisse, 1979). Underlying the high tide of the popularity of Africans in Europe was the notion that Christian Africans could serve as allies against the Muslim encirclement of Christendom.

The priest-king Prester John was imagined to be a descendant of one of the Three Kings who came from afar to worship the Christ child; he was held to be the king of a legendary Christian kingdom located somewhere on the far side of the Muslim domains. The legend, which emerged in the twelfth century in the form of the fake 'Letter of Prester John', may be related to attempts on the part of Latin Christians to resume relations with the Nestorian Christians, who had spread in many directions. Accordingly, the legendary kingdom of Prester John was placed now in Turkey, then in Cathay (where Marco Polo went to look for him), or in Ethiopia, where the Kopts had kept the Christian Church intact: 'It is possible that the original of this legendary priest-king was one of the Christian rulers of Abyssinia, who successors were certainly identified with him in the fifteenth century. But in Polo's time his realm was generally believed to be somewhere in the Far East' (Latham, 1958, p. 22).

The small black pages who figure in portraits of European dignitaries from the seventeenth century onwards are derived from Arab and Moorish culture, as an early form of Orientalism and cultural borrowing. The black servant became a status symbol in rich households, first in Venice and Spain and later in northern Europe.

In the Renaissance genre of the Paradoxa, far-away cultures, real or imaginary, were used as means to criticize prevailing customs and ideas, and to provide amusing conversation items. The 'noble savage' of America performed this function, as did later the 'Persians' in Montesquieu's *Lettres Persanes*. From the time that Europe established direct contact with Asia and Africa, rather than mediated through the Arab world, new patterns of osmosis set in with wide and profound ramifications for European culture.

Chinoiserie

China's reputation in Europe is virtually as old as the Silk Roads, the ancient East-West connections. After Marco Polo's travels to the Cathay of Kublai Khan in the thirteenth century, China spoke loudly to the European imagination. In 1620 Francis Bacon observed that three inventions, printing, gunpowder and the compass, 'changed the appearance and state of the whole world' (in Merson, 1989, p. 82). All three had been invented in China and had been passed on to Europe directly (gunpowder) or indirectly (compass, via Arab intermediaries).

The routes of European expansion are sprinkled with chinoiserie. On their ships and in their factories the East Indies Companies used Chinese export porcelain. The consumption of tea (later coffee and cocoa) created a demand for cups, teapots and plates, and as the beverages were Oriental, so was the 'china' from which they were drunk. It was not until the eighteenth century that Europeans were able to manufacture porcelain themselves (Temple, 1986, pp. 91–4).

China, admired for its rational despotism, inspired many Enlightenment themes. China and Asia generally, however, from the seventeenth century onwards, fulfilled different roles in France and Britain. In France, admiration for Asia was a weapon used by reformers and radicals, whereas in Britain, Asia often figured in the repertoire of the traditionalists, not of the radicals. The interpretation of Greece as an outpost of *Oriental* civilization – advanced by contemporary critics of Eurocentrism – was cited already in the late seventeenth century by William Temple, a self-confessed 'ancient'. In his 'Essay of ancient and modern learning' he noted, 'For whoever observed the account already given of the ancient Indian and Chinese learning and opinions will easily find among them the seeds of all those Grecian productions and institutions.' China in his words was 'the greatest, richest and most populous kingdom now known in the world' (in Marshall and Williams, 1982, pp. 132, 133). Temple's disciple Jonathan Swift shared his admiration for China and displayed close affinities with Confucian culture.

In France, the Physiocrats liked to imagine Louis XV as a Chinese emperor and themselves as literati. As Bernal notes, 'Under their auspices China made a major cultural impact on France, and many if not most of the centralizing and rationalizing political and economic reforms of the mid-eighteenth century followed Chinese models' (1987, pp. 172–3). *Philosophes* such as Voltaire, Diderot and Quesnay upheld China as the model for Europe to follow. There were also actual specific borrowings. 'By the end of the eighteenth century, even before the French Revolution in 1789, Talleyrand had adopted the Chinese system of a written examination of civil servants, a practice which was later taken up elsewhere in Europe' (Merson, 1989, p. 122). The rationalization of public administration, according to Weber one of the hallmarks of modernity, was originally based on the example of China. The Chinese examination system foreshadowed Parsons' universalism and achieved status.

Joseph Needham's studies on Chinese science and technology document its extraordinary advances. In a popularizing account of Needham's findings, Robert Temple states:

> It is just as much a surprise for the Chinese as for Westerners to realize that modern agriculture, modern shipping, the modern oil industry, modern astronomical observatories, modern music, decimal mathematics, paper money, umbrellas, fishing reels, wheel barrows, multi-stage rockets, guns, underwater mines, poison gas, parachutes, hot-air balloons, manned flight, brandy, whisky, the game of chess, printing, and even the essential design of the steam engine, all came from China.(Temple, 1986, p. 9; cf. Needham, 1981)

However, whether these were first invented in China or 'came from China' are quite different points, which are not always clarified in the studies.

Egyptianism

In the eighteenth century a vogue for ancient Egypt set in. The cult of Louis XIV as *roi soleil*, instituted in 1661, has explicit Greek (Apollo) and Roman (Augustus) overtones, but possibly also Egyptian references in the theme of sun worship, worship of Ra. The Egyptian revival had its beginnings in Rome in the eighteenth century – witness the obelisks of baroque Rome. In France, it dates from Napoleon's campaign in Egypt (1798). Freemasonry at the time included many progressives, and Masonic myth, imagery and architecture displayed a predilection for Egyptian motifs (Bernal, 1987, pp. 173–7). Masonic Egyptophilia is on display in Mozart's *Zauberflöte* (1791) (Kreidt, 1987, pp. 60–75). Cagliostro sought to 'Egyptianize' Freemasonry, and in the wake of Napoleon's campaign 'Egyptian rites' proliferated in French masonry (Chailley, 1972, p. 59).

Whereas Turkish and Chinese motifs retreated along with rococo, Egyptian styles merged with neoclassicism and survived as an architectural style that was held to be particularly appropriate for libraries, museums, schools, prisons and cemetery gates, as well as synagogues and Masonic temples. With their monumental geometry, Egyptian buildings seemed like archaic predecessors of classicism. By their evocation of eternity they were held to inspire 'elevated' sentiments and a pedagogically appropriate sense of awe, and as such they were also highly appropriate for demonstrating state power, as numerous monuments in the Paris city scape, particularly from Napoleon's empire, testify (Koppelkamm, 1987, p. 20).

Fashion followed conquest, and in the footsteps of Napoleon's campaign in Egypt came the upsurge of Orientalism, particularly in France, as in the works of Flaubert, Nerval, Delacroix, Ingres and many others (Said, 1985; Kabbani, 1986). In 1811 Carl Maria von Weber composed his operetta *Abu Hassan*. Between 1812 and 1823 Rossini alone wrote eight operas with an 'Oriental' theme, *Ciro in Babilonia, Tancredi, L'Italiana in Algeri, Il Turco in Italia, Armida, Mosè in Egitto, Maometto II* and *Semiramide* (Kreidt, 1987, p. 76).

India

India has been of particular importance to Germany and England. Indian philosophies left a clear mark on German Idealist philosophy. In the words of Dietmar Rothermund, 'The philosophical interest in India is deeply related to the rise of the German Idealism' (1986, p. 4). Friedrich Schlegel's *Uber die Sprache und Weisheit der Indier* (1808) set the tone for an admiration that knew no limit: 'Everything, absolutely everything is of Indian origin' (in Bernal, 1987, p. 230). Schopenhauer's *Die Welt als Wille und Vorstellung* could pass for a late Vedanta text. In a lecture in Bombay in 1893, Schopenhauer's disciple Paul Deussen drew attention to 'the concordance of Indian, Grecian and German metaphysics; the world is maya, is illusion, says Cankara, it is a world of shadows, not of realities, says Plato, it is "appearance only, not the thing in itself" says Kant' ('The philosophy of the Vedanta in its relations with the Occidental metaphysics', quoted in

Rothermund, 1986, p. 4). As the easternmost country of the West, Germany traditionally displayed great receptivity to and affinity with Oriental influences. The medieval alliance between the Holy Roman Empire and Byzantium forms part of this (Heer, 1966), and so does the German preoccupation with Venice – Europe's primary point of reception of Oriental influences, as well as the *oculus totius Occidentis* – as with Goethe, Wagner and Thomas Mann. The preoccupation of German archaeologists (Winckelmann) and philologists (Nietzsche) with ancient Greece, Troy and Mycenae is also part of Germany's habit of 'looking East'.

English views on India went through several stages. The generation of Warren Hastings initiated a tradition of scholarly study of India by British officials. William Jones founded the Asiatick Society of Bengal in 1784, under whose auspices many Sanskrit texts such as the *Bhagavad Gita* were translated into English. His views on Sanskrit echo William Temple's views on the status of China and India relative to the Greeks and Romans, a hundred years earlier: 'The *Sanscrit* language, whatever be its antiquity, is of a wonderful structure; more perfect than the *Greek*, more copious than the *Latin*, and more exquisitely refined than either' (in Said, 1985, p. 79). But once the reformers set foot in India in the 1820s, the attitudes turned to disillusionment with India and to British *mission civilisatrice* to combat oriental despotism, Hindu idolatry and rural stagnation (Parry, 1971, pp. 415–24; Archer and Lightbown, 1982).

Cultural dialectics

Let us turn to more recent dynamics and to the phenomena of European cultural 'cannibalism' and European cultural 'indigestion'. The late nineteenth century, the epoch of the New Imperialism, saw a true crescendo of Asian and African influxes in European culture:

As the imperial age progressed, non-western elements came increasingly to the fore within western culture. Toward the turn of the century, when western imperialism and colonialism were at their peak and chauvinism and racism at their most intense, ironically, the non-western orientations in western culture rose to unprecedented levels as well. (Nederveen Pieterse, 1989/ 1990, p. 371)

'Culture' and Thomas Cook (established 1869), organizer of tours to Morocco or Egypt, Persia or Palestine, became twin terms. Operas and plays display the Afro-Asiatic influences in interior Europe – *Aida* (Verdi's tribute to the opening of the Suez Canal in 1869), *The Queen of Sheba, Oberon, Moses, Ceasar and Cleopatra* and *Harem*.

Japonisme exercised a major, threefold influence – on the Arts and Crafts movement, which set the stage for Design and Jugendstil; on the avant-garde movement in painting, which opened the way to modernism; and on high fashion, where it set the tone for a decade or longer (Berger, 1987). Impressionism, Monet, Van Gogh, Toulouse-Lautrec, Whistler, Degas and, in decorative arts, art nouveau, are familiar examples of this influence.

Painters and poets journeyed to pre-industrial lands and depicted them as erotic havens and counterpoints to *fin de siècle* Europe – Paul Gauguin to Tahiti, Henri Matisse to Morocco, and Arthur Rimbaud, Pierre Loti and André Gide to black Africa. After the *fin de siècle* it became customary for Western artists to pass through the ethnological museum on the way to the studio. *L'art nègre*, fauvisme, Matisse, Picasso, cubism and, in a different way, Douanier le Rousseau are examples of this trend. Of course, this concerns a much wider radius – witness, for instance, Debussy's interest in black American music and Javanese gamelan, Dvořak's interest in black American music (*Symphonie der Neuen Welt* and *Negerkwartett*, both composed before 1900), the influence of Andalusian flamenco on Ravel, the influence of Javanese and Japanese art on the work of Jan Toorop, and Artaud's interest in Balinese theatre.

Many expressions which are considered specifically *national* traits in fact exemplify Asian or African influences. Thus Dutch Delft Blue ceramics imitated Chinese porcelains in terms of styles, shapes, motifs and colours. What is known in art history as the 'Belgian line' was developed by the painter Henry van de Velde from Japanese inspirations (Berger, 1987, p. 198).

The politics of reception

One of the questions that arises concerns the difference in the patterns of osmosis between Western and non-Western worlds in the eras *before* and *after* European or Western hegemony. The cutting point in my view is not 1500, where many such stories begin (as with Marx and Wallerstein), but 1800. In brief, prior to 1800 Europe remains predominantly in a learning mode *vis-à-vis* non-European worlds. The worlds of Islam, Byzantium, the Ottoman empire, China, India and Persia are models to learn from, and/or dreamlands, lands of fulfilment, their tales passed on like the *Thousand and One Nights*. They are idealized as utopias, like the kingdom of Prester John, in which biblical or classical reveries are projected, as new Edens or a new Golden Land, such as America. One of these learning modes is defensive assimilation: non-European cultures are assimilated so that Europe (in the process of constructing itself) can better arm and defend itself against them.

After hegemony, or after 1800, a different pattern sets in. Actual borrowing goes on as before, but the attitudes have changed. Negative appraisals of non-European worlds, which had been there all along, come to the foreground and European self-congratulation sets the tone. A significant turning point, for instance, is the change in attitudes towards China, which after 1800 is increasingly viewed as a land of stagnation, corruption and decay. The Opium Wars exemplify this attitude and seal China's fate. The imaginaries shift from utopia to dystopia- as in the case of the noble savages who from Romantic heroes undergo a metamorphosis to 'deeply sunk heathens' in their representation by Christian missionaries. The dreamlands and Edens that were romanticized before are now recast in ominous and and frightening tones: the Orient is recreated as lands of decay, decadence and despotism; *Arabia felix* is fortunate no longer. Africa, once the cherished land of Ethiopianism and Prester John, of magnificent Timbuctoo and the golden trade of the Moors, is recast as the Dark Continent. The attitudes are those of demonization and the politics are of domination.

Native cultures are distorted: borrowing goes on, but now as alienation, appropriation and plunder. The terms of recognition narrow: non-European influences are recognized mainly in the 'weak', 'feminine' sides of European culture, in art, religion, fashion and design. European industrialization incorporated the craft techniques of pre-industrial cultures and adapted them to the industrial process. Thus the highly sophisticated paisley pattern (Gombrich, 1979, p. 139) in British textiles has been taken from Indian textiles. Dutch textile manufacturers adapted Javanese batik to an industrial process of wax printing, added African motifs and patterns, and have been selling the cloth throughout Africa. In this particular context, North-South relations are an instance of the general phenomenon of ambivalent relations between the dominant mode of production and its predecessor, shifting between contempt and nostalgia, aversion and idealization.

There is a European tradition, when such non-European influences are observed at all, of making disparaging remarks about them.

They are dismissed at the same time as being acknowledged, marginalized the moment they are noticed, disqualified in the very terms of appreciation. This ambivalence recurs time and again: an example is the observation by the 'progressive' British historian Victor Kiernan:

> twentieth-century Europe has become more the same, more one whole, but also less European; it has been 'going native', most of all in its morals, as illustrated by the near-nudity of the modern, white woman by contrast with the missionary horror of unclothed native life a century ago. (Kiernan, 1981, pp. 55–6)

Let us note that 'Europe' is taken for granted here, as a singular entity which in the twentieth century has become 'less European'. This kind of grudging ambivalence towards non-European cultures and their influence on Europe is an instance of a deeper ambivalence, which also turns up with European culture itself. Sometimes 'wild' or 'primitive' are taken as badges of honour, tokens of disaffection with dominant culture – in the tradition of critical utopia and militant alienation.

Non-European cultures are often equated with their manifest status *within* Europe as *exotic* cultures; accordingly, the complex web of actual South-North intercultural relations is *reduced* to the single dimension of the exotic.[2] What most often predominates in the appraisal of the exotic in contemporary eyes is the *erotic*. This is another way of assessing the influence of non-Western cultures in centre-periphery terms: the exotic is a peripheral mode – of adornment, décor, curiosity, entertainment, titillation – and therefore the centre ground of European culture, values and achievements is never in doubt. The terms of analysis set a discursive framework which is impossible to transcend. A related approach is to view the influence of non-European culture in terms of fashions or fads referred to earlier (chinoiserie and turquerie are examples), or in terms which denote psychological anomaly, such as mania or obsession (Egyptomania, Turcomania) (e.g. Sweetman, 1987). The *basic* identity of European culture remains sheltered from 'foreign' influence, for the terminology portrays non-European contributions as indulgences or deviations on the part of Europeans; in addition, non-European contributions are denigrated or trivialized because of their association with the anomalous psychological state.

Another term used to denote non-European influences in Western culture is *incorporation*. Thus in world-system theory, Europe or the West as the 'modern world system' 'incorporates' 'external areas' (Wallerstein, 1974). This is a profound misrepresentation of historical dynamics: what is missed is that 'Europe' did not simply take in non-European influences, but was constituted by them, that 'Europe' itself is a creation out of global influences (cf. Bergesen, 1990).

The various assessments usually assume that non-European influences were marginal in relation to the real *modern* identity of Europe. It is ironical, then, if it turns out that many trend-setting expressions of precisely this modern identity – in architecture, design, painting and abstract art – are in fact modelled on the 'archaic', premodern cultures and traditions which the 'modern age' so looks down on. This involves, *inter alia*, and besides the role of japonisme and *l'art nègre* mentioned above, the influence of abstract Arabic art and decorative motifs on Kandinsky and others of the Bauhaus and the Stijl (Weisberger, 1985). The modern shopping mall is an elaboration of the nineteenth-century glass-roofed shopping arcade, which is a European adaptation of an oriental example, the bazaar or kasbah (Bédarida, 1985, p. 103).

These cultural exchanges and dialectics are not without their problems. The eminent Indian artist K. G. Subramanyan observes that 'neither East nor West is what it used to be' (1987, p. 73). He mentions the mistakes in interpretation which have occurred in the reception of non-Western art among Western artists and notes, conversely, 'our own knowledge of Eastern culture has been shaped by western interpretations'. Susantha Goonatilake (1982, 1991) argues that, because of the overriding Western influence, Third World scholars have lost touch with their scientific traditions.

Where does this leave European culture? The best French restaurant is now in Tokyo (James, 1989). The finest European classical music may soon be performed in Japan. Some of the choicest works of European fine arts are *en route* to Japan. In this context, globalization makes for new horizons. Globalization is not simply cultural imperialism and does not necessarily make for monoculture; rather, it produces 'third cultures' and new syntheses, such as World Music, the *Magiciens de la terre* exhibition in Paris, 'Punjabi Pop' (Zwerin, 1990), etc.

Is all that this adds up to merely a culinary and decorative integration of global culture? Are food, fashion, music and entertainment exotic wallpaper on the walls of hegemonic culture? Are plunder, simplification and distortion of non-Western cultural elements the dominant patterns? Are creative adaptation and fusion still rare? Perhaps. The problem is that precisely because of the official and élite-distorted definition of what European or Western culture is – in the USA it is referred to as 'from Plato to Nato' (McBride, 1988) –

the extent of actual creative intercultural interplay cannot even be visible.

From the above it follows that to a considerable extent what we call European civilization is actually a universal human heritage which for historical, political and geographical reasons comes to us in the guise of a European or Western synthesis. The lineages are intercontinental, the synthesis is European. That the synthesis is European is significant, but that the lineages are intercontinental is likewise meaningful. With respect to the relations between East and West, Robert Temple observes that

> the East and the West are not as far apart in spirit or in fact as most of us have been led, by appearances, to believe, and that the East and the West *are already combined* in a synthesis so powerful and so pronounced that it is all-pervading. Within this synthesis we live our daily lives, and from it there is no escape. The modern world *is* a combination of Eastern and Western ingredients which are inextricably fused. (1986, p. 9)

The specificity of European development

To deconstruct Europe is to deconstruct modernity, its leading self-definition. This is a theme in postmodernism. The postmodern critique of modernity, however, remains so far largely a critique internal to Europe, a Western quiz with Western answers to Western questions. As postmodernity it implies and presumes modernity. This debate is conducted almost entirely with the backs turned to the South. Hence it is necessary to follow a different route: the way to come to terms with the specifity of Europe is to explain the singularity of its development, in contrast to that of other continents: in a word, unpacking the specificity of European development.

The Renaissance, the Enlightenment, the age of the democratic revolution, industrialization or, according to a general shorthand, modernization – why in Europe? In answering this we have essentially two options: an explanation which interprets this development in terms of factors endogenous or exogenous to Europe. The endogenous approach argues for the singularity or uniqueness of Europe, which easily leads to chauvinism

- on sociopolitical grounds (Occidental freedom);

- on topological, climatological grounds: the 'too hot for civilization' argument of Bodin, Montesquieu and Buffon;
- on religious grounds: the blessing of Jafeth and the curse of Ham, or Calvinism and the Protestant ethic;
- on grounds of race: virtues of the white or Caucasian race, other peoples being less gifted by nature;
- or, more drastically, on grounds of polygenism: other cultures, other species.

Ultimately these are all variations on the theme of European apartheid or 'separate development'. An influential argument of a different kind is that Europe developed the way it did because empire and central authority did not develop as much in Europe as it did elsewhere. European feudalism, then, was a manifestation of European backwardness and, on account of this, greater local autonomy was possible. We find this thesis in the work of Samir Amin (1989): the incomplete development (*inachevé*) of the tribute-paying mode of production. This resembles the classic argument of the autonomy of the towns as the decisive factor in European development. Essentially both of these are variations on the classic theme of Occidental liberty, now restated in terms of the 'privilege of backwardness'. There are other regions and periods, however, where the tribute-paying mode remained undeveloped or broke down, such as during times of imperial interregnum or transition, or because of geographical remoteness, as in Indo-China, south India, the Malay world and parts of Africa. But it is in Europe that certain developments took place. Thus, if relevant, this explanation is at least incomplete. Hence to this sociopolitical argument let us add another dimension which takes into account exogenous influences and is not mentioned as often in this context: geographical and historical circumstances.

Geography: Europe as part of Eurasia, the 'cap d'Asie' (Valéry), and the place from which there is only one way further: westward. History: Europeans driven westward because in the fifteenth century the ways south and east were closed by the world of Islam and pressures from the Seljuk and Ottoman Turks. The prosperity of the Islamic world has been based on its middleman position among three continents – the Silk Roads from Asia, the gold trade from Africa, and the caravan trade linked up with Europe. From the sixteenth century onwards, Europe, driven on to the ocean because all land routes were blocked, achieved a middleman position among *four* continents. This is the era of Atlantic Europe, no longer Mediterranean Europe. For three hundred years, roughly from 1500 to 1800, this gave Europe no more than a marginal position in other continents – geographically, economically, militarily and culturally marginal. By then the multiplier effects of three hundred years of this globally central position began to add up, to a level of capital accumulation and cultural development that made the industrial revolution possible. Europe's global lead in a sense only begins then. Thesis: what is specific about Europe is the combination of elements, not the elements themselves. Each of these can be found in other cultures too, but due to geographical and historical circumstances they came to an effective synthesis in Europe. Of course, this is only a skeletal explanation which does not account for the *nature* of the European synthesis; for this, other elements would have to be brought in, such as the role of Christianity (e.g. Mann, 1986, ch. 15), the development of science and the relationship between science and religion.

Upon closer consideration each of the celebrated stations of Europe – Greece, Rome, Christianity, Renaissance, Enlightenment – turns out to be a moment of cultural mixing: Greece, an outpost of Egyptian, Phoenician and Asian civilization; Rome, strongly indebted to Greece, Egypt and Carthage; Christianity, an Asian religion originally, whose non-European career with Byzantium, the Nestorians and Gnostics at times loomed larger than the career of European, i.e. Latin, Christendom; the Renaissance, a recovery of Hellenic civilization passed on through Arabic civilization and deeply engaged with non-European cultures; the Enlightenment, another period wide open to non-European influences, from China to Egypt, as evident not only in the Romantic movement, the other face of the Enlightenment, but also in the cultural lineages of the modernization programmes of Reason.

The most celebrated European philosophies, political principles, forms of knowledge, technologies, art and styles turn out upon closer examination to be multicultural in character, origin and composition. Reviewing the realities of multicultural Europe and the West, we witness the universal character of human culture not as something abstract and remote, but as an everyday reality. The Occident was historically multicultural long before it became demographically multicultural. The cultural osmosis with non-Western worlds is the corollary of Europe's structural middleman position in global commerce and intercourse over many centuries. Imperialism, domination and imposition are but one side of the story, relatively late and of brief duration; absorption, assimilation and adaptation are the other side of the coin, obscured by the narcissism of imperialism. European culture is a hybrid culture.

Notes

This paper was originally delivered as a lecture at St Patrick's College, Maynooth, the University College of Cork, De Horst, Driebergen and the University of the Western Cape, Cape Town, in 1992. I am indebted to Wim Wertheim for information on Dvořak and Debussy and to Robin Blackburn for comments on an earlier version. This is a revised version of the text published in the Occasional Paper Series of the Department of Sociology, University College of Cork, Ireland, 1992.

1   The '1500 complex' is discussed in Nederveen Pieterse (1989/1900, ch. 1). An interesting exception is Gills and Frank (1990).
2   Examples of focusing on the exotic in otherwise first-rate studies are Rousseau and Porter (1990) and the exhibition and catalogue series of the *Württembergische Kunstverein* in Stuttgart, *Exotische Welten, Europäische Phantasien* (1987).

References

Amin, Samir (1989) *Eurocentrism*, London: Zed Press.
Archer, M., and Lightbown, R. (1982) *India Observed: India as Viewed by British Artists 1760–1860*, London: Victoria and Albert Museum.
Barraclough, G. (1979) *Turning Points in World History*, London: Thames and Hudson.
Bédarida, F. (1985) 'Population and the urban explosion', in Briggs, A. (ed.), *The Nineteenth Century*, New York: Bonanza Books.
Berger, K. (1987) 'Dreimal Japonismus', in *Exotische Welten – Europäische Phantasien*, Stuttgart: Cantz.
Bergesen, A. (1990) 'Turning world system theory on its head', in Featherstone, M. (ed.), *Global Culture*, London: Sage.
Bernal, Martin (1987) *Black Athena: The Afroasiatic Roots of Classical Civilisation*, Vol. 1, London: Free Association Press.
Bishop, A. J. (1990) 'Western mathematics: the secret weapon of cultural imperialism', *Race and Class*, vol. 32, no. 2.
Chailley, J. (1972) *The Magic Flute: Masonic Opera*, London: Gollancz.
Cipolla, C. M. (1980) *Before the Industrial Revolution: European Society and Economy, 1000–1700*, 2nd edn, New York: Norton.
Clark, K. (1969) *Civilisation: A Personal View*, New York: Harper and Row.
Devisse, Jean (1979) *The Image of the Black in Western Art*, Vol. 2: *From the Early Christian Era to the 'Age of Discovery'*, Pt 1: 'From the demonic threat to the incarnation of sainthood', New York: William Morrow.
Diop, Cheik Anta (1991) *Civilization or Barbarism: An Authentic Anthropology*, Chicago: Lawrence Hill (original French edition 1981).

Gheverghese Joseph, G. (1987) 'Foundations of Eurocentrism in mathematics', *Race and Class*, vol. 28, no. 3.

Gheverghese Joseph, G. (1991) *The Crest of the Peacock: Non-European Roots of Mathematics*, London: IB Tauris.

Gills, B. K., and Frank, A. G. (1990) 'The cumulation of accumulation: theses and research agenda for 5000 years of world system history', *Dialectical Anthropology*, vol. 15.

Girouard, Mark (1988) 'In fee to the gorgeous East', *Times Literary Supplement*, 27 May–2 June.

Gombrich, E. H. (1979) *The Sense of Order: A Study in the Psychology of Decorative Art*, Oxford: Phaidon.

Goonatilake, S. (1982) *Crippled Minds: An Exploration into Colonial Culture*, New Delhi: Vikas.

Goonatilake, S. (1991) *The Evolution of Information: Lineages in Gene, Culture and Artefact*, London: Pinter.

Heer, F. (1966) *The Intellectual History of Europe*, New York: World Publishing.

Hobsbawm, E. J. (1987) *The Age of Empire, 1875–1914*, London: Weidenfeld and Nicolson.

James, B. (1989) 'Creating *la crème de la France* in Tokyo', *International Herald Tribune*, 5 December.

Kabbani, Rana (1986) *Europe's Myths of Orient*, London: Pandora.

Kiernan, V. G. (1981) 'Europe in the colonial mirror', *History of European Ideas*, vol. 1, no. 1.

Koppelkamm, S. (1987) *Exotische Architekturen im 18. und 19. Jahrhundert*, Berlin: Ernst & Sohn.

Kopplin, Monica (1987) 'Turcica und Turquerien', in *Exotische Welten – Europäische Phantasien*, Stuttgart: Cantz.

Kreidt, D. (1987) *Exotische Figuren und Motive im Europäischen Theater*, Stuttgart: Cantz.

Latham, R. (1958) 'Introduction', in *The Travels of Marco Polo*, Harmondsworth: Penguin.

Linton, Ralph (1936) *The Study of Man*, New York: Appleton Century Croft.

Mann, Michael (1986) *The Sources of Social Power*, Cambridge: Cambridge University Press.

Marshall, P. J., and Williams, G. (1982) *The Great Map of Mankind: British Perceptions of the World in the Age of Enlightenment*, London: Dent.

McBride, Elissa (1988) 'Western Civ: from Plato to Nato', *The Activist*, no. 21.

McNeill, W. (1982) *The Pursuit of Power*, Chicago: University of Chicago Press.

Merson, J. (1989) *Roads to Xanadu: East and West in the Making of the Modern World*, London: Weidenfeld and Nicolson.

Mokhtar, G. (ed.) (1990) *Ancient Civilizations of Africa* Vol. 2: *General History of Africa*, Paris and London: UNESCO and James Currey.

Nederveen Pieterse, Jan (1989;1900) *Empire and Emancipation*, New York/London, Praeger/Pluto Press.

Nederveen Pieterse, Jan (1991) 'Dilemmas of development discourse: the crisis of developmentalism and the comparative method', *Development and Change*, vol. 22, no. 1.

Nederveen Pieterse, Jan (1992) *White on Black: Images of Africa and Blacks in Western Popular Culture*, New Haven and London: Yale University Press.

Needham, Joseph (1981) *Science in Traditional China*, Cambridge, Mass.: Harvard University Press.

Needham, Joseph (1987) *Heavenly Clockwork: The Great Astronomical Clocks of Medieval China*, Cambridge: Cambridge University Press.

Parry, J. H. (1971) *Trade and Dominion: The European Overseas Empires in the Eighteenth Century*, London: Weidenfeld and Nicolson.

Raphael, C. (1985) *The Road from Babylon: The Story of Sephardi and Oriental Jews*, New York: Harper and Row.

Reynolds, R. (1949) *Beards*, New York: Harcourt, Brace, Jovanovitch.

Rothermund, D. (1986) *The German Intellectual Quest for India*, New Delhi: Manohar.

Rousseau, G. S., and Porter, R. (eds) (1990) *Exoticism in the Enlightenment*, Manchester: Manchester University Press.

Said, E. W. (1985) *Orientalism*, Harmondsworth: Penguin.

Schiffer, R. (1982) *Turkey Romanticized: Images of the Turks in Early 19th century English Travel Literature*, Bochum: Studienverlag Brockmeyer.

Schöning-Kalender, Claudia (1987) 'Türkisches gestern und heute: verschwindet die Exotik bei Anwesenheit der "Exoten"?', in *Exotische Welten- Europäische Phantasien*, Stuttgart: Cantz.

Sertima, Ivan Van (ed.) (1989) *Egypt Revisited*, 2nd edn, New Brunswick, NJ: Transaction Books.

Subramanyan, K. G. (1987) *The Living Tradition: Perspectives on Modern Indian Art*, Calcutta: Seagull Books.

Sweetman, J. (1987) *The Oriental Obsession: Islamic Inspiration in British and American Art and Architecture, 1500–1920*, Cambridge: Cambridge University Press.

Tanja, J. (1987) 'Brabantse Monsieurs, Vlaemsche Yveraars en Hollandtsche Botticheyt: Het beeld van de Zuidnederlandse immigranten in de Noordelijke Nederlanden, 1580–1630', in *Vreemd Gespuis*, Amsterdam: Ambo.

Temple, R. K. G. (1986) *China, Land of Discovery and Invention*, Wellingborough: Patrick Stevens.

Theunissen, H. (ed.) (1989) *Topkapie & Turkomanie*, Amsterdam: Bataafsche Leeuw.

Toynbee, A. (1972) *A Study of History*, London: Thames and Hudson.

Wallerstein, I. M. (1974) *The Modern World-System*, New York: Academic Press.

Weisberger, E. (ed.) (1985) *The Spiritual in Art: Abstract Painting 1890–1985*, Los Angeles/New York.

Zwerin, M. (1990) 'Taking "Punjabi Pop" around the world', *International Herald Tribune*, 8 February.

4

EGYPT IN AMERICA: *BLACK ATHENA*, RACISM AND COLONIAL DISCOURSE

Robert Young

Introduction

Colonial discourse analysis was initiated as an academic sub-discipline within literary and cultural theory by Edward Said's *Orientalism* (Said, 1978). This is not to suggest that colonialism had not been studied before then, but it was Said who shifted the study of colonialism among cultural critics towards its *discursive* operations, showing the intimate connection between the language and forms of knowledge developed for the study of cultures and the history of colonialism and imperialism. This meant that the kinds of concepts and representations used in literary texts, travel writings, memoirs and academic studies across a range of disciplines in the humanities and social sciences could be analysed as a means of understanding the diverse ideological practices of colonialism. Said's Foucauldian emphasis on the way in which Orientalism developed as a discursive construction, so that its language and conceptual structure determined both what could be said and what recognized as truth, demonstrated that all other perspectives on colonialism share and have to deal with a common discursive medium: the language used to describe or analyse colonialism is not transparent, innocent, ahistorical or merely instrumental. Colonial discourse analysis therefore looks at the wide variety of texts of colonialism as something more than mere documentation or 'evidence', and also emphasizes and analyses the ways in which colonialism not only involved a military or economic activity, but permeated forms of knowledge which, if unchallenged, may continue to be the very ones through which we try to analyse and understand colonialism itself.

Said's emphasis on Orientalism as a discourse had two main implications. First, the charting of the complicity of Western literary and academic knowledge with the history of European colonialism emphasized the ways in which seemingly impartial, objective academic disciplines had in fact colluded with, and indeed been instrumental in, the production of actual forms of colonial subjugation and administration. *Orientalism* provided powerful evidence of the complicity between politics and knowledge. Said's more controversial contention was that the discursive construction of Orientalism was self-generating, and bore little if any relation to the actuality of its putative object, 'the Orient'. This has been the most disputed aspect of his thesis and the most difficult for people to accept. At the same time, it has been one which, at worst, has allowed a certain lack of historical specificity. After all, if Orientalist discourse is a form of Western fantasy that can say nothing about actuality, while at the same time its determining cultural pressure means that those in the West cannot but use it, then any obligation to address the reality of the historical conditions of colonialism can be safely discarded. Thus colonial discourse analysis has meant that we have learnt a lot about the fantasmatics of colonial *discourse*, but at the same time that we have been prevented by definition from knowing about the actual conditions such discourse was framed to describe, analyse or control.

The totalizing direction of Said's argument in *Orientalism* was quickly challenged by Homi K. Bhabha, who maintained that Said assumed too readily that an unequivocal intention on the part of the West was always realized through its discursive productions (Bhabha, 1983). Bhabha called attention to the moment in which Said briefly, but in an undeveloped way, set up the possibility of Orientalism working at two conflictual levels, and in a significant but uncharacteristic invocation of psychoanalysis, distinguished between a 'manifest' Orientalism, the conscious body of 'scientific' knowledge about the Orient, and a 'latent' Orientalism, an unconscious positivity of fantasy and desire. Bhabha's outstanding contribution was to develop the implications of this idea by emphasizing the extent to which the two levels fused and were, in operation, indistinguishable. He showed how colonial discourse of whatever kind operated not only as an instrumental construction of knowledge, but also according to the ambivalent protocols of fantasy and desire. In subsequent work,

Bhabha has been concerned to demonstrate the constitutive ambivalence that rests at the heart of colonial discursive production, an
ambivalence that its appearance in a non-European context only
accentuated. He has exhibited through a series of analyses the ways
in which European colonial discourse – whether it be governmental
decree, district officers' reports, or missionary accounts – is effectively
decentred from its position of power and authority. This occurs at
times by its taking on an increasing hybridity when placed in a colonial
context, at other times through the exploitation by the colonized
themselves of the equivocations and contradictions that are all too
apparent in the more hostile and challenging criteria of its alien
surroundings. If Said shows that misrelation is the anagrammatic secret
of Orientalism, Bhabha demonstrates that oscillation is that of the
colonialist.

By contrast, Gayatri Chakravorty Spivak has been concerned to
emphasize, against Said, the possibility of counter-knowledges such
as those constructed around the criteria of the journal *Subaltern Studies*
(Spivak, 1985, 1987, 1990: Guha, 1982). If the desire of today's anti-
colonial historian is to retrieve a subaltern history that rewrites the
received account both of the colonizing academics and of the native
ruling élite, Spivak stresses the pitfalls and aporias that even radical
historiography can remain blind to. She instances examples of histories
that continue to be ignored, such as those of native subaltern women.
Taken always as an object of knowledge, by colonial and indigenous
rulers who are as masculinist as each other, the subaltern women is
written, argued about, even legislated for, but allowed no discursive
position from which to speak herself. She therefore tends to be absent
from the documentary archives, and writing her history has to involve
a particular effort of retrieval. This focus on the kinds of exclusion
produced not only by colonialism itself but even by current forms of
understanding is typical of Spivak's more general concern with what
she considers to be the continuing epistemic violence that is practised
in the exercise of Western forms of thought upon the East. Equally
importantly, Spivak has championed with a remarkable degree of
success the cause of minority groups excluded or neglected by contemporary academic, particularly feminist, practices. It is typical of
the relentlessly questioning nature of her work, however, that she has
recently been concerned with an interrogation of, as she sees it,
the increasing commodification of the category of 'marginality' itself
(Spivak, 1991).

These positions have been elaborated and developed by a number
of other critics, but it would be true to say that Said, Bhabha and

Spivak constitute the holy trinity of colonial discourse analysis, and have to be acknowledged as central to the field (Young, 1990). While there has been a remarkable, indeed quite staggering, growth of critics researching in this area, an increasing tendency has been to produce new archival material rather than to develop further the theoretical parameters set up by Said *et al*. The major challenge has come from critics such as Chandra Talpade Mohanty, Benita Parry and Aijaz Ahmad, who have criticized a certain textualism and idealism in colonial discourse analysis which, they allege, occurs at the expense of materialist historical enquiry (Mohanty, 1984; Parry, 1987; Ahmad, 1992). There is a considerable cogency to some of these objections, the underlying message of which probably has less to do with Said's own work than with its influence, and the sense that from a theoretical perspective colonial discourse analysis has reached a stage where it is itself in danger of becoming oddly stagnated, and as reified in its approach – and therefore in what it can possibly produce at the level of analysis – as the colonial discourse which it analyses. Critics have reached something of an impasse with regard to the theoretical questions involved in the analysis of colonial discourse, and at times this has meant a certain complacency about or neglect of the problems of the methodologies that have been developed.

Black Athena and geopolitics

From a theoretical point of view, this situation could be said to have occurred because the analytic paradigms developed for other literatures or continents have not been strong enough to challenge the discursive model of Said. I want now to consider a book which holds out the promise of providing a different possibility for the theoretical paradigm of colonial discourse analysis, Martin Bernal's controversial *Black Athena*, a book whose impact can be compared only to that of *Orientalism* (Bernal, 1987, 1991). Bernal does not claim to be providing an analysis of colonialism as such, but colonialism of a more far-reaching kind proves to be fundamental to his analysis. *Black Athena* is important first of all because it moves the question of Africa to the centre of both historical and intellectual enquiry in the history of Western knowledge. For reasons that will become clear, the book is hostile to the nineteenth-century obsession with India. As Said shows, 'the Orient' itself tended to move eastwards with the historical movement of exploration and colonization. But the decline of interest in the Middle East in the nineteenth century can also be attributed to other factors. *Black Athena* argues that the waning of attention and prestige accorded to the Middle East corresponded to an increasing denigration of Semitic and African culture, the reasons for which were largely racist. The prestige of India, by contrast, developed with the notion of its common 'Aryan' stock with Europeans. Even today India quite clearly retains that position of pride of place, the jewel in the crown of colonial discourse analysis.

Black Athena's significance derives not only from its hotly contested claims to revise some of the fundamental historical assumptions of classics and archaeology. Its more far-reaching contemporary cultural and political importance stems from its implied reappraisal of Black history, not only making it central to any account of the origins of European civilization, but also powerfully strengthening its still marginalized institutional academic standing. The book thus makes a dynamic intervention in the current reappraisals of the bases of Western knowledge. *Black Athena*'s value also derives from the fact that it provides the most detailed and comprehensive demonstration to date of the way in which the allegedly objective historical scholarship of apparently non-political academic disciplines, classics and archaeology, were in fact determined by their own cultural and political values. Bernal corroborates Said's claim that all knowledge is interested, but connects this more specifically to questions of racism. Bernal's book suggests that the parameters that have already been set up defining the limits of colonial discourse need to be extended much more widely into the history of academic disciplines. *Black Athena* holds out the much more disturbing possibility that all Western knowledge is, directly or indirectly, a form of colonial discourse.

Bernal begins by making the provocative claim that the classical and archaeological scholarship of the nineteenth and twentieth centuries has been racially biased. He supports this argument with a historical analysis which demonstrates that the formation of classics as an academic discipline in the nineteenth century was based on the deployment of a new form of historical scholarship that significantly modified the story of the origins of Greek civilization that had hitherto been accepted for the previous two thousand years. In the place of the 'ancient model' of the dependence of Greece on Egyptian culture, nineteenth-century academics substituted what Bernal calls the 'Aryan model' which denied that the Greeks had received any cultural influence at all, either from the Semitic or African cultures of the Phoenicians or from the Egyptians, and held instead that Greek culture was, essentially, self-generated. This is the paradigm which, he alleges, with its cultural and racial assumptions intact, has broadly speaking stayed in place ever since. The main argument of *Black Athena*, then, as Bernal himself summarizes it, is that

> the Ancient Model was destroyed and replaced by the Aryan Model not because of any internal deficiencies, nor because the Aryan Model explained anything better or more plausibly; what it did do, however, was make the history of Greece and its relations to Egypt and the Levant conform to the world-view of the nineteenth century and, specifically, to its systematic racism. (Bernal, 1987, p. 442)

The hostile reaction of classicists to *Black Athena* is hardly surprising and recalls that of Orientalists to Said's *Orientalism*. Whether Bernal's claims can be sustained at their broad-stroke level of generality is doubtless open to question. It is not my intention here to consider the argument among classicists, archaeologists or historians about whether Bernal is right or wrong. I want to focus instead on his methodological claims and look more closely at the contemporary political implications of his argument.

Bernal calls volume 1 of *Black Athena* 'The Fabrication of Ancient Greece 1785–1985', and maintains that this involves the process of the Aryan model of the Romantics (Greece as a self-generated pure origin, both of itself and of European culture) superseding the traditional view of Greece's heavy dependence on Egyptian philosophy, science and knowledge. The argument of the book, therefore, is that – with some modifications – the traditional view is in fact true, and that of the Romantics false. This means that there is a crucial difference between Bernal's project and Said's in *Orientalism*. For Said, 'the Orient' is a Western projection on to the East that has no corresponding actuality or reality that can be set against it to put the record straight, the reason being that the very notion of the Orient is itself a piece of Orientalism. This leads Said to develop the problematics of the whole question of representation to the point where he finds himself entangled in the anthropological quandary of whether it is possible to represent other cultures properly at all. Bernal, by contrast, says that we *can* know the truth about ancient Greece. Despite his appeal to Kuhn, ultimately it is not just a question of models or of representation. It is a matter of evidence, and he offers us, therefore, a return to historical truth. This sets up the interesting possibility that what Said describes in *Orientalism* is not just a discursive projection but a Romantic fantasy that could, after all, be corrected by a return to the historical actuality. Anthropology, too, would once again be able to know and to represent its object. Moreover, the revalidation of the ancient model also means that *Black Athena* impinges on the symptomatic moment of anthropology in which indigenous and Western academic knowledges confront each other. Bernal's validation of the former offers a way of breaking our contemporary habit of even now seeing the so-called native as an object but not as a source of knowledge. This still operates as a general rule for non-Western forms of knowledge, particularly within the academic institution.

The problem with the book arises, however, from a related anthropological quandary: the position of the observer. In volume 1, Bernal makes his case via a sociology of knowledge which differentiates between 'internal' arguments – pure scholarship – and 'external' arguments, where knowledge is seen in an interested relation to its own contemporary politics and other equally politicized disciplines (ethnology, anthropology, eugenics, etc.). Bernal argues that, from a historical perspective, the ultimate justification for the first can always be found in the second – except in his own case. Here Bernal's old-fashioned and in many ways refreshing appeal to evidence, with its accompanying distinction between true and false history, means that he must also maintain a split between scholarship and politics, despite his eloquent simultaneous demonstration of its impossibility. His own illustrations of how facts are always imbricated with values begs the question of the status of his own 'facts'. The recently published *Black Athena* volume 2, which contains 'the evidence', has confirmed that Bernal cannot himself successfully lay claim to the very notion of disinterested scholarship that he shows to be impossible for everyone else (Young, 1993). Unlike J. D. Bernal's comparable project in *The Social Function of Science*, there is no Marxism available here to enable Martin Bernal to separate the metaphysical elements from science (Bernal, 1939). Bernal does not after all, then, succeed in returning to an empirical methodology that could set us free from the problems set up by Said.

Despite its methodological difficulties, however, *Black Athena* remains important for three reasons: first because it puts Africa as central to the question of Western knowledge; second because it poses far-reaching questions about the status of academic learning and its policing of the borders between proper and improper knowledge (including *Black Athena* itself); and third because, far more than *Orientalism*, it puts the question of race at the centre of its enquiry. In short, Bernal's most significant intervention, though to some extent unacknowledged even by himself, is the fact that he places race, racism and the racialization of knowledge at the core of his argument.

The question of the status of Egypt

Black Athena itself, and its subsequent reception, is testimony to the problem of the legitimation of knowledge and the degree to which political considerations perform this function. One of the many paradoxes of Bernal's book is that, whereas public interest is focused on its more general implications, which go well beyond the immediate detail of the material discussed, Bernal himself wants to keep fairly rigorously to the parameters of his specific topic. In fact, despite his own strictures on classics, Bernal remains predominantly concerned to set his own argument within the limits of the field.

This avoidance of the book's contemporary political implications is most apparent in the question of the status of Egypt. As we have seen, Bernal's argument is that in the early nineteenth century Greece replaced Egypt as the origin of European civilization. This shift was achieved not through documentary or archaeological evidence, but via the prestige of linguistics, with the discovery of the Indo-European family of Aryan languages. Bernal argues that the motivation that lay behind this was the desire to give European civilization a European and not an African origin, a move which he connects to the development of scientific theories of racism in the nineteenth century. This shift from Egypt to Greece simultaneously involved a denigration and indeed denial of the history and civilization of Africa.

Egypt, in Bernal's argument, is undoubtedly a fulcrum for this antagonism between Europe and Africa, and therefore also between white and black. Bernal himself shows that since classical times there has been a highly contested debate about whether the Egyptians were 'essentially African', whether they were white or black. Clearly, in terms of the book's political argument, this question is a crucial one – for if the Egyptians were not African, if they were not black, then the wider cultural consequences of the whole argument of *Black Athena* for our own contemporary cultural politics would collapse. Bernal himself, however, restricts his comments to the guarded remark that 'the Ancient Egyptians ... though their colour was uncertain, lived in Africa' (Bernal, 1987, p. 440). Despite its critical significance for the argument of the book, Bernal plays the question down.

The problem is that he is trying to have it both ways. For Bernal, the point that the Egyptians were racially mixed makes their identification as black problematic; he addresses the issue by recourse to literal descriptions of skin colour. What he does not consider is the fundamental point that today's term, 'Black', was developed not to describe skin colour in any literal way, but rather to characterize a political category of oppression. This points up the problems of the political use of the term 'Black' to describe peoples of different historical epochs who were not oppressed by white society, or, to put it another way, it emphasizes the historical specificity of today's racial politics. The tendency to assimilate the Egyptian history of thousands of years ago to our own contemporary political issues and values obviously runs the risk of hypostatizing a transhistorical essence of 'Blackness' – because historically speaking, even if the Egyptians were black, the meaning of Blackness could clearly not be the same then as it is now. Any tendency to assimilate the Egyptian history of thousands of years ago to our contemporary political issues is thus as full of pitfalls as of potential. On the other hand, Bernal himself shows that this very historical identification of the Egyptians as African and black was itself the reason why they were written out of European cultural history in the nineteenth century. In exactly the same way, it is because the book is considered to be saying something about the history of Black civilizations that it has made such a significant intervention in the realm of today's cultural politics. Moreover, by calling it *Black Athena*, Bernal himself in fact directly invokes such an implication. All of which shows the continuing impossibility of trying to separate scholarship from politics. Despite its powerful demonstration of how this has operated historically, *Black Athena* insists on maintaining a sphinx-like silence about its own relation to today's contemporary cultural politics. This scholarly stance does not, however, prevent the meaning of *Black Athena* from being inextricably bound up with the racial politics of the past two hundred years.

The reception of *Black Athena* suggests that today's racial politics still work through a polarization between Black and white, just as we talk of colonizer and colonized, of self and Other. This remorseless dialectalization is characteristic of twentieth-century accounts of race, racial difference and racial identity, and suggests that they are in certain respects less different from those of the nineteenth century than is often assumed. The obviously necessary but easy dismissals of Victorian expressions of racial superiority mean that we are also often unaware of the links between contemporary cultural discourses and earlier racialist thinking. In fact I would suggest that oddly enough what had remained least visible to colonial discourse analysis is the question of race. Most of us, of course, work on the assumption that racism can always be found in the colonial arena, and a certain safety and comfortable moral rectitude can be found by citing glaring examples of racist sentiment in any analysis. So we have not missed the fact that most colonial discourse is racist in today's terms. What I would argue, however, is that nineteenth-century ideas about race have not been taken seriously – precisely because we consider the racist assumptions of the Victorians to be so morally wrong, the most objectionable part of their culture. We therefore tend to neglect a fundamental aspect of the framework of colonialism: namely, racialism as a *theoretical* discourse of the nineteenth century.

This discourse continues to impinge upon our own. Much of what we now discuss in terms of ethnicity and cultural difference fell in those times under the category of race: our aversion and nervousness about 'race' means that we tend to ignore its own theoretical foundation and, as a corollary, fail to examine the links between our own contemporary cultural theorizations and those of the rejected past. The distinguishing characteristic of the analysis of colonial discourse today is that we like to talk about colonialism as if it were not us: we are 'postcolonial'.

Egypt in America

Bernal's reticence about the cultural conditions of his own book's production and reception is striking given the American context in which he is writing. In keeping with his tendency to play down the contribution of African-American writers who contested the de-Africanization of Egypt, in all his detailed, laborious discussions of racialism in nineteenth-century academia, particularly in relation to Egyptology, Bernal nowhere discusses the 'American School' of anthropology which was instrumental from the 1840s onwards in promoting in Europe as well as the USA, what was claimed to be the modern, scientific account of racial difference. This lacuna is all the more curious given the significant role played by the history of Egypt in that racial theory. The arguments are thus already local and determined: Egypt has been a contested category in the racial politics of America for over a hundred and fifty years.

Bernal demonstrates how European scholars from the Romantic period onwards tended to argue that Greek civilization was essentially self-generated and owed nothing to that of Egypt. If so, then why, one might ask, did later scholars seek to prove that Egyptian civilization had itself been white rather than black? Bernal's answer is racism: '*If it has been scientifically 'proved' that Blacks were biologically incapable of civilization, how could one explain Ancient Egypt – which was inconveniently placed on the African continent?*' (Bernal, 1987, p. 241, italics in original). The immediate solution was to make Egypt white.

But what Bernal does not point out is that there are two distinct arguments being made here in relation to Egypt. One is about the non-Egyptian origins of Greek (and therefore European) civilization. The other has nothing to do with Greece at all, but is focused instead on the 'problem' of Egypt producing a civilization as such. This second issue was developed not by classicists (who, after all, had proved that Egypt was irrelevant), but by archaeologists and anthropologists who were engaged in developing racial theory. The point here is that they could never convincingly argue their thesis of the inherent biological inferiority of the black race while Egypt remained an African civilization. What Bernal does not say is that it was in the USA that the most concerted effort took place to prove that Egyptian civilization had not been African. The reason for this was straightforward: the desire to produce a scholarly, academic justification for slavery.

The debates about slavery that preceded and accompanied the American Civil War were themselves to be significant not only in the USA but in Britain too, and succeeded in changing the terms of debates about race. An important factor here was the comparative ease with which black and white were divided and set against each other in the American accounts: this apparently absolute antithesis then became the dominant theoretical model for all the relations of the white to the non-white world, neatly coinciding with popular racism, which is really only ever interested in distinguishing between black and white. Thus instead of the general schema of degrees of difference between the races that had formerly dominated ethnology, the new model set up whites as absolute and distinct, and considered all non-white races only in terms of how much they deviated from the illustrious Caucasian standard.

With this new model, moreover, a more constitutive difference, of species, became the central focus of racial theory. The reason for this was simple. The constitution of the United States proclaimed that all men were born equal: the institution of slavery clearly constituted a flagrant breach of that principle. However, if there were different species of man, with black people classified as a lower species that did not share all the human characteristics, then it could be argued that constitutional equality did not apply to them. We thus find a concerted effort gathering pace from the 1840s to establish the doctrine of polygenesis – that is, that blacks and whites constituted different species – in the place of monogenesis, according to which all humans were considered one species, their differences being explained by the effects of climate and environment.

The debate focused on two related questions, one cultural, one biological: these two aspects always went hand in hand and always had to be assessed simultaneously. The cultural question was whether there had ever been a Black civilization (if not, this would substantiate claims about the superiority of the white race, and the inherent inferiority of the black). The biological question was whether the hybrid offspring of unions between the two races were fertile or not (if not, this would show that they were different species, for the test of two animals being of different species was that any hybrid between them was infertile). For this reason, the major emphasis in writing about race in this period gets placed on the history of Black civilizations (particularly Egypt), and the question of hybridity in human reproduction. The success of the American anthropologists J. C. Nott and George R. Gliddon's *Types of Mankind* (1854), which went into eight editions by 1860, was doubtless the result of a particular combination of skills that united both these areas: Nott was a physician, Gliddon an Egyptologist. The significance of their work was the way they brought the scientific and the cultural together in order to promulgate an indistinguishably scientific and cultural theory of race.

Improbably, therefore, biology and Egyptology *together* constituted the basis of the new 'scientific' racial theory. Egypt, as the earliest civilization, developed in Africa, clearly represented the major potential stumbling block to the claim for the permanent inferiority of the black race, which, it was alleged, had never created or produced anything whatsoever of value. As Gliddon made clear in his best-selling *Ancient Egypt* (1843), those who advocated an African Egypt were in effect also advocating 'the African origin of civilization', with the unwelcome consequence that 'we, who trace back to Egypt the origin of every art and science known in antiquity, have to thank the sable Negro, or the dusky Berber, for the first gleams of knowledge and invention' (Gliddon, 1843, pp. 58–9). It was therefore essential to prove that the Egyptians were Caucasians. The whitening of Egypt that Bernal points to in *Black Athena* thus here finds its rationale not in a general conspiracy of European racism in nineteenth-century academia, but in the particular context of nineteenth-century American racial theory in its attempt to justify and rationalize slavery in the years leading up to the American Civil War.

Nott and Gliddon substantiated their argument that 'Egypt was originally peopled by the Caucasian race' by recourse to the phrenological researches of their fellow American S. G. Morton (also an anatomist and Egyptologist), whose *Crania Ægyptiaca* was published in 1844. Morton's phrenological investigations in Egypt were widely taken to have proved that the ancient Egyptians were Caucasians. It had, in fact been Gliddon himself who had provided the Egyptian skills for Morton's research, urging him to use his anatomical and craniological skills to prove the Caucasian basis of Egyptian civilization. He wrote to Morton in 1841:

> I am hostile to the opinion of the *African* origin of the Egyptians. I mean of the *high caste* – kings, priests, and military . . . We, as hieroglyphists, know Egypt better *now*, than all the Greek authors or the Romans. On this ground, unless you are convinced from Comparative Anatomy, with which science I am totally unacquainted, and be backed by such evidence as is incontrovertible, I urge your pausing, and considering why the Egyptians may not be of Asiatic, and perhaps of Arabic descent; an idea which, I fancy, from the tenor of your letters, is your present conclusion. At any rate, they are not, and never were, Africans, still less Negroes. (Nott and Gliddon, 1848, pp. xxxvixxxvii)

Morton agreed, and in 1844 himself argued that 'Negroes were numerous in Egypt, but their social position in ancient times was the same as it is now, that of servants and slaves' (Morton, 1844, p. 66; cf. Nott, 1844, p. 16). Here, then, was an ancient historical precedent for a white society with black slaves: Morton, Nott and Gliddon deployed their account of Egypt to justify the natural place of 'Negroes' in their own Southern society, and to argue for the everlasting nature of racial social relations. In *Types of Mankind*, Nott and Gliddon asserted the permanent difference between the races, their mutual antagonism and the necessity of their enduring separation, by invoking the category of 'types', first introduced by Cuvier, to claim the fixed nature of the different races. Placing great emphasis on the evidence of Egyptian illustrations and skulls that were five thousand years old, Nott and Gliddon claimed to have established proof of 'the permanency of types', and thus could argue that the Caucasian and Negro races were as different in ancient Egypt as in the America of the 1840s.

In 1844, in one of a series of popular lectures on what he privately described as 'niggerology' (Gould, 1984, p. 49), Nott began by emphasizing the crucial role that Egypt played in his racial theory:

> Before entering upon the Natural History of the human race, it is indispensably necessary, as a preliminary step, to examine some points in chronology, and to take a glance at the early history of Egypt. I must show that the Caucasian or white, and the Negro races were distinct at a very remote date, and *that the Egyptians were Caucasians*. Unless this point can be established the contest must be abandoned. (Nott, 1844, p. 8, italics in original)

Nott here offers an argument familiar to readers of *Black Athena*, though it will seldom be found stated in so bald and explicit a fashion in Bernal's book:

> the conclusion to my mind is irresistible, that the civilization of Egypt is attributable to these Caucasian heads; because civilization does not now and never has as far as we know from history, been carried to this perfection by any other race than the Caucasian – how can any reasoning mind come to any other conclusion?
>
> It is clear then that history, the Egyptian Monuments, her paintings and sculptures, the examination of skulls by Cuvier, Morton and others, analogy, and every thing else connected with this country, combine to prove beyond possible doubt, that the Ancient Egyptian race were Caucasians. (p. 12)

But in Nott's account, the significance of the Caucasian identity of the ancient Egyptians is developed into an important corollary that constitutes the always-present other side of racial theory:

> Positive historical facts prove too, that Egypt has been conquered in early times by various inferior tribes, and the blood of her people adulterated . . . even the pure blood of Greece and Rome could not wash out the black stain, both moral and physical, which she had received.
>
> Naturalists have strangely overlooked the effects of mixing races, when the illustrations drawn from the crossing of animals speak so plainly – man physically is, but an animal at best, with the same physiological laws which govern others.
>
> This adulteration of blood is the reason why Egypt and the Barbary States can never rise again, until the present races are exterminated, and the Caucasian substituted.
>
> Wherever in the history of the world the inferior races have conquered and mixed in with the Caucasian, the latter have sunk into barbarism. (p. 16)

Having claimed, like Schlegel and others before him, that Egyptian civilization was the product of the arrival of Aryans from India, the question that Nott here addresses is how that theory can be squared with the racial identity of modern Egyptians. The fact that by the nineteenth century Egypt's population was clearly made up of a mixture of Arabs and Africans is held not to disprove the Caucasian thesis, but rather to explain Egypt's long decline. In language that closely anticipates that of Gobineau (an edited English version of whose work Nott quickly arranged to be published in America) (Gobineau, 1856), Nott claims that the Aryans created Egyptian civilization, and that the subsequent mixing of races debased it and brought about its fall. He then concludes that all mixture of Caucasian races has caused them to sink into 'barbarism', thus extending his theory of Egyptian history into a general historical theory of the rise and fall of nations according to the principle of race.

For Nott, the ultimate white supremacist, the Aryans did everything alone, and the mixing of races brought about degeneration, infertility and barbarism. Egypt will never rise again, until its present mixed population is 'exterminated'. Nott comments in his Preface that 'the parts which treat of the effect of the crossing of races, are those to which I wish to draw more particular attention, as these facts have not heretofore been sufficiently considered' (Nott, 1844, p. 1). Clearly, the mixing of races and racial extermination was a question preoccupying him, for in the same year he had published an article entitled 'The mulatto a hybrid-probable extermination of the two races if the whites and blacks are allowed to marry'. Here the argument took a contemporary swerve in the direction of the doctrine of polygenesis, addressing the vexed question of the fertility of interracial unions. Nott claimed that observation in the United States showed that mulattos were less fertile than whites or blacks, and argued as a consequence that if a general mixing of races took place, the USA would degenerate not only culturally, but also physically (Banton, 1987, pp. 40–1). In maintaining the reduced fertility of mulattos, Nott thus put the emphasis less on any threatened degeneration of American culture than on the idea that sexual interaction between white and black would cause the American people to decline and literally die out altogether. Sexuality and miscegenation thus occupy a core position in his covert defence of the 'peculiar institution'.

For despite the success of the notion of 'type' in the popular mind as a way of distinguishing between races (and classes), Nott and Gliddon's argument, though clearly useful for the Southern defence of slavery, remained vulnerable to the question of hybridity. Sex was less easy to contain than ancient Egypt. Notwithstanding their fundamental claim for the permanence of types across the ages, it is noticeable that in *Types of Mankind*, Nott and Gliddon also feel obliged to repeat the threat of the ghastly effects of miscegenation:

> It seems . . . certain, however, in human physical history, that the superior race must inevitably become deteriorated by an intermixture with the inferior . . . through the operation of the laws of Hybridity alone, the human family might possibly become exterminated by a thorough amalgamation of all the various types of mankind now existing on earth. (Nott and Gliddon, 1854, p. 407)

They thus make a double argument: the difference between the species of men is permanent, a permanence preserved through the laws of hybridity by the degeneration and eventual infertility of any crossing between them. Conversely, however, it is maintained that any breakdown of the social divisions between black and white in American society, which it was always assumed would lead inevitably to widespread interracial unions, would therefore cause the eventual extermination of the whole nation. The more racial theory proposed permanent racial difference at the level of an absolute specific distinctness, the more obsessed its upholders became with the questions of hybridity and the prospect of interracial sex.

Hybridity and miscegenation

If it was in the United States that we find the greatest obsession and paranoia about hybridity, it was the American fantasmatic ideology of race, posing as scientific truth in the guise of ethnology, 'the science of races', that from the 1840s onwards provided the theoretical justification for European colonialism, just as it did for slavery in the USA. In the endless discussions of questions of miscegenation in nineteenth-century racial theory, however, we can see the soft underbelly of white-black power relations, whereby cultures in their colonial operation become hybridized, alienated and potentially threatening to their European originals. The detail with which miscegenation was discussed and thought through can be seen in Tschudi's table (Figure 1), reproduced in Nott and Gliddon, and here taken from Robert Brown's four-volume survey, *The Races of Mankind* (Brown, 1873–9, vol. II, p. 6).

Here the curious evaluative comments about the children of different proportions of mixed race that increasingly supplement the second column show the influence of contemporary anthropological tables of the different mental and physical qualities of the races. (It is no doubt symptomatic that, despite its exhaustive categorizations, the coupling of any 'Indian' or 'Negro' father with a white mother is completely excluded: the whole process is theoretically not reversible.) We can read this table of miscegenation or 'mongrelity' as an analytic account of the intricate gradations of cultural as well as racial fusion, regarded as a process of degeneration that mocked the nineteenth century's imperial 'diffusion' model of the spread of cultures with confusion, subverted the evolutionary comparative method of anthropology, and beyond these held out the threat of undoing the whole progressive

Nothing could perhaps better illustrate the mongrel character of the Spanish-American population than by saying that twenty-three crosses can be determined, and have received names. They are as follows:—

PARENTS		CHILDREN
White father and negro	mother	mulatto
" " Indian	"	mestiza
Indian " negro	"	chino
White " mulatto	"	cuarteron
White " mestiza	"	creole (pale-brownish complexion)
" " chino	"	chino-blanco
" " cuarterona	"	quintero
" " quintera	"	white
Negro " Indian	"	zambo
" " mulatto	"	zambo-negro
" " mestiza	"	mulatto-oscuro
" " chino	"	zambo-chino
" " zamba	"	zambo-negro (perfectly black)

PARENTS		CHILDREN
Negro father and quintera	mother	mulatto (rather dark)
Indian " mulatto	"	chino-oscuro
" " mestiza	"	mestizo-claro (frequently very beautiful)
" " chino	"	chino-cola
" " zamba	"	zambo-claro
" " chino-cola	"	Indian (with frizzly hair)
" " quintera	"	mestizo (rather brown)
Mulatto " zamba	"	zambo (a miserable race)
" " mestiza	"	chino (rather clear complexion)
" " chino	"	chino (rather dark)

In America the terms mulatto, quadroon, and octoroon are commonly used to express the possession of a half, a fourth, or an eighth of black blood, and the nomenclature goes no further, but experienced observers can detect much more minute quantities. A person with one half of Indian blood is usually styled a half-caste, or more commonly a half-breed. The term is used, however, very vaguely to denote the presence of a greater or less amount of white blood.

Figure 1

paradigm of Western civilization. Here theories of racial difference as degeneration themselves fused with the increasing cultural pessimism of the late nineteenth century and the claim that the world itself – that is, the West – was degenerating.

In recent years a whole range of disciplines has been concerned with the question of the exclusion and representation of 'the Other', of inside/outside notions of Otherness, or of the difficulties, so painful for anthropology, of self-Other relations. Brown's finely gradated table, by contrast, suggests that racism, and therefore perhaps colonialism, also worked according to a different paradigm than ours (still in fact present today, but hidden), of diversity and inequality. Deleuze and Guattari get it right in the course of a discussion of Christ's face in a scene from Giotto's *The Life of St Francis*:

> If the face is in fact Christ, in other words, your average ordinary White Man, then the first deviances, the first divergence-types are racial: yellow man, black man ... European racism as the white man's claim has never operated by exclusion, or by the designation of someone as Other ... Racism operates by the determination of degrees of deviance in relation to the White-Man face, which endeavours to integrate non-conforming traits into increasingly eccentric and backward waves ... From the viewpoint of racism, there is no exterior, there are no people on the outside. There are only people who should be like us and whose crime is not to be. (Deleuze and Guattari, 1988, p. 178).

Nineteenth-century racism was constructed through the 'computation of normalities' and 'degrees of deviance': a race, Deleuze and Guattari observe, 'is defined not by its purity but rather by the impurity conferred upon it by a system of domination. Bastard and mixed-blood are the true names of race' (p. 379).

What is most striking is that the 'scientific' account of racial difference is in fact focused on an extraordinary, nightmare vision of fertility, a frenetic panorama of frenzied, interminable copulation between races. Racial theory projects a dynamic phantasmagoria of the coupling, coalescence and fusing that give rise to the infinite motley variety of interbreeding and the melange, miscegenation, mongrelity, hybridization of its offspring – half-blood, half-caste, half-breed, Eurasian, creole, mulatto, mestiza, chino, zambo, terceron, quarteron, quinteron, quadroon, octoroon ... Nineteenth-century theories of race did not just consist of essentializing differentiations between white and black: they were about people having sex – interminably adulterating, aleatory, illicit, interracial sex.

But this steamy model of mixture was not a simple sexual or

even cultural matter: in many ways it preserved the older commercial discourse that it superseded. It is clear that the forms of sexual exchange brought about by colonialism were themselves both mirrors and consequences of the forms of economic exchange that constituted the basis of colonial relations. That extended exchange of property which began with small trading posts and the visiting slave ships originated, indeed, as much as an exchange of bodies as of goods, rather of bodies as goods: as in that paradigm of respectability, marriage, the economic and sexual exchange were intimately bound up, coupled with each other, from the very first. It was therefore wholly appropriate that sexual exchange, and its miscegenated product, should be the dominant paradigm through which the economic and cultural forms of colonialism were theorized. Perhaps this begins to explain why our own forms of racism remain so intimately bound up with sexuality and desire. At the same time, it is striking that our own contemporary cultural theory remains equally preoccupied with the concept of hybridity. Its translation from the biological to the cultural sphere would be more reassuring if the biological and cultural had not always been inextricably intertwined. The fantasy of those working in cultural studies and colonial discourse analysis in the Western academy is that we have managed to free ourselves from the hybrid commerce of colonialism, as from every other aspect of the colonial legacy.

References

Ahmad, Aijaz (1992) *In Theory: Classes, Nations, Literatures*, London: Verso.

Banton, Michael (1987) *Racial Theories*, Cambridge: Cambridge University Press.

Bernal, J. D. (1939) *The Social Function of Science*, London: Routledge.

Bernal, Martin (1987) *Black Athena: The Afroasiatic Roots of Classical Civilization*. Vol. 1: *The Fabrication of Ancient Greece 1785–1985*, London: Free Association Books.

Bernal, Martin (1991) *Black Athena: The Afroasiatic Roots of Classical Civilization*. Vol. 2: *The Archaeological and Documentary Evidence*, London: Free Association Books.

Bhabha, Homi K. (1983) 'Difference, discrimination, and the discourse of colonialism', in Barker, F., Hulme, P., Iversen, M., and Loxley, D. (eds), *The Politics of Theory*, Colchester: University of Essex.

Brown, Robert (1873–9) *The Races of Mankind*, 4 vols, London: Cassell, Petter and Galpin.

Deleuze, Gilles, and Guattari, Félix (1988) *A Thousand Plateaus: Capitalism and Schizophrenia*, trans. Brian Massumi, London: Athlone.

Gliddon, George R. (1843) *Ancient Egypt. A Series of Chapters on Early Egyptian*

History, Archaeology, and other Subjects, connected with Hieroglyphical Literature, 12th edn (1848) revised and corrected, with an appendix, Philadelphia: Peterson.

Gobineau, Arthur de (1856) *The Moral and Intellectual Diversity of Races, with Particular Reference to their Respective Influence in the Civil and Political History of Mankind. With an analytical introduction and copious historical notes, by H. Hotz. To which is added an Appendix containing a summary of the latest scientific facts bearing upon the question of the unity or plurality of species. By J. C. Nott, MD, of Mobile*, Philadelphia: Lippincott.

Gould, Stephen Jay (1984) *The Mismeasure of Man*, Harmondsworth: Penguin.

Guha, Ranajit (1982) 'On some aspects of the historiography of colonial India', in Guha, Ramajit (ed.) *Subaltern Studies*, Vol 1, Delhi: Oxford University Press.

Mohanty, Chandra Talpade (1984) 'Under Western eyes: feminist scholarship and colonial discourses', *Boundary 2*, vol. 12, no. 3 vol. 13, no. 1.

Morton, Samuel George (1844) *Crania Ægyptiaca; or, Observations on Egyptian Ethnography, derived from Anatomy, History, and the Monuments*, Philadelphia: Pennington.

Nott, Josiah C. (1844) *Two Lectures on the Natural History of the Caucasian and Negro Races*, Mobile: Dade and Thompson.

Nott, Josiah, C., and Gliddon, George R. (1854) *Types of Mankind: or, Ethnological Researches, Based upon the Ancient Monuments, Paintings, Sculptures, and Crania of Races, and upon their Natural, Geographical, Philological, and Biblical History: illustrated by Selections from the inedited papers of Samuel George Morton, MD*, London: Trubner; Paris: Bossange; Philadelphia: Lippincott.

Parry, Benita (1987) 'Problems in current theories of colonial discourse', *Oxford Literary Review*, vol. 9.

Said, Edward (1978) *Orientalism*, London: Routledge and Kegan Paul.

Spivak, Gayatri Chakravorty (1985) 'Can the subaltern speak? Speculations on widow sacrifice', *Wedge*, vols 7/8.

Spivak, Gayatri Chakravorty (1987) *In Other Worlds: Essays in Cultural Politics*, New York: Methuen.

Spivak, Gayatri Chakravorty (1990) *The Post-Colonial Critic*, London: Routledge.

Spivak, Gayatri Chakravorty (1991) 'Theory in the margin: Coetzee's *Foe* reading Defoe's *Crusoe and Roxana*', in Arac, Jonathan, and Johnson, Barbara (eds), *Consequences of Theory*, Baltimore: Johns Hopkins Press.

Young, Robert (1990) *White Mythologies: Writing History and the West*, London: Routledge.

Young, Robert (1993) '*Black Athena*: the politics of scholarship', *Science as Culture*, vol. 4, part 2, no. 19.

Part III

RACISM AND MODERNITY IN
EUROPE

5

RACISM IN EUROPE: UNITY AND DIVERSITY

Michel Wieviorka

Observing growing racist tendencies that affect most European countries, an increasing number of scholars feel an urgent need for a
comparative reflexion that may bring answers to a central question:
over and beyond the empirical evidence of differences, is there not a
certain unity in contemporary racism in Europe? Is it not possible to
elaborate a reasoned set of hypotheses that could account for most
national racist experiences in Europe, while shedding some light on
their specificities?

European unification, in so far as it exists, and the growth of racism
are obviously distinct phenomena, and it would be artificial to try and
connect them too directly. The most usual frame of reference for any
research about racism and race relations remains national. And even
the vocabulary or, more deeply, the analytical and cultural categories
that we use when dealing with this issue vary so widely from one
country to another that we meet considerable difficulties when trying
to translate precise terms. There may be large differences in language,
and words with negative connotations in one country will have positive
ones in another. Nobody in France, for instance, would use the
expression *relations de race*, which would be regarded as racist, although
it is commonly employed in the United Kingdom.

The key preliminary task, therefore, is not to contribute direct
empirical knowledge about the various expressions of racism in
Europe, as can be found, for instance, in the important survey of
'Racism and xenophobia' published in 1989 by the European Community (CCE, 1989). Nor is the initial task to compare elementary

forms of racism, such as harassment, stereotypes, discrimination or political racism in a certain number of countries, in order to prove that they are more or less similar, or that they follow a similar evolution. Rather the problem is primarily conceptual. If we want to test the idea of a certain unity of contemporary racism in Europe, we must elaborate sociological and historical hypotheses, and then apply them to the facts that we are able to collect. Thus the most difficult aspect of a comparative approach is not to find data, but to organize it with well-thought-out hypotheses.

My own hypotheses can be formulated in two different ways, one of which is relatively abstract and the other more concrete.

Racism and modernity

An initial formulation of the problematic, in effect, consists in the construction of a global argument enabling us to demonstrate that racism is inseparable from modernity, as the latter developed from European origins, and from its present crisis (Wieviorka, 1992a). Racism, both as a set of ideologies and specious scientific doctrines, and as a set of concrete manifestations of violence, humiliation and discrimination, really gathered momentum in the context of the immense changes of which Europe was the centre after the Renaissance. It developed further in modern times, with the huge migrations, the extension of trading relationships, the industrialization of Western society and colonization. But racism, in its links with modernity, cannot be reduced to a single logic, and even seems to correspond to processes which are sometimes so distinct that numerous demands are made for the discussion of racisms in the plural. This in fact gives rise to a debate the terms of which are badly posed. It is effectively possible to set up an integrated, global argument in which the various forms of racism, including anti-semitism, find their theoretical place, and which goes in the direction of a sociological, even anthropological, unity of racism. One can also consider each of these forms in its historical specificity, which goes in the opposite direction. Both approaches are legitimate and complementary, but since we are thinking here about the unity of contemporary forms of racism in Europe, it is clear that we should privilege the former. This leads us to distinguish four main lines of argument which cross the space of racism in its relation to modernity.

In the first instance, as the companion of modernity triumphant, racism is universalist, denouncing, crushing and despising different identities. Whence the apparition of inferior 'races' as an obstacle to the process of expansion, in particular colonial expansion, or destined to be exploited in the name of their supposed inferiority.

Next, linked to processes of downward social mobility, or exclusion, racism is the expression, as well as the refusal, of a situation in which the actor positively values modernity, but lives, or is afraid he/she will be exposed to a form of expulsion which will marginalize him/her. The actor then assumes a reflex or an attitude of 'poor white', particularly common in contexts of economic crises or of retraction from the labour market. Racism here is a perversion of a demand to participate in modernity and an opposition to the effective modalities of its functioning.

A third line of argument corresponds not to a positive valorization of modernity, the rise of which must be ensured, or from which one refuses to be excluded, but to appeals to identity or to tradition which are opposed to modernity. The nation, religion and the community then act as markers of identity, thus giving rise to a racism which attacks those who are assumed to be the vectors of a detested modernity. The Jews are often the incarnation of these vectors, as are, in some circumstances, those Asian minorities who are perceived as being particularly economically active. Finally, racism can correspond to anti- or non-modern positions, which are displayed not against groups incarnating modernity, but against groups defined themselves by an identity without any reference to modernity. It expresses, or is an extension of, intercultural, intercommunity, interethnic or similar tensions.

It is therefore possible to represent the space of racism around four cardinal points:

Modernity against identities

Identities against identities   Identities against modernity

Modernity against modernity

In a space of this type, the racist actors do not necessarily occupy one single position, and their speech and their behaviour are frequently syncretic and vary over time. There are even sometimes paradoxical mixtures of these various positions, when people, for instance, reproach a racialized group with symbolizing at the same time modernity and traditional values which they consider deny modernity: in the past, but also today, Jews, in many cases, fulfil this double function (Wieviorka, 1992b). They are hated in the name of their supposed identification with political power, money, the mass-media and a cosmopolitan internationalism, but also because of their difference, their visibility, their nationalism and support or belonging to the state of Israel, or because they flaunt their cultural traditions or their religion.

This theoretical construction of the space of racism may help us to answer our question. In effect, it enables us to read the European experience, and above all its recent evolution. The latter has long been dominated, on the one hand, by a racism of the universalist, colonial type and, on the other hand, by oppositions to modernity which have assumed the form of anti-Semitism; today, much more than previously, it is directed by the fear or reality of exclusion and downward social mobility, and on the other by tensions around identity and vague fears of which the most decisive concern the question of belonging to the nation.

Formation and restructuration of the European model of national societies

The argument outlined above can be completed by a much more concrete historical analysis of the recent evolution of most of the major western European countries. The latter, throughout this century, and up to the 1960s or 1970s, can be defined on the basis of a model which integrates three elements which are then weakened and destructured, reinvigorating the question of racism.

The era of integration

In most western European countries, racism, before the Second World War, was a spectacular and massive phenomenon, much more widespread than today. Colonial racism postulated the inferiority of colonized people of 'races', and modern anti-Semitism gave a new and active dimension to former anti-Judaïsm. This is why we must introduce a sense of relativity into our perceptions of contemporary racism. This is why we must also think in terms of periods, with the idea of a certain unity in time for the phenomenon that we are discussing. This idea means not that there is no continuity in racist doctrines, ideologies, prejudice or more concrete expressions, but that a new era in the history of racism began with the retreat, as Elazar Barkan (1992) says, of scientific racism, the end of decolonization, and, above all, the 'economic crisis' that has in fact meant the beginning of the decline of industrial societies.

Until that time, i.e. the 1960s and 1970s, most European countries had succeeded, to a greater or a lesser extent, depending on the country, in integrating three basic components of their collective life: *an industrial society, an egalitarian state* and *a national identity.*

Most European countries have been industrial societies: that is, they have had a set of social relations rooted in industrial labour and organization. From this point of view, they have been characterized by a structural conflict, which opposed the working-class movement and the masters of industry, but which extended far beyond workshops and factories. This conflict gave the middle classes a possibility to define themselves by either a positive or negative relationship towards the working-class movement. It brought to unemployed people the hope and sometimes the reality of being helped by this movement. It was also the source of important political debates dealing with the 'social question'. Furthermore, it influenced intellectual and cultural life profoundly, and acted as a point of reference for many actors, in the city, in universities, in religious movements and elsewhere.

European countries, and this is the second basic component of our model of analysis, have also been able to create and develop institutions which aimed at ensuring that egalitarian treatment was imparted to all citizens as individuals. The state has generally taken over various aspects of social welfare and security. It has become a welfare state. The state also introduced or defended a distance between religion and politics. Although countries such as Spain, Portugal and Greece have recently experienced dictatorial regimes, states in Europe have generally behaved, since the Second World War, as warrants for democracy.

Lastly, most European countries have given a central importance to their national identity. This identity has usually included two different aspects, sometimes contradictory, sometimes complementary. On one hand, the idea of a nation has corresponded to the assertion of a culture, a language, a historical past and traditions, with some tendencies to emphasize primordial ties and call for a biological definition loaded with racism, xenophobia and anti-Semitism. On the other hand, the nation has also been defined in a more positive way, as bound to the general progress of mankind and to universal values that could be defined in economic, political or ethical terms. In this last perspective, a nation is related to reason, progress, democracy of human rights.

Industrial society, state and *nation*: these three basic elements have never been consonant with their highest theoretical image. One can easily show the weakness of the working-class movement in some countries, or its constant subordination to political forces, the limits of the welfare state everywhere in the past, and the domination of the reactionary and xenophobic aspects of nationalism in many circumstances. Moreover, some European countries have defined themselves as bi- or plurinational. But since we recognize these limits, and since we recognize many differences between countries, we can admit, without the danger of creating a myth, that our three basic elements are typical of European countries until the 1960s and 1970s. Not only have they characterized three countries, but they have also been relatively strongly articulated, so much so that various terms are used to express this articulation: for instance, integration, nation-state and national society. We must be very cautious and avoid developing the artificial or mythical image of countries perfectly suited to the triple and integrated figure of an industrial society, a two-dimensional nation and a modern and egalitarian state. But our representation of the past is useful in considering the evolution of the last twenty or thirty years, an evolution which is no doubt dominated by the growing weakness and dissociation of our three basic elements.

The era of destructuration

All European countries are experiencing today a huge transformation which affects the three components of our reflection, and defines what I have called, in the case of France, '*une grande mutation*' (Wieviorka, 1992c).

Industrial societies are living their historical decline, and this phenomenon should not be reduced to the spectacular closing of workshops and factories. More important in our perspective is the decay of the working-class movement as a social movement. In the past, the working-class movement was, to various degrees, capable of incorporating in a single action collective behaviour corresponding to three major levels. There could be limited demands, struggles based on the professional defence of political demands, dealt with by the institutional system, and, at the highest level of its project, orientations challenging the control and the direction of progress and of industry. These orientations are quite out of place today: the working-class movement is breaking up, and this decomposition produces various effects (Touraine *et al.*, 1987). Among workers, there is a strengthening of tendencies towards corporatism and selfishness – those workers who still have a certain capacity of action, because of their skill or their strategic position in their firm, develop struggles in the name of their own interests, and not in the name of more general or universal ones.

Sometimes workers' demands can no longer be taken up by the trade unions, which have been considerably weakened. This can result in violent forms of behaviour, or in spontaneous forms of organization, such as the recent 'co-ordinations' in France, which are easily infiltrated by extremist ideologies.

In such a context, the middle classes no longer have to define themselves by reference to class conflicts, and they tend to oscillate between, on the one hand, unrestrained individualism and, on the other, populism or national-populism, the latter being particularly strong among those who experience downward mobility or social exclusion. These two distinct phenomena are closely related to social and economic dualization. In the past, most people could have a strong feeling of belonging to a society, 'down' as workers, or 'up' as éites or middle classes. Today, a good number of people are 'in', and constitute a large middle class, including those workers who have access to jobs, consumption, health or education for their children, while a growing proportion of people are 'out', excluded and marginalized.

Such an evolution may lead to renewed expressions of racism. Those who are 'out', or fear to be, have a feeling of injustice and loss of previous social identity. They think the government and the politicians are responsible for their situation, and may develop populist discourses and attitudes in which anti-migrant or ethnic minorities racism can take place. They then impute their misfortune to migrants, even if these migrants share the same experience. And those who are 'in' may develop more subtle forms of racism, trying to secure themselves with a colour bar or by individual or collective behaviours that create social and racial segregation and build symbolic but also real barriers. Furthermore, the logic of segregation, particularly at the political level, is always likely to become indistinguishable from a national and populist form of discourse which amalgamates the fears, anger and frustrations of the excluded and the social self-centredness of those who wish to defend their status and their way of life. This merging therefore gives a result which is only paradoxical in appearance, since it results in an identical form of racism in those people who have experienced living with, or close to, immigrants or similar categories of people, and in those who have not actually done so, but who have heard about it through the mass-media or from rumours.

A second element of destructuration deals with the state and public institutions, which encounter increasing difficulties in trying to respect egalitarian principles, or in acting as welfare states. Everywhere in Europe, the number of unemployed people has grown, creating not only a great many personal dramas, but also a fiscal crisis of the state. The problems of financing old-age pensions, the health care system, state education and unemployment benefits are becoming increasingly acute, while at the same time there is a rising feeling of insecurity which is attributed, once again, to immigrants. The latter are then perceived in racist terms, accused not only of taking advantage of social institutions and using them to their own ends, but also of benefiting from too much attention from the state. At the same time, the ruling classes have been tempted since the 1970s by liberal policies which in fact ratify and reinforce exclusion and marginalization.

The crisis of the state and the institutions is a phenomena which must be analytically distinguished from the decline of industrial society and the dualization which results from its decline. But the two phenomena are linked. Just as the welfare state owes a great deal, in its formation, to the social and political discussions which are inseparable from the history of the working class, which is particularly clear in the countries endowed with strong social democracy, so too the crisis of the welfare state and the institutions owes a great deal to the destructuration not only of these discussions and conflicts, but also of the principal actor which informed them, the working-class movement.

A third aspect of the recent evolution concerns the national issue, which becomes nodal – all the more so as social issues are not politically treated as such. In most European countries, political debates about nation, nationality and citizenship are activated. In such a context, nationalism loses its open and progressive dimensions, and its relationship with universal values, and is less and less linked with ideas such as progress, reason or democracy. National identity is increasingly loaded with xenophobia and racism. This tendency gains impetus with the emergence or growth of other identities among groups that are defined, or that define themselves, as communities, whether religious, ethnic, national or regional. There is a kind of spiral, a dialectic of identities, in which each affirmation of a specific identity involves other communitarian affirmations among other groups. Nationalism and, more generally speaking, communal identities do not necessarily mean racism. But as Etienne Balibar explains, racism is always a virtuality (Balibar and Wallerstein, 1988).

This virtuality is not nurtured uniquely by the presence, at times exaggerated and fantasized, of a more or less visible immigration. It also owes a considerable amount to phenomena which may even have nothing to do with it. Thus national identity is reinforced in its most alarming aspects when national culture appears to be threatened by the superficial and hypermodern character of an international culture which originates primarily in America, by the political construction of Europe or, again, by the globalization of the economy.

At the same time, it becomes more and more difficult to assert that society, state and nation form an integrated whole. Those who call for universal values, human rights and equality, who believe that each individual should have equal opportunities to work, make money and then participate fully in cultural and political life – in other words, those who identity themselves with modernity – are less and less able to meet and even to understand those who have the feeling of being excluded from modern life, who fear for their participation in economic, cultural and political life, and who retire within their national identity. In extreme cases, social and economic participation are no longer linked with the feeling of belonging to a nation, the latter being what remains when the former becomes impossible. Reason, progress and development become divorced from nation, identity and subjectivity, and in this split, racism may easily develop.

In the past, industrial society often offered workers disastrous conditions of work and existence. But the working-class movement, as well as the rulers of industry, believed in progress and reason, and while they were opposed in a structural conflict, this was precisely because they both valorized the idea of progress through industrial production, and both claimed that they should direct it. The nation, and its state, as Ernest Gellner explains (1983) were supposed to be the best frame for modernization, and sometimes the state not only brought favourable conditions, but also claimed to be the main agent of development. Nationalism could be the ideology linked to that perspective, and not only a reactionary or traditionalist force. Today, waters divide. Nationalism is mainly expressed by social and political groups frightened by the internationalization of the economy and culture. It is increasingly differentialist, and racism develops as social problems such as exclusion and downward mobility grow, and as anxiety develops in regard to national identity.

The categories of the sociological analysis of racism

The argument outlined above is historical and sociologial in nature, but a closer examination of the contemporary phenomena of racism requires explicitness in the instruments and, therefore, the categories of analysis of racism properly speaking (Wieviorka, 1991).

The two logics of racism

Contemporary sociological literature increasingly insists on the idea of changing forms of racism. Some scholars, relying on American studies, oppose the old 'flagrant' racism to the 'subtle' new versions (Pettigrew, 1993). Others emphasize a crucial distinction, which could, in an extreme interpretation, lead to the idea of two distinct kinds of racism. Following authors such as Martin Barker or Pierre-André Taguieff, we should distinguish between a classical, inegalitarian racism and a new, differentialist one (Barker, 1981; Taguieff, 1988). The first kind considers the Other as an inferior being, who may find a place in society, but the lowest one. There is room for inferior people in this perspective, as long as they can be exploited and relegated to unpleasant and badly paid tasks. The second kind considers the Other as fundamentally different, which means that he/she has no place in society, that he/she is a danger, an invader, who should be kept at some distance, expelled or possibly destroyed. The point is that for many scholars the new racism, sometimes also referred to as cultural racism, is the main one in the contemporary world, while the inegalitarian one becomes secondary.

As long as this remark is intended as a statement of historical fact, based on the observation of empirical realities of present-day racism, it is acceptable. But it must not take the place of a general theory of racism. First, cultural or differentialist perspectives in racism are not new. It is difficult to speak of Nazism, for instance, without introducing the idea that anti-Semitism in the Third Reich was deeply informed by these perspectives. Jews were said to corrupt Aryan culture and race, and the 'final solution' planned not to assign them to the lowest place in society, but to destroy them. Second, the opposition between the two main logics of racism should not conceal the main fact, which is that a purely cultural definition of the Other, as well as a purely social one, dissolves the idea of race. On one hand, Claude Levi-Strauss is not a racist when he emphasizes cultural differentiation. One is a racist only when there is any reference to race in a cultural opposition, when beneath culture we can, explicitly or implicitly, find nature: that is, in an organicist or genetic representation of the Other as well as oneself. On the other hand, when the Other is defined only as socially inferior, exploited or marginalized, the reference to race may disappear or become, as William J. Wilson suggests (1978), less significant.

In fact, in most experiences of racism, the two logics coexist, and racism appears as a combination of them both. There are not two racisms, but one, with various versions of the association of cultural differentialism and social inegalitarianism. The general analysis that has been presented for contemporary Europe helps us to refuse the idea of a pure, cultural racism, corresponding to a new paradigm that would have taken the place of an old one. The sources of European contemporary racism, as I have suggested, are in the crisis of national identities and in the dualization of societies, which favour a differentialist logic. But the are also connected with phenomena of downward social mobility and economic crisis, which lead to populism and exasperation and have an important dimension in appeals for an unequal treatment of migrants.

Two main levels

As I have indicated in a recent book (Wieviorka, 1991), we may distinguish four levels in racism. The way that experiences of racism are articulated at the different levels where they act may change with their historical evolution. Our distinction is analytical, and should help us as a sociological tool.

A first level refers to weak and inarticulated forms of racism, whatever they may consist of: opinions and prejudice, which are more xenophobic and populist than, strictly speaking, racist; and diffuse violence, limited expression of institutional discrimination or diffusion of racial doctrines, etc. At this first level, racism is not a central issue and it is so limited, quantitatively and qualitatively, that I have chosen to use the term *infraracism* to characterize it.

We may speak of *split racism* at a second level, in reference to forms of racism which are still weak and inarticulate, but stronger and more obvious. At this stage, racism becomes a central issue, but does not give the image of a unified and integrated phenomenon, mainly because of the lack of a strong political expression.

We may speak of *political racism*, precisely, when political and intellectual debates and real political forces bring a dual principle of unity to the phenomenon. On one hand, they give it an ideological structure, so that all its expressions seem to converge and define a unique set of problems; on the other hand, they offer it practical forms of organization.

At the fourth level, we may call *total racism* those situations in which the state itself is based on racist principles. There is nowadays no real threat of total racism in our countries, and we may now simplify the distinction into four levels of racism by reducing them to two main ones, the *infrapolitical* level, including infra and split racisms, and the *political* one.

We can now come back to our general analysis of European contemporary racism and be more precise. This rise of the phenomenon, following what was previously said, is due to the evolution of three basic elements, and to their destructuration. We may add that it appears first at an infrapolitical level, and that it then ascends to the political level, with variations from one country to another.

In certain cases, a rather important political party appears and develops quickly, as in France with the *Front National*. In other cases, such a party appears but quickly declines, which means not that racism necessarily stays at the infrapolitical level, but that it informs political debates without being the flag of one precise strong organization – this could define the English experience. But above all, the analytical distinction into levels enables us to introduce a central question: is there not throughout Europe the same danger of seeing political actors capable of taking over and of directing infrapolitical racism?

On the one hand, we observe in several countries the growing influence of racist ideologies, but also of political organizations which are no longer small groups of activists and which may occupy an important space in political life. The French *Front National* appears as a leader in Europe, and sometimes as a model, but other parties or movements should be quoted too: the *Deutsche Volksunion* and the *Demokratische Partei Deutschlands* in Germany; the FPO in Austria, which gained 22.6 per cent of the votes in the November 1991 elections in Vienna; the *Vlaams Blok* in Flanders, with twelve members of Parliament since November 1991; and the Italian Leagues.

One must be careful, however, not to exaggerate. The more extreme-right parties occupy an important place, the more they appear as populist rather than purely racist. Racism, strictly speaking, is only one element, and sometimes a minor one, along with strong nationalism or regionalism. Moreover, political and electoral successes force these parties to look respectable, and avoid overtly flagrant expressions of racism.

On the other hand, racism appears in non-political contexts, when prejudice and hostile attitudes to migrants develop, when social and racial segregation is increasingly visible (which is the case in France, where the issue of racism is constantly related to the so-called urban crisis and 'the suburban problem'), when violent actions develop, sometimes with a terrorist aspect, when various institutions including the police have a responsibility for its growth, when discrimination is obvious (for instance, in relation to housing or employment), and when the media contributes to the extension of prejudice. In such a perspective, all the European democracies have to face the same problem. There is a growing opportunity for extreme-right forces to capitalize on fears, frustrations, unsatisfied social demands and feelings of threat to national identity. Even worse, there is a danger that these forces will introduce new elements into infrapolitical racism. This is the case in France, for instance, where popular racism is strongly hostile to migrants, to black people and to gypsies, rather than to Jews, and where the *Front National* tries constantly to instill anti-Semitism.

More generally, there is still a real distance between infrapolitical and political racism, and this means that racism is not so much a widely extended ideology offering people a general framework in which to interpret their own lives and personal experiences, but rather a set of prejudices and practices that are rooted in these concrete lives and experiences, and which could possibly evolve.

In the present state of things, the development is dominated by a process of populist fusion in which popular affects and political discourse converge, but which, paradoxically, protects our societies from extreme and large-scale racist episodes. However, populism is never a stable phenomenon and is always potentially open to more frightening processes.

The diversity of European racist experiences

In contemporary Europe, our general analysis does not apply everywhere in the same way. Many factors intervene, which do not invalidate our global hypothesis, but which oblige us to introduce much more diversified images.

Some are related to the social history of each country, to its industrialization, or to the making of its working-class movement.

Some are related to its political history, to the making of its state, institutions and political system, and, possibly, to its dictatorial or totalitarian recent past. Some also deal with the specificity of its culture and national identity, and with its international past. Countries that have experience colonization and decolonization, or that have to face domestic tensions due to what many nationalist actors and intellectuals have called 'internal colonialism' differ between themselves, and from countries that are not concerned with these issues. For many years, some European countries have experienced the presence of migrants who have been attracted by agriculture and industry, or who came for other reasons, including political ones. Others, like Italy, are only now discovering this phenomenon.

The list of factors of this kind could certainly be extended, but the most important thing is to see that they each affect at least one of the three basic elements of our global analysis. The latter insists on the twofold idea of a process in which, in the first place, industrial society breaks down, the egalitarian state enters into crisis and the nation becomes paralysed in differentialist and defensive terms; and in which, secondly, these three elements are increasingly dissociated. The pattern of this process of destructuration and dissociation depends on the various capacities of resistance to decline or crisis of each basic element, and consequently on the various factors listed above.

In Germany, for instance, industrial society adapted to the change more efficiently than elsewhere. Trade unions, and mainly the DGB, maintain a much higher capacity for action and bargaining than most of their counterparts in the world. Before the fall of the Berlin Wall, West Germany had a state and a political system which seemed less affected by the crisis than other countries, and it is only recently, with the huge price of the reunification with East Germany, that fiscal and political problems developed and took on acute forms. At the same time, the third element of our general analysis, the national issue, appears as a crucial topic. Racist and neo-Nazi violence, and the extension of skinhead groups, express primarily symbolic and concrete difficulties in implementing national unification, and are particularly important in the former East Germany, where immense social tensions and fears for the future are interpreted within the category of nation. The centrality of this issue is also important in Austria. In these two countries, the experience of the 1930s and 1940s informs present political debates, and references to a national culture and identity are so significant that theoretical priority should be given to the national issue. The strength of popular and political anti-Semitism in these countries reinforces this point; it strongly supports the hypothesis of anti-modern attitudes linked to a traditional nationalism, or to its revival due to the economic crises that transform social demands into nationalist and racist attitudes.

In Italy, to introduce a different case, the decline of industrial society and the crises of trade unions are obvious, but they do not constitute the main problem. In this country, national unification came late, and localism or regionalism are strong, but they do not constitute the heart of the problem. Analysing the emergence of racism in Italy, interest must focus on the crisis of the state, of institutions and of the political system, which is expressed by the recent electoral successes of the Leagues in the northern part of the country, by the incapacity of the state to deal with the mafia, and by the renewal of debates concerning the *mezzogiorno*. Italy has long been a country of emigration, and is just discovering that it has now become a country of immigration. The first expressions of racism should not be overestimated. The Leagues are much more populist than racist, and concrete discrimination and acts of violence are not so frequent. When they appear, they express a will for the economic inferiorization of black or Arab migrants; they are not strongly linked to a cultural and differentialist affirmation. The possible extension of the racist phenomenon, at least at the political and ideological level, should be analysed in terms of the crisis of the state and the political system. This implies paying special attention to intellectual and political actors, who in Italy sometimes have a paradoxical role: by importing, mainly from France, the issue of anti-racism in a context of weak forms or racism, and by developing the image of a differentialist racism. While the main popular expressions are inegalitarian, they are perhaps creating a self-fulfilling prophecy.

In other countries such as France, Belgium or the United Kingdom, there is a temptation to use as a starting point for analysis the decay of industrial society and the decline of the working-class movement, one consequence of this being that migrants are defined less as workers and more as members of religious or ethnic communities, even if the very existence of these communities may be overestimated. But French, Belgian and British experiences deserve in fact an analysis that is directly three-dimensional and that gives equal importance to the decomposition of industrial society, to the crises of the state and institutions, and to the national issue. Let us add that, at least in the Belgian and British cases, the unit for analysis of racism should not be the whole country, but smaller entities, so that differences between, for instance, Scotland and England, or Flanders

and Wallony could be seriously taken into account: English nationalism, for example, is much closer to xenophobia and racism than
Scottish nationalism.

There are therefore considerable differences between countries,
but these do not fundamentally challenge our global analysis. Each
national experience must be approached in its three-dimensionality,
even if, depending on the country, it is better at the outset to focus
thinking on only one or other of the three basic elements in our
argument. In any event, it is effectively the image of the dissociation
of these three elements – society, the state and the nation – which is
the origin of the spread of racism.

References

Balibar Etienne, and Wallerstein, Immanuel (1988) *Race, classe, nation*, Paris: La
  Découverte.
Barkan, Elazar (1992) *The Retreat of Scientific Racism*, Cambridge: Cambridge Uni-
  versity Press.
Barker, Martin (1981) *The New Racism*, London: Junction Books.
CCE (1989) *Eurobaromètre: L'opinion publique dans la Communauté Européenne*,
  Brussels: Commission des Communautés Européennes.
Gellner, Ernest (1983) *Nations and Nationalism*, Oxford: Blackwell.
Pettigrew, Thomas, and Meertens R. F. (1993) 'Le racisme voilé: composants et
  mesure', in *Racisme et Modernité* (under the direction of M. Wieviorka), Paris:
  La Découverte.
Taguieff, Pierre-André (1988) *La force du préjugé*, Paris: La Découverte.
Touraine, Alain, Wieviorka, Michel, and Dubet François (1987) *The Working Class
  Movement*, Cambridge: Cambridge University Press.
Wieviorka, Michel (1991) *L'espace du racisme*, Paris: Seuil.
Wieviorka, Michel (1992a) 'Racism and modernity', paper presented at the Con-
  gress of the American Sociological Association, Pittsburgh.
Wieviorka, Michel (1992b) 'Analyse sociologique et historique de l'antésimitisme
  en Pologne', *Cahiers Internationaux de Sociologie*, vol. 93, pp. 237–49.
Wieviorka, Michel (ed.) (1992c) *La France raciste*, Paris: Seuil.
Wilson, William J. (1978) *The Declining Significance of Race*, Chicago: University of
  Chicago Press.

6

EXPLAINING RACISM IN CONTEMPORARY EUROPE

Robert Miles

Introduction

Much of the recent British discussion about the relationship between the restructing of Europe and the expression of racism has a predominantly negative tone. On the left, the view that the Single European Act will create a 'Fortress Europe' is hegemonic, and carries the implication that European integration should be opposed because it is reinforcing the expression of racism. There is truth in these arguments, but there is also mystification because of a failure to comprehend the contradictory nature of the process. In order to join those seeking to demystify the debate (Dummett, 1991), but with a different emphasis (cf. Blackburn, 1992, pp.28–35), it is proposed here that the contemporary conjuncture provides us with an opportunity to reassess the explanations that have been offered for the expression of racism. When we extend the parameters of our analysis beyond the boundary of the nation-state in which it was formulated, we find that it carries the imprint of a nationalized history, an imprint that may obscure the specificities of historical development in other European nation-states (Bovenkerk et al., 1990).

Looking for 'race' in Europe

It has become common for British sociologists and anti-racist activists to claim that 'race' should now be analysed in a European context

(e.g. Allen and Macey, 1990). The immediate stimulus to this escalat-
ing interest in developing a 'European perspective' on 'race' is the
Single European Act, implemented on 1 January 1993 (e.g. Gordon,
1989; Ardittis, 1990): some writers have concluded that it signals the
creation of a new Euro-racism (Sivanandan, 1990a, pp. 153–60). While
agreeing that the Act marks an important transition in the historical
development of capitalism, and in the relationship between capitalism
and the nation-state in Europe, I have expressed elsewhere (Miles,
1992a, 1992b) some reservations about this interpretation. I amplify
these reservations here by contesting the arguments of those who
now seek to analyse 'race' in a European context.

The need to generate a European perspective on racism provides
further reasons why it is erroneous to reify 'race' as an analytical
concept (cf. Miles, 1982, 1993). As British attention shifts away from
the USA and South Africa as comparators, Europe should not be
interpreted as a new context within which to revive the sociology of
'race relations'; rather, the development of a comparative analysis
of racism in Europe highlights the poverty and insularity of the British
sociology of 'race relations'. Hence, the objective should be to analyse
the evolving transformation and re-creation of Europe in order to
further the demise of the 'race relations' problematic (for a recent
attempt at revival, see Banton, 1991).

I am conscious of travelling a familiar and well-worn road, or revisit-
ing a site where many have previously paid their respects. Once again,
it is necessary to reconsider the meaning and significance of the idea
of 'race'. This is because some seem to have not yet made the
journey: for example, Allen and Macey claim fallaciously that British
sociologists have 'hardly begun' the task of 'problematising and the-
orising public discourses on race and ethnic relations' (1990, p.376).
They ignore a decade's productive analysis (e.g. Miles, 1982, 1984,
1989; Fields, 1982, 1990; Cohen, 1988; Goldberg, 1990). Moreover,
those acquainted with the French literature will know that similar
arguments predate this Britain and American work by another decade
(e.g. Guillaumin, 1972a, 1972b, 1980, 1988). Others have been there
too, although they have drawn different conclusions (CCCS, 1982;
Gilroy, 1987) about the implications of their critical evaluations of
public discourse.

In the first instance, the issue concerns the epistemological status
of the idea of 'race'. The fact that the idea of 'race' has no biological
object in the sense defined by nineteen-century science is broadly
accepted by most sociologists. Nevertheless, there are exceptions.
For example, in a recent paper published in a leading international

sociological journal, a social scientist proposed that the *only* appropriate use of the notion of 'race' is to refer to 'humans who share genetically inherited features based on long periods of in-breeding' (Riggs, 1991, p. 444). This is a reminder of the persistence even within the social sciences of use of the idea of 'race' to refer to a presumed biological reality, and therefore of the need for conceptual rigour.

Certainly, the idea of 'race' is woven into everyday understandings and legislation, and into practices of resistance, in the UK in such a way that the belief that there really are distinct 'races' is sustained. Does it follow that this everyday reality should be captured by and encapsulated in a sociology of 'race relations', that the idea of 'race' should be accorded the status of an analytical concept? I have argued elsewhere that the answer to this question should be a negative (Miles, 1982, 1984, 1993). Here, I augment these arguments.

In the UK, the political consequences of New Commonwealth migration are widely understood through the ideological prism of the idea of 'race'. In commonsense terms, 'coloured immigration' is thought to have brought to the UK a 'race problem'. One solution has been to improve social relations between the 'races' by legislation in the form of the Race Relations Acts, which have sought to reduce 'racial discrimination' and promote 'equal opportunity'. As a result, 'race' is defined as a political issue: political parties formulate and advocate policies on 'race', and politicians can choose or refuse to play the 'race' card. In these and other ways, the ideological notion of 'race' is embedded in the British political process and political culture, giving specific meaning to the apparently general problems of 'law and order', 'immigration', 'mugging', etc.

With the recent *re-creation* of a European political space (for there is nothing new about the idea of Europe), British political parties and activitists have endeavoured to occupy that space, and define issues within it. Sections of the left have demanded that there should be a 'race' perspective, a 'race' politics, within Europe. This is commonly legitimated by the claim that the UK is the only nation-state within the European Community (EC) with 'race' legislation, i.e. the three Race Relations Acts and the Public Order legislation. Although there are well-founded doubts about the effectiveness of the legislation in achieving its objectives (e.g. Jenkins and Solomos, 1989), it is nevertheless argued that it has at least an important symbolic value in reinforcing the principle of 'equality' or 'equal opportunity'. The conclusion is that the EC and the European Parliament should devise and implement legislation on 'race' which embodies at least the most positive attributes of British legislation.

Factually, the claim is, at best, a half-truth. Much depends upon what is meant by 'within the European Community'. There are two bodies of specifically (supranational) European law which exist alongside, and partly above, the law of the individual nation states which constitute the EC. Concerning European law, it is true that there are few or no specific provisions concerning racialized discrimination in, for example, the European Convention on Human Rights and in the legislation and directives of the EC (Dummett, 1991; Lester, 1992). But the situation is more complicated when one examines the law of individual nation-states. In Germany, Belgium, France and the Netherlands, there are either constitutional principles or individual laws which either declare opposition to racism and racialized exclusion or make racist discourses and actions illegal, or which state the principle of equality of treatment (Costa-Lascoux, 1991; Lloyd, 1991, pp. 69–70).

Furthermore, advocates of the view that Europe needs a 'race' perspective fail to comprehend the variation in the manner in which the political process has been signified as a result of the articulation of racism. Within Europe, the political process has been racialized in different ways and with different consequences. In Germany, the last person to agitate in favour of a 'race' perspective was Adolf Hitler. The attempt by the Nazi regime thoroughly to racialize the German social formation in the 1930s (see Burleigh and Wipperman, 1991) has ensured, since the defeat of fascism, that *any* attempt to use the discourse of 'race' is suffused with the meanings instilled and legitimated by fascism. In the public domain, any use of the idea of 'race' is therefore illegitimate. This is despite the fact that belief in the existence of biological 'races' (in the form of the triadic differentiation of the human population into three 'races': Caucasian, Negroid and Mongoloid) is part of everyday common sense. It is also widely believed that all those resident in Germany are 'of the same Caucasian race'. Hence, for potentially contradictory reasons, a proposal to formulate legislation to regulate relations between 'races' would receive little support in Germany.

Since 1945, the ideological complex which has been constituted around immigration, and its political consequences, has differed from one nation-state to another. But with the exception of the UK, the content of the ideological response, from both above and below, to large-scale labour migration has not pivoted on the discourse of 'race'. In France, the political debate has been organized by the ideas of *immigrées*, *étrangers*, *nationalité* and *citoyenneté*. In the Netherlands, the political debate has centred around the notions of *minderheid* and *immigratie*. And, in Germany, the key concepts have been *Gastarbeiter* and *Ausländer*. These distinctions are not absolute: notions of 'race', of 'ethnic minority', etc. sometimes appear, explicitly and implicitly, in each of these nationally distinct cultural complexes, but they are constituted and contextualized in different ways, occupying a particular place and having a specific meaning within a distinct hierarchy of elements. As a result, it is difficult to translate each of these national discourses directly into the terms of another because the meaning of even the apparently common elements is structured in part by the place they occupy in the nationalized ensemble.

This is not a matter of superficially different discourses referring in fact to 'the same thing'. Rather, what these diverse discourses reveal (or perhaps refract) are the different ideological mechanisms, the disparate political structures and institutions, which have coalesced in the course of the constitution of social formations as distinct *nation*-states, each of which has its own internal historical and cultural dynamic (e.g. Lloyd, 1991, p. 64) that is not reducible to the mode of production. There are differences not only in the way in which each nation is imagined, but also in the way in which each has been constructed concretely, materially, in law and in institutions, in the process of government. Especially relevant in this context is the way in which this is refracted in differences in law on nationality and citizenship. In Germany, citizenship has become based exclusively upon biological descent, reflecting the dominance of an essentialist, ethnocultural conception of the nation, and the evolution of a specific state strategy intended to ensure the structural marginalization of immigrant populations. By comparison, in France, the values of universalism and rationalism have become allied with that of assimilation, with the result that citizenship is allocated by the state primarily on the basis of the principle of *jus soli* (e.g. Noiriel, 1988; Hailbronner, 1989; Räthzel, 1990; Brubaker, 1990).

Yet, at another level of abstraction, there is a sense in which the process and the institutions are the same: the bourgeois nation-state within western Europe constitutes a specific historical and politico-spatial form, and all instances therefore share a set of common features. For example, each nation-state has a set of criteria to determine 'belonging', to define the conditions of membership of the nation: each has criteria by which the state assigns to individuals the attribute of nationality and the rights and obligations of citizenship. But the phenomenal forms in which these 'universal' categories appear differ, reflecting the reality of distinct processes of nationalization.

The analytical problem is as follows: can one analyse comparatively these distinct realities using a conceptual language derived from the phenomenal, commonsense understandings that have been generated in a single nation-state? Those who demand a 'race' perspective on Europe assume that the answer is affirmative. I disagree: such a perspective not only reifies the idea of 'race', but also overrides the distinction between essential relations and the phenomenal form, thereby obscuring the specific ideological content of the political process in each European social formation. These differences have real consequences, as comparison of the consequences of French an German law on nationality and citizenship demonstrates.

The significances of recognizing the specificity of the nationaliz-ation process can be demonstrated in another way. Sivanandan claimed that in the mid–1980s there had been a 'degradation of the black struggle' in Britain (1990a, pp. 77–122): he argued that the ideological category of 'black' no longer signified the existence of a coherent community organized in and through struggle against racism and capitalism. One of the symptoms of this decline was the bifurcation of 'black struggle' into distinct Asian and Afro-Caribbean ethnic struggles. We might now add that the coherence of the Asian struggle is in doubt in the light of the heightened significance of an Islamic identity following the 'Rushdie Affair'. While the collapse of the 'black' struggle in Britain is a fact, the explanation can be contested from different directions: other writers have suggested that the distinct histories and cultures of British citizens of Afro-Caribbean and South Asian origin (Gilroy, 1987, p. 39; Modood, 1988; James, 1989, 1992; Eade, 1990) are at least as important as any 'divide and rule' strategy implemented by the state (Sivanandan 1990a, p. 85).

Whatever the explanation, it is clear that the idea of 'black' denotes a particular, rather than a universal, political perspective and strategy of resistance. It is spatially, culturally and historically specific. Its origin lies in part with the struggle for equality on the part of those citizens of the Untied States who trace their cultural and spatial origins, via a history of exploitation as a source of unfree labour, to Africa. It is also to be found in anti-colonial struggles in Africa, where ideas of blackness and négritude have been central (see, for example, the work of Fanon). The specificity of the category 'black' is overdet-ermined by the fact that it was forged to resist a specific racist dis-course and imagery which linked notions such as slave, 'Negro' and African with the ideology of 'race'. The radical category of 'black', by inverting and resignifying the racist discourse in a different evaluative framework, nevertheless reproduced elements of that discourse and thereby reinforced a particular cultural history and tradition. Those racialized Others in Europe who can successfully imagine another, non-African tradition or origin may find little that is meaningful in the celebration of the history of slavery, albeit a celebration that highlights the resistance to it. Indeed, those Others may ally themselves with racist discourses which draw on this history in order to distance themselves from those who label themselves as 'blacks'.

Attempts to universalize the category 'black' have achieved a certain success. In England during the 1970s and 1980s, it became a matter of common sense within radical circles that 'blackness' was not a reference to skin colour *per se*, but was rather an expression of a common experience of exclusion and of a common political identity forged through resistance to that exclusion (Brah, 1992, pp. 127–31). In such instances, 'black' becomes a metaphor. That the significance of the metaphor is conjuncturally specific is suggested by the fact that there are other identities and cultural traditions available to those who feel and who are excluded by racism (Modood, 1988; Eade, 1990), identities and traditions which have come to coexist with (but which often override) a 'black' identity since the mid–1980s.

The specificity of 'blackness' as a symbol and site of resistance is also revealed by the adoption of a European perspective. Where there are people who can trace their origin back to Africa, as there are in France, Germany and the Netherlands, then it can have significance. For example, in the light of the history of French colonialism in Africa and in the Caribbean, there are French citizens who can and do claim an African heritage and tradition. But Africa is a large continent, with different cultural histories. And there are large parts of North and West Africa where there has been a link between histories of resistance to colonialism and Islam, or where postcolonial politics have taken a form where Islam has become a symbol of resistance to anti-democratic and semi-feudal domination. In contemporary France (e.g. Leveau and Kepel,1988; Hargreaves, 1991; Wihtol de Wenden, 1991, 1992), either the category of Islam, or symbols alluding to an identity with the Maghreb (including the example of *les beurs*), have greater potential to supply meaningful signs of resistance for such people than those of *noir* and *nègritude*. Indeed, in the light of the French tradition of *assimilation* and of the contradictions entailed in stressing differences (e.g. Taguieff, 1987), some French political movements seek to highlight the extent to which the 'second generation' of migrants are already 'integrated' into French society (e.g. France-Plus).

The point is also illustrated by Germany, where people of Turkish nationality constitute the largest proportion of *Ausländer*: they have considerable difficulty in imagining their origin as being in Africa. And, while there are some 200,000 'black' German nationals, the extent to which they use the discourse of 'blackness' to organize themselves politically is not clear. Such organization as does occur in an expression of a specific experience of exclusion (one which *is* directly comparable to the British situation, at least in so far as those concerned are nationals and citizens), but it does not provide an immediate point of contact with either the cultural history of the politico-legal situation of the 4 million foreigners who are permanently resident in Germany.

In the light of this evidence, the argument can be expressed in another way. During the 1980s, some have proposed the retention of 'race' as an analytical category in order to recognize a particular mode of political and cultural resistance. As a result, the concept of 'racial formation' has become influential because it draws attention to the fact that the idea of 'race' can function as a site of mobilization against racist exclusionary practices (Omi and Winant, 1986; Gilroy, 1987; Small 1991). The concept of racialization can also be used to comprehend this process (Miles, 1989), but that is a secondary issue here. For the sake of argument, let us accept that the idea of 'racial formation' can have as its object 'the release of political forces which define themselves and organize around notions of "race"' (Gilroy, 1987, p. 38). Ideas of contingency, struggle and transformation are central to this concept. Logically, advocates of this position can therefore be expected to accept that it is an open question as to whether the multitude of 'minorities' in Europe choose to resist their position and experience of subordination by means of the idea of 'race'. Just as its limits are becoming increasingly apparent in the UK, an in-depth evaluation of the European situation will serve to reinforce the conclusion that it is a culturally specific, and politically limited, mode of organization and resistance.

But my disagreement with the imposition of a 'race' perspective on Europe is not dependent upon the meanings of discourses alone. Discourses are embedded in historically constituted social structures and social relations, from which they derive their meaning. There is one dimension of these structures and relations which warrants attention here. A large number, but far from all (Kay and Miles, 1992), post–1950 migrants to Britain arrived as British subjects, albeit British subjects of colonial origin, an origin that was, at best, regarded as 'second class'. This was to be confirmed by the simultaneous narrowing and widening of the category of British nationality by a succession of immigration and nationality Acts from 1962 onwards, which reinforced 'whiteness' as a central symbol of Britishness (e.g. Miles and Phizacklea, 1984). Yet, while many millions of British subjects elsewhere in the world found themselves deprived of this status, those who arrived before 1962 (along with, for example, many hundreds of thousands of family members who entered later) were legally included within the boundary of the British nation as nationals and citizens. A struggle against racism began simultaneously with their arrival: they were aided in that struggle by the fact that, as British subjects, they had full and equal rights of political participation.

This makes the 'British case' specific, at least relatively speaking. Certain migrations to other European nation-states parallel those from the Caribbean and the Indian sub-continent to Britain: for example, until 1975, the population of Surinam were Dutch nationals and citizens (NSCGP, 1979, p. 51), while between 1947 and 1962, the population of Algeria possessed French nationality and citizenship (Adler, 1977, pp. 60, 72–5). Consequently, on arrival in the Netherlands and France respectively, Surinamese and Algerian migrants could exercise the same rights as the already resident population. But the majority of migrants to western Europe since 1945 have been, juridically speaking, 'foreigners', who thereby possess comparatively limited and qualified rights of political participation and representation (Hammer, 1985; Layton-Henry, 1990). Their contemporary exclusion and position of inequality may be motivated and effected in part by racism, but it is overdetermined by the mediation of the legal category of nationality, which expresses their legal status as 'foreigners'. The contemporary struggle around the 'immigrant presence' in Germany, France, Belgium and the Netherlands therefore includes the attempt by certain political movements to redefine the nature and meaning of citizenship by first divorcing it from the category of nationality (e.g. Silverman, 1991, 1992). An attempt to impose a 'race perspective' on this struggle will, at best, be rewarded with puzzled incomprehension.

The terrain of citizenship can be approached from the specificities of the British situation, and hence from a different direction. For the British situation, seen in comparative European perspective, demonstrates that possession of the rights of citizenship does not ensure for racialized populations of recent migrant origin a position of equality with their fellow citizen. The 'facts of racial disadvantage', as they are often signified, are well researched in Britain (e.g. Brown, 1984), although they do not reveal a simple 'black and white' picture (Miles, 1987b; Modood, 1991). The category of citizenship can then be problematized on the grounds that formal legal equality as citizen is contradicted by the facts of material inequality. And a struggle to

redefine the meaning and content of citizenship in order to connect
it with the achievement of material equality extends a link not only
to the ongoing struggle over the meaning of citizenship elsewhere in
Europe, but also to those other ('white') sections of the British population who are, to varying degrees, living the same material realities
of inequality, albeit for partly different reasons. In sum, rather than
advise other Europeans to discover, impose and legislate a 'race'
perspective for the 'new Europe', we could enter the European debate
about the meanings of citizenship, democracy and equality in the
'new Europe' (e.g. Balibar, 1992). This provides a common terrain on
which to articulate a multitude of specific oppressions.

Naming and explaining racism

Everywhere in Europe, racism seems to be on the increase, and there
are strong temptations (and good reasons) to seek a European-wide
explanation, one that considers European nation-states to be structured by common processes which apply throughout Europe. How
well placed are British researchers to contribute to this explanation?
The argument of the preceding section is that many are limited by
the conceptual baggage of 'race' that they have inherited from the
'race relations' problematic and that they seem unable to reject. There
is a further limitation: in order to join the debates about racism in
Europe, it is necessary to have an adequate explanation for the
expression of racism within the UK. Progress on this matter is uneven,
in part because much of the recent debate has focused on *naming*
rather than *explaining* racism.

Over the past two decades, a major focus of the British debate
about the concept of racism has concerned the attributes of its object
(Miles, 1989). There is general unanimity that, during the nineteenth
and early twentieth centuries, the concept of racism had a clearly
identifiable object: namely, the belief that the human species consists
of a number of distinct and hierarchically biological types, each of
which has a naturally endowed character and destiny. This belief
was legitimated by scientific knowledge (Banton, 1987; Stepan, 1982;
Barkan, 1992). In the light of the history of German fascism and the
termination of European colonialism, claims that particular populations are 'racially superior' or 'racially inferior' are no longer integral
to official justifications of inequality and discriminatory treatment. For
some writers, this means that racism is no longer the dominant ideology that it once was: for them, the age of racism has come to an end.

Others reject the implicit assumption that the concept of racism refers to a single, one-dimensional and rigid ideology. They argue that there are many different *racisms*, that each is historically specific to a particular conjucture, and that the 'old' biological racism of the nineteenth century has been replaced by a 'new' racism. This is a European debate: in most of the nation-states of north-west Europe, there has been a discussion about whether or not a new or neoracism, has been formulated in the past two decades (e.g. Barker, 1981; Taguieff, 1987; Balibar and Wallerstein, 1988; Balibar, 1991; Kalpaka and Räthzel, 1986). We can characterize this debate as one that concerns the *naming* of racism.

Those involved in the debate have been preoccupied with defining the characteristics of racism, and especially the 'new racism', that refracts contemporary material conditions. I prefer to replace the chronological distinction between the 'old' and the 'new' racism with the new analytical distinction between an *inegalitarian* and a *differentialist* racism (Taguieff, 1987), although acknowledging that this distinction is not as precise as its creator presumes. Nevertheless, once the 'new racism' has been discovered to exist, the analytical task is usually thought to be over. The naming of racism is equivalent to condemning racism, such is the value content of the concept. All that remains is to 'root it out'. The key to achieving this final act of ideological 'cleansing' is to have the 'correct' anti-racist strategy.

In this struggle for 'correctness', at least one matter is often forgotten. The concern to *name* racism tends to displace the concern to *explain* racism. But what are its conditions of existence? Why does it assume such important in contemporary capitalist social formations in Europe? These are difficult questions, yet our answers to them have as much significance for formulating an adequate anti-racist strategy as does the naming of racism. In so far as answers to them have been implicit in the kinds of anti-racist work that have been initiated during the 1980s in the UK, and in so far as that work has not achieved a great deal of success in 'defeating the beast', it is time to retrieve and re-evaluate them (Rattansi, 1992, pp. 29–41; Cohen, 1992).

The colonial paradigm: its significance and limits

There is nothing (yet) in contemporary Europe to compare with the totalizing racialization of the German nation-states that occurred during the 1930s under fascism. The fascist state racialized intentionally the political process and the imagination of the nature and charac-

ter of the German nation, with consequences that are well known.
Elsewhere in Europe, other right-wing forces achieved supremacy,
even if racism was less central to their rise and to their rule. This
history of European fascism has shaped post–1945 state legitimations
of the exercise of power, and of politics that are intended to sustain
domination and to ensure the reproduction of the inequalities central
to the capitalist mode of production. As the end of the twentieth
century approaches, the state in Europe remains enmeshed ideo-
logically in a rhetoric of human rights and a liberal variant of anti-
racism. While this certainly does not prevent either a resort to racist
practices, or the 'toleration' of the expression of racism within civil
society, it does impose a restriction on the manner in which, and
perhaps the extent to which, the state can racialize the nation-states
of western Europe. This explains, in part, the incomplete shift from
an inegalitarian to a differentialist racism.

Any discussion about the determination of contemporary racisms
should take account of this historicity of the expression of racism
within Europe. Even if the 'new racism' were really 'new', it would
have been preceded by an 'old' racism, and both racisms need to be
explained. In other words, any conjunctural explanation for contemporary racisms should not contradict the explanation for the expression
of racism in European nation-states during the first half of the twentieth century and, indeed, before then. Even if there are certain characteristics specific to late-twentieth-century capitalist social formations,
they cannot alone explain contemporary racisms because those racisms
are not unique. Racism is a historical phenomenon and so an explanation for it must have a historical dimension.

This is one strength of the predominant, if not the sole, explanation
offered for the expression of racism in the post–1945 United Kingdom.
The *colonial paradigm of racism* proposes that racism has its origin
largely or wholly in the colonial project: racism was created to legitimate colonial exploitation, and sometimes the genocide of colonized
populations, by typifying those populations as 'inferior races' in order
to resolve the contradiction between the universalizing humanism of
the Enlightenment and the manifestly inhuman treatment of the
colonized. When previously colonized populations arrived to fill vacant
positions in the British labour market after 1945, colonial images were
retrieved and reconstructed in order to perpetuate their subordinate
position, not only in the labour market, but in all the major social
institutions, and to construct a commonsense explanation for the
political crisis of the 1970s (see Lawrence, 1982; Sivanandan, 1982,
1990a).

The colonial paradigm offers a consummate historical explanation (cf. Miles, 1982). Moreover, its explanatory power transcends the boundary of the British nation-state. Spain, Portugal, France, the Netherlands and Belgium were also colonial powers: differentially, they participated in the formation and maintenance of European hegemony within the emergent world economy from the sixteenth to the early twentieth centuries. As a result, in all five nation-states, the contemporary expression of a particular racism can be explained in part by the reproduction and mutation of racist images of the colonized Other. Yet, as an explanation for historical *and* contemporary racisms in Europe, the colonial paradigm can only be a partial explanation: it is silent concerning the *interior* racisms that predominated within Europe before the Second World War, most notably racist anti-Semitism. This silence is mirrored by attempts to explain the predominance of racist anti-Semitism within Europe during the late nineteenth and the first half of the twentieth centuries. For example, Mosse (1978) has nothing to say about colonialism because the Jews and 'gypsies' of Europe were not colonized minorities required to supply unfree labour, at least not before the 1930s.

The inevitable silence of the colonial paradigm concerning the racialization of Jews (and other *interior* minorities within Europe: see Miles, 1991) since the second half of the nineteenth century is often 'resolved' by drawing a distinction between racism and anti-Semitism. There is some historical substance to this distinction in so far as, historically, the differentiation and exclusion of Jews includes a negative religious signification which is precapitalist in origin. But the existence of a similar precapitalist negative image of Islam has not prevented many from claiming that the contemporary exclusion of Muslims in Europe is racist. It is a historical fact that the Jews were one of the objects of the racialization of the world that occurred in the name of science during the nineteenth and early twentieth centuries (Mosse, 1978). Moreover, like other excluded and inferiorized populations, many Jews embraced the idea of 'race' as a self-description (Marrus, 1971, pp. 10–27), a fact that prompts the observation that the process that some define as 'racial formation' has an extensive history. And scientific racism was a central dimension of the evolution in the policy towards the Jews in fascist Germany (Burleigh and Wippermann, 1991, pp. 23–73). In so far as there are specific determinants of the construction of the Jew as a racialized Other in the course of the past century or more, these can be expressed in the idea that anti-Semitic racism is one of the modalities of racism (cf. Holmes, 1979; Cohen, 1988; Kushner, 1989; Kushner and Lunn, 1989).

If the distinction between racism and anti-Semitism cannot be sustained, then we need more than the colonial paradigm to explain historical racisms in Europe. This applies equally to contemporary racisms. The largest and most economically advanced capitalist nation-state in contemporary Europe (Germany) was never a major colonial power, and only a small part of post–1945 migration to Germany has a colonial origin. Yet, racism was a central dimension of German fascism (and of collaboration with fascism during the German occupation of the Netherlands, France and Belgium) while, in contemporary Germany, racism stimulates a great deal of political activity within both formal and informal politics (e.g. Räthzel, 1991). The historical and contemporary expression of racisms in Europe therefore presents a major challenge to the hegemonic position of the colonial paradigm, by exposing the failure of theories of racism to confront not only the realities of anti-Semitic racism, but also a number of other interior racisms.

There is a further problem with the colonial paradigm: while it offers an explanation for the *origin* of a specific modality of racism, it does not necessarily offer an explanation for the *reproduction* and *transmutation* of colonial imagery. Why is it that a historically constituted ideology has retained a capacity to explain and structure the social world, even after its scientific legitimation has been largely discredited, with the result that it has been reconstituted as a differentialist rather than an inegalitarian racism? One way of answering such a question is to argue that there are certain features of the contemporary conjuncture, of the current state of development of the capitalist mode of production and of the nation form, which facilitate or 'require' the reproduction of racism. This would provide a conjunctural explanation, but it would not necessarily explain the historical continuity of racism in Europe.

On the origin and reproduction of racism

The idea that a *European racism* has recently come into existence has intellectual and political currency at the moment (Sivanandan, 1988; Balibar, 1991). Unfortunately, this notion can obscure more than it reveals if it is used prior to a more thorough theoretical reflection (Miles, 1992a). It is commonly employed to homogenize and totalize a wide range of ideologies and practices in an undefined number of European nation-states, ideologies and practices which are not necessarily new and whose interrelationship needs to be demonstrated rather than assumed. Physical attacks on North African migrants in Italy, increased electoral support for the *Front National* in France, the involvement of skinheads in neo-Nazi political movements in Germany, police harassment of young people of Caribbean origin in the UK, the identification of Jews as 'the enemy within' in Poland, the attempt to harmonize visa policies within the European Community: these phenomena are collectively identified as evidence for the existence of a new European racism.

But nothing is actually *explained* by this act of labelling: disparate events and ideologies are categorized as expressions of the same phenomenon as if the connections were self-evident. This labelling reveals little about, for example, the reasons why North African migrants have been recently brutally attacked on the streets of Italian cities. It *may* be that the presence of such people is signified as illegitimate by the Italian state or by some Italian citizens because it is mistakenly believed that Italy is a European nation-state which is the 'home' of people who are exclusively Christian and who have somatic characteristics that can be described as 'white'. If so, then we can legitimately talk of a *racist construct of the idea of Europe*. And while there are good reasons to expect to find such a racialized concept in other European nation-states (Pieterse, 1991), its origin requires careful explanation. Moreover, the existence of such an ideology does not, by itself, necessarily explain the violence: the ideological motivation could be grounded in a racialized conception of Italy as a distinct *nation-state*.

While the necessary theoretical and historical work is carried out to refine and limit the parameters of a concept of European racism, there are advantages in posing the question as 'simply' one of explaining the expression of racism in the nation-states of contemporary Europe. Yet this formulation needs further clarification because there is nothing new about the expression of racism in Europe. We might then pose two analytically distinct questions. What are the origins of racism in Europe? And what are the reasons for its renewed and restructured expression in the late twentieth century? In other words, what are its conditions of existence, and what are the conditions for its (expanded?) reproduction?

The colonial paradigm of racism *externalizes* the explanation for the origin of racism beyond Europe. By implication, if emergent European states and merchant capitalist classes had not created a world economy by organizing commodity production in the Americas and beyond, then racism would not have been 'invented': in the absence of the exploitation of an unfree labour force beyond Europe, there would have been no inequality to legitimate. Yet colonialism is a historical fact, and colonial racism can be explained, in part, by references to the exigencies of the colonial situation. But as we have seen, not all western European nation-states have a significant colonial history, and there are other non-colonial racisms whose existence requires explanation. Moreover, there remains the possibility of explaining the existence of racisms in general, of identifying what all racisms have in common to warrant categorization as instances of the same phenomenon, and then seeking to discover their general conditions of existence.

Part of the explanation for the origin of racism can be found by taking account of the historical development of capitalism *within* Europe: indeed, the debate about the origin of racism during the late 1930s placed primary emphasis upon the evolution of nationalism within Europe as the *explanadum* (see Miles, 1991). In other words, if we were to resurrect the question that asks whether or not we can explain racism as embedded uniquely in the historical evolution of capitalist social formations (an explanation that suggests that racism is a 'normal' feature of these social formations rather than an 'atypical' response to crisis), then the significance of colonialism would be contextualized relative to its role in the historical evolution of capitalism and the nation-state within Europe. The intention is not to revive the 'traditional' Marxist argument that racism is 'only' a utilitarian invention of the bourgeoisie to divide the working class and to legitimate colonialism. Rather, the argument is historical and structural, and relies principally upon the assumption that racism is not only contradictory in its 'nature' (Cohen, 1992; Rattansi, 1992) and in its consequences (see Miles, 1989, pp. 99–100), but also has its origin in a set of contradictions.

The thesis is that racism can be explained as integral to the historical evolution of capitalist social formations because of three (analytically distinct, but in reality closely interrelated) structural contradictions. The effects of these contradictions are mediated by the constant transformation of all social relations on an increasingly world scale. Historically, the capitalist mode of production is unique in that it induces a permanent and continuous transformation of all social relations (cf. Sayer, 1991, pp. 9–13). Social transformation, the 'uninterrupted disturbance of all social conditions' (Marx and Engels, 1968, p. 38), is not an abnormal condition, a sign of crisis: rather, it is a constant, a characteristic of the essence of capitalism as a revolutionary mode of production. Hence, the consequences for social reproduction and human experience (uncertainty, contingency, anomie, temporality, rootlessness, etc.) are structurally determined and not conjunctural phenomena.

The first contradiction is that between, on the one hand, the universalizing and equalizing tendencies embodied in the commodity form and in the tendency towards the 'commodification of everything' (cf. Wallerstein, 1988) and, on the other, the necessary reproduction of social inequality, not only between classes but also that expressed in uneven spatial development. For those whose political and economic interests are rooted in the reproduction of capitalist social formations, this contradiction can be mediated ideologically by the naturalization of social inequality and uneven development: racisms (as one form of naturalization) can therefore 'fix' economic and political disadvantage 'in nature' by attributing specified social collectivities with essential attributes. This is especially evident in the process of constituting and legitimating relations of production, hence the argument that racism can be analysed as a relation of production (Miles, 1987a, pp. 186–95), but is not confined to this 'economic' process. Equally, those who have resisted the transformations inherent in the capital accumulation process (e.g. the landed aristocracy) have turned to ideas of 'nature' and of the threat of 'degeneration' to claim an inherent 'right to rule'.

The second contradiction is between these same universalizing tendencies and the reality of extensive cultural diversity rooted in the disaggregation of social formations, within which material reproduction was socially organized prior to the development of the capitalist mode of production, and which have been reproduced parallel with that development while those social formations have not been fully incorporated into the capitalist world economy. Indeed, certain 'backward' cultural, political and economic forms have been strategically reproduced in certain conjunctures in order to assist the advance of the capitalist mode of production in other spatial sites. In different ways, those social formations sustaining cultural diversity have been interpreted as the symbol, and indeed the object, of resistance to the encroachment of capitalist relations of production, but also as unacceptable barriers to the spread of those same universalizing relations of production, as 'primitive' forms which must be 'transcended' in the name of the principle of 'progress' that simultaneously obscures and expresses the expansion of generalized commodity production. In both instances, racism ensures that the differences alluded to (both real and imagined) are naturalized and interpreted as evidence of either the essential difference of, or the inferiority of, the social collectivities whose existence is rendered synonymous with the social formation.

The third contradiction is that between the universalizing tendencies and the nationalization of social formations: that is, the creation of the nation-state as the main political form within which capitalist relations of production have been partially 'confined'. Historically, the development of the capitalist mode of production was situated in specific spatial locations which were incrementally secured by a strong state that was able to create an 'internal' order, to protect the activities of the emergent bourgeois class beyond the boundary of that order, and to repel any assault upon that territory by competing units of capital (e.g. Corrigan and Sayer, 1985). The nation form and the consolidation of capitalist relations of production within its boundary (often in association with commodity production located beyond its boundary) ensured that the nation-state became a formidable economic and political force, inducing incipient bourgeoisies elsewhere to reproduce the form in order to ensure their competitive existence (Nairn, 1981). Thus, the extension of capitalism on a world scale, the creation of a universal economic system, has been accompanied by the political fragmentation of the world, by the creation of discrete 'nations', each supposedly expressing a unique essence and each producing nationalized and racialized subjects.

In other words, racisms only became possible in Europe following the transcendence of feudal, 'unfree social relations, of unequal class relations sanctioned by sacred ideologies, by beliefs about a divine 'order of things' which fixed social relations as a static order (but also a temporal order, given the assumption of the immediacy of the Day of Judgement). As a result of the parallel humanizing of the human subject (an ideological process that simultaneously 'reduced' all human beings to the same formal status as equal beings, and also created the possibility of being 'non-human' or *untermensch*), and of the rationalizing and universalizing tendencies of the commodity and the market, legitimations for the persistence of inequality became internalized in the 'nature' of certain kinds of human being who were the subjects of domination (cf. Guillaumin, 1988). While these emergent racisms drew upon precapitalist images of the Other (Miles, 1989, pp. 11–40), they were, in another sense, unique and specific to the emergent capitalist social formations *because* those formations were structurally unique, and embodied a historically specific set of contradictions which were not reducible to the mode of production.

By locating the explanation for racisms in a field of contradictions, the latter maps a terrain of struggle: hence, if racism is explained as a response to the contradiction between, on the one hand, universalism and humanism and, on the other, the reproduction of social inequality and exploitation, then one has simultaneously theorized the possibility that racism will be challenged by opposing social forces: not only by those whose position of inequality is naturalized by racism, but by all those dominated by the state that secures the reproduction of the capitalist mode of production. That is to say, if we explain racism as a product of contradictions, then those same contradictions also explain the existence of anti-racism, the struggle against not just the naturalization of difference to legitimate inequality, but also, potentially, inequality itself. The precise relationship *between* racism and anti-racism is always a conjunctural matter, a relationship that can be determined only by a concrete analysis of the balance of forces in an evolving historical situation. This is equally true for the assessment of the relative significance and influence of racism, and of anti-racism, *within* a social formation.

This is a preliminary and schematic summary of an argument that requires elaboration. Its significance here is that, by providing an explanation for the origin of racism within capitalist social formations, it provides an important part of the explanation for the existence of racism within European nation-states. Racism and the struggle against racism, therefore constitute a continuous thread running through the historical evolution of European nation-states, not because racism is 'natural', but because of the existence of a set of contradictions inherent in the historical evolution of the capitalist mode of production. The thread is always more or less evident: what remains to be determined are the conditions under which it is reproduced, and under which it becomes more or less evident.

In identifying certain of these conditions in the section that follows, I am not proposing a holistic explanation for the expression of contemporary racism in Europe. Having for a long time argued that racism is a contradictory ideology that cannot be explained as the direct outcome of structural and historical forces (cf. Phizacklea and Miles, 1979; Miles, 1989, 1993), I concur with those who have called recently for an explicit recognition of the multiple determination of racism, one that draws upon not only historical materialism but also psychoanalysis. It is indeed necessary to discover the necessary complementarity between, on the one hand, the historical and structural determinants and, on the other, the 'micro-foundations of racist ideologies' which explain 'the deeper reaches of the racist imagination' (Cohen, 1992; p. 96). In focusing here upon the former dimension of this complementary, I acknowledge the incompleteness of the explanation because of the silence concerning the 'micro-foundations'. Equally, there is a perilous silence in that perspective which remains enclosed within presentism and the fragility, fluidity and multiplicity of subjectivity.

Explaining racism in contemporary European nation-states

An answer to the specific problem identified above depends in part upon periodization: when did racism again become a major force in European nation-states after 1945? Many would argue that this happened during the 1970s and 1980s (although there are good reasons to propose an earlier date). These years coincide with either the evolution of the economic crisis of world capitalism, or (to cite an alternative theoretical paradigm) the creation of a 'post-industrial' or 'postmodern' society, evident specifically in the deindustrialization of western Europe and in the disappearance of the working class both as a class and as the primary political actor.

Thus, in Britain, the 'rise of racism' has been explained as a response by the state to the emergence of an organic crisis of British capitalism, a response that entailed the reworking of a racialized image of the colonial Other (CCCS, 1982). Wieviorka (1991a, pp. 149–219, 1992, pp. 25–41, and in this volume) has explained the 'rise of racism' in France as a response to the creation of a post-industrial society (cf. Lapeyronnie, 1992). This argument warrants special attention because Wieviorka asserts that his explanation for the pivotal influence of racism in France during the 1980s can be generalized to account for the heightened expression of racism throughout Europe (Wieviorka, 1991b).

He argues that the French social formation has undergone *une grande mutation* during the past two decades, a metamorphosis marked by the dissipation of industrial society and of the working-class movement. This transition to post-industrialism has been accompanied by the decline of 'Great Power' nationalism, the crisis of the Republican state (evident in mass unemployment and the struggle over *laïcité*) and the supplanting of collectivism by individualism and subjectivism. Wieviorka emphasizes that these changes do not mark a crisis, but rather constitute a rupture in social development: post-industrial society is a qualitatively different type of society in comparison with the industrial societies of the late nineteenth and most of the twentieth centuries. In so far as this metamorphosis of the French social formation is common to other nation-states in western Europe, an explanation for contemporary racism in France is an explanation for the expression of racism throughout contemporary Europe.

How do these changes explain contemporary racism? Wieviorka's argument is that *la grande mutation* has created instability and disorganization within the nation-state, and has resulted in *dualization* (understood as the division of a previously unitary social order into two separate parts, the 'haves' and the 'have nots'). Racism fills the vacuum created by social change, especially for the 'have nots': disorder and racism are therefore theorized as elective affinities. The decline of the working-class movement has entailed the collapse of 'old' hopes and meanings, and so a search for 'new' ways of projecting the self into the future by reference to the past. Among the ideological objects available to those searching for new individual and subjective meanings are those of ethnicity and 'race': thus, 'ethnic revival' and racism permit, at least in thought, a reorganization of society and a resolution of the angst of the ever more fragile ego.

The pertinence of this explanation for the alleged renewed significance of racism within Europe since the 1970s depends in part upon the general validity of the 'post-industrial society' thesis: if one can show that the processes referred to as *la grande mutation* are not historically unique, then, at least by themselves, they cannot explain the contemporary expression of racism. As I have already argued, the capitalist mode of production is, by definition, characterized by continuous transformation of all social relations (Marx and Engels, 1968, p. 38; Sayer, 1991, pp. 9–13). Consequently, the fact of transformation that 'typified' the decades of the 1970s and 1980s is not unique.

The entire period since 1945 has been characterized by constant change. The reconstruction of the capitalist mode of production after the devastation caused by the war, the reorganization of the labour process consequent upon the changing ratio of constant to variable capital, the emergence of 'internal' labour shortages and the evolution of large-scale labour migrations, and the extension of commodity production and consumption: these and other changes amount to a continuous process of transformation within the social formations of western Europe during the decades of the 1950s and 1960s. And, if we extend our analysis further back in time, a further series of changes are revealed. Hence, if social change is a structural feature of capitalist social formations, it can only ever be a general precondition for the increased expression of racism, never in itself a sufficient condition.

It is true that the social formations of western Europe have undergone a set of structural changes as a result of the crisis of accumulation that commenced in the early 1970s: large sectors of industrial production have been abolished, while those that remain have experienced a reorganization of the labour process and the further substitution of constant for variable capital. As a result, there has been a decline in the absolute and relative numbers of manual workers employed in manufacturing industries, an increase in the proportion of the employed population in the service sector, and an increase in the relative surplus population. But as the twentieth century draws to a close, the social formations of Europe continue to be structured by wage labour as the primary relation of exploitation, and by generalized commodity production and consumption (cf. Lash and Urry, 1987). Much (although not all) of that industrial production has become increasingly mechanized, even automated, and a considerable part of it has been relocated outside the boundary of Europe to spatial sites where 'primitive accumulation' often continues unabated. As a result, European nation-states are even more dependent upon industrial commodity production (and the consumption thereof) than they were at the beginning of the century.

Hence, we can conceive of these social formations as 'post-industrial' only if we abstract them from the ever-tighter web of connections that constitute them as integral to the world economic system within which industrialization and proletarianization remain central features (cf. Sivanandan, 1990b). The consequences of the collapse of 'really existing socialism' reinforce the significance of this: eastern Europe is a major new site for the extension of the capitalist mode of production, not least because it 'offers' a new source of comparatively cheap labour and an extension of the market for commodity production.

Moreover, the export of industrial production to the peripheries of the world economic system is partly counterbalanced by a 'reverse' movement, a reconcentration at the centre of the world economic system of certain kinds of industrial production, alongside an expansion of a range of 'industrialized' service and clerical functions necessary to the control and servicing of the world economic system (Sassen, 1988, 1991). Furthermore, uneven development within the centre means that previous countries of emigration (Italy, Spain and Portugal) have recently become countries of immigration in order to provide labour for construction, agricultural production and tourism (Simon, 1987; Miles, 1992b). These changes are accompanied by continuing migrations (often, but not always, 'illegal' or clandestine) from periphery to centre. While these developments are not reconstituting the class of manual wage labourers employed *en masse* in large industrial factories (but rather involve small-scale, 'domestic' production, as well as 'high-tech' production of consumer durables with a very high organic composition of capital), they do entail the reconstitution of a form of factory or industrial production in certain sectors within Europe and North America (e.g. Phizacklea, 1990). In other words, several of the transformations referred to by Wieviorka as *la grande mutation* can be theorized as evidence of the restructuring of the capitalist world economy, which has, as its consequence, a *disorganization of capitalism*, a process that includes the *reconstitution* of the proletariat in terms of skill, gender, ethnic origin, national status and space. Certainly, this is a transformation of considerable significance, but it does not entail the creation of a wholly new set of social relations, of a new type of society.

For example, there is nothing new about dualization: the object of this concept does not identify contemporary capitalist social formations as historically unique. The evidence cited by Wieviorka can be retheorized by reference to Marx's claim that the capitalist mode of production reproduces simultaneously a relative surplus population, which is absolutely impoverished in periods of crisis, and a working class which is always relatively impoverished (Mandel, 1976, pp. 69–72). Thus, contemporary Europe only reconfirms that the capitalist mode of production effects, necessarily and simultaneously within the social formations that it structures, an expansion in collective wealth and the reproduction of those sites in class relations which are filled by people who receive only the socially defined minimum necessary to sustain human life. Absolutely, because of the consequences of capital accumulation, the socially defined reproduction costs of those who occupy these sites within western Europe are greater than a century ago, but relatively, there remains a vast gap between those minimum costs and the resources devoted to the reproduction of the ruling class and of the capitalist mode of production itself.

What sites in class relations are identified by this argument, and which 'agents' fill them? The wages of large sections of the semi- and unskilled working class have always ensured that their income for reproduction is close to or below the socially defined minimum. For those who occupy the ranks of the relative surplus population, the 'welfare state' has, for much of the twentieth century (at least in north-west Europe), ensured that the socially defined minimum was made available to them, although the capacity of the state to sustain this is now in question as the numbers of people defined as 'surplus to requirements' has increased over the past decade and in parallel with the fiscal crisis of the state. The 'have nots' of the dualization

thesis include, therefore, those who occupy a specific set of class sites
defined and reproduced by the capitalist mode of production: namely,
the semi- and unskilled proletariat and the relative surplus population.
These class locations are certainly not unique to the late twentieth
century.

There is another level of argument concerning the dualization
thesis. Wallerstein (1983) has noted that, in the history of the evolution
of the world capitalist system, only a minority of the population living
within it has been employed formally as wage labourers: that is, in
the history of capitalism, the majority of the population has never
'worked' and has had not prospect of 'working'. One does not have
to accept world-systems theory *in toto* to note that this is the case for
the social formations of contemporary Europe and, therefore, that this
is not a unique feature of the conjuncture. The argument can be
reinforced by observing that, within political relations, the majority of
the population has only been included formally within civil society
with the winning of the vote for women. In sum, the fact of dualization
is a historical constant, although its extent is historically variable.

However, the gender and cultural profile, and legal status, of those
people who occupy the class sites of the manual proletariat and the
reserve army of labour, and who have been permitted by the state to
become 'equal participants' or 'full citizens' in civil society, has
changed since 1945, partly as a result of the increased employment
of women and partly as a result of migration. Concerning the latter,
this highlights the significance of the nation form, for the national
boundary of this social formation defines the migrant Other (or rather
certain migrant Others) as *de jure* or *de facto* aliens, human beings
whose Otherness is allegedly embodied in the signified marks of
alienness, the marks of culture and phenotype in varying combination
which are thought to prevent 'them' from becoming 'like us'. These
variously differentiated Others usually occupy several sites in class
relations alongside those who have been nationalized at an earlier
phase of historical development and who therefore provide a measure
of Otherness, but the former occupy a distinct politicolegal and ideological position.

To this point, I have outlined a set of general difficulties with the
post-industrial society thesis. But the critique extends to include some
more specific problems concerning the explanation for the political
significance of racism. First, why were the decades of the 1950s and
1960s, dominated as they were by social change, not also characterized
by a search for racist identities? An answer might be found in the
claim that these were decades of apparently unproblematic capitalist

expansion and accumulation when the organized working class improved its material conditions, decades of transformation which therefore did not require a 'retreat into the past' to rediscover 'old certainties' because the future appeared to offer further material improvement.

However, capitalist expansion was far from unproblematic, as the economic crisis of 1967/68 and the trade union and political struggles throughout the period demonstrate. Moreover, is it true that, through-out this period of continuous change, the organized working class was a bulwark against the ever-present potential for a resort to 'regressive' ideologies ad strategies? The implication of the 'post-industrialism' thesis is that the expression of racism only increased following the decline of the organized (male) factory proletariat. This is contradicted by the fact that the organized male working class has played a major role in articulating racism and enforcing systems of racist exclusion in the workplace and beyond during the period of capitalist expansion and change between the early 19 50s and the early 1970s. Long before the transformations referred to by the notion of 'post-industrialism', sections of the organized working class in western Europe were enforcing a racialized hierarchy in the labour market and beyond (e.g. Castles and Kosack, 1973), often with the complicity of the state.

This should not be surprising. The notion of the organized working class presumes, but is often silent about, the political parameters within which it is organized. Historically, it is the nation form that has constituted the site of, and therefore the parameters for, legitimate political organization. With the initial admission of the male proletariat as a licensed actor to the bourgeois political arena during the nine-teenth century, its political consciousness and practice were formally constrained by the boundary of the nation-state. Indeed, the organized working class existed as a legitimate political force only in so far as it subordinated its interests and practice to the state: this subordination was often transformed into an active identification with the state and with the imagined community of nation that the state constructed. Furthermore, nationality became a criterion to determine inclusion in or exclusion from the labour market, and as a result 'aliens' were excluded from the 'benefits' of citizenship.

In so far as all expressions of nationalism potentially or necessarily embody a racism (cf. Miles, 1987c; Balibar, 1988), one can expect the organized working class, once committed to the defence of the interests of the nationalized working class *contra* all external economic and political forces, to seek to protect and advance these interests by measures that often express racism. In sum, the diminution of the male factory proletariat has not created a space which racism can now fill because fractions of the organized working class have, to a varying extent, always articulated and realized (to varying extents) a racism in order to defend perceived economic interests.

There is a further difficulty with the argument that the 'disappearance' of the organized industrial proletariat has created a vacuum which racism fills because it offers a new identity. The contemporary conjuncture is also characterized by the involvement of large numbers of people in various kinds of anti-racist politics: the decade of the 1980s in France is replete with examples (Hargreaves, 1991). If social dislocation explains the increasing articulation of racism, how can we explain its antimony, the existence of anti-racist movements of various kinds? In other words, how can we explain the fact that, in the context of *la grande mutation*, so many people abstain from seeking, or actively reject, a new identity in racism? Of special importance here are those political movements that have grown out of the migration and settlement of many populations from beyond Europe since the 1950s. The argument of the previous section offers an explanation, but Wieviorka's exegesis for the expression of racism seems to preclude the possibility of anti-racist ideology and political practice.

Historically, what is conjuncturally novel about the past two decades is not an increase in racism *per se* (for there are other conjunctures where racism was a major political force), but the intensification of ideological and political struggle around the expression of a racism that often claims not to be a racism, in a context where an anti-racist politics has a potential to weld together a range of social forces in opposition. It is necessary to be reminded that the hegemonic power of racism only began to be dissolved *within* Europe in the 1930s: of course, beyond Europe, racism had been opposed in many ways before the 1930s, but the struggle against fascism proved decisive, as is demonstrated by the critique of scientific racism (Barkan, 1992). Indeed, this is signified by the invention of the concept of *racism* during the 1920s and 1930s. In the wake of the post–1945 revelations about the Nazi concentration and death camps, and the ideological work of UNESCO in discrediting inegalitarian racism, anti-racist struggles gained a novel legitimacy and power, both at the centre (e.g. the USA) and the periphery (e.g. the colonies of European nation-states) of the world economic system. It is because of their legitimacy and partial successes that we have witnessed certain transformations in the expression of racism, specifically the partial shift from an inegalitarian to a differentialist racism.

Despite these difficulties, Wieviorka's thesis challenges us to seek an explanation for the contemporary expression of racism within Europe which is grounded in a general theory of European capitalist social formations and their place in the capitalist world economy. But this must be a theory which takes adequate account of the specificities of the historical development of individual nation-states as well as of the general transformations (economic and political) of the capitalist world economy. Wieviorka is acutely aware of the significance of the former (1991b) and, in the case of France, he highlights the crisis of the Republican state and of French national identity. These specific crises are reproduced, but in different phenomenal forms, elsewhere in Europe, and this then returns us to consideration of the importance of the thesis that links the intensification of the expression of racism with the organic crisis of the nationalized social formation. Here my argument, and that of Wieviorka, share a common terrain, even if the reasoning is somewhat different.

Conclusion

What, then, is the most important change that explains the increasing political struggle around racism within western Europe at the end of the twentieth century? A central actor in this struggle is the state (Bovenkerk *et al.*, 1990). And the role of the state in the articulation of racism is not only a response to the organic crisis within capitalist social formations subsequent to the crisis of accumulation that began at different times in different nation-state (e.g. CCCS, 1982, pp. 9–46). It is also a response to the increasing marginalization of the nation-state in its existing form as a result of the transnational functioning of the largest units of capital within the capitalist world economic system.

Above, I have acknowledged that there has been a reorganization of the capitalist mode of production within European nation-states, arguing that this collectivity cannot be abstracted from the world economic system. The increasing mobility (in both scale and velocity) of capital, commodities and human beings across national boundaries highlights the extent to which the nation-state is not 'post-industrial', but rather is increasingly pervious to (or unable to restrain) international (and industrial) intrusions of various kinds, and their multiple consequences. Thus, the commodities consumed in the nation-states of western Europe are ever more likely to be produced in other nation-states within and beyond Europe, the resident population of these nation-states is ever more likely to include people who do not possess the rights of citizenship that are granted to nationals and who have a different ethnic origin, and the population formally engaged in wage labour is ever more likely either to be employed by a trans-national company based outside the nation-state or to have conditions of existence influenced by international capital.

In other words, it has become increasingly evident at the phenom-enal level that the nation form no longer 'contains' the effects of the capitalist mode of production. Yet the nation-state remains the struc-ture within which the subordinate classes are required to organize themselves politically, and within which they are constructed ideo-logically by the state as nationalized subjects. It is at the moment that the nation-state becomes increasingly unviable as a political structure, increasingly disorganized internally, that a defence of its existence is mounted by governments within Europe. This defence seeks to sus-tain the partial fiction that the nation is 'sovereign' when it has already ceded considerable sovereignty to a supranational structure, one designed to provide a political framework within which European capital can remain competitive with capital located in the USA and Japan (Ross, 1992), and when it has largely lost the power to control large-scale movements of international capital across national boundaries.

The effects of this change are overdetermined by the restructuring of capitalism within the nation-states of western Europe, a restructur-ing that has been accompanied by a large increase in the size of the relative surplus population (for whom the 'new world order' means exclusion and deprivation), and by the cyclical functioning of the capitalist mode of production. The increased expression of, and articu-lation between, nationalism and racism can be explained by this conjunctural ensemble of economic, political and ideological relations.

If the racist imagination 'works' by turning 'the world upside down . . . through a conservative appropriation of existing structures and discourses of power' (Cohen, 1992, p. 90), then (in alliance with nationalism) it can become an especially powerful ideological force in such a conjuncture. This is because it offers an explanation, from which arises a political strategy, that conceives an external threat to 'our' existence, in the body or essence of a racialized Other (e.g. *les Arabs*, the Jews, 'Third World' refugees) which 'we' must regain control over by more state power, but at a time when much of the power of the state in so many economic and political arenas has already ebbed away. For example, having voluntarily ceded the power to use nationality as a criterion by which to control movements of population across national boundaries for citizens of member states of the EC, the European states envisage the threat of a racialized Other whose entry (or whose commodities) must be controlled at a time when the ease of movement (not least because of the massive capital investment in systems of international transportation and communication) makes control under conditions of competitive individualism ever more difficult. It is a classic inversion in which the imagination denies the real conditions of existence of both Us and Other in order, at least in thought, to freeze the 'uninterrupted disturbance of all social conditions' by the exercise of state power.

'All' that remains to be done is to trace the historically specific evolution of this conjunctural ensemble within each of the nation-states of Europe (e.g. Silverman, 1992), and to correlate this explanation for the reproduction of racism at the end of the twentieth century with that offered for the origin of racism in capitalist social formations.

Note

Different versions of this paper were prepared for presentation at the Annual Conference of the British Sociological Association at the University of Kent, 7–9 April 1992, and at the Annual Conference of the American Sociological Association in Pittsburg, 18–24 August 1992. I wish to thank Max Silverman for his constructive comments on an earlier draft.

References

Adler, S. (1977) *International Migration and Dependence*, Farnborough: Gower.

Allen, S., and Macey, M. (1990) 'Race and ethnicity in the European context', *British Journal of Sociology*, vol. 41, no. 3.

Ardittis, S. (1990) 'Labour migration and the single European market: a synthetic and prospective note', *International Sociology*, vol. 5, no. 4.

Balibar, E. (1988) 'Y a-t-il un "Néo-Racisme?" ' in Balibar, E., and Wallerstein, I. (1988) *Race, nation, classe: Les identités ambiguës*, Paris: La Découverte.

Balibar, E. (1991) '*Es gibt keinen Staat in Europa*: Racism and Politics in Europe Today', *New Left Review*, no. 186.

Balibar, E. (1992) *Les Frontières de la Démocratie*, Paris: La Découverte.

Balibar, E., and Wallerstein, I. (1988) *Race, nation, classe: Les identités ambiguës*, Paris: La Découverte.

Banton, M. (1987) *Racial Theories*, Cambridge: Cambridge University Press.

Banton, M. (1991) 'The race relations problematic', *British Journal of Sociology*, vol. 42, no. 1.

Barkan, E. (1992) *The Retreat of Scientific Racism: Changing Concepts of Race in Britain and the United States Between the World Wars*, Cambridge: Cambridge University Press.

Barker, M. (1981) *The New Racism*, London: Junction Books.

Blackburn, R. (1992) 'The ruins of Westminster', *New Left Review*, no. 191.

Bovenkerk, F., Miles, R., and Verbunt, G. (1990) 'Racism, migration and the state in western Europe: a case for comparative analysis', *International Sociology*, vol. 5, no. 4.

Brah, A. (1992) 'Difference, diversity and differentiation', in Donald, J., and Rattansi, A. (eds), *'Race', Culture and Difference*, London: Sage.

Brown, C. (1984) *Black and White Britain: The Third PSI Survey*, Aldershot: Gower.

Brubaker, R. (1990) 'Immigration, citizenship, and the nation-state in France and Germany: a comparative historical analysis', *International Sociology*, vol. 5, no. 4.

Burleigh, M., and Wipperman, W. (1991) *The Racial State: Germany 1933–1945*, Cambridge: Cambridge University Press.

Castles, S., and Kosack, G. (1973) *Immigrant Workers and Class Structure in Western Europe*, London: Oxford University Press.

CCCS (1982) *The Empire Strikes Back: Race and Racism in 70s Britain*, London: Hutchinson/Centre for Contemporary Cultural Studies.

Cohen, P. (1988) 'The perversions of inheritance: studies in the making of multi-racist Britain', in Cohen, P., and Bains, H. S. (eds), *Multi-Racist Britain*, London: Macmillan.

Cohen, P. (1992) ' "It's racism what dunnit": hidden narratives in theories of racism', in Donald, J., and Rattans, A. (eds), *'Race', Culture and Difference*, London: Sage.

Corrigan, P., and Sayer, D. (1985) *The Great Arch: English State Formation as Cultural Revolution*, Oxford: Blackwell.

Costa-Lascoux, J. (1991) 'Des Lois Contre le Racisme', in Taguieff, P. A. (ed.), *Face Au Racisme*, Vol. 2: *Analyses, Hypothèses, Perspectives*, Paris: La Découverte.

Dummett, A. (1991) 'Europe? Which Europe?', *New Community*, vol. 18, no. 1.

Eade, J. (1990) 'Nationalism and the quest for authenticity: the Bangladeshis in Tower Hamlets', *New Community*, vol. 16, no. 4.

Fields, B. J. (1982) 'Ideology and race in American History', in Kousser, J. M., and McPherson, J. M. (eds), *Region, Race and Reconstruction: Essays in Honour of C. Vann Woodward*, New York: Oxford University Press.

Fields, B. J. (1990) 'Slavery, race and ideology in the United States of America', *New Left Review*, no. 181.

Gilroy, P. (1987) *'There Ain't No Black in the Union Jack': The Cultural Politics of Race and Nation*, London: Hutchinson.

Goldberg, D. T. (ed.) (1990) *Anatomy of Racism*, Minneapolis: University of Minnesota Press.

Gordon, P. (1989) *Fortress Europe? The Meaning of 1992*, London: Runnymede Trust.

Guillaumin, C. (1972a) *L'Idéologie Raciste: Genèse et Langage Actuel*, Paris: Mouton.

Guillaumin, C. (1972b) 'Caractères spécifiques de l'idéologie raciste', *Cahiers Internationaux de Sociology*, vol. 53.

Guillaumin, C. (1980) 'The idea of race and its elevation to autonomous scientific and legal status', in UNESCO, *Sociological Theories: Race and Colonialism*, Paris: UNESCO.

Guillaumin, C. (1988) 'Race and nature: the system of marks', *Feminist Issues*, 1988.

Hailbronner, K. (1989) 'Citizenship and nationhood in Germany', in Brubaker, W. R. (ed.), *Immigration and the Politics of Citizenship in Europe and North America*, Lanham: University Press of America.

Hammar, T. (ed.) (1985) *European Immigration Policy: A Comparative Study*, Cambridge: Cambridge University Press.

Hargreaves, A. G. (1991) 'The political mobilisation of the North African community in France', *Ethnic and Racial Studies*, vol. 14, no. 3.

Holmes, C. (1979) *Anti-Semitism in British Society 1876–1939*, London: Edward Arnold.

James, W. (1989) 'The making of black identities', in Samuel, R. (ed.), *Patriotism: The Making and Unmaking of British National Identity*, Vol. 2: *Minorities and Outsiders*, London: Routledge.

James, W. (1992) 'Migration, racism and identity: the Caribbean experience in Britain', *New Left Review*, no. 193.

Jenkins, R., and Solomons, J. (eds) (1989) *Racism and Equal Opportunity Policies in the 1980s*, Cambridge: Cambridge University Press.

Kalpaka, A., and Räthzel, N. (1986) *Die Schwierigkeit, nicht rassistisch zu sein*, Berlin: Express Edition.

Kay, D., and Miles, R. (1992) *Refugees or Migrant Workers? The Recruitment of Displaced Persons for British Industry 1946–1951*, London: Routledge.

Kushner, T. (1989) *The Persistence of Prejudice: Anti-Semitism in British Society During the Second World War*, Manchester: Manchester University Press.

Kushner, T., and Lunn, K. (1989) (eds) *Traditions of Intolerance*, Manchester: Manchester University Press.

Lapeyronnie, D. (1992) 'L'exclusion et le mépris', *Les Temps Modernes*, vols 545/546.

Lash, S., and Urry, J. (1987) *The End of Organised Capitalism*, Cambridge: Polity Press.

Lawrence, E. (1982) 'Just plain common sense: the 'roots' of racism', in CCCS, *The Empire Strikes Back: Race and Racism in 70s Britain*, London: Hutchinson/Centre for Contemporary Cultural Studies.

Layton-Henry, Z. (ed.) (1990) *The Political Rights of Migrant Workers in Western Europe*, London: Sage.

Lester, A. (1992) 'Race and law: the European vacuum', *The Runnymede Bulletin*, vol. 252.

Leveau, R., and Kepel, G. (eds) (1988) *Les Musulmans dans la Société Français*, Paris: Presses de la FNSP.

Lloyd, C. (1991) 'Concepts, models and anti-racist strategies in Britain and France', *New Community*, vol. 18, no. 1.

Mandel, E. (1976) 'Introduction', in Marx K. *Capital*, Vol. 1, Harmondsworth: Penguin.

Marrus, M. R. (1971) *The Politics of Assimilation: A Study of the French Jewish Community at the Time of the Drefus Affair*, Oxford: Clarendon Press.

Marx, K., and Engels, F. (1968) 'The manifesto of the Communist Party' in Marx, K., and Engels, F., *Selected Works*, London: Lawrence and Wishart.

Miles, R. (1982) *Racism and Migrant Labour: A Critical Text*, London: Routledge and Kegan Paul.

Miles, R. (1984) 'Marxism versus the "sociology of race relations?" ', *Ethnic and Racial Studies*, vol. 7, no. 2.

Miles, R. (1987a) *Capitalism and Unfree Labour: Anomally or Necessity?*, London: Tavistock.

Miles, R. (1987b) 'Class relations and racism in Britain in the 1980s', *Revue Européenne des Migrations Internationales*, vol. 3, nos 1/2.

Miles, R. (1987c) 'Recent Marxist theories of nationalism and the issue of racism', *British Journal of Sociology*, vol. 38, no. 1.

Miles, R. (1989) *Racism*, London: Routledge.

Miles, R. (1991) 'Die Idee der "Rasse" und Theorien über Rassismus: Überlegungen zur britischen Diskussion', in Bielefeld, U. (ed.), *Das Eigene und das Fremde: Neuer Rassismus in der Alten Welt*, Hamburg: Junius Verlag.

Miles, R. (1992a) 'Le racisme européen dans son context historique: Reflexions sur l'articulation du racisme et du nationalisme', *Genèses*, vol. 8.

Miles, R. (1992b) 'Migration, racism and the nation state in contemporary Europe', in Satzewich, V. (ed.), *Deconstructing the Nation: Immigration, Multiculturism and Racism in 90s Canada*, Toronto: Garamond Press.

Miles, R. (1993) *Racism After 'Race Relations'*, London: Routledge.

Miles, R., and Phizacklea, A. (1984) *White Man's Country: Racism in British Politics*, London: Pluto Press.

Modood, T. (1988) ' "Black," racial equality and Asian identity', *New Community*, vol. 14, no. 3.

Modood, T. (1991) 'The Indian economic success: a challenge to some race relations assumptions', *Policy and Politics*, vol. 19, no. 3.

Mosse, G. L. (1978) *Toward the Final Solution: A History of European Racism*, London: Dent.

Nairn, T. (1981) *The Break-up of Britain*, London: Verso.

Noiriel, G. (1988) *Le Creuset Français*, Paris: Seuil.

NSCGP (1979) *Ethnic Minorities*, Den Haag: Netherlands Scientific Council for Government Policy.

Omi, M., and Winant, H. (1986) *Racial Formation in the United States: From the 1960s to the 1980s*, New York: Routledge and Kegan Paul.

Phizacklea, A. (1990) *Unpacking the Fashion Industry: Gender, Racism and Class in Production*, London: Routledge.

Phizacklea, A., and Miles, R. (1979) 'Working class racist beliefs in the inner city', in Miles, R., and Phizacklea, A. (eds), *Racism and Political Action in Britain*, London: Routledge and Kegan Paul.

Pieterse, J. N. (1991) 'Fictions of Europe', *Race and Class*, vol. 32, no. 3.

Räthzel, N. (1991) 'Germany: one race, one nation?', *Race and Class*, vol. 32, no. 3.

Rattansi, A. (1992) 'Changing the subject? Racism, culture and education', in Donald, J., and Rattansi, A. (eds), *'Race', Culture and Difference*, London: Sage.

Riggs, F. W. (1991) 'Ethnicity, nationalism, race, minority: a semantic/onomantic exercise (part two)', *International Sociology*, vol. 6, no. 4.

Ross, G. (1992) 'Confronting the new Europe', *New Left Review*, no. 191.

Sassen, S. (1988) *The Mobility of Labor and Capital: A Study in International Investment and Labor Flow*, Cambridge: Cambridge University Press.
Sassen, S. (1991) *The Global City: New York, London, Tokyo*, Princeton: Princeton University Press.
Sayer, D. (1991) *Capitalism and Modernity: An Excurses on Marx and Weber*, London: Routledge.
Silverman, M. (1991) 'Citizenship and the nation state', *Ethnic and Racial Studies*, vol. 14, no. 3.
Silverman, M. (1992) *Deconstructing the Nation: Immigration, Racism and Citizenship in Modern France*, London: Routledge.
Simon, G. (1987) 'Migration in southern Europe: an overview', in OECD, *The Future of Migration*, Paris: OECD.
Sivanandan, A. (1982) *A Different Hunger: Writings on Black Resistance*, London: Pluto Press.
Sivanandan, A. (1988) 'The new racism', *New Statesman and Society*, 4 November.
Sivanandan, A. (1990a) *Communities of Resistance: Writings on Black Struggles for Socialism*, London: Verso.
Sivanandan, A. (1990b) 'All that melts into air is solid: the hokum of New Times', *Race and Class*, vol. 31, no. 3.
Small, S. (1991) 'Racialised relations in Liverpool: a contemporary anomaly', *New Community*, vol. 17, no. 4.
Stepan, N. (1982) *The Idea of Race in Science: Great Britain, 1800–1945*, London: Macmillan.
Taguieff, P. -A. (1987) *La Force du Préjugé: Essai sur le racisme et ses doubles*, Paris: La Découverte.
Wallerstein, I. (1983) *Historical Capitalism*, London, Verso.
Wallerstein, I. (1988) 'Universalisme, racisme, sexisme: les tensions idéologiques du capitalisme', in Balibar, E., and Wallerstein, I., *Race, nation, classe: Les Identités ambiguës*, Paris: La Découverte.
Wihtol de Wenden, C. (1991) 'Immigration policy and the issue of nationality', *Ethnic and Racial Studies*, vol. 14, no. 3.
Wihtol de Wenden, C. (1992) 'Les associations "beur" et immigrées, leurs leaders, leurs stratégies', *Regards sur l'Actualité*, vol. 178.
Wieviorka, M. (1991a) *L'Espace du Racisme*, Paris: Seuil.
Wieviorka, M. (1991b) 'Tendencies to racism in Europe: is the French experience unique or exemplary?' paper presented to a conference on 'Racism and Migration in Europe in the 1990s', 20–22 September.
Wieviorka, M. (1992) *La France Raciste*, Paris: Seuil.

7

UNIVERSALISM AND DIFFERENCE: THE CRISIS OF ANTI-RACISM IN THE UK AND FRANCE

Cathie Lloyd

Introduction: the crisis in anti-racism?

It has been widely argued that the anti-racist movement in France is suffering a crisis (Taguieff, 1991). I suggest here that something similar has been happening in the UK, but that it has been less openly acknowledged. The crisis in anti-racism has taken different forms in the UK and in France, but there are interesting parallels. The crisis is in part an aspect of the general crisis of the left, and associated values, particularly of modernity and universalism. In both countries, the 'left' has traditionally been identified with anti-racism (although this is a complex relationship, as outlined by Guiral (1977)).[1] Thus the fragmentation of the left in recent years, particularly through the loss of confidence in the Enlightenment values of progress, and the dissolution of many left structures have sapped the vitality of anti-racist movements. In a weakened state, these movements are less able to confront the massive rise in racism and fascism, shown by recent events in Germany, but also in ex-Yugoslavia with 'ethnic cleansing', and in Holland, Belgium and France with the rise of new extreme-right parties. In the UK, racial violence is extremely widespread despite vigorous campaigning and policy making over many years.[2]

This paper focuses on the basis of anti-racist beliefs and discourses:

for instance, the ideas of human equality, universalism, and faith in the inevitability of progress and the possibility of the improvement of humanity. These ideas are particularly relevant to France, where much anti-racist discourse still resounds to the great names of the Enlightenment, and where it is claimed that the first anti-racists were some of the *philosophes* and revolutionaries of the eighteenth century (in particular the Abbé Gregoire).[3]

In the UK, the problems of the anti-racist movements revolve around the weaknesses of the left, especially its exclusion from power, which has increased defensiveness, narrow labourism, lack of will and divisions in the left and encouraged a long-standing split between black and white approaches to organization (Heineman, 1972).

In both countries there has been a contestation of ideas, particularly since the 1970s, involving a challenge to 'left universalism' based on the assertion of the importance of authentic experience (France) and the politics of identity (the UK). The argument here is that there can be fundamental (or significant) differences between individual experiences or cultures, and that minority cultures should be safeguarded. One problem that becomes evident, I would argue, is that the roots of Enlightenment universalism are full of contradictions and limitations, which suggest that universalism was (paradoxically) particular and Eurocentric (and even perhaps narrower than this). The ideas of the Enlightenment (especially in France) have been sites of considerable struggle, so that today they are appropriated in a number of different and complex ways.

In this paper I will argue that it is important to assess critically the theoretical and conceptual framework of anti-racist organizations. Many of the central contradictions in the French and British movements revolve around questions of 'identity' or 'difference' versus universalism in an apparent dichotomy. This may mean an uncomfortable questioning of former certainties. However, I will also try to show that these discourses of 'difference' or of 'identity politics' bring with them their own problems and contradictions. Both *differentialism/particularism* and *universalism* are the subjects of myth-making, a process whereby grand ideas are appropriated and reforged through reference to heroic struggles of the past. It thus becomes difficult but necessary to disentangle the different aspects of myth and appropriation.

The debates about the 'crisis of anti-racism' in the UK and France suggest parallels and divergences. The French contributors to this debate have considered questions raised by the crisis of anti-racism at high levels of theoretical complexity, and the French debate could usefully inform the British one because it is dealing with shared fundamental issues. I suggest that the two experiences illustrate serious problems with both particularist notions of difference or identity and universalism, but that within the debates are the seeds of some very exciting new ways to redefine the project of anti-racism as one relating to social and political rights and citizenship.

One might expect that the influence of universalist discourses in the French left and anti-racist movements would make it resistant to notions of 'difference' and 'identity'. After all, put simply, the universalist view holds that all people are equal and that differences exist 'only' on the surface as a result of different experiences and histories. In much Enlightenment thought we are told either that people are all capable (through learning) of achieving the highest levels of 'civilisation' or that modern (European) humanity has degenerated from a common state of innocence. This admittedly is to caricature and simplify the different arguments of the *philosophes*. What is important, however, is that aspects of their thought have become part of the general culture, particularly through the period of the French Revolution, the transforming and purifying revolutionary mission of the Jacobins, and struggles in the nineteenth and twentieth centuries to legitimize successive regimes and movements by reference to these 'founding myths'. Along the way, these ideas themselves have been appropriated to make them fit realities for which they were not originally conceived. To give one example, it is frequently claimed[4] that the Abbé Gregoire was 'the first anti-racist'. However, despite his contributions to the anti-slavery movement and Jewish emancipation, 'anti-racism' as such did not exist in his days. There are obvious problems with retrospective claims such as these, which are frequently made by contemporary anti-racists for figures such as Gregoire.

On the left, 'universalism' in the nineteenth century was used to argue for the essential unity of the working class. The special role of the working class was to act as an agency for the achievement of an equal society. Divisions between workers were the result of the way capitalists used foreign labour to undercut indigenous wages. This type of argument thus denies the possibility of working-class racism and, where conflicts do arise, refuses to confront them by displacing the argument. There are other difficulties in the use of this type of argument, particularly in relation to the growth of fascism in the 1930s (for example, the 'class against class' position in which working-class support for fascism was ignored and which focused instead on 'social democrats' as 'social fascists') and the debates on the left about the 'correct' position to take up in relation to colonial liberation movements. The ambivalence of the French Communist Party to Algerian nationalism is of great relevance here (Joly, 1991; Hamon and Rotman, 1979). I will not deal with these issues here, but rather will look briefly at a more recent example of this argument in anti-racism in the 1970s and 1980s.

I refer to an ongoing study of the way in which ideas of identity and difference have interacted with ideas of universalism in the written materials and practices of one of the older French anti-racist movements, the Mouvement Contre le Racisme et Pour l'Amitié entre les Peuples (MRAP).[5] Initially, the main way in which 'identity' is expressed in its activities and publications is in a rather folkloric manner, through cultural demonstrations on gala solidarity evenings, with 'ethnic food', music, song and dancing. However, through the 1970s with the settlement and feminization of the migrant population, there is a discernible shift, a change in the way people in France are thinking and acting in relation to 'immigrants' (particularly those from North Africa) living in France. From units of labour, families 'become visible', and the question of living together in close quarters becomes important. Thus the way in which immigrants, especially those from North Africa, are socially constructed changes during this period. What is interesting is the way in which the anti-racist movement changes in response to this.

The early references in MRAP publications (*Droit et Liberté*) point to the need to understand the problems and the culture of immigrants in order to help deal with discrimination. At the same time, the theme of cultural diversity is frequently present in the practice of the anti-racist movement, with cultural evenings in local committees particularly important in the solidarity aspects of anti-racism. Education is seen as an important tool to overcome the 'fear of difference', and anti-racist education is used to help to understand and accept 'the Other'.[6] There are a number of interesting points here: in particular, the way in which the construction of 'the Other' entails an assumption of a community of 'we' who are 'not Other'. One editorial encourages the reader who may be going on holiday to reflect on the societies being visited and to be aware of the relationships involved in mass tourism. In this, the MRAP is responding to the new intellectual climate after 1968, which must have been a difficult adjustment especially for those MRAP activists who were close to the Communist Party.

The transition is, however, incomplete. The more traditional anti-racist arguments are still frequently used in the 1980s: that racism is an attempt to divide the working class (which has a universalist

mission), and that an assertion of anti-racism is part of the revolutionary and republican traditions of liberty, equality and fraternity, and
the Declaration of the Rights of Man. I would argue that there was
an attempt at a synthesis, particularly in the MRAP, between the
universal and the particular, embodied in the slogan 'equally in difference'.

This linkage was expressed in an important statement by the movement's then President (Professor F. Gremy) in November 1980 (*Droit
et Liberté*, 1980). An announcement was made of the launch of a new
monthly publication, significantly titled *Differences*, and a change in
the title of the MRAP from 'Mouvement Contre le Racisme, l'Anti-
Semitisme et Pour la Paix' to 'Mouvement Contre le Racisme et
pour l'Amitié entre les Peuples'.[7] The suppression of a reference to
opposition to anti-Semitism is made on the grounds that racism cannot
be divided, and that it is important to recognize other important
manifestations of racism, particularly against North Africans. The
introduction of the words 'friendship between peoples' was to replace
a commitment to 'peace' as something more active. It also introduces
the theme of cultural diversity:

> For us racism is not simply an unjust and murderous ideology but it is
> fundamentally an impoverishment. Each culture brings to the human sym-
> phony, sonorities and harmonies proper to itself. In praising difference, we
> should see not an appeal for separation and ignorance but an appeal for
> exchange, dialogue and fraternity.

Here then is an attempt to bring together the two discourses of
universalism and difference. Racism cannot be divided, and there
should be no special case (hence the dropping of the reference to
anti-Semitism). However, part of the reason given for the change of
name is the realization of another specific racism, against North Africans. There is an attempt to argue that, through celebrating
humanity's differences, universal values (particularly fraternity) can
be realized. While there is one racism to be combated, there is a
plurality of 'peoples'.

In the UK, the debate about the future of anti-racism is narrower,
perhaps more 'practical', with two main focuses: the internal problems
of the anti-racist movement, and the shortcomings of policies to overcome discrimination. The development of ethnic classification and
terminology as a site of considerable struggles in the 1980s has encouraged the fragmentation of groups and has led some to speak of

themselves as belonging to a 'race'. For instance, recently the Commission for Racial Equality consulted its local organizations about their names and the preferred title (to replace Community Relations Councils) was Race Equality Councils). If we accept that classificatory discourses are important (and this is the point of the fierce debates around them), then anti-racists should be very concerned at this re-emergence of the term 'race', which is something which ultimately can never be appropriated for any other purpose than to attempt to justify racism. The danger is that the use of the term will play into the hands of racists. What do people in the UK mean when they talk about 'race equality', given the contradictory logic of this term? We neglect to confront the term 'race' at our peril.

The major debates in the UK about the nature of post-industrial society/post-Fordism which took place in the late 1980s and early 1990s (using French postmodernist references, but with the main impact coming considerably later than in France, which makes this comparison so intriguing) largely passed by the implications about the growth of racism[8] and focused instead on the fragmentation of identity, which separated the implications of social change from its economic base. While I would not argue for a crude economic determinism, there has been in the debate a neglect of the broad dimensions of economic equality. For instance, there are very few studies of the interface between the experience of racism and poverty (Cook and Watt, 1992). The debate about 'post-industrial society' rarely takes into consideration growing global inequality and Third World immiseration. The emphasis on the idea that the personal is political pulled anti-racism away from its linkages with the community and relocated it at the individual level. Sivanandan (1990, pp. 38–9) pointed to the emptiness of this position: 'carried to its logical conclusion, just to be black, for instance, was politics enough: because it was in one's blackness that one was aggressed, just to be black was to make a statement against such aggression', and suggested that this was a 'way out' for the 'emerging black middle class of functionaries and intellectuals'. This argument is also pursued by Gilroy (1992) in a rather different analysis, in which he points to 'many voices from within the black communities themselves which have needed no prompting to develop their own fascination with ethnic differences and thus reduce political definitions of "race" to a narcissistic celebration of culture and identity'. In attempting to escape from one reduction (the economic), there is a danger of falling into another, on the basis of essentialized difference (Crosby, 1992).

The UK and France: different traditions of anti-racism

There are some important common themes in discussions in the UK and France, such as the nature of the changes in contemporary society and the way to understand them, and the relationship between a traditionally universalist left anti-racism (in a crisis of self-doubt), particularism and difference. However, these issues are born out of quite different traditions of political debate and anti-racist organization.

It is to the question of different traditions of anti-racism that I will now turn. These traditions reflect to some extent the positions of the populations and social actors concerned in anti-racist work, and the growth of state structures and interventions in this area which, especially in the UK, has had an effect on the activity and organization of voluntary structures. In the UK, I will argue, the theme is increasingly related to racialized relations, while in France issues are related to new conceptions of citizens' rights.

In the UK, through the implementation of the Race Relations Acts, especially the 1976 Act, the state has played a leading role in developing anti-discrimination, multi-ethnic and 'anti-racist' policies. The 'race relations project' has been affected as a result of its being implemented during a period of growing social inequality and as part of a wider state policy of 'integration and control' (Lloyd, 1993). The Race Relations Acts in the UK came into effect at a time when there were efforts to form a national anti-racist, umbrella-style civil rights movement. The failure of the Campaign Against Racial Discrimination (CARD) in the 1960s illustrates the general difficulties of establishing a broad anti-racist movement in the UK, (Heineman, 1972). There were problems of a fundamental clash between reformists and radicals; the paternalism of white social democrats; and divisions between 'immigrant' groupings, in an attempt to establish an overambitious campaign with ill-defined goals.

The influence of developments in the USA led to attempts to transplant experiments which were continuously being outdated by transatlantic experiences. The efforts of other anti-racists to mediate between these antagonistic groupings were neutralized. These conflicts seem regularly to resurface in anti-racist organizations in the UK.

Divisions within the anti-racist/anti-fascist movement again began to emerge in the 1970s, despite massive mobilizations in opposition to National Front campaigning activity. Many questions which exercised French anti-racists in the 1980s, particularly over the limits of popular campaigning and their relationship with the media, and the development of 'Rock against Police' into the mega-concerts of SOS-Racisme, were rehearsed ten years earlier in British experience of 'Rock against Racism'. Gilroy's analysis of *Temporary Hoarding*, the punk-oriented journal of Rock Against Racism, which tapped into a popular culture similar to the early issues of *CARF*, suggests (Gilroy 1987, p. 129) that the anti-racist project was beginning to address 'universalist' questions, if only by a rearticulation of consumerist impulses through pop culture for radical ends:

> it makes racism central to radical or revolutionary sentiment not because it was the most important dimension to life in the declining UK but because it was a moment in the process of social and political struggle where the system as a whole was vulnerable, where its irrationality, bias and brutality could be demonstrated to exist. It was the proof that everything that the left had said about capitalism in general and Britain in particular was true.

Fundamental disagreements about tactics quickly surfaced between those who wished to privilege defeating the National Front electorally and those with longer-term aims involving grass-roots organization against racism (*CARF* 1977), which might have given rise to a structure similar to the MRAP's today. Sectarianism and unwillingness to listen to the experiences of black anti-racists within the white left exacerbated tensions, which ultimately blew organizations apart. Contemporary debates between the Anti-Racist Alliance, Anti-Nazi League and Anti-Fascist Alliance are reproducing those of the 1970s without apparently trying to draw lessons from them, but also within the new dynamic of a much stronger challenge from black leadership.

The 1980s was the decade of 'municipal anti-racism' led by the Greater London Council (GLC). After 1981 most left-wing (Labour) local authorities adopted policies to encourage the employment and promotion of 'ethnic minorities' and to take their special needs into account. Major debates took place about the way to tackle 'institutional racism', with strongly held positions about the respective merits of multiculturalism versus anti-racism.

However, the enactment of 'correct' policies at local level was fraught with difficulties. For instance, in the field of education there has been a complex reaction on the part of white parents (sometimes but not always fuelled by the organized extreme right) against anti-racist curricula. Following the killing of Ahmed Ullah in a Manchester school playground, the Burnage Report (Macdonald, 1990) concluded that the anti-racist strategy adopted by the school was seen as concerning black but not white pupils and parents, and assumed that white people could not be anti-racist.

John LaRose (1992, p. 41), in discussing the intolerance of what he calls 'symbolic anti-racists' (i.e. those based in local authority race units) in preventing the views of white anti-racists from being expressed, writes:

> I have been to meetings, numerous meetings in this country over the years, where a white worker gets up and begins to speak, and he says something about blacks and this and that, and immediately the whole meeting prevents him from continuing to speak; so you don't ever hear what his real grievances are . . . The middle classes tend with their liberalism to believe that they are being antiracist by preventing white workers from explaining their grievances and discussing their grievances openly, as they should, in meetings with black people, with Asian people, white people, with anybody, for example, who is interested in bringing about serious antiracism, racial equality and social justice.

The growth of a 'race relations industry' armed with a carefully tuned set of policies for different ethnic groups has in the UK eclipsed the role of association,[9] many of which have in any case been sucked into competing for local authority grants a process (like in France)[10] which has necessitated accommodation and conformity with certain norms. The incorporation of independent community-based groups reduces the number of voices which can be heard, and tends to shape policies in a certain mould. Much theoretical literature about anti-racism does not address movements, but rather different levels of state policy.

The bitterness of the debate in the UK dividing people according to ethnic origin has deepened in the 1990s. I would argue here with Miles (see this volume) among many others that the experience of 'race relations' policies in the 1980s has reinforced the racialization of social relations in contemporary Britain. I would add that this has been exacerbated by the neglect and gross insensitivity of the white 'left'.[11] Tendencies which Heineman in 1972 described as tearing apart the CARD, particularly the gulf between the patronizing 'ownership' of white left-liberals and black radicals, have been strengthened. Thus, we have seen different parts of the anti-racist movement at bitter loggerheads about the legitimacy of their respective organizations or affiliations, sectarianism, specific attitudes to black leadership, the nature of the 'main enemy', and the relationship between anti-racism and community (Platt, 1992; Wadsworth, 1992; *Searchlight*, 1992; *CARF*, 1992).

The 1992 uprising in Los Angeles, USA, where much of the notion of 'equal opportunities' originated (Sooben, 1991) also underlines these concerns. It does not seem that the recent riots in US cities will lead to a radical reappraisal of the policies which have failed to deal with inequality and racism. Jesse Jackson has pointed to the need for a much wider agenda, which I think could relocate the role of anti-racism (Jackson, 1992). He writes:

> For years, racism has helped to camouflage the growing desperation in our society. The poor were assumed to be black and brown, lazy and dissolute, different... But most poor people are white not black or brown. Most poor people work every day that they can. They need more opportunity not more indignity.
>
> Now, once again, the riots in Los Angeles and elsewhere remind us just how incalculable the costs of neglect are. In the end as Dr King taught us: 'The agony of the poor impoverishes the rich; the betterment of the poor enriches the rich. We are inevitably our brother's keeper because we are our brother's brother. We truly have no other choice.'

Jackson is using a broadly Universalist (Christian) discourse here. His comments about the way in which black and white poverty are interlinked but covered up by racism connects with findings in the UK critical of anti-racism. The US experience must make us question the gains made in recent years, and pose the question of what 'equal opportunities' can mean in a context of growing inequality (what the French call a society à deux vitesses).

The 'crisis of anti-racism' in France is taking place in a rather different structure. The 1972 Law Against Racism did not create an enforcement body like the CRE,[12] but was rather the product of concerted campaigning and lobbying by established anti-racist organizations, notably the MRAP (MRAP, 1984) but also other organizations such as the Ligue des Droits de l'Homme. Since 1981, when Mitterrand made it easier for foreigners to form associations, there has been a massive expansion of associations particularly linked to the younger generation born in France, the most well known of which is SOS-Racisme. Some of these have now been established long enough to be able to take on cases under the 1972 law.

As in the UK, associations have been incorporated into the state mechanisms through competition for grants, which has had a distorting effect to their activities. In some instances, it was felt that anti-racists were being used in party political manipulations, as during the March 1992 regional elections when anti-racists mobilized across France to oppose Front National election meetings, but were 'warned off' when they began to succeed. The role of SOS-Racisme and France Plus as vectors of Socialist government policy have been hotly debated, and there is considerable evidence for this.[13] In the past few years there has been a greater involvement of the state in the assessment of 'integration' policies, with annual reports from the Haut Conseil à l'Integration (1991a, 1991b, 1992) and the Commission Consultative des Droits de l'Homme (1991, 1992).

In France, the crisis on the left, the decline of the French Communist Party (PCF), wide-spread unemployment, industrial restructuring and the crisis in education have created massive social deprivation and alienation. Anti-racists have also had to confront their failure to prevent the rise of the Front National, a mass movement which has used new right discourse increasingly, in recent years to deny its racist and fascist core.

The crisis of strategy: which racism?

If we can talk about different traditions in the UK and France, it is also clear that there are similar problems. In both countries, a central question is the nature of the racism to be confronted, and therefore the appropriate combative strategy. The success of the right has also highlighted the inadequacy of what the French see as the 'failure' of their traditional models of integration (Schnapper, 1991; Noiriel, 1991), which are linked in the debate to the decay of key social institutions such as the family, the education system, employment, trade unions and political parties (especially the PCF). Debate in France has to a large extent engaged outwards, perhaps partly as a result of the relationship between the anti-racists and intellectuals/ researchers in France and the role of intellectuals in public life (Benabdessadok, 1992). Anti-racism is also seen as occupying a central place in political debate, to be linked with questions of national identity and citizenship.

I think that this is an important difference with the UK, where the debate focuses largely on problems with the anti-racist policies adopted by public authorities (Jenkins and Solomos, 1987; Gilroy, 1992), and debates within and between anti-racist organizations (*Searchlight*, 1992; *CARF*, 1992),[14] rather than an analysis of how to explain the continued existence of racism. Miles (this volume) expresses this as 'labelling' rather than 'explaining' racism.

The British debate about multiculturalism has highlighted the way in which state policies fail to differentiate between different aspects of cultures, which may have unacceptable consequences for parts of a group. This was well illustrated during the debates around the Rushdie Affair, and continues to be manifest in attitudes to 'minority religions'. If 'minorities' are viewed in the UK as homogeneous groups defined solely by their religion, this enables religious leaders to 'edge themselves into positions of political as well as spiritual leadership, defining the community's agenda and power structure, and negotiating with the state for resources' (Bard, 1992). This development has a particularly pernicious effect on women (Yuval-Davis, 1992), whose social marginalization is often not challenged by traditionalist multi-culturalism. Anti-racists, it is argued, have disenfranchised themselves from adopting a position on these issues, by privileging the struggle against 'racism' over the support for oppressed groups, by failing to understand the implications of religious fundamentalisms and by their distance from the 'minority groups' on whose behalf they mobilize.

Multicultural policies have been criticized as tending to encourage the development of simplistic models of 'minority' cultures and the formation of 'instant experts'. There are reasons for this inward approach – particularly the way in which governmental power has been exercised since 1979 – but it is a weakness of which we need to be aware, rather than allowing it to continue to immobilize debate. This is one of the reasons why discussion about the French experience is useful and illuminating.

The French 'model of integration',[15] which until recently operated through a fairly liberal access to nationality and citizenship (particularly the *jus solis* principle), is seen to be failing at a time when many French-born young people whose parents were immigrants are demanding their rights and a proper recognition of their position within French society. This is evident in the different grass-roots organizations from which sprang the 'marches for equality' of the early 1980s. The older anti-racist movements faced not only the problem of how to respond to the challenge of the new forms which young people created, but also the problem of how to act when the social framework which in the past formed the base of their activity had gone. One crucial debate which is just starting in the French anti-racist movement is what precisely are the limits and boundaries of anti-racism.

There is a perceived danger that the broad anti-racist movements will try to fill the vacuum left by the decayed primary and local institutions (the family, education and community-based organiza-tions, even political parties), particularly through the activities of their local committees. There is concern that the specific struggle against racism will be absorbed by the wider social issues which desperately need an answer, and that the anti-racism movement will be under pressure to turn itself into a sort of substitute political party, and lose its specific role. This could be very damaging to a national organization like the MRAP, which includes members from different political parties, positions and religious perspectives. The situation is rendered more complicated because there is considerable evidence that the Front National has itself stepped into the vacuum, providing day-to-day support for people in marginal positions (those suffering unemployment, bad housing, insecurity, etc.) who have been abandoned by the main political parties (Tristan, 1987).[16]

In attempting to mobilize against the Front National, anti-racists in France have gone perhaps further than in the UK in discussing the implications of the new right. In the early 1980s, as we have seen, organizations were continuously referring back to traditional anti-racist ideas of the 1930s, 1940s and 1950s to explain what and why they should mobilize. This needs to be understood in the context of the violence used by extreme-right groups particularly in the late 1970s and early 1980s.[17]

However, in the 1980s the anti-racists had to take account of two important factors. First, the main everyday target for racial violence and Front National propaganda were 'immigrants' from North Africa and the reference point was *Algerie française* and France's imperial greatness rather than 'Hitlerian Nazism', although of course there were links between the two in France.[18] Second, the discourse of the extreme right was changing, partly to accommodate to the postwar period in which biological racism was less acceptable and scientifically disproved (UNESCO, 1980). A culturally based racism mirrored the discourse of the anti-racists (particularly the post–1968 'Third Worldists') in claiming the 'right to difference'. Thus the Front National could claim that it was against racism, but particularly racism against the French. Le Pen's famous comment illustrates this well: 'I prefer my daughters to my nieces and my nieces to my neighbours like everyone else . . . all men are the same'.[19]

To anti-racists, part of the problem with the Front National's new discourse is that it is no longer possible simply to label the party because of its leader's fascist past, however important this may be. To many Front National voters, the sort of discourse I have just cited is common sense and reassuring. When this discourse is deployed, anti-racist 'demonizing' of the Front National seems to be counterproductive, although the current levels of racial violence in France point to an extremely serious situation (Guidice, 1992). While there are many other, more convincing explanations for the rise of populist racism, there is a genuine problem: the failure to address the issues being currently raised by the Front National. Clearly, the nature of the 'racist' being opposed needs to be looked at again more carefully.

There is one powerful strand in critique of the anti-racists which suggests that their mistaken strategy in drawing attention and overreacting to racists is responsible for the rise of the Front National. A partial explanation is suggested by Taguieff (1991), who indicates the way in which anti-racist activity has become routinized, dominated by a teleological conception of 'racial prejudice' which traces a continuous link between a negative attitude towards 'Others' and racism as a system of extermination. This is well portrayed by an MRAP poster of the early 1980s, which was headed 'Attention! Racism Leads to Fascism!'. It portrayed a male figure (probably of North African origin) fleeing from an aggressor who was wearing a military helmet and wielding a club, across a vast urban space reminiscent of the Nuremberg rallies and with swastikas festooned on a monolith. How were people to relate this dramatic representation to the racism which they would encounter in their everyday lives and which has sustained the Front National?

Taguieff (1991) argues that the crisis of anti-racism lies in the lack of a clear understanding of the racism(s) which has (have) to be fought. He distinguishes three types of anti-racism:

1 The economic reductionist view of racism, which reduced racism to a mode of legitimation of capitalist exploitation, and the linked belief that racism will disappear with imperialism.[20]
2 A demonological anti-racism, in which racism incarnates absolute evil.
3 A rationalist pedagogical anti-racism, based on the idea that racism was a biological reductionism that could be 'disproved' and therefore eliminated by science or education.

As a result of these views it was thought that, if the notion of racial hierarchy had no scientific or economic basis, it could be expected to go away. What happened in anti-racist discourse was a sort of 'demonizing disqualification' (Taguieff, 1991, p. 31) which attempted to dispel racism by repeating rational arguments and disqualifying racists as 'bad' (or ignorant) scientists. The influence of cultural relativism meant that to reject racism was to reject all forms of ethnocentrism; the 'real' anti-racism became a sort of cultural relativism. Ideas of identity and differentialism were acceptable because they were consonant with individualist values (crucial, as we have seen, to social integration in France), a 'return to roots' and the abandonment of ideas of universality. Taguieff argues strongly that the fundamental mistake of the anti-racists was to fail to understand the way in which their project was being undermined by the new right, whose new racism was also based on the principle of the radical difference (here on the incommensurability) or different cultural forms.

In a recent essay, Stuart Hall (1992) debates this same issue but in a British context and argues:

> The fact that this grounding of ethnicity in difference was deployed, in the discourse of racism, as a means of disavowing the realities of racism and repression does not mean that we can permit the term to be permanently colonized. That appropriation will have to be contested, the term disarticulated from its position in the discourse of 'multi-culturalism' and transcoded, just as we previously had to recuperate the term 'black', from its place in a system of negative equivalences. (p. 257)

It seems to me that there are several initial problems with this brave project. First, in neither the French nor the British context have anti-racists fully grappled with the implications of the broader constituency made available to organizations like the Front National through their new-found discourse claiming respectability. Until this is further advanced, it will be difficult to change the terms of the debate. And to attempt to do so may be dangerous without taking up a strong position against the new right. Furthermore, the example given of a renegotiated term, 'black', was successful only for a limited period and space. New challenges are now present for anti-racists in Europe (Miles, 1992).[21]

Conclusion

It may be becoming clear that, in discussing anti-racism in the UK and France, one is dealing with similar problems and difficulties. In both countries there is an increase in racism and new demands are being placed on anti-racist organizations. In both situations there are new actors present: in the UK, the Anti Racist Alliance has a very different approach to leadership questions than had organizations in the past; while in France, associations are often established on the basis of generation and 'experience', based on identity. Weakened by the crisis of the left, and unable to overcome the contradictions of universalism/particularism, anti-racist organizations have found it difficult to respond to the new right.

In the UK, much of the recent struggle has taken place around the policies of equal opportunity and multiculturalism, while in France independent anti-racist organizations remain at the centre of the debate, although government policies on 'integration' are also an important issue. In one sense the debate in France is much broader, and it is more conscious that it encompasses implications for society as a whole. This is partly due to the Enlightenment universalist tradition, which was particularly important in the immediate postwar years in 'reconstructing' the French nation after the profound divisions caused by the Occupation, Vichy and the Resistance.[22]

As I have already suggested, there are problems here in the way in which the Enlightenment is used to 'legitimate' anti-racism. It is unsound to try to transplant an eighteenth-century world-view to justify contemporary positions. Considerable scholarship has also pointed to the contradictory, partial and ambiguous Enlightenment view of societies and peoples outside Europe (Duchet, 1971; Sala-Molins, 1988). Some writings suggest an extraordinarily wide concept of humanity, particularly in speculations about the 'natural man'. Montesquieu thought that the African's physical characteristics prevented him from feeling any sympathy for their enslavement:

> those concerned are black from head to toe and they have such flat noses that it is impossible to feel sorry for them. One cannot get into one's mind that god, who is a very wise being should have put a soul, above all a good soul, in a body that was entirely black. (Montesquieu, 1989, pp. 249–50)

Voltaire's attachment to polygenism led him to attempt to identify the 'singularities' for the basis of races, and he rejects the view that the *sauvage* has anything to teach about the dilemmas of contemporary man (for instance, in his short story 'L'Ingenu', 1966), which had been suggested earlier by Montaigne's profoundly humanist essay 'Des Cannibales' (1972).

It is apparent on closer study that, while the 'official discourse' of anti-racism is one of universalism, there are various important subtexts or counter-themes which are used as part of common sense without stock of their implications for the general model. I am arguing here that it would be wrong to oversimplify the French position by suggesting that the model of 'universalism' encompasses all.

As indicated in the analysis of the MRAP, there is an uneasy 'cohabitation' between universalism and cultural relativism, as expressed by the slogan 'equality in difference' often deployed by the MRAP. At the same time, there are many specific themes around different groups of people and discriminations: for instance, Jewish people and their experience of anti-Semitism, North Africans and the conflict over decolonization, particularly the Algerian war, and people from the Dominions and Overseas Territories (DOM-TOM) who have French citizenship but who experience considerable discrimination (Condon and Ogden, 1991; Ravel, 1987). Contract workers from West Africa, travellers, refugees and others have different statuses again.

On the other hand, the British debate is not without its appeals to universalism. For instance, Sivanandan (1990, p. 22) argues that

> the joint struggles of refugee, migrant and black groups in Britain not only help to sustain the links between racism and imperialism and between racial oppression and class exploitation, but have also been at the forefront of the attempts to build a network of European groups against a new European racism . . .

He suggests that a broad community base ('organic in the sense of sharing a common life'), linking civil society in a complex web of struggle with the state, works towards a wider political movement commensurate with our times.

This vision seems to share a common concern with that of Sami Nair (1992), who argues that in the French context it is important to effect four fundamental changes: first, to refocus the question of French identity to take account of the profound transformations of the global social system; second, to make the integration of marginalized groups a matter of common right rather than extraordinary regulation; third, to define clear egalitarian rules about religious representation in the French secular space; and fourth, to reproblematize the way in which the nation is represented in order to make a space for diversity of origin.

It is clear that Nari and Sivanandan are thinking about profound changes for the nature of citizenship and nation-states. There are concerns particular to the different positions in France and the UK which mean that their focus is different. This brings me to my central argument. What I am suggesting (Lloyd, 1991)[23] is that each national debate has its own particularity, including its own contradictions (Silverman, 1992), but that there will be common themes and common problems. It may be necessary to construct a new framework for the 1990s, particularly in the broader European context. For instance, if the basis of universalist ideas of equality, liberty and fraternity cannot be transposed to contemporary struggles, and are unable either to help confront racism (which they largely predated) or inspire people, then as Balibar argues, we need to 'transform what we mean by universalism' (Balibar, 1989, p. 21). This entails fundamental changes in our understanding of citizenship and political participation, which is on the agenda for anti-racists because of Fortress Europe (Balibar, 1991).

Nair (1992) is thinking along similar lines when he surveys the potential for conflict between North and South, South and East, with continuing global inequality and pressure on migration to Europe in the 1990s. He argues that to get out of the vicious circle of development aid, and the fear of new immigration, what is needed is to take up the great idea of equality, beginning with a fundamental change to the concept of citizenship, giving civic rights to all people living in France regardless of their nationality. He sees in this the possibility of reopening a debate to strengthen and bring into the contemporary world the ideas of the Enlightenment. These ideas inspired many anti-colonial nationalisms and this source could be rediscovered.

Finally, this entails a realization that what has been criticized recently as 'universalist' was in fact highly particularist, and that those values of humanism, liberty, equality and fraternity will have to be fundamentally rethought if they are to provide a new basis for a European and international anti-racism.

Notes

1   Guiral (1977) points to the complexity of the attitudes of the left towards the categories 'race' and 'racism'. While left ideology rejects racism on the basis that all people are born equal in right, things are less clear in practice. In particular, that part of the left which inherited aspects of Jacobinism has been reluctant to accept human differences, and has stressed the superiority of the French Enlightenment message in an assimilationist approach. Neither is the left free of 'scientific' racism, anti-Catholicism (anti-Latin) racism or anti-Semitism.

2   To give one recent example, in the week when right-wing youth were besieging asylum-seekers in Rostock in Germany, no national media coverage was given to arson attacks on a mosque in Charlton, East London, near the headquarters of the British National Party (see Baxter, 1992).

3   Gregoire (1750–1831) was a representative of the clergy in the revolutionary Estates General and became a member of the Convention in 1790. He was an active member of the Societé des Amis des Noirs and advocated the abolition of the slave trade and a gradual transition from colonial slavery by

building up an intermediary stratum of 'people of colour'. When slavery was abolished, however, on the 16th Pluviose of Year 2 of the French Republic (4 February 1794), following Toussaint L'Ouverture's successful uprising, Gregoire was horrified as he believed that a long period of apprenticeship for liberty was required. He remarked that suddenly to emancipate black slaves was equivalent to beating a pregnant woman so that she could give premature birth. Gregoire was also involved in campaigning for the emancipation of the Jews in France. Overall it would seem that, although he was relatively progressive for his time, Gregoire cannot be seen as an entirely unproblematic example of an early anti-racist.

4 For example, in the publications of the Movement Against Racism (MRAP) Gregoire occupies a particular place, although other Enlightenment figures are frequently cited, as are other anti-slavery campaigners, particularly Victor Schoelcher. See, for instance, *Droit et Liberté* between June 1950 and 1980, and *Différences*, September 1992, where there are numerous references to different aspects of Gregoire's work (writings on human emancipation, slavery and Jewish emancipation) as one who would have been associated with anti-racist thought, and one of the first anti-racists.

5 MRAP was formed in 1949 from the illegal MNCR (Mouvement National Contre le Racisme) and the UJRE (Union des Juifs pour la Resistance et l'Entre'aide). It was linked to resistance organizations which had tried to warn the Jewish population of what was really happening in concentration camps and saved many Jewish children from the Vichy-Occupation regimes. Since then the MRAP has gone through many transformations in its orientations. It has a network of some 250 local committees with a federal structure, and a number of national subject committees. There are approximately 4,700 members (Documents of the MRAP National Congress, 10–12 April 1992, Saint Denis, Paris).

6 See review of Marcou *Le Racisme et l'enfance* in *Droit et Liberté*, no. 335, Dec. 1974-Jan. 1975, which argues for 'le droit à la différence, le droit d'autri de vivre avec des coutumes, des traditions, des modes de comportement qui ne sont pas "les notres" '.

7 The old title in English reads 'Movement Against Racism, Anti-Semitism and for Peace' and the new, 'Movement Against Racism and for Friendship between Peoples'.

8 For instance, there was very little on this issue with bearing on anti-racism in the pages of *Marxism Today*, although the implications of this critique have been drawn out by Sivanandan (1990) in particular, that the analysis of identity must eventually return to the analysis of the economic (pp. 28–9).

9 For instance, 'broker' community-based organizations such as the West Indian Standing Conference are cited (Goulborne, 1988) as having been 'bypassed' by the development of state-funded agencies, such as the Commission for Racial Equality and local authority race relations units, which have channelled off some of its representational functions but also many of its potential leaders.

10 The Social Action Fund (FAS) was established in 1958, at first just for Algerians and since 1964–6 for all 'immigrant' workers. It provides grants for immigrant associations and anti-racist groups.

11 Without going into too much detail here, the response to the Rushdie Affair, failure to mobilize around issues of great importance to black communities (such as policing and criminalization), and intransigence towards black organizations in trade unions and political parties would all be examples of an inability to accommodate. There are signs that similar mistakes are being made in France.

12 In 1972 there was no proposal for an enforcement body, partly because the Law Against Racism was to operate through existing associations and partly because the idea of a semi-autonomous statutory body such as the CRE would not have been acceptable in the then right-wing dominated French political system. While the law was unopposed in the National Assembly, there was little evidence that mainstream politics was prepared to give resources to an anti-discrimination body.

13 For instance, on 14 July 1992, SOS-Rascisme was given a huge government grant for a concert with the theme 'Our mates' Europe', which stressed an alternative dimension to the republican values expressed traditionally in the Bastille Day military parade. It coincided with the government's plea for a 'yes' vote for Europe in the referendum.

14 In particular, see *CARF*, no. 6, Jan./Feb. 1992, which outlines the need to respond to new forms of racism and to learn from the limitations of past anti-fascist struggles, maintaining the need for a grass-roots movement which 'must fight racism and therefore fascism'. 'Rumbled', *Searchlight*, April 1992, attacks the Anti Nazi League for failing to understand the contemporary neofascist movement, and accuses it of political opportunism in its relaunch. A number of critiques of anti-racist policies are brought together by Donald and Rattansi (1992), but they do not address the question of anti-racist social movements.

15 Much has been written about the 'French model of integration'. Silverman (1992, p. 123) argues that there is no clear break between the ideas of integration and assimilation. Integration involves individual adhesion to society and 'an equality in rights but not necessarily a conformity in culture'.

16 Ann Tristan is a journalist who posed as an unemployed typist in Marseille and entered into contract and activity with the Front National. Her book emphasizes that, while there is a hard-core of violent neofascists, beneath the surface, the majority of people to whom the Front National appeals are 'ordinary' working-class French whose lives have been ravaged by economic change and who find immigrants an easy scapegoat (Tristan, 1987). She showed, however, that the Front National was able to enter a local community by taking up small grievances and acting on behalf of people, thus gradually extending its influence.

17 There were bomb attacks on anti-racist offices, and considerable neo-Nazi terrorist violence (the bombing of the synagogues on the rue Copernic and the rue des Rosiers, and attacks on immigrant workers hostels). Like the Anti-Nazi League of the late 1970s in Britain, the emphasis was on showing the Nazi past of Le Pen, and the strongest mobilizations and reactions were in the context of 'classic' anti-Semitic Nazism.

18 The most striking link is in the role of Maurice Papon, responsible for Jewish affairs in Bordeaux in the 1940s, and prefect of police in Paris in the 1960s

at the time of the Algerian war. He was responsible for a murderous suppression of a peaceful demonstration by the National Liberation Front against curfews of Algerians on 17 October 1961, which for many years was a taboo subject (Lloyd and Waters, 1991).

19 Interview on FR3 Saturday, 9 December 1989, reported in *Libération*, 9 December 1989.

20 For instance, the General Declaration of the Cultural Congress of Havana, Cuba, 4–11 January 1968.

21 Miles (1992) shows that the idea of 'black' as a site of resistance gained much of its strength from its claims to be a metaphor, but conjunctural and specific, and currently subject to increasing challenge.

22 I am not suggesting here that the French Republic prior to 1939 was a homogenous entity. There were profound divisions in France after 1789 over issues such as the position of the Church, colonialism, anti-Semitism (evidenced in the Dreyfus Affair) and fundamental ideas of the Republic.

23 I have argued that in making comparisons we need 'to bear in mind the surrounding political landscape', differences in terminology, and the historical, cultural and politico-philosophical contexts (Lloyd, 1991).

References

Balibar, E. (1989) 'Le racisme: encore un universalisme', *Mots*, no. 18, March.

Balibar, E. (1991) 'Racism and politics in Europe today', *New Left Review*, no. 186, March/April.

Bard, J. (1992) 'The priests have it', *New Statesman and Society*, 1 May.

Baxter, S. (1992) 'Face to face with fascism', *New Statesman and Society*, 4 September.

Benabdessadok, C. (1992) 'Anti-Racisme: Le point de vue de PA Taguieff', *Differences*, no. 127, April.

CARF (1977) (Series 1), October/November.

CARF (1992) (Series 2) January/February.

Commission Consultative des Droits de l'Homme (1991), *1990: La Lutte Contre le Racisme et la Xenophobie*, Paris: Documentation Français.

Commission Consultative des Droits de l'Homme (1992), *1991: La Lutte Contre le Racisme et la Xenophobie*, Paris: Documentation Français.

Condon, S. A. and Ogden, P. E. (1991) 'Afro-Caribbean migrants in France: employment, state policy and the migration process', *Transactions of the Institute of British Geographers*, vol. 16, pp. 440–57.

Cook, H., and Watt, S. (1992) 'Racism, women and poverty', in Glendenning, C., and Millar, J. (eds), *Women and Poverty in Britain: The 1990s*, Hemel Hempstead: Harvester.

Crosby, C. (1992) 'Dealing with difference', in Butler, J., and Scott, J. (eds), *Feminists Theorise the Political* London: Routledge.

Donald, J., and Rattansi, A. (1992) *'Race', Culture and Difference*, London: Sage.

Droit et Liberté (1980) no. 396, November/December.

Duchet, M. (1971) *Anthropologie et histoire au siècle des lumières*, Paris: Maspero.

Gilroy, P. (1987) *There Ain't No Black in the Union Jack*, London: Hutchinson.

Gilroy, P. (1992) 'The end of anti-racism', in Donald, J., and Rattansi, A. (eds), *'Race', Culture and Difference*, London: Sage.

Goulbourne, H. (1988) 'West Indian political leadership in Britain', The Byfield Memorial Lecture 1987, Occasional Papers in Ethnic Relations, no. 4, CRER, University of Warwick.

Guidice, F. (1992) *Arabacides*, Paris: La Découverte.

Guiral, P. (1977) 'Idée de race et pensée politique en France (gauche et droite) au XIXème siècle', in Guiral, P., *et al.* (eds) *L'idée de Race dans la pensée politique français contemporaine*, Paris: Gallimard.

Hall, S. (1992) 'New ethnicities', in Donald, J. and Rattansi, A. (eds), *'Race', Culture and Difference*, London: Sage.

Hamon, H., Rotman, P. (1979) *Les porteurs de valises: La résistance français à la guerre d'Algérie*, Albin Michel.

Haut Conseil à l'Intégration (1991a) *Premier Rapport*, February.

Haut Conseil à l'Intégration (1991b) *La Connaissance de l'Immigration et de l'Intégration*, November.

Haut Conseil à l'Intégration (1992) *Conditions Juridiques et Culturelles de l'Intégration*, January.

Heineman (1972) *The Politics of the Powerless: A Study of the Campaign Against Racial Discrimination*, Oxford: Oxford University Press/IRR.

Jackson, J. (1992) 'Fire and loathing', *Guardian*, 5 May.

Jenkins, R., and Solomos, J. (1987) *Racism and Equal Opportunity Policies in the 1980s*, Cambridge: Cambridge University Press.

Joly, D. (1991) *The French Communist Party and the Algerian War*, London: Macmillan.

LaRose, J. (ed.) (1992) *Racism, Nazism, Fascism and Racial Attacks*, Paris: European Action for Racial Equality and Social Justice.

Lloyd, C. (1991) 'Concepts, models and anti-racist strategies in Britain and France', *New Community*, vol. 18, no. 1.

Lloyd, C. (forthcoming) 'National approaches to immigration and minority policy', in Rex, J., and Drury, B. (eds), *The Mobilisation of Ethnic Minorities and Ethnic Social Movements in Europe*, Centre for Research in Ethnic Relations, University of Warwick.

Lloyd, C., and Waters, H. (1991) 'France: one culture, one people?', *Race and Class*, vol. 32, no. 3.

Macdonald, I., Bhavnani, R., Khan, L., and John, G. (1989) *Murder in the Playground*, London: Longsight Press.

Miles, R. (1992) 'Migration, racism and the nation state in contemporary Europe', in Satzewich, V. (ed.), *Deconstructing the Nation: Immigration, Multi-Culturalism and Racism in 90s Canada*, Toronto: Garamond Press.

Montaigne, L. (1972) 'Des Cannibales', in *Essais*, vol. 1, Paris: Fayard.

Montesquieu, (1989) *The Spirit of the Laws* (ed. and trans. by S. Cohler, J. Miller and M. Stone), Cambridge: Cambridge University Press.

MRAP (1984) *Chronique du Flagrante Racisme*, Paris: La Découverte.

Nair, S. (1992) *Le regard des Vainquers*, Paris: Grasset.

Noiriel, G. (1988) *Le Creuset Français*, Paris: Seuil.

Platt, S. (1992) 'Race wars', *New Statesman and Society*, 28 February.

Ravel, J. (1987) 'Un peu moins français que les autres?', *Differences*, no. 64, February.

Sala-Molins, L. (1988) *Le Code Noir*, Paris: PUF.

Schnapper, D. (1991) *La France de l'Integration*, Paris: Gallimard.

Searchlight (1992) Editorial: 'Rumbled', April.

Silverman, A. (1992) *Deconstructing the Nation: Immigration, Racism and Citizenship in Modern France*, London: Routledge.

Sivanandan, A. (1990) 'All that melts into air is solid: the hokum of New Times', *Race and Class*, vol. 31, no. 30.

Sooben, P. A. (1991) 'The origins of the Race Relations Act', *Research Papers in Ethnic Relations*, no. 12, CRER, University of Warwick.

Taguieff, P.-A. (1991) 'Les metamorphoses idéologiques du racisme et la crise de l'anti-racisme', in Taguieff, P.-A. (ed.), *Face au Racisme*, Vol. 2: *Hypothèses, Perspectives*, Paris: La Découverte.

Tristan, A. (1987) *Au Front*, Paris: Gallimard.

UNESCO (1980) *Sociological Theories of Race and Colonialism*, Paris: UNESCO.

Voltaire (1966) 'L'Ingenu' in *Romans et Contes*, Paris: G.-F. Flamarrion.

Yuval-Davis, N. (1992) 'Fundamentalism, multi-culturalism and women', in Donald, J., and Rattansi, A. (eds), *'Race', Culture and Difference*, London: Sage.

Wadsworth, M. (1992) 'Letter', *New Statesmen and Society*, 6 March.

Part IV

RACIALIZED IDENTITIES, LOCAL AND GLOBAL

8

RACISM, MENTAL ILLN[...]
THE POLITICS OF IDENTI[...]

Sallie Westwood

Introduction

The politics of identities is foregrounded in current attempts to revision the political agenda within the deformation of the West and the new global configurations. A new complexity has to be confronted in which all certainties of essentialist politics and grand narratives are fractured. We have to find a route through the fissures and towards a politics of identities that is articulated with a growing number of 'sites' in which this politics is discursively created. My concern in this paper is to elaborate some of the ways in which it is possible to analyse and understand a current politics while that politics is being generated and sustained, within the specific context of the struggles around racism and mental illness. In part this is a politics of the new social movements – a term much debated, but nevertheless useful in signalling the ways in which political action has been generated by women and men creating new collective identities and political subjects within civil society, often against the state. But the issues raised by the encounter between those of African-Caribbean and Asian descent in Britain and psychiatry as discourse and practice prompt a reconstruction of the most complex of issues for the politics of identities, the racialized articulation between the psychic and the social. In addition, the discussion seeks ways in which to explore the inverson of centre/periphery by bringing the margin to the centre. It thus contests the position in which the mentally ill of African-Caribbean and Asian descent are placed, offering instead a speaking position tioned by subjects. The paper begins with the continuing story of the encounter between racism and psychiatric discourses, one part of the way in which European identities have been constructed within the binary of the West and the Rest.

Racism and psychiatry

In 1988 Glyn Harrison and his colleagues in Nottingham, UK, published the results of an extended study of the incidence of schizophrenia among the African-Caribbean population of Nottingham (Harrison *et al.*, 1988). The study is the most recent in a series of studies reviewed by Ineichen (1989) which all suggest 'that rates of diagnosed schizophrenia among both British born and migrant Afro-Caribbeans are high'. The results from the Nottingham study showed an especially high incidence of schizophrenia among young black British subjects in the 16–29 age range, which was eighteen times the rate in the 'general population'. Across the age range the study showed a rate twelve to thirteen times higher among African-Caribbeans. The research was widely reported in the press and fuelled controversy and media interest in the relationship between racism and mental illness. Critics, like Sashidharan (*Guardian*, 4 November 1988), pointed to the inadequacy of the database, the difficulties surrounding diagnosis and the question of misdiagnosis in a racist society. Harrison defended his results as scientifically sound, but did point to the inner-city location of many young black people where rates of schizophrenia are generally higher. He and his co-workers also acknowledged the possible role of 'discrimination' (rather than racism) in the generation of schizophrenia. 'Such experiences of discrimination (Burke, 1984) may have schizophrenia evoking effects and could have played a significant role in the higher rates reported here', and Harrison *et al.* continue, 'It is possible that individuals genetically or constitutionally vulnerable to schizophrenia on account of selection factors in their parents are especially sensitive to these forms of social stress' (Harrison *et al.*, 1988, p. 654).

The study, and the controversy surrounding it, have a long history in psychiatry which is reproduced in this contemporary version through the attention to the incidence of mental illness among black people *vis-à-vis* white people and the reference to genetics.[1] The attention to 'discrimination', however, is a shift that has been inserted into psychiatric discourse by black and Asian psychiatrists like Aggrey Burke, Suman Fernando and Sashidharan through debates that have been part of the Trans-Cultural Psychiatry Association, alongside the growing political debates within black communities about the role of psychiatry in the lives of black people. Constraints of space within this essay do not permit a long and detailed account of these debates (see Mercer, 1986) or the historical relationship between psychiatric discourses and the histories of racist discourses in Europe and the United States of America. On both sides of the Atlantic concern has been expressed and elaborated through contributions such as Thomas and Sillen, *Racism and Psychiatry* (1972) and the more recent British work from Fernando, *Race, Culture and Psychiatry* (1988). In tandem with these contributions there has been a renewed interest in the work of Franz Fanon. The histories of psychiatry are redolent with the themes raised by Harrison's study, the attention to the incidence of mental illness among black people, the calling up of genetics/ nurture as explanations, and the presentation of psychiatry as scientific. But as Fernando's account of this history makes clear, the call to science cannot absolve psychiatry:

> Psychiatry prides itself on having a background of basic sciences on which to draw. To start with, these were Anatomy and Physiology, but more recently Psychology and Sociology have come to the fore. Historically speaking two important sets of ideas came into psychiatry from the basic sciences. First, the view that black people are born with inferior brains and limited capacity for growth; and secondly, that their personalities tend to be abnormal or deviant because of nature (genetic endowment) and/or nurture (upbringing). The influence of these themes . . . was overt in the nineteenth century, but although less obvious since the war, shows a tenacious persistence into the present. (Fernando, 1988, p. 17)

The views to which Fernando calls attention were part of the rise of nineteenth-century 'scientific racism', which guided the account of the world generated in Europe as a precursor to full-blow imperialism. But the clear contradiction between the initially morphological view and the later genotypical view which disproved the biological account of 'races' was largely ignored and, more contradictory still, the model of genetic typifications has passed into the common sense and the science base of psychiatry and psychology: for example, in the work of Jensen and Eysenck. Racism, as Fernando (1988) points out, in both its 'scientific' and its commonsense variants has become part of psychiatry. But it is also clear that psychiatry is not unitary and that within psychiatry the debates between social and medically based psychiatry have also highlighted the role of racism and sexism, and the class position of subjects in relation to a multidimensional account of mental illness. Given the long history of the relationship between medical anthropology and psychiatry, it is not surprising that 'culture' and 'ethnicity' should figure strongly in these accounts, but this too proves to be an ambiguous coupling in two ways. The first of these is the long history of discourses on culture and civilization in psychiatry. Early psychiatrists felt moved to comment on the state of the world at a time when much of the anthropological evidence for this world was highly dubious, and, equally, they felt moved to comment on the mental lives of African and Asian peoples as a way of placing the European mind in relation to a global account of mentalities. It is not surprising, given the historical conjuncture, that this should have given rise to a view of the superiority of European minds and cultures and the development of a link between 'civilization' and sensibilities which produced the now famous account of melancholia as the English disease, related to the superior (as they were seen) levels of development in England in the nineteenth century. These accounts, which seem today to be mere curiosities, the products of ignorance and prejudice, are not, however, so innocent – like the early anthropological accounts that privileged exotica and the search for more and more 'extraordinary' symptoms, as they seemed to the Western gaze (Littlewood, 1988). The current interest in 'culture' in relation to mental illness has clear resonances with the culturalist discourses that position black and Asian people as the Others of Western societies (Bhabha, 1983). Reviewing the encounter between psychiatry and black people, and the renewed interest in the insertion of 'culture' as a means of understanding this encounter, Mercer (1986, p. 139) comments:

> At this point, the culturalist system of representation of differences functions to bring the encounter with the black subject in line with the professional ethos of efficient, therapeutic doctor-patient communication. The project of transcultural psychiatry constructs a culturalist framework of knowledge that objectifies the 'culture' of the black patient and subjectifies that 'culture' in order to make the individual personality or identity of the patient relevant to psychiatric intervention. Its culturalism expands the range of points of psychiatric intervention and deepens the mode of intervention by 'individualizing the subject'.

These culturalist discourses also have resonances with the earlier constructions of 'Englishness' and the links between the 'race', the nation, national characteristics and, as it was thought, forms of mental illness.

These accounts help to frame the response from psychiatry in terms of patient care and the encounters between black and white in mental health care. The notion that racism has a major impact on the mental health of black people is the subject of considerable dispute. However, it is clear that black and Asian psychiatrists give a centrality to racism in the genesis of mental illness and distress, and in confronting racism as a part of the route out of illness and distress. Thus, in opposition to Harrison *et al.*'s account of racism as an additional stress, Fernando (1986, p. 130) writes: 'racism is not just an added stress to black and ethnic minorities, but a pathogen that generates depression in the individual', and he continues: 'Racism causes depression by promoting blows to self-esteem, inducing experiences of loss, and placing individuals in a position of helplessness' (p. 132). Similarly, in concluding an account of the impact of racism on mental health, Aggrey Burke (1986, p. 154) writes:

> The evidence points to the conclusion that racism does lead to mental illness; firstly, by fermenting and maintaining social deprivation and so impairing chances of attaining mental health; secondly, by institutional factors which have the effect of with-holding care; thirdly, by bully-boy/girl strategies of humiliating Blacks into subordination and inflicting sado-masochistic attacks on them; and finally, when this fails, by implementing methods of social/ medical control.

The issues raised by Fernando and Burke are complex and not easily amenable to discussion in a short paper In part the questions raised by the relationship between racism and mental illness are epistemological issues that go to the very core of our understandings of the psyche, subjectivities, rationality and the discourses and practices of psychiatry and psychotherapy. Black psychiatrists, of whom there are very few, and some Asian psychiatrists are convinced of the link through their work in clinical practice and their politics as black and Asian people in British society, and I too am convinced of the link by my own much more limited involvement with the politics of black mental health. Thus, the paper both accepts the proposition and seeks to problematize the relationship between racism and mental illness. In so doing, it explores this juxtaposition through the analysis of a series of 'narratives of sickness' generated from black and Asian people diagnosed as schizophrenic, in relation to an account of racism which foregrounds the ideological construction of the nation, discourses on belonging and, tentatively, the poststructuralist account of decentred subjects. It does not seek to offer a fully theorized account of the relationship. The paper is, therefore, a tentative and exploratory essay *en route*, I hope, to greater understanding.

The attention to racism has activated a network of black and Asian community groups, concerned with racism and the politics of psychiatry, which have highlighted the use of involuntary admissions to hospitals under Section 2 of the Mental Health Act 1983, the complexities of diagnosis and the issue of misdiagnosis, and the stereotypes used to construct black people as 'dangerous' rather than ill. And, like previous critiques of psychiatry, this analysis has sought to expose the link between psychiatry and the state, and the power of psychiatry in relation to issues of civil liberties and human rights. This is part of the broader concern evidenced among black and Asian people on the whole question of the relationships between the state, state agencies and black and Asian people, and how far state interventions via these agencies constitute forms of surveillance and discipline. In this respect, the issues raised can be characterized as one part of the biopolitics to which Foucault alerts us in his series of studies of the rise of modern institutions and the disciplinary and 'individualizing' discourses that constitute medical and psychiatric knowledges. A Foucauldian account of racism is also helpful because it shifts the field of vision beyond the specific institutional sites in which racism is deployed, to the generality and diffuseness of racism as a regime of power which is constitutive of subjects, subjectivities and resistance. This moves us closer to the issues involved in the relationship between racism, black and Asian people and mental illness. Thus, racism in Britain is, as Cohen (1988, p. 63) comments: 'not something "tacked on" to English history by virtue of its imperialist phase, one of its aberrant moments; it is constitutive of what has become known as the British Way of Life'.

Narratives of sickness

Fernando and Burke refer to both the institutional and the psychic impacts of racism in relation to black and Asian people, and it was in relation to both these aspects and the rising levels of concern and politicization around these issues that I came together with members of the Black Mental Health Group in Leicester, Janet Couloute, Suki Desai, Paul Matthew and Annette Piper, and we embarked upon a research project which sought to consider the experiences that local black and Asian people had had in relation to the psychiatric services available. The substantive material was collected via a series of extended interviews which produced 'narratives of sickness' and invited black and Asian people diagnosed as schizophrenic, and those suffering from depression, to reconstruct an account of their illness and its impact on their lives (Westwood *et al.*, 1989). In this paper I want to concentrate on the narratives related to those diagnosed as schizophrenic, and to try to relate these to the current debates that surround psychiatry and the complexities of understanding racism and the politics of identities in the UK.Thus, the voices that speak in relation to the experience of mental illness and the attempt to make sense of that experience are not part of a sample; nor do they seek to 'represent' the black experience in Britain. The voices are one part of that experience and not its totality.

The concentration upon 'narratives' is in direct opposition to 'cases' and was one way in which the research sought to give voice to the black and Asian mentally ill, to break the silence, and thereby to empower those whose overwhelming sense was one of disempowerment. Those who agreed to talk with us were encouraged to do so via a series of community networks and not a clearly articulated database. The insights gained from this way of working relate, in part, to the ways in which we choose to interpret and, therefore, reconstruct the narratives to which we have access.

All the subjects, seventeen in total, had been diagnosed as schizophrenic. Schizophrenia is itself contested terrain and the subject of considerable debate (Birchwood *et al.*, 1988; Warner, 1985), especially in relation to black people where questions over diagnosis and/or misdiagnosis are at issue. The condition is marked by auditory hallucinations, delusions of influence and thought disorder diagnosed in relation to the PSE (Present State Examination) and DSM111 which has been used to limit the diagnosis. Our research had no access to clinical notes or the diagnostic process, so we were unable to enter this terrain – a crucial arena in which the power of psychiatry, through categorization, is exercised. From the accounts, and the questions that people asked, it was clear that the label 'schizophrenia' was mystifying and objectifying for the people so diagnosed, who, at the same time, recognized a need for help, that they were distressed, could not 'cope', or were ill. Those interviewed included eleven men and six women: three people were of Asian descent, one woman and two men, while the majority were of African-Caribbean descent, and one woman had a white mother and a black father. Of those of African-Caribbean descent, half were born in the Caribbean and half in the UK, while one Asian man was born in Uganda and the Asian woman was born in Kenya. The age range was 20 to 47 and half were below the age of 30. The discussion therefore relates to black (in the political sense) working-class lives in postwar Britain, lives marked by migration and rapid changes.

The black and Asian people who shared their biographies wanted very much to be heard, despite their nervousness and hesitancy about identification: 'I'm talking to you because I want to be heard' was repeated in a variety of ways in the context of an experience of treatment that this group of black and Asian people often viewed as objectifying. By asking for their own accounts of their illness, the research insisted upon their integrity as 'knowing subjects'. But in reconstructing and generating these representations, it was also very clear that there was immense pain: pain in the memories of lives often shattered by severe illness and surrounded by misunderstandings and a deep loneliness. As Homi Bhabha (1986, p. xxiii) reminds us:

> Remembering is never a quiet act of introspection or retrospection. It is a painful re-membering, a putting together of the dismembered past to make sense of the trauma of the present . . . It is such a memory of the history of race and racism, colonialism and the question of cultural identity, that Fanon reveals with greater profundity and poetry than any other writer.

The narratives with which this paper is concerned are also profoundly touched by the issues raised in the poetry of Fanon's writings.

What, then, were people telling us about their lives? Every account is unique and yet the commonalities are equally striking. Through all the accounts there was a desire to be heard, and in this a desire to be recognized, to be real and to be valued as a unique person, a creative entity. It could be said to be intimately linked to Fanon's question: what does the black man want? But it is only a partial answer to such a profound question. It does raise, however, one of the important contradictions of being black and Asian in British society – to be simultaneously visible and subject to the 'Empire of the gaze', while being rendered invisible as creative individuals. As Foucault (1977, p. 187) writes: 'It is the fact of being constantly seen, of being able always to be seen that maintains the disciplined individual in his subjection.' Equally, this applies to the person who is defined as mentally ill and subject to psychiatric regimes. But the 'disciplined individual' has many ways in which to resist the 'Empire of the gaze' not only through active resistance, but also in relation to the struggle for self and for meanings. Thus, at the core of the accounts was the struggle for meaning amid events that often proved exceptionally opaque. The struggle is also for order in a world where it often seems illusory. Thus, although re-membering was often a painful resistance, it was felt to be healing and helpful. It is also clear that the many insights developed in these conversations were indeed the material of therapeutic encounters, although no one in this group was ever offered therapy as a path or an aid to recovery or the management of their illness. Nevertheless, it calls into serious doubt (like the work at Bradford and Nasfiyat, the intercultural therapy centre) the common sense within psychiatry that black and Asian patients do not want to talk about their distress, or that they are more likely to express distress in somatic ways and are therefore less well suited to the talking therapies and the language of 'the self'. These are too easily seen, on the culturalist model, as being the monopoly of the West.

The other issue that consistently emerges from the narratives is the issue of racism in its institutional and commonsense variants, within a great diversity of contexts and through everyone's lives, from school to hospital, as children and as adults. Recalling racist incidents provoked anger and defiance, but also pain and hurt in equal measure. While specific incidents of racism were recalled, however, it is the argument of this paper that the impact of racism is considerably more complex than the denial of services or name-calling in the playground, and that it has to be understood both contextually and as a regime of power, in which the constructions of inclusion and exclusion that emanate from specific discourses generated around the nation are crucial. These discourses which have a bearing upon the generation of identities are not just 'out there', but they are part of the psychic structures of individuals and are deeply resilient. One of the most telling comments came from John (all names used have been changed), who complained about racist name-calling on the ward after he was hospitalized. He concluded: 'I couldn't believe it, even mad people hate us.' As he explained, he had posited either a commonality among the mad or that racist and culturalist repertoires were extinguished with madness, but it was not so: racism remained in place while thoughts travelled, and delusions were generated and reproduced. Thus even those on the side of 'unreason', the 'not-normal', maintained the normality of racism. For John it added to the deep loneliness of hospitalization and a further withdrawal from social contacts.

Loneliness was a shared feature of the accounts and is common to the lives of the mentally ill, black and white. For half of the people we talked to, their first sense of a deep loneliness had come with the process of migration. They, like many of their countrymen and women, had travelled across the world in relation to the economic restructuring of the postwar period and the demand for workers in the reconstruction of the UK, or, as in the case of Usha and Aziz, because of the political traumas of East Africa in the postcolonial period. But the move to the UK was not always experienced in this way, as Alison's mother recalled: 'The Queen came to Barbados and invited us to Britain.' The gentility of the way in which this is expressed and the familiar terms that make coming to Britain like an invitation to tea were devastatingly ruptured on arrival by the hostility and harshness of life in the UK. The older generation commented on their sense of shock at the racism in the country, and the ways in which black people were locked out of skilled work, directed towards lower-level training in the NHS and had difficulties in finding housing and friends.

One of the consequences of these difficulties was that the children of these early migrants stayed longer in the Caribbean than their parents had intended they should, and so they too faced the trauma of migration. Elroy and Leon, for example, both had happy memories of childhood days in the Caribbean with their grandmothers, and considerable pain and loss when they left this behind and came to parents and siblings they did not know. Coupled with this was the sense that they had not been wanted in the UK. As Elroy said, 'My parents didn't want me and I didn't want to come. I liked life in Barbados. I knew the life there. They brought me here and then my dad went back to Barbados anyway.' Leon echoed similar views: 'I remember the meals my gran used to cook for me, and going for a swim and having friends, and the sun. It was a lovely place. I don't know what I am doing here.' Paul, who came as a teenager, said, 'I used to cry myself to sleep every night for months. It was all so strange and people were so unfriendly. I didn't know any white people and then I came here and, of course, there are white people everywhere.'

Given the overt hostility encountered by Leon, Elroy and Paul as they entered school and tried to live in their neighbourhoods and with their now estranged families, it is not surprising that their memories of the Caribbean are 'sweet' and that the past and not the present is known as a time of happiness and belonging, one in which they were loved and felt at home in the world. The burden of this knowledge is felt keenly by their mothers, who have seen them through their illness and to whom they are still close. James's mother, for example, often wonders whether bringing James to the UK was the right thing to do: 'He never wanted to come. He wanted to stay with his gran. He didn't believe we wanted him but we did, it just took so long for things to settle down here.' Parents are a contradictory element in all our lives and no less in these accounts: both sources of support and sources of shame, because many felt that they had failed their parents, most especially their mothers. There was a strong sense that somehow they should have had the strength of the older generation, and that illness was a sign of their weakness and inability to cope in the UK. For some it was brothers and sisters who were sources of support.

Childhood was remembered with pleasure and happiness whether in Leicester kicking a football or in Uganda. Schooling was a much more contradictory experience, marked by racist abuse, defeats in the classroom and academic disappointment, except for Janet who did well at school and went on to a London polytechnic because she wanted to teach – a career now thwarted by illness. The majority went from school into manual work, but for some illness intervened before they joined the labour market. None of the group was employed at the time of the interviews.

The onset of schizophrenia manifests in diverse, dramatic and insidious ways. Relatives and sufferers struggled to understand sudden immobilization, terror or incomprehensible utterances and behaviours, but as they moved from one situation to the next and consistently sought help and advice from GPs, social workers, local hospitals, neighbours and friends, they found themselves bereft and forced back on the police. This left them feeling punitive and disloyal to their sons and daughters, sisters and brothers. For many of the young black men, the police were their route into the asylum and they were conscious of the role of the police and the custodial nature of their initial entry into psychiatric care. The role of the police in the patient career is not one necessarily sought by the police themselves, who, by their own admission, feel ill-equipped to deal with mental illness. It is a measure of the isolation of carers that the police were the last on the list and the only ones to turn up. But their interventions left everyone in the families affected feeling bruised and often regretting the involvement of the police.

Relatives and patients then had to encounter hospital staff and, while they came to recognize nurses, they generally had no contact with the psychiatrists – except for one mother who was exceptionally persistent and insisted on seeing and hearing the views of the psychiatrists. For most there was drug therapy and a diagnosis: schizophrenia. No one ever tried to explain what this meant, what kind of prognosis it offered or how it should be managed. Relatives and those who had now become patients were left to cope, often in deep loneliness, in institutions that reminded them that among the mentally ill they were 'different', marginalized and subject to the racism of staff and patients. There was, it seemed, no one to talk to, no one to explain anything and no sympathy or empathy. The experience of hospital was marked by a deepening loneliness: 'Everyone with their own problem and no one to talk to', 'I was so lonely' and 'No one to talk to' are typical comments, and as Elroy's mother chillingly observed, 'My boy, he just wanted someone to talk to, but they electrify him.'

The politics of identities

The extracts from the narratives foreground the inadequacies of psychiatric and social services responses to the black and Asian mentally ill. They are one moment in the encounter between black and Asian people and the institutional life of the UK more generally. The Burnage Report (Macdonald *et al.*, 1989) studies of racism in education (e.g. Rattansi, 1988), the literature on relations between black people and the police (IRR, 1986) and the recent report from NAHA (1989) on the health service: all these accounts detail racism in the UK, and the ways in which these encounters reinforce among British black and Asian subjects a sense of exclusion and unbelonging.

In order to explore this and to make the connections with issues of identities and subjectivities, it is useful to turn to the more recent work on the relationship between the social and ideological construction of the British nation and racism (Gilroy, 1987; Hall, 1987, 1989; Cohen, 1988), and the ways in which this, too, is 'narrated' via the media, public and political discourses and the English literary canon, recently explored in Bhabha (1990). In addition, there is the attempt by Boyne and Rattansi (1990) to unravel the conditions of postmodernity, which make marginality central to the experience of postmodernity and in which the self is no longer centred, unified and in place, but is multiple, shifting and decentred. Together these foreground the current debate on British identity, setting up an opposition between the grand narrative of 'Britishness', founded on the hegemony of Englishness, and the subordination of the multiplicity of ethnic identities that constitute British society today and have done so historically. This grand narrative also includes, importantly, notions of tolerance and fair play, and the presentation of the UK as home to refugees and migrants. Anderson's account of the nation highlights the way in which the nation is an 'imagined political community' (Anderson, 1983, p. 15), but it is no less real or powerful for being imagined or symbolic. In the UK, the nation is generated from a mythical account of some unbroken Anglo-Saxon past in relation to the dominance of the English state and the English language over time, which has secured the hegemony of Englishness and subordinated Irish, Welsh and Scottish nationalism, although, quite clearly, they have not gone away. This 'fictive' account of Britishness has also been tied to notions of 'race', via eugenics, state interventions and the language of 'this island race', the 'British race'. 'Race' and nation were articulated, during Thatcherism, with notions of culture – the infamous 'swamping' statement. The Falklands War allowed a specific moment in which jingoism and British nationalism were rife. The account of the nation privileges one ethnicity over a multiplicity of ethnicities to the point where the ethnicity of the dominant group disappears. Thus, in the UK, 'ethnic' is used to refer to minorities, but not to the English. Such an account of the nation is marked by exclusion in relation to peoples other than the dominant group, who are indeed characterized as 'Others' and known through their 'Otherness'.

The social and ideological construction of the nation does not succeed without an articulation with the state and the whole panoply of legal and institutional arrangements which define nationals and aliens and generate laws around nationality and immigration. What is quite clear in the UK is that these laws operate against black and Asian people and that they have become, during this century, more and more exclusive. The examples of their abuse and exclusivity are well documented, especially in relation to women (Klug, 1989). Thus the state and the nation have a crucial role in the politics of identities, and this is not lost on the UK's black and Asian population, struggling to reunite families divided by the law or to seek entry to the UK on the basis of historical ties. While these discourses impress upon black and Asian peoples an insistent language of unbelonging and marginality, and the idea that the UK can never be home and a place of safety and acceptance, the story is more complex still, as Cohen (1988) suggests in his analysis of the 'nationalism of the neighbourhood'. While state and national structures, and the institutions of British life, point to the outsider status of the ethnically diverse population that is the United Kingdom, this is reinforced at the local level in terms of space and place, and regional and class cultures into which black populations have come through migration and birth. These coming togethers have, however, generated the contradictory response articulated by Stuart Hall (1987, p. 44):

I've been puzzled by the fact that young black people in London today are marginalized, fragmented, unenfranchised, disadvantaged and dispersed. And yet, they look as if they own the territory. Somehow, they too, in spite of everything are centered, in place: without much material support, it's true, but nevertheless they occupy a new kind of space at the centre.

This is a contradictory statement in more ways than one. It may well be that the 'as if' of the statement is a crucial caveat that needs to be foregrounded. Alternatively, given the view that we are all now decentred and not in place, the view of the decentred subject may require some revision in relation to the creative ways in which people generate spaces and places in relation to the positions that are offered by ethnic and cultural inscriptions.

As in London, so in Leicester, where a confident and settled black and Asian population lay claim to the city, its institutions, power structures and geographical and social space, because the old national story, despite Thatcherism's articulations of commonsense racism with the power of public discourses and the state, cannot hold. The situation is, in fact, much closer to the postmodern account, which suggests that the extraordinary economic, political and cultural upheavals of the twentieth century make migrants of us all, and give us the complex biographies expressed in the growing hyphenated identities of Black British and Asian British among many complex and shifting identities.

These self-designations speak also for the growing understanding that identities and selves are not the stable entities of the Enlightenment philosophers' imaginings, but are shifting, unstable and multiple selves (Hall, 1987). This does not mean that decentred selves are not positioned by histories, ethnicities and cultures. In fact, as Hall points out, this is probably the moment at which we should reclaim ethnicity, much in the way that blackness was reappropriated through the 1960s into the 1980s. Similarly, cultures and cultural identities should be understood not as inert categories or scripts constantly reproduced from one generation to the next, but as dynamic multitextured productions subject to constant change and revision. Such a view is at a considerable distance from the current version of ethnicities, which rests strongly on a series of ethnic stereotypes that usually incorporate contradictions while fixing individuals in relation to static cultural attributes. This is, in fact, a reworking of the morphological account of 'races', where individuals sharing racial characteristics were constructed in the Western gaze, not as individuals but as representing a 'race'. So today, a Gujarati, a Jamaican or a Hindu is seen to be representative of a fixed set of cultural attributes which takes no

account of the dynamic and shifting nature of cultures and the inter-
actions between class, ethnicity, gender, region and many more forms
of cultural configuration that are living parts of British society.

Such an account of racism, sometimes called the 'new racism' (but
this is contentious given its resonances with the older and extant
versions), has a special resonance for the narratives that this paper
has, all too briefly, discussed. First, there is the strong sense of
exclusion that permeates the accounts with its sense of unbelonging,
carrying echoes of the title of Paul Gilroy's book, *There Ain't No Black
in the Union Jack* (famous initially as a racist football chant), which
reminds black people that 'British' means 'white'. The official discourses that surround the nation and the exclusionary practices of the
state provide a place for subjects of the narratives as 'Others', outside
the 'ideal community'. Thus, difference is made both visible and
invisible simultaneously, and black and Asian individuals are seen for
what they represent rather than who they are. The narrators were
acutely aware of this process and the ways in which it decentred them
and refracted the complex identities that they presented. The sense
of exclusion and invisibility was further exacerbated by the difficulties
with which some encountered their families, and by the reconstruction
of family life in the UK within the context of migration and separation.
The sense of loss and pain cannot be underestimated; nor can the
ways in which the political economy of migration, with its emphasis
upon labour power and black people as workers for the British economy, made invisible black women as mothers and black men as
fathers, and both as family members.

The experience of exclusion and marginalization sets up the question: why? This in itself prompts another narrative on the self, on
identity and the place of blackness within this. Thus, Elroy asks,
'Why do these things happen to me? Is it because I am black? White
people hate black people.' Elroy had plenty of evidence to support
the notion that being black had a great deal to do with the course of
his life and his encounters with white institutions and white people.
At his first court appearance, the magistrate referred to him as a 'black
menace'; later, in secure units and hospital, he had to contend with
being called 'nigger', 'sambo' and 'black bastard', and he responded
with the question: 'Is it because I am a black man that they treat me
like this?' For Leon the sense of unease was expressed through the
language of belonging. As his mother commented, 'Leon always
talked a lot about not belonging.' But Leon used this creatively and
sought his own history and a sense of place, first through a familiarity
with black history and political struggles via the works of Malcolm X

and Angela Davis, and then through a conversion to Islam, which was for him a liberating experience: 'I had no mental chains, I had thrown these off when I embraced Islam.' Leon's pursuit of place and meaning, and of a sense of identity within this, continues through confinement, drug therapy and illness. Janet expressed her misgivings about being a black woman: 'I don't enjoy being a black woman. Given the chance I would change that.' The directness of her statement makes transparent the complexities of what she is saying and how she views life for a black woman in Britain.

These statements suggest that the place claimed by the young black people of Hall's text has eluded some of those black people we interviewed, and that to be black and mentally ill is to be positioned in relation to a multiplicity of cross-cutting regimes of power that define, confine and exclude, and which promote a fictional account of the self as being whole, stable and tied to being white (male) and British. When the question 'Why?' is asked, it is directed not to the terrain of mental illness, but to racism, to being black in Britain. Thus, for the black mentally ill, racism becomes the modality through which mental illness is represented, and this is reinforced by psychiatric discourses and practices. The deep ambivalence that surrounds blackness in some of these accounts resonates with Fanon's writings. 'The Fact of Blackness' (Fanon, 1986: pp. 109–10) opens: 'I came into the world imbued with the will to find a meaning in things, my spirit filled with the desire to attain to the source of the world, and then I found that I was an object in the midst of other objects'. Fanon continues: 'For not only must the black man be black; he must be black in relation to the white man.'[2]

Fanon's moving and poetic discourse on blackness and objectification speaks to a Foucauldian understanding of racism as a regime of power constitutive of subjects – subjects decentred via the 'Empire of the gaze' which refracts the black subjects' humanity, constantly generating visibility on another's terms and invisibility via objectifications. But Fanon's discourse is not a discourse of powerlessness and defeat. For him there is a way through the cultural imperialism of the self and a way towards some true humanity: 'It is through the effort to recapture the self and to scrutinize the self, it is through the lasting tension of their freedom that men will be able to create the ideal conditions for a human world.' This humanist plea, for it is deeply that, is given a new inflection through the current attention to difference and its centrality in the politics of identity, because it cannot be a difference denied or devalued. Ultimately, we can only know the world through difference. As Hall (1987, p. 45) points out: 'I believe it is an immensely important gain when one recognizes that all identity is constructed across difference and begins to live with the politics of difference'; or as Fanon writes (1988, p. 214):

As soon as I DESIRE I am asking to be considered. I am not merely here and now, sealed into thingness. I am for somewhere else and something else. I demand that notice be taken of my negating activity insofar as I pursue something other than life; insofar as I do battle for the creation of a human world – that is of a world of reciprocal recognitions.

Conclusion

The foregoing analysis has sought ways in which to begin to tease out the complexities of the links between racism and mental illness, by juxtaposing 'narratives of sickness' with a very limited account of the current debates around the nation, nationalism, racism and British identity. The argument has sought ways in which to use the insights offered by a poststructuralist reading of the self and subjectivities as decentred. The analysis suggests that the decentring that is a crucial part of the black and Asian experience in the UK is a part of, but distinctive in relation to, the generalized postmodern experience of decentring common to us all. This is because of the regime of power that is racism and the ways in which black and Asian subjects are positioned within this regime. Furthermore, the black and Asian mentally ill are 'individualized' by two mutually reinforcing regimes of power – racism and psychiatry – both of which are exclusionary and pathologizing. This raises as highly problematic the search for belonging, place and safety, and suggests that these are productions, the outcomes of struggles. Thus, we return to Fanon conscious that his work related to colonial relations and not to postcolonial Britain, but, more importantly, aware that power relations were central to his analysis, as they are currently central to the politics of black mental health and to the politics of identities in the UK. Without a recognition of these power relations, there can be no 'reciprocal recognitions'.

Notes

I am deeply grateful to all those who agreed to be interviewed and to Janet, Suki, Paul and Annette with whom I shared so much. The Black Mental Health Group has now raised funds through the IAP to set up an inner-city resource for the black and Asian mentally ill and their carers.

The research discussed in this paper is part of a larger project on *Racism and the Politics of Mental Health* (forthcoming).

1   Black and African-Caribbean are used interchangeably in this paper. The Black Mental Health Group uses Black inclusively to signal a politically forged identity between African-Caribbean and Asian peoples.
2   Fanon uses 'man' throughout his writings in part as an inclusive term which raises problems of gender difference, but also because his writing is deeply personal.

References

Anderson, B. (1983) *Imagined Communities: Reflections on the Origin and Spread of Nationalism*, London: Verso.

Bhabha, H. (1983) 'The Other question', *Screen*, vol. 24 no. 6.

Bhabha. H. (1986) 'Remembering Fanon', Foreword to Frantz Fanon's *Black Skin, White Masks*, London: Pluto Press.

Bhabha, H. (ed.) (1990) *Nation and Narration*, London: Routledge.

Birchwood, M., Hallett, S., and Preston, M. (1988) *Schizophrenia: An Integrated Approach to Research and Treatment*, London and New York: Longman.

Boyne, R., and Rattansi, A., (eds) (1990) *Postmodernism and Society*, London: Macmillan.

Burke, A. (ed.) (1984) *Transcultural Psychiatry: Racism and Mental Illness* (30th anniversary issue of the *International Journal of Social Psychiatry*.

Burke, A. (1986) 'Racism, prejudice and mental illness' in Cox, J. (ed.), *Transcultural Psychiatry*, London: Croom Helm.

Cohen, P. (1988) 'The perversions of inheritance: studies in the making of multi-racist Britain', in Cohen, P. and Bains, H. (eds), *Multi-Racist Britain*, London: Macmillan.

Eggleston, J., Dunn, D., Anjali, M., and Wright, C. (1986) *Education For Some*, Stoke: Trentham Books.

Fanon, F. (1986) *Black Skin, White Masks*, London: Pluto Press.

Fernando, S. (1986) 'Depression in ethnic minorities', in Cox, J. (ed.), *Transcultural Psychiatry*, London: Croom Helm.

Fernando, S. (1988) *Race, Culture and Psychiatry*, London: Croom Helm.

Foucault, M. (1977) *Discipline and Punish*, London: Allen Lane.

Gilroy, P. (1987) *'There Ain't No Black in the Union Jack': The Cultural Politics of Race and Racism*, London: Hutchinson.

Hall, S. (1987) 'Minimal selves', *Identity*, ICA Document 6, London: Institute of Contemporary Arts.

Hall, S. (1989) 'New ethnicities' *Black Film, Black Cinema*, ICA Document 7, London: Institute of Contemporary Arts.

Harrison, G., Owens, D., Holton, A., Neilson, D., and Boot, D. (1988) 'A prospective study of severe mental disorder in Afro-Caribbean patients', *Psychological Medicine*, vol. 18.

Ineichen, B. (1989) 'Afro-Caribbeans and the incidence of schizophrenia: a review', *New Community*, vol. 5, no. 3.

IRR (1986) *Policing Against Black People*, London: Institute of Race Relations.

Klug, F. (1989) 'Oh to be in England: The British case study', in Yuval-Davis, N., and Anthias, F. (eds), *Woman-Nation-State*, London: Macmillan.

Littlewood, R. (1986) 'Anthropology and British psychiatry', *Anthropology Today*, vol. 2, no. 1.

Macdonald, I., Bhavnani, R., Khan, L., and John, G. (1989) *Murder in The Playground*, London: Longsight Press.

Mercer, K. (1986) 'Racism and transcultural psychiatry', in Miller, P. and Rose, N. (eds), *The Power of Psychiatry*, Cambridge: Polity Press.

NAHA (1989) *Action Not Words*, London: National Association of Health Authorities.

Rattansi, A. (1988)' "Race", education and British society', in Dale, R., Ferguson, R., and Robinson, A. (eds), *Frameworks for Teaching*, London: Hodder and Stoughton.

Thomas, A., and Sillen, S. (1972) *Racism and Psychiatry*, New York: Brunner/Mazel.

Warner, R. (1985) *Recovery From Schizophrenia: Psychiatry and Political Economy*, London: Routledge.

Westwood, S., Coulote, J., Desai, S., Matthew, P., and Piper, A. (1989) *Sadness in My Heart: Racism and Mental Illness*, Leicester: Leicester Black Mental Health Group/University of Leicester.

9

RACIAL FORMATION AND HEGEMONY: GLOBAL AND LOCAL DEVELOPMENTS

Howard Winant

Introduction

Race in all its forms continues to preoccupy us, to surprise us, to shape our world. In North America, the political clamour and deep cultural divisions over race stubbornly refuse to subside. Throughout the Americas, the anniversary of European conquest is more deeply resisted than celebrated, for the arrival of Europe in the 'new world' was a foundational racial event which echoes down the centuries to us today. In Africa, we observe the crumbling of apartheid and its likely replacement by something more 'American': will the African National Congress's goal of a 'non-racialist' South Africa prove chimerical? In Europe, the permanent installation of African, Turkish and Asian immigrants is reshaping national identities as much as the inexorable drive towards integration: to what extent, and in what form, will the venerable currents of exclusivism and neofascism reappear as the cold war and the Soviet presence fade into the past? On the Pacific rim of Asia, the Chinese and Japanese struggle anew with problems of heterogeneity and pluralism, often imbued with racial themes. While perhaps more properly defined as 'ethnic', ferocious conflicts taking place at the fringes of the 'developed' world, from South and South-East Asia to the Middle East, from Burundi to Burma, from Azerbaijan to Bosnia, exhibit at least 'protoracial' features. Arguably the world today is a vast racial battlefield.

But what is this quality we call 'race'? At once evanescent and ferocious, ephemeral and intense, conspicuous and unspecifiable, race is a fascinating and terrible problem precisely because of its slippery and contradictory character. It is nothing but a contradiction, an absent presence, a present absence. Race partakes of liminality: it is a 'threshold' phenomenon, a quality which, in Althusser's terms, is 'always already present'. There is a recognizably 'interior' side to race – for anyone raised in a racialized social order – in which one's identity is indelibly marked, indeed formed, by the phenomenon.

At the same time, there is the near ubiquity of racial order, racial 'structuration' of society, however various and flexible its particular forms. Here we see the 'exterior' side of race: in social policy and political organization, where it takes such forms as exclusion/inclusion, pluralism/assimilation, or even genocide; in collective action, both institutionalized and spontaneous; and in the political economies of localities, nations and the globe, where it determines patterns of inequality and stratification.

This paper is an effort to specify some of the racial dimensions of *hegemony* in the contemporary world, by which I mean chiefly the post-Marxist world. It is necessarily a preliminary effort and chiefly a theoretical one. The argument is organized as follows. First, I present a view of hegemony which dispenses with any notion of core agency (i.e. Gramsci's 'fundamental class'), and focuses instead on the inter-related structural and signifying dimensions of hegemony.[1] Such a view, necessarily schematic and open to all sorts of theoretical objections, retains from Gramsci a deep concern with hegemony as politics; it adopts from numerous poststructuralist currents an abiding interest in meaning and interpretation (Young, 1990).

Next I argue for a particular theoretical approach, *racial formation theory*, as the most useful framework with which to analyse contemporary racial phenomena within this view of hegemony (Omi and Winant, 1994). This approach understands race as pervasive throughout social life; it recognizes the expansion and intensification of racial phenomena in the contemporary world; and it suggests a new conception of racial time, one which combines genealogical and contingent temporalities.

From this perspective, the link between race and hegemony can be more deeply explored. The epochal process which has constructed and reconstructed the meaning of race, and which has over and over again engraved racial signifiers on social and political institutions, collectivities and individuals, continues to do so in the present. The study of racial phenomena is particularly relevant in a global political economy where class-based politics are weakening, and where flows of people, capital and ideas are ever more rapid. Racial identities are transnational and some form of racial difference nearly universal; they are also highly personal and experiential, an instantly recognizable part of who one is. Thus race is a simultaneously global and local phenomenon, politically contested from the largest to the smallest of social terrains.

Having established this framework for thinking about race in terms of hegemony, I next consider the *global and local dimensions* of contemporary racial formation processes. After general discussions of each of these dimensions, I present two 'case studies' of sorts. In respect to the global scope of racial formation, I focus on the internationalization of the race-class relationship. I am particularly interested here in the re-emergence of fascism, and in the capacity of radical democratic movements to defeat it. I focus attention on a local instance of racial formation processes: the dramatic transformation of racial identities in the United States in the wake of the civil rights reforms of the 1960s.

Theorizing hegemony

For present purposes, hegemony may be defined as a form of rule that operates by constructing its subjects and incorporating contestation. In this interpretation, hegemony can be strongly distinguished from domination because under hegemonic conditions opposition and difference are not repressed, excluded or silenced (at least not primarily). Rather they are inserted, often after suitable modification, within a 'modern' (or perhaps 'postmodern') social order. Hegemony therefore involves a splitting or doubling of opposition, which simultaneously wins and loses, gains entrance into the 'halls of power' and is co-opted, 'crosses over' into mainstream culture and is deprived of its critical content.

Hegemony organizes various themes, axes and cleavages, which can be characterized, but not fully captured analytically, by using familiar terms: race, gender, class and neocolonialism might be the top categories on the present epoch's list. Such concepts are essentially metaphors for institutionalized social relationships which combine processes of exploitation and domination on the one hand, with processes of subjectification and objectification – that is, with struggles over meaning and identity – on the other.

For simplicity's sake, and leaving many important questions out for the moment, let us call the former set of questions, in which we can include mainstream and/or radical views of politics and economics, the *structural* dimensions of hegemony. These include organized political processes of various kinds (elections, workplace struggles, policy-making), as well as distributional conflicts and the institutionalized aspects of social movements of all types, ranging from national liberation to civil rights and feminism.

Struggles over meaning and identity I shall awkwardly call the *signification* dimensions of hegemony. By this I mean the 'cultural' and 'social psychological' processes of identity-formation and socialization through which, and however unstably, individuals and collectivities are constructed and assigned their structural locations in society: as rulers, subordinates, nurturers, natives, 'political classes', etc.

Of course, the frameworks of 'culture' and 'social psychology' do not adequately capture the complex struggles over political meanings and concepts, over the representations of power and identity which have been central to both Gramscian and poststructuralist political theory. Nor does this division between structure and signification adequately address all cases of identity-formation and collective action. For example, the volatility with which collectively can emerge or disintegrate in everyday experience, and the complex interplay of political themes and personal identifications such quotidian events imply, cannot be theorized adequately by the crude dichotomy proposed here. One thinks of Sartre's discussion of the interplay of 'fused' and 'serial' identities in the *Critique of Dialectical Reason* (1976) or of Bhabha's analysis of the parodic and subversive themes in the discursive practices of the colonized (Bhabha, in press). Nor do I wish to suggest an undue benignity in the operations of hegemony: no hegemonic system incorporates *all* its opposition. If we look at racial issues, there is certainly plenty of room in societies across the globe for exclusion, segregation, discrimination, malevolence, ignorance and outright violence. To suggest that a general trend may be detected, however, from domination to hegemony, away from outright coercion and towards 'consent' (in the Gramscian sense) as a more effective form of rule, is not to argue that violence and repression are on the wane, either in racial matters or in other spheres of conflict. Would that this were so.

But I do not wish to be detained here. The point is clear enough: hegemony is a form of rule in which the subjective dimensions of politics expand significantly. An effective hegemony constructs its own subjects; an effective counter-hegemony subverts those subjectivities; it disrupts and reinterprets the seemingly unified conceptions, memories, symbols and identities of the 'establishment' against which it contends.

Finally, it bears repeating that hegemony both structures *and* signifies. In concrete experience there is no break between say, 'economic' and 'cultural' life. Inequality, for example, is a complex sociopolitical phenomenon that 'socializes' individuals and groups, that stigmatizes the many and exalts the few, deeply identifying us, distinguishing us and allowing us to interpret our world. Inequality has to be 'policed', not only in the literal sense, that of controlling the opposition which injustice tends to stimulate, but also in the cultural sense. Inequality requires constant interpretation. Why is there poverty amid plenty? How can the 'North' justify its excesses before the impoverished and increasingly desperate 'South'? How much responsibility do the poor bear – how much do 'I' bear for my own poverty?

Thus any theory of hegemony begins by recognizing that institution and interpretation, structure and culture, society and self are concretely linked, that they are in fact congruent at the level of experience, of material life. Their distinction can only be a conceptual one, useful for purposes of analysis only.

Racial formation

Racial formation theory was developed as a response to postwar understandings of race, both mainstream and radical, which practised 'reductionism': by this I mean the explanation of racial phenomena as manifestations of some other, supposedly more significant, social relationship. Examples of racial reductionism include treatments of racial dynamics as epiphenomena of class relationships, or as the result of 'national oppression' or as variations on the ethnicity paradigm established in the early twentieth-century USA after successive waves of European immigration.

In contrast to these approaches, racial formation theory suggests that race has become a fundamental organizing principle of contemporary social life. At its most basic level, race can be defined as *a concept which signifies and symbolizes sociopolitical conflicts and interests in reference to different types of human bodies*. Although the concept of race appeals to biologically based human characteristics (so-called phenotypes), selection of these particular human features for purposes of racial signification is always and necessarily a social and historical process. There is no biological basis for distinguishing human groups along the lines of 'race', and the sociohistorical categories employed to differentiate among these groups reveal themselves, upon serious examination, to be imprecise and arbitrary. Indeed, we can speak of racial formation as a *process* precisely because the inherently capricious and erratic nature of racial categories forces their constant rearticulation and reformulation – their social construction – in respect to the changing historical contexts in which they are invoked.

The implications of this view are manifold. First, race is understood as a phenomenon whose *meaning pervades social life*. Race operates both micro- and macro-socially: not only the individual psyche and relationships among individuals, but also collective identities and social structures, are racially constituted. Because race is not a 'natural' attribute, but a socially and historically constructed one, the racial dimensions of social structures, identities and signification systems must be understood as flexible and contested. They are often explicitly, but always at least implicity, political terrain.

Second, racial formation theory addresses the surprising *expansion and intensification* of racial phenomena occurring in the contemporary world, the new global context of race mentioned earlier. This is discussed more extensively below, but can be crudely formulated here in terms of the cross-cutting nature of racial identities. Race is a transnational, interclass phenomenon, not simply in the abstract, but concretely. The legacies of enslavement and colonization have established powerful (though not unproblematic) linkages between dispersed communities – often geographically distant from one another, often citizens of distinct nation-states – who share some experience of racially organized subjection. The same shared experiences can create cross-class solidarities which defy the supposed 'rational expectations' of both mainstream and Marxist economic analyses.

Third, racial formation theory suggests a *new conception of racial time*. At least two dimensions of time can be distinguished, one genealogical, one contingent. In *genealogical* terms, the social construction of race is a millennial phenomenon, whose origins lie in an immense historical rupture encompassing the rise of Europe, the onset of African enslavement, the *conquista* and colonization of the western hemisphere, and the subjugation of much of Asia. Across the centuries, there has been never-ending dispute over the meaning of race, controversy which was integral to the struggles of the oppressed and enslaved with their rulers. By now we have substantial scholarship on these matters which quite effectively explains the framing of supposedly unified collective identities (e.g. Europe) in terms of externalized 'others' (Todorov, 1985; Connolly, 1991). The temporal dimensions of this account are in my view extremely significant.

'Western' or colonial time completed its synchronization of the globe during the nineteenth century, demarcating human 'difference' in terms of the traditional or primitive versus the modern (Wolf, 1982). Complicit in the racialization of time were not only the propagandists of colonialism, but also the great social theorists of modernity. Weber's 'spirit of capitalism', Durkheim's account of the division of labour and the wellsprings of sociocultural solidarity, and Marx's analysis of the brutal but also ultimately progressive extension of the capitalist mode of production to the 'ends of the earth' (consider the subtext of this term: where does the earth begin?) all privileged European time. Just as, for example, the writers of the *Annales* school sought to locate the deep logic of historical time in the means by which material life was produced – diet, shoes, etc – so we might usefully think of a racial *longue durée* in which the slow inscription of phenotypical signification took place upon the human body, in and through conquest and enslavement to be sure, but also as an enormous act of expression, of narration.

Another type of historical time accessible to racial formation theory is that of *contingency*. Particular racial meanings and social structures are always context-driven. The presence of a racial order consolidated by coercion (e.g. the antebellum South, classical colonial rule in Africa) grants little political terrain to racial conflict. In such an absolutist context, I suggest, the racial order is 'naturalized' and publicly unproblematic. Racial time can appear nearly frozen – until the repressive social order is shattered by violence, the only meaningful form of resistance. In such situations, the dominant groups seek to monopolize not only the means of violence, but those of knowledge;[2] opposition is marginalized and may be rendered nearly invisible until, like the dream deferred, it explodes.

On the other hand, once they abandon the *Herrenvolk* mode, democratic politics are forced to develop more hegemonic forms of racial rule. That is, they must incorporate their racial oppositions, make concessions to their demands, and engage in ever-widening debate about the meaning of race in society. In such a context, the racial order is necessarily and publicly problematic, resistance to racial oppression becomes increasingly multiform, and racial time appears to move swiftly indeed. North Americans have only to consider the rapidly moving events of the last quarter century to ratify this perception. Contemporary African and European racial time is also accelerating daily.

To summarize, racial formation theory as presented here is compatible with the decentered conception of hegemony outlined above: it resists the temptation to dismiss race as an 'illusion', mere 'ideology', while at the same time rejecting any objectivist or essentialist interpretation of the concept.[3]

The global dimensions of racial formation

I have already suggested that, on a global comparative scale, the continuing and indeed expanding significance of race has defied the predictions of most high officials, as well as most social critics and movement leaders. Until quite recently, mainstream economists and Marxists, liberals and conservatives, ethnicity theorists and nationalists, all expected the dissolution of race in some greater entity: free market or class struggle, cultural pluralism or nation-state. Although the full implications of the endurance of racialized societies and identities have yet to be plumbed, it is clear enough that the heyday of liberalism, modernism and Marxism is finished. Far from appearing as an aberrant phenomenon, a survival of more benighted times, the fact of racial phenomena now seems rather overwhelming. Their perseverance seems rather less mysterious than belief in their imminent superannuation, which today seems almost wilfully naive.

Yet the 'elementary forms of racial life' vary tremendously from one culture, one society, to another. To what extent can a theory of racial formation address the bewildering variety of racialized experiences, identities and social structures on a global scale?

Once more easily seen in terms of imperial reach, in terms of colonization, conquest and migration, the geography of race is becoming *globalized* and thus accessible to a new kind of comparative analysis. This only becomes possible now, at a historical moment when the distinction 'developed/underdeveloped' has been definitively overcome. Obviously by this I do not mean that now there are no disparities between North and South, rich and poor. I mean that the movement of capital and labour has internationalized all nations, all regions. Today we have reached the point where 'the empire strikes back' (CCCS, 1982), as former (neo)colonial subjects, now redefined as 'immigrants', challenge the majoritarian status of the formerly metropolitan group (the whites, the Europeans, the Americans or French, etc.). While ex-colonial subjects immigrate to the metropolises, the formerly well-paying and supposedly secure jobs of metropolitan workers emigrate toward the former colonies, there to exploit a more vulnerable labour force congregated on export platforms, herded into industrial enclaves designed to produce cheaply for the 'developed' countries.

Culturally too the internationalization of race proceeds apace. Such phenomena as the rise of 'diasporic' models of blackness, the creation of 'panethnic' communities of Latinos and Asians (in such countries as the UK or the USA), and the breakdown of borders in both Europe and North America, all seem to be hybridizing and racializing previously national polities, cultures and identities. Because of these transformations the comparisons of local social/political orders based on race becomes possible. Likewise for the first time we can begin to think of variations in racial identity not as deviations from some supposedly modal (and actually quasi-imperial) norm, but as a flexible set of context-specific *repertoires*. As a final note, the dissolution of the transparent racial identity of the formerly dominant group – that is to say, the increasing racialization of whites in Europe and the USA – must also be recognized as proceeding from the increasingly globalized dimensions of race.

A global case: the internationalization of the race-class relationship

The deep mutuality inherent in the race-class relationship is well established. Colonialism and empire were constructed from the fusion of these two materials. Race is no mere byproduct of capitalism, as reductionist theories would have it; rather, capitalism is a racial entity. Without its ability to racialize those whom it exploited, capitalism could not have accumulated the wealth needed to subdue the world. In this matter Marx's famous denunciation is fully justified:

> The discovery of gold and silver in America, the extirpation, enslavement, and entombment in mines of the aboriginal population, the beginning of the conquest and looting of the East Indies, the turning of Africa into a warren for the commercial hunting of blackskins, signalized the rosy dawn of the era of capitalist production. These idyllic proceedings are the chief momenta of primitive accumulation. (Marx, 1967, p. 751)[4]

Can anyone seriously argue today that these 'idyllic proceedings', these multiple enslavements, this series of fatal plagues, these orgies of cultural deracination, would even have been attempted, let alone successfully accomplished, if their intended victims had been other

Europeans?[5] In my view the mere origin of capitalism in racially rationalized conquest definitively refutes all class reductionisms of race.

Yet of course the genealogy of race, replete with variations on this theme of 'racial capitalism', proceeds unbroken up to the present (West, 1987). Every secondary labour market, every ghetto, casbah and native reserve, every segregated neighbourhood testifies, in this account, to the interdependence of class and race. So what's new? On what basis can I claim that today we are witnessing the internationalization of the relationship between race and class?

I have already suggested that today hegemony takes a decentered form, one which is not organized around a fundamental class antagonism. This is not merely a theoretical revision of Gramsci, but also reflects a new historical moment in which class antagonisms are definitively displaced from the central political significance they have occupied since, say, 1848 – since the end of 'the age of revolution' (Hobsbawm, 1962; Mouffe and Laclau, 1985). There are many signs of this: the incoherence and consequent popular rejection of 'actually existing' (or should we say 'recently existed'?) socialism, the reversal of capitalist development in 'the South', the internal rot affecting all the so-called 'developed' countries.

This decentering of hegemony means that other antagonisms, differences other than class, which were always present but lacked visibility and politicization due to the apparent centrality of class struggle, can now come to the fore. The increasing significance of race (and gender as well) is in part caused by the declining significance of class. Class politics, class struggle, are preponderantly white, male politics, and have by now been extensively criticized as such.

To be sure, the predominance of class on the political stage was always uneven: in the USA, the inability of a true class-based politics to develop cast some early suspicions on the supposed universality of this 'motor of history' (Sombart, 1976). The sustained ferocity of racial antagonisms, their presence from the beginning of the colonial period (in respect to native peoples), and early unification of colour and enslavement (in respect to African peoples), made the phrase 'American exceptionalism' something of a cliché in Marxist analysis. The early emergence of feminism as an offspring of abolitionism rather than as a key factor in socialism also signified the relative weakness of class politics in the USA. In the colonial and neocolonial world, the nationalist forms in which politics were arranged always clashed with Marxist logic, even when their practitioners were avowed Marx-

ist-Leninists. Class as the 'fundamental contradiction' of the modern
world was, then, something of a European framework.

This situation has been complicated even further in the present,
as the structural legacies of 'northern' dominance begin to erode. The
luxury of corporatist pacts between capital, labour and the state,
trading off wage gains for productivity increases, is effectively at an
end. The ability of established unions and their political representa-
tives to speak for their national working classes is at best stretched to
its limit, and frequently ruptured. The capacity of political democracy
to discipline capital – to restrict capital flight, for example – to levy
effective taxes on capital, or to enact environmental or social legislation perceived by capital as disadvantageous has declined dramatically.

Political battle lines are being redrawn in many countries as the
new dimensions of the relationship between race and class, the racial
dimensions of capitalism, are recognized. Mobilization of white
racial antagonisms has proved indispensable for the 'respectable' right,
and even for some sectors of the left, in many 'northern' countries.
In the USA it has been an indispensable feature of Republican presi-
dential politics since 1964.

Conversely, there now arises the difficult task of mobilizing (in
some cases, newly) heterogeneous racial minorities in order to counter
this trend. This task falls to social movements, for all too often
established social democratic and trade union groups seek principally
to defend the interests of their traditional, white constituencies. Such
defensiveness is going to accelerate the dissolution of class politics, if
only because the presence of large numbers of immigrant workers
portends radical demographic shifts in the 'developed' world. In a
quarter-century whites may be a minority in the USA. In a quarter-
century substantial racially defined minorities will exist in integrated
Europe; although nowhere near approaching the numbers that exist
in the USA, these Asian or African immigrants and their descendants
will have to be reckoned with.

The political logic that this situation presages, I think, goes well
beyond the mere interpenetration and increasing complexity of the
relationship between race and class. What it foreshadows is nothing
less than a global struggle between fascism and democracy.

Unquestionably, a clear potential exists for the *resurgence of fascism*.
Organized fascist movements already exist in most countries, as does
a fascist international of sorts. Contemporary fascism lacks a great
deal of ideological depth and consistency, but what internal coherence
it does have derives directly from its appeals to racial fear. Such

positions are all too familiar: the racial enemy, often in league with the Jew, is a parasite upon the national body, a despoiler of sacred national and cultural traditions; the country is in danger of being 'swamped' by immigrants; the key institutions of society have already been subverted; only through a massive appeal to the true, hard-working folk 'who built this country' (white, French, American, English, Christian, etc.), only by return to the 'traditional' values, can we restore the grandeur ... In its aspirations to hegemony, fascism too must construct its subjects: they are the producers, the patriots, the 'true' Americans, Frenchmen, etc. The nation has been betrayed by its 'Others', people who are different, who do not really belong in the fatherland, who do not believe in hard work.

Fascism's potential constituencies are the displaced workers, the downwardly mobile members of the middle classes, those whose vulnerabilities are most clearly articulated by what Ronald Walters has called (in the US context) 'white racial nationalism' (Walters, 1987). The ideological narrative addressed to them can take various forms; it can be 'coded' as a sub-text for elections and propaganda, or it can be grunted or shouted while carrying out beatings or lynchings, defacing synagogues, or attacking immigrant workers' hostels or neighbourhoods. What is crucial is its reliance on politics of resentment, fear and exclusion, its ability to link race and class (and often, gender as well), and its hunger for an authoritarian solution to uncertainty and vulnerability.

Confronting the resurgence of fascism is the potential for *radical democracy*. Radical democracy must compete with authoritarianism of all sorts to articulate an open and plural vision of politics. I have argued that, as the relative significance of class declines, other forms of social organization, in particular racial and gender differences, come to the fore. These differences constitute the very opposite of the authoritarian order which racial reaction seeks to create through its politics of exclusion and repression. They counterpose the possibility of inclusion to that of exclusion; they oppose repression with self-expression. Radical democracy potentially represents a subversive, as well as celebratory, counter-hegemonic tendency: for those who were never effectively addressed by mainstream politics, for the millions whom class politics either excluded outright or included only indirectly, radical democracy and the 'politics of difference' offer a precious glimmer of recognition.

Yet if it is effectively to counter reactionary and authoritarian initiatives based on race – initiatives which have had considerable success in France, Britain, Germany and the USA among other countries –

radical democratic politics will have to acknowledge the fears to which the right appeals. That is, radical democratic politics must link race (and gender) with class more effectively through inclusion than reactionary politics can do through exclusion. There are, I suggest, two keys to this process, one social structural and the other a matter of signification, of interpretation of identities and cultural meanings.

On the social structural side, radical democratic politics must articulate concepts of *social and economic justice, fairness and equality*. There are substantial historical precedents, as well as powerful political arguments, for this connection. In many countries, deep democratic traditions can be mobilized in favour of social justice and fairness, especially when combined with long-standing class-based demands for greater economic equality and redistribution. Recent decades have been marked by the diminution of living standards in most countries of the so-called West; popular antagonism to this trend is high. Additionally, a radical democratic articulation of race and class must acknowledge that racial minority status still serves as a negative marker, a stigma, in the class formation process. All across the globe, dark skin still correlates with poverty.[6] Thus class position is in many respects racially assigned. It follows from this that radical democratic challengers should reopen the question of discrimination as a racial process with class consequences.

On the side of signification, radical democratic politics *must acknowledge and accept the uncertainty and fragility of social and cultural identities*, and the fears that threats to these identities can produce (Przeworski, 1986). This can be done without the flirtation with neoconservatism evident even on the left (Sleeper, 1990); a more effective approach evokes the ethical dimensions of the racial crisis, and asks to what extent we permit ourselves to know the racialized Other (West, 1991; Lechner, 1988). Such a politics invites us to examine the contingency and multiplicity of our own identities. No individual belongs to 'just' one socially constructed category: each has her/his racial, gender, class-based, national identities, and that is just a start of the list. Nor are these categories uniform or stable; we are Whitmanesque, we contain multitudes. To recognize our many selves is to understand the vast social construction which is not only the individual, but history itself, the present as history. A radical democratic politics must invite us to comprehend this.

But merely issuing the invitation is not enough; indeed I suggest that the earlier postwar social movements organized around race, gender, peace, etc. in fact did this and no more, thus setting themselves up for the blacklash that subsequently engulfed them. Why?

Because to understand the fragility of our identities can be profoundly disconcerting, especially in the absence of a political and moral vision in which the individual and the group can see themselves included, supported and contributing to the construction of a better society. To counter the authoritarian interpretation of fear and uncertainty, to resist the imposition of exclusive and repressive models of order, a radical democratic politics must acknowledge fear and uncertainty, while at the same time offering a way to accept and interpret these emotions publicly and collectively. Not through repression, but through knowledge of the differences within ourselves can we achieve the solidarity with others which, though necessarily partial, is essential for the creation of a more just and free world.

The local dimensions of racial formation

The argument so far has focused largely on the contemporary amplification of racial conflict across the globe. It would be a mistake, however, to assume any overarching uniformity in this upsurge of tension over, and heightened awareness of, racial matters. Applying the model of hegemony I have advanced here, which focuses on the interaction of social structure and signification, it is logical to expect a great deal of variation among local racial orders. Of course, each nation-state, each political system, each cultural complex, necessarily constructs a uniquely racialized social structure, a particular complex of racial meanings and identities. Thus the global similarities, the increasing internationalization of race, can be understood only in terms of prevalent patterns, general tendencies; in no sense can such generalizations substitute for detailed analyses of local racial formations.

With what questions should we approach the examination of particular racial formation processes? Many variables, particularly structural ones, are already familiar: in what way are the social dynamics of race affected by such demographic patterns as immigration and fertility rates? What is the extent of racial inequality, of stratification by race, and what trends are evident in its development? To what extent are racial equality and social justice concerns incorporated into the national policy agenda? How do social and political institutions mediate racial divisions and conflicts? In what way has the mutation or even outright decay of previously effective political forms – such as various versions of socialism, nationalism and developmentalism – refocused racial politics and policies? Answers to these and many other similar questions can give a good empirical view of the local social structure of race.

None of these questions, of course, addresses such questions as the meaning of race, the boundaries of racial identity, or the means by which these meanings and boundaries are defined and changed. To examine such issues we must turn to the problem of signification:; that is, to the way in which hegemonic sociopolitical orders construct their subjects. Here our empirical focus is necessarily imprecise: what is the degree of variability in racial identities, both collective and individual? To what extent is race 'essentialized', 'biologized' in a given society? How much autonomy is available to the individual in the construction and selection of racial identities? In what ways are traditional forms of racial representation – for example, in religion, art or science – undergoing modification?

Here we are asking questions about signification which also have crucial structural implications. When we enquire, for example, as to how much flexibility a national-popular culture allows in the constitution of racial groups, we are in practice examining the state, various 'ideological apparatuses', institutions of socialization, etc. Are there rigid, caste-like colour lines as in apartheid? This is as much a political economic question as a cultural one. Is mobility possible among racially defined subordinate groups? The answer to this question depends not only on their degree of organization and political capabilities, but on their access to the means of representation and rearticulation, their capacities, indeed, for parody and subversion (Bhabha, in press).

Furthermore, the dynamics of racial signification are necessarily *relational*. How much autonomy does the individual have to choose her/his racial location? To what extent is national identity bound up with racial identity? The construction of racial meanings is about the positionality of groups (and individuals) *vis-à-vis* one another: identity is constituted through differentiation, difference through identification (Connolly, 1991). Thus the increasing empowerment of a racial minority formerly subject to intense exclusion and discrimination will engender an 'identity crisis' for the group formerly more absolutely superordinate. Here the interdependence of the structural and signification dimensions of hegemony is clearly demonstrated. Examples of these kinds of shift might include minority enfranchisement, upward economic mobility, or increased access to cultural fora such as media and curriculum. The USA, South Africa, the UK and many other countries furnish ready contemporary cases. In the following section, I discuss some of these processes with particular reference to present-day developments in US racial formation processes.

A local case: the transformaton of racial identity in the United States

US racial identities have been drastically reshaped in the post-civil rights era. The very categories and concepts with which we think about race have changed: such terms as 'Latino', 'Hispanic', 'African-American' and 'Asian American' hardly existed a quarter-century ago, when the black movement was at its height. Tremendous battles have been fought about the very names we use for racial subjects.[7]

Elsewhere I have written extensively on these matters (Omi and Winant, 1994; Winant, 1990; Omi and Winant, 1991). Here I will simply sketch out some of the ways in which shifting racial identities themselves are constantly being transformed. As I have argued, there is a necessary reciprocity in the process of racial formation: because we identify ourselves racially by differentiating ourselves from others, a change in one group's boundaries or self-understanding cannot occur without affecting those of other groups. In examining these shifts, we can see the way that hegemony has been increasingly racialized, not only on a global scale as I have indicated above, but also in the local setting of the USA.

The first thing we notice about post-civil rights era racial dynamics is the increasing prominence of the 'brown' and 'yellow' groups on the US racial spectrum. That is, the presence and visibility of Latinos/Hispanics, and of Asian Americans, has increased. This is due to two factors: demographic shifts, of course, and the phenomenon of *panethnicity*, a term which refers to the construction of new racialized subjects from groups whose previous ethnic identities were separate and distinct.

Latino/Hispanic and Asian American groups are increasing their numbers in the USA. Generally high rates of immigration and fertility account for this transition. The effects of this demographic shift, all on its own, are profound. For example, as new or greatly expanded ethnic enclaves spring up in major cities, the pressures on neighbouring groups increase, heightening resentments and tensions. New immigrants may bring intense competitive pressures into particular sectors of the labour force, as Latinos have done in the construction trades. They may come to dominate particular economic niches which are classically those of 'middleman minorities'. Thus we see the expansion of Asian American retail purveyors in low-income, often black neighbourhoods.[8]

Panethnicity is an even more intriguing phenomenon. In the wake of the civil rights movement, distinct Asian ethnic groups, primarily

Chinese, Japanese, Filipino and Korean Americans, began to assert
their common identity as Asian Americans. Latinos/Hispanics and
Native Americans did the same. The labels these groups adopted
reflected their recognition of the similar treatment they had historically encountered at the hands of state institutions and the population
at large. Different Asian ethnic groups, for example, had been subject
to exclusionary immigration laws, restrictive naturalization laws, labour
market segmentation and patterns of ghettoization by a polity and
culture which treated all Asians as alike. Native Americans had suf-
fered abrogation of treaty rights, assaults on what remained of their
territories and unremitting efforts to coerce assimiliation: of children,
religion and custom. The emergence of panethnic identities involved
the muting of profound cultural and linguistic differences. Panethnicity was a contradictory and flexible phenomenon: it created new
racial subjects by minimizing significant historical differences and
antagonisms among distinct ethnic groups. It permitted the insertion
en bloc of new immigrants into the pre-existing US racial order. It also
provided a crucial rallying point for raising political consciousness
about the problems of minority ethnic communities, and for asserting
demands on state institutions in the post-civil rights era (Lopez and
Espiritu, 1990).

A second dramatic transformation of US racial identities took the
form of *heightened class divisions within the black community* in the post-
civil rights period. The importance of class factors in shaping the
African-American experience is nothing new (DuBois, [1899] 1967;
Frazier, 1957). The profound deepening of these distinctions in the
wake of the civil rights reforms was, however, largely unanticipated.
Previous conflicts between the 'black bourgeoisie' and the 'black
masses' had occurred in a context of nearly complete segregation.
However much these two sectors of the community viewed each other
with suspicion and mistrust, they were forced to live together, and
frequently to ally, against the system of white supremacy.

But the destruction of legally sanctioned segregation made mobility
possible for the few, and rationalized the abandonment of the many.
Twenty-five years after the enactment of major civil rights reforms,
the African-American community is both the beneficiary and victim
of its own success. A community once knitted together by survival
imperatives in a segregated society, and bound up by internal 'thick'
relationships of intracommunal labour, commerce, residence and
religion, has now been dispersed. This dispersion has occurred primarily along *class* lines. African-Americans who could take advantage of
the slow but real lowering of racial barriers in education, employment

and housing have been able to achieve an unprecedented degree of upward mobility. This does not mean that they are shielded from discriminatory acts, or that they have abandoned their identification as 'black'. But it does mean that they are living in a far more integrated world, and that racial identity and racism no longer determine their fates or futures as inexorably as before (Landry, 1987). At the same time, capital flight and fiscal crisis have further impoverished low-skilled and undereducated African-Americans, leading to the much-publicized problem of the 'underclass', or 'ghetto poor' (Wilson, 1987, 1991; Jencks, 1992).

A key result of the intensification of class distinctions among blacks, then, is their *differential racialization* along lines of class. By this I mean that, while racial identity of course retains its salience in shaping the life-chances and experiences of blacks (as it does for all North Americans), its significance as a determinant of identity now varies with class to an unprecedented degree. This differential racialization has important consequences for individual identity, collective consciousness and political organization. For the African-American middle class, it generates profound ambivalence and anxiety about race (Poussaint, quoted in Garreau, 1987). For example, middle-class blacks can achieve significant levels of economic security, but are not able to escape discriminatory treatment (Feagin, 1991). By contrast, the ghetto poor, excluded from the labour market and thus marginalized by the class system, are ever more monolithically racialized. The middle-class ambivalence about racial identity contrasts sharply with the bitter frustration and pervasive violence through which impoverished ghetto youth experience their blackness. And the black working class is defeated in two ways at once by the contrasting experiences which bracket it.

This argument does not seek to minimize the continuing significance of race. I simply suggest that today, more than at any other time in US history, the experiential dimension of race varies significantly with class. The ongoing discrimination faced by the black middle class is certainly a serious problem (Feagin, 1991; Williams, 1991).[9] In many ways no African-American, however affluent, can feel as secure as even the average white: for example, in an encounter with the police (Dunne, 1991). Yet the malevolent attentions of floor-walkers in Bloomingdales cannot be compared with those of the Los Angeles Police Department.

A final instance of the transformation of racial identities in the USA is the *incipient crisis of whiteness*. Here too there is a demographic component: whites do not immigrate in large numbers, and white fertility rates are low. In various areas of the country, whites may not constitute a majority for long; nor can they expect to exercise the unquestioned racial domination of the past (Roediger, 1991). As previous assumptions erode, white identity loses its transparency, the easy elision with 'racelessness' that accompanies racial dominance. Today the very meaning of 'whiteness' has become a matter of anxiety and concern. In this respect, whites too have been racialized in the post-civil rights era.

The major response to these anxieties has been resistance to such reforms as affirmative action policies. Many whites, especially those most vulnerable to increased competition for jobs, access to education or moderately priced housing, now feel that it is they, and not racially defined minorities, who are discriminated against by state policies designed to promote racial equality. While an overwhelming majority of whites favour egalitarian principles, according to survey data, only a minority support state policies aimed at implementing such principles (Schuman *et al.*, 1985). As one respondent opined in a recent study, the 'average American white guy' gets a 'raw deal' from the government because 'blacks get advantages, Hispanics get advantages, Orientals get advantages. Everybody but the white male race gets advantages now' (Greenberg, 1985, p. 70).

The idea that whiteness could be a *handicap* is quite unprecedented. Under conditions of white supremacy, for example, the meaning of whiteness was relatively unproblematic. In the aftermath of the civil rights challenge, though, it became necessary to evaluate more seriously the nature of whiteness.

One early response asserted the primacy of ethnicity over race. In this account, there was no such thing as a homogeneous white majority. Many whites were really minorities in their own right, 'unmeltable' ethnic minorities (Novak, 1972). More recent research, however, suggests that most whites do not experience their ethnicity as a definitive aspect of their social identity. They perceive it dimly and irregularly, picking and choosing among its varied strands to exercise, as Mary Waters (1990) suggests, an 'ethnic option'. The specifically ethnic components of white identity are fast receding with each generation's additional remove from the old country. Unable to speak the language of their immigrant forebears, uncommitted to ethnic endogamy and unaware of their ancestors' traditions (if in fact they can still identify their ancestors as, say, Polish or Scottish, rather than a combination of four or five European – and non-European – groups), whites undergo a racializing panethnicity as 'Euro-Americans' (Alba, 1990).

The 'twilight of white ethnicity' in a racially defined and increasingly polarized environment means that white racial identity will grow in salience. The racialization process for whites is very evident on university campuses, as white students encounter a heightened awareness of race which calls their own identity into question. Students quoted in a recent study on racial diversity (Institute for the Study of Social Change, 1990) conducted at the University of California at Berkeley illustrate the new conflictual nature of white identity:

> Many whites don't feel like they have an ethnic identity at all and I pretty much feel that way too. It's not something that bothers me tremendously but I think that maybe I could be missing something that other people have, that I am not experiencing. (p. 52)

> Being white means that you're less likely to get financial aid ... It means that there are all sorts of tutoring groups and special programs that you can't get into, because you're not a minority. (p. 50)

> If you want to go with the stereotypes, Asians are the smart people, the Blacks are great athletes, what is white? We're just here. We're the oppressors of the nation. (p. 52)

Here we see many of the themes and dilemmas of white identity in the post-civil rights period: the 'absence' of a clear culture and identity, the 'disadvantages' of being white with respect to the distribution of resources, and the stigma of being perceived as the 'oppressors of the nation'.

The big question remains how white identity will be articulated in the coming period. What political and ideological elements will be called into service in the refashioning of whiteness? Already far-right political actors such as David Duke actively seek to organize whites to defend their supposedly threatened racial privileges, all in the name of equality. Such racist populism is not very different from the demagogic use of the code word 'quotas' by Jesse Helms and George Bush to attract white votes.

On the other hand, white resentments cannot be wholly dismissed; they are not solely the result of racist demagogy or a last gasp attempt to retain some vestige of racial privilege. Such sentiments also express loyalty to an idealized and seemingly threatened civic culture in which *individual equality* was enshrined as a core democratic principle. That culture was never guaranteed to most whites, much less to non-whites, but it was espoused across the political and cultural spectrum as a central ideal. At present it seems to many Americans to be a receding ideal, obscured by hypocrisy and greed. The future avoidance of racial polarization may depend on resuscitating and rearticulating that vision to include race-specific demands in a society of greater social justice for all. This implies the radical democratic vision discussed above, in which greater equality permits more flexibility and uncertainty about individual, and collective, racial identity and its meaning.

These short 'case studies' demonstrate not only the adaptability and centrality of race in the contemporary USA, but also the linkages between racial formation processes and hegemonic ones. Demographic shifts, political realignments and economic pressures – both global and national – all profoundly affect the nature of racial identity in this one local, albeit important, setting. I have focused on racial identity as a dimension of hegemony, in order to demonstrate the continuing crisis that besets our notions of who we are and of what our all-too-easy racial categorization signifies. I submit that today effective political opposition demands the ruthless critique not just of inequality, not only of the lack of political representation, not simply of social policies of 'benign neglect' (or, in some cases, 'malign neglect'), but also of the system of racial signification itself. The 'common sense' notions that one understands the meaning of race in one's society, and that one could be 'comfortable' with one's racial identity, need to be exposed as supports of the local hegemonic order, in whatever country they appear.

Notes

1 This approach obviously involves an interpretation of Gramsci which cannot be spelled out within the limits of the present essay. The Gramsci literature is vast and rewarding for students of race. I rely here upon Gramsci (1971), Hall (1986) and Mouffe and Laclau (1985). I have also found useful material in Guha (1982).

2 The efforts of Southern slaveholders to maintain illiteracy among the slaves, and to ban all news about slave insurrections and the Haitian revolution, exemplify this form of rule.

3 'To say that "race" is a biological fiction is not to deny that it has real material effects in the world; nor is it to suggest that "race" should disappear from our critical vocabularies. Clearly it is no more adequate to hold that "race" is itself merely an empty effect than it is to suggest that "race" is solely a matter of skin colour. What is called for is a closer look at the production of racial subjects, at what forces organize, administer, and produce racial identities. What is called for is an approach which intervenes in the essentialist/constructivist polemic that has hitherto imprisoned "race" in a rigidified and falsifying logic' (Fuss, 1989, p. 92).

4 As I have noted, even Marx frequently legitimated such processes as the

inevitable and ultimately beneficial birth-pangs of classlessness – by way of the ceaselessly revolutionary bourgeoisie.

5 The two types of primitive accumulation detailed in Marx's *Capital* – the conquest already mentioned and the destruction of the English peasantry known as 'enclosure' – clearly are not parallel in terms of their destructiveness and brutality. For all the miseries brought upon the nascent English working class by the onset of capitalism, enclosure cannot be described as genocidal. Conquest cannot be understood in any other way.

6 In 1989, US blacks were almost three times as likely to be poor as whites. The median income of black families was 56 per cent that of white families; 44 per cent of black children lived in poverty in 1989, as compared to 16 per cent of white children (Bureau of the Census, 1990). Latino median income is about two-thirds that of whites, and Latinos are roughly twice as likely to be poor as whites, although this group is far more stratified than are blacks (Bean and Tienda, 1987). Similar variations exist for Asians (O'Hare and Felt, 1991). For Native Americans, poverty rates approach or exceed those of blacks: median family income in 1980 was $13,678, as compared to $19,917 for whites; native peoples were 2.5 times more likely than whites to be living in poverty (Bureau of the Census, 1989).

7 Even the presence or absence of a hyphen in a commonly accepted racial term can be cause for concern, due to its implications for hybridity in concepts of identity. African-Americans want to retain the hyphen; Asian Americans to drop it.

8 In these communities, certain enterprises such as groceries and convenience stores can be financed with the small amounts of capital often brought by Asian immigrants from the home country; such businesses are labour-intensive and can be operated as family enterprises. Relatively low capital requirements and higher risks of crime both attract immigrant entrepreneurs and alienate more established businesspeople. These conditions also channel community resentments, particularly in the ghetto, towards immigrant Asian entrepreneurs. One byproduct of these demographic patterns, then, is new varieties of neighbourhood racial tension.

9 Indeed the failure effectively to consolidate the status of the black middle class as 'junior partner' to the white establishment has been analysed as the key factor generating black nationalism (Frazier, 1957).

References

Alba, Richard, D. (1990) *Ethnic Identity: The Transformation of White America*, New Haven: Yale University Press.

Bean, Frank D., and Tienda, Marta (1987) *The Hispanic Population of the United States*, New York: Russell Sage Foundation.

Bhabha, Homi K. (in press) *The Location of Culture*, New York: Routledge.

CCCS (1982) *The Empire Strikes Back: Race and Racism in 70s Britain* (London: Hutchinson/Centre for Contemporary Cultural Studies).

Connolly, William E. (1991) *Identity/Difference: Democratic Negotiations of Political Paradox*, Ithaca: Cornell University Press.

DuBois, W. E. B. [1899] (1967) *The Philadelphia Negro: A Social Study*, New York: Schocken.

Dunne, John Gregory (1991) 'Law and disorder in Los Angeles', *New York Review of Books* 10 and 24 October.

Feagin, Joe R. (1991) 'The continuing significance of race: antiblack discrimination in public places', *American Sociological Review*, vol. 56, no. 1.

Frazier, E. Franklin (1957) *Black Bourgeoisie*, New York: The Free Press.

Fuss, Diana (1989) *Essentially Speaking: Feminism, Nature, and Difference*, New York: Routledge.

Garreau, Joel (1987) 'Competing bonds of race and class', *Washington Post*, 30 November.

Gramsci, Antonio (1971) *Selections from the Prison Notebooks* (ed. by Geoffrey Nowell-Smith and Quentin Hoare) New York: International Publishers.

Greenberg, Stanley, B. (1985) *Report on Democratic Defection*, an unpublished report prepared for the Michigan House Democratic Campaign Committee.

Guha, Ranajit (ed.) (1982) *Subaltern Studies*, vol. 1, Delhi: Oxford University Press.

Hall, Stuart (1986) 'Gramsci's relevance for the study of race and ethnicity, *Journal of Communication Inquiry*, vol. 10, no. 2.

Hobsbawm, Eric J. (1962) *The Age of Revolution: 1789–1848*, New York: New American Library.

Institute for the Study of Social Change (1990) *The Diversity Project: An Interim Report to the Chancellor*, Berkeley: University of California.

Jencks, Christopher (1992) *Rethinking Social Policy: Race, Poverty, and the Underclass*, Cambridge, Mass.: Harvard University Press.

Landry, Bart (1987) *The New Black Middle Class*, Berkeley: University of California Press.

Lechner, Norbert (1988) *Los Patios Interiores de la Democracia: Subjetividad y Politica*, Santiago: FLACSO.

Lopez, David and Espiritu, Yen (1990) 'Panethnicity in the United States: A theoretical framework, *Ethnic and Racial Studies*, vol. 13.

Marx, Karl (1967) *Capital*, vol. 1, New York: International Publishers.

Mouffe, Chantal, and Laclau, Ernesto (1985) *Hegemony and Socialist Strategy: Towards a Radical Democratic Politics*, London: Verso.

Novak, Michael (1972) *The Rise of the Unmeltable Ethnics*, New York: Macmillan.

O'Hare, William P., and Felt, Judy (1991) 'Asian Americans: America's fastest growing minority group', Population Trends and Public Policy Occasional Papers no. 19, Washington, DC: Population Reference Bureau.

Omi, Michael, and Winant, Howard (1994) *Racial Formation in the Unites States: From the 1960s to the 1990s*, New York: Routledge.

Omi, Michael, and Winant, Howard (1991) 'Contesting the meaning of race in the post-civil rights era', paper presented at the annual meetings of the American Sociological Association, August.

Przeworski, Adam (1986) 'Some problems in the study of the transition to democracy', in O'Donnell G., Schmitter, P., and Whitehead, L. (eds), *Transitions From Authoritarian Rule: Comparative Perspectives*, Baltimore: Johns Hopkins University Press.

Roediger, David (1991) *The Wages of Whiteness: Race and the Making of the American Working Class*, London: Verso.

Sartre, Jean-Paul, (1976) *Critique of Dialectical Reason*, Vol. 1: *Theory of Practical Ensembles* (trans. Alan Sheridan Smith), London: New Left Books.

Schuman, Howard, Steeh, C., and Bobo, L. (1985) *Racial Attitudes in America: Trends and Interpretations*, Cambridge, Mass.: Harvard University Press.

Sleeper, Jim (1990) *The Closest of Strangers: Liberalism and the Politics of Race in New York*, New York: W. W. Norton.

Sombart, Werner [1896] (1976) *Why Is There No Socialism in the United States?* (trans. Patricia Hocking and C. T. Husbands), White Plains: International Arts and Sciences Press.

Todorov, Tsvetan (1985) *The Conquest of America: The Question of the Other* (trans. Richard Howard), New York: Harper and Row.

US Bureau of the Census (1989) *Current Population Reports*, P–60, no. 168, Washington, DC: GPO.

US Bureau of the Census (1990) *Statistical Abstract of the United States*, Washington, DC: GPO.

Walters, Ronald (1987) White racial nationalism in the United States, *Without Prejudice*, vol. 1, no. 1.

Waters, Mary C. (1990) *Ethnic Options: Choosing Identities in America*, Berkeley: University of California Press.

West, Cornel (1987) 'Race and social theory: towards a genealogical materialist analysis, in Davies, M., Marable, M., Pfeil, F., and Sprinkler, M. (eds), *The Year Left 2*, London: Verso.

West, Cornel (1991) 'Nihilism in Black America', *Dissent*, vol. 38, no. 2.

Williams, Lena (1991), 'When blacks shop, bias often accompanies sale', *New York Times*, 30 April.

Wilson, William Julius, (1987) *The Truly Disadvantaged: The Inner City, the Underclass, and Public Policy* Chicago: University of Chicago Press.

Wilson, William Julius (1991) 'Studying inner-city social dislocations', *American Sociological Review*, vol. 56, no. 1.

Winant, Howard (1990) 'Postmodern racial politics: difference and inequality', *Socialist Review*, January-March.

Wolf, Eric (1982) *Europe and the People Without History*, Berkeley: University of California Press.

Young, Robert M. (1990) *White Mythologies: Writing History and the West*, New York: Routledge.

INDEX